LIFE IN AN ENGLISH VILLAGE

Photo by]   [*Watson, Frome.*

AN OLD INHABITANT.

Frontispiece.

LIFE IN AN
ENGLISH VILLAGE

AN ECONOMIC AND HISTORICAL
SURVEY OF THE PARISH OF
CORSLEY IN WILTSHIRE

BY

M. F. DAVIES

T. FISHER UNWIN
LONDON: ADELPHI TERRACE
LEIPSIC: INSELSTRASSE 20
MCMIX

A6316410

PREFACE

In 1905, when a student at the London School of Economics, it was suggested to me by Mr. and Mrs. Sidney Webb that I should pursue my studies of economic history and social science by making an investigation into the history and present conditions of the parish in which I was living, and it is upon the research and investigations begun at that time that this monograph is based.

Everything that may be of value in the book is due to some suggestion of Mr. or Mrs. Sidney Webb, while to my own mistakes and failures in filling in outlines sketched by them must be ascribed all its shortcomings.

To Mr. and Mrs. Webb, moreover, I owe the most valuable advice on how to investigate and where to look for possible sources of information, historical or otherwise.

My thanks are due to many of the lecturers and staff of the London School of Economics for advice and criticism, especially to Mr. Hubert Hall, Dr. Lilian Knowles, and Mr. J. McKillop.

I am indebted to the Marquis of Bath for allowing me to examine various documents at the Longleat Estate Office, relating to the history of Corsley.

To the Rev. J. T. Kershaw I owe thanks for various references to manorial and ecclesiastical records.

I have to thank Canon Christopher Wordsworth, Mr. C. N. Phipps, Miss M. Calthrop, and many others for valuable information, advice, or the loan of documents or books, and Miss Winifred Mitchell for reading the proofs.

Last, but not least, my most hearty thanks are due to many friends and neighbours in Corsley, who do not wish to be mentioned by name, but without whose extremely valuable co-operation no attempt could have been made to describe village life in the nineteenth century and at the present day.

MAUD F. DAVIES.

CONTENTS

PART II

CORSLEY IN THE PRESENT

APPENDICES

LIST OF ILLUSTRATIONS

LIFE IN AN ENGLISH VILLAGE

PART I

CORSLEY IN THE PAST

Life in an English Village

THE PARISH UNDER CLEY HILL

BEYOND the far western border of Salisbury Plain, dividing the chalk Downs, which descend to it with a sweeping curve, from the rich, wooded vales of Somersetshire, lies a shelf or plateau, some four hundred feet below the Downs, and midway between their summits and the sea, but with a wide view over the yet lower lying valley to the'west.

On this shelf, which is composed of a rich and fertile sandy soil, the parish of Corsley is situated, extending over an area of 4¾ square miles.[1]

Towards the eastern margin of the parish an oval-shaped hill rises abruptly from the plain, and stands, facing the downs, two miles distant, resembling them in every feature of substance and form, an isolated fragment, which has somehow been separated from the main body and left stranded on a foreign soil.

The eastern boundary of Corsley parish passes over

---

[1] The exact area is 3,056 statute acres. At the census of 1881 the area was 2,580 statute acres, or 4 square miles ; but between 1881 and 1891 part of Norton Bavant was transferred to Corsley parish (Census Report, 1891, vol. ii. p. 394).

this hill, whose name, Cley Hill, is probably a Celtic
and Saxon reduplication, and from its summit we may
obtain a wide view of the environments, while the
parish itself lies spread below us to the west.

Facing eastward we see the rolling Downs, extending line beyond line to the far horizon.   Through
their centre the River Wylie has cut a broad
valley, down which it finds its way to meet the
southern Avon, a valley now traversed by the high-
road and the line of the Great Western Railway
from Warminster to Salisbury.

Near at hand, in the mouth of the valley, with a
background of green hills and woods, lies Warminster, plainly distinguishable, with its churches,
while to the left lime-quarriers have cut the Down
into perpendicular white cliffs.   This little town,
about two miles distant as the crow flies, was formerly
the principal corn-market of the West of England,
and is one of the four places where the Wiltshire
Quarter Sessions are held.   The level land between
Cley Hill and the Downs, to the north-east, is
occupied by Norridge Wood.

Round Cley Hill the high ground forms a rough
semicircle from north and east to south, where,
divided from us, as we stand on the hilltop, by a
narrow gap, through which the roadway from Frome
to Warminster passes, the land rises fully to the
height of the neighbouring grassy Downs, its true
relationship to the latter being veiled by a rich cover-
ing of pines and deciduous trees, of rhododendron and
azalea; for the whole tract to the south of Corsley
belongs to the famous park and woods of Longleat,
once within the bounds of the ancient Forest of Selwood, the beauty of its splendid timber and rich pastures being wonderfully enhanced by the broken and
hilly character of the ground, which lends itself to

their full display, besides affording more distant views of surprising beauty.

Turning back to the north, we see at the foot of the Downs, four miles away, the market town of Westbury, with red smoke emerging from the chimneys of the iron-works. The main line of the Great Western Railway to Weymouth and Cornwall passes through Westbury, thence running on into Somersetshire, where it touches Frome.

This latter picturesque old town lies for the most part buried from our sight in a cuplike valley four miles distant to the west, those dwellings only which are situated on the hilltops around it meeting the eye from where we stand. Midway between Frome and Cley Hill runs the line of division between Wiltshire and Somersetshire, this line coinciding with the western boundary of Corsley parish.

Beyond Frome, across the broad valley of the Bristol Avon, is a line of low hills, bounding the view on the western horizon. Behind these lie the coal-mines of Radstock, important to the parish of Corsley on account of the considerable business which is carried on by the inhabitants in transporting timber thither and returning with coal, timber having, during the nineteenth century, taken the place in this trans-action of the corn from Warminster market, which for many centuries was carried at first on pack-horses, later in wagons, to feed the populous cities of Bristol and Bath.

Having surveyed the environment, we may now turn our eyes downwards to the parish at our feet.

Cley Hill and the ridge in Longleat woods form part of the watershed between the rivers of the south on the one hand which flow into the English Channel, and on the other the rivers of the west flowing northwards into the Bristol Channel.

Two tiny streams rise and flow westward through Corsley. Small as they are, these little brooks serve to feed the rich and valuable water meadows which lie along their margin.

Between these streams, which run near the northern and southern borders of the parish, the land falls gently from the foot of the steep chalk hills, for Cley Hill has a diminutive companion to the north. Round the hills is a belt of arable land ;[1] next to this a fine pasture, with here and there an arable field, extending westward for a mile or so, intersected by well-timbered hedgerows and small copses ; then, beyond, the ground falls out of sight in broken valleys, which verge on the Somersetshire country.

The visitor who climbs to the summit of the hill usually inquires, after a survey, " Where is the village? "—the remarkable fact being that, with a population of from seven hundred to eight hundred, there is no village, properly speaking. The dwellings lie scattered over the area, in hamlets, in groups of two or three, or in solitary houses.

One group is formed by the parish church, a farmhouse, once the manor-house, and the parish school, no other dwellings being found here.

Sturford Mead, one of the larger houses of the parish, forms the nucleus to a group of houses and cottages, as well as being in close vicinity to Whitbourne Springs and other hamlets.

Corsley House, and the smaller residence of Sandhayes, on the other hand, form isolated groups in central Corsley, with a few cottages only in their neighbourhood.

The numerous farmhouses lie scattered over the parish, some isolated, as Cley Hill Farm, one of the historical houses of the parish ; others in the midst of

[1] Part of this was laid down to grass in 1907.

the hamlets ; others, again, near the hamlets, or with a few cottages grouped round them.

The bulk of the cottage population is distributed in, roughly speaking, nine principal hamlets, besides several smaller ones, and many quite isolated pairs of cottages, or even single dwellings. These hamlets are sometimes fairly compact groups, such as Corsley Heath or Leighs Green ; sometimes they are a collection of scattered or straggling dwellings, such as Dartford or Whitbourne Moor. None deserves the name of a village. There is, however, one village, situated on high ground to the north of the parish, named Chapmanslade. Curiously enough this typical village, consisting mainly of a long row of houses on either side of the village street, is not a distinct parish at all, but is divided up among three or four neighbouring parishes. The street runs east and west, and the houses to the south of the street belong to Corsley. This village, though without separate parochial rights, forms a distinct centre of social life. It has its own church, its own chapels, its school, and its police-constable, all, however, situated or resident on the northern side, and, therefore, not in our parish. It has also three public-houses, two of these being on the Corsley side of the street.

In Corsley there is no such nucleus, the parish church and school being situated in one hamlet, the Church of St. Mary and the Baptist chapel in a second at Temple, the post-office, police-constable, and a public-house in a third at Corsley Heath, a Wesleyan chapel and a public-house in a fourth at Lane End, and another public-house in a fifth hamlet at Leighs Green.

For the position of the various hamlets and houses in Corsley the reader must be referred to the map. Speaking broadly, the population is collected along the western and southern borders, extending from Chapmanslade in the north-west, southward in the hamlets of Huntley, Leighs Green, Lane End, and Dartford, then passing east from the two latter, in Corsley Heath, Whitbourne Moor, Temple, Longhedge, and Whitbourne Springs.

No large hamlets lie in the north-easterly and central portion of the parish, and this distribution of the population dates back to feudal times, when the three great common fields lay under Cley Hill and to the north, while the hill itself was doubtless a sheepwalk, as it is to-day, and the homesteads belonging to the several manors which shared the common fields were distributed in the more sheltered nooks of the westward and southern districts. For all the evidence we have points to the fact that the more exposed hamlets, such as Corsley Heath and Longhedge, are of much more recent origin than those in the cups of the valleys like Whitbourne, Temple, and Leighs Green.

It is tempting, though perhaps somewhat rash, to speculate how it was that the dwellings of Corsley came to be scattered over its area in a fashion dissimilar to that of neighbouring parishes.

Professor Maitland, in "Domesday Book and Beyond," describes two main types of parishes, the nucleated village and the parish of scattered hamlets and homesteads, and he suggests that the village of nucleated type may have been founded by Germanic settlers, while the scattered village owes its characteristics to a Celtic origin.[1]

Again, he throws out a hint that where within historical times large tracts of forest land have existed hamlets rather than villages may be found.[2]

[1] F. W. Maitland, "Domesday Book and Beyond," p. 15.
[2] Ibid. p. 16.

The peculiar distribution of the dwellings in Corsley may be due to either or both of these causes.

There was, in olden times, a Celtic settlement upon the summit of Cley Hill,[1] which is still surrounded by the lines of its entrenchments, and crowned by two barrows, one of which was anciently used for sepulchral purposes.[2]

It is for antiquaries to discuss the probability of this Celtic settlement having extended into the valleys at the foot of the hill, and the ancient Britons having thus been, as Professor Maitland suggests, the originators of a type of parish which appears to be unique in the district.

This view is given colour by the fact that when the common fields were enclosed in the eighteenth century the award map shows that these were divided up into irregular strips and patches, quite unlike the regular rectangular strips of other common fields of the district. This would appear to be an indication of Celtic origin.

But whether or no the Celts in this district forsook the hilltops for the plain, the second cause suggested by Professor Maitland must undoubtedly have played a part in shaping the form of Corsley, which was within the bounds of the ancient royal forest of Selwood until the seventeenth century.[3] In the reign of King Edward I. the office of bailiff or forester of the forest was granted at a rent of £10 per annum to Sir Reginald de Kingston, whose family are affirmed by Canon Jackson to have resided in Corsley itself.[4] Sir Reginald, in the following reign,

[1] Sir Richard Colt Hoare, "History of Ancient Wilts," Hundred of Warminster, p 51.   [2] *Ibid.*

[3] *Wilts Archæol. Mag.* xxiii. p. 289. Depositions as to the extent of Selwood Forest, taken about A.D. 1620-30.

[4] *Wilts Archæol. Mag.* xxiii. p. 286.

petitioned for a reduction of his rent, as the extent
of the forest had been so reduced as to result in a loss
instead of a profit to the bailiff. An inquisition held
at Longbridge Deverel found that the £10 had been
raised only by violent acts of extortion and by
seizing the grain of poor people ; [1] the rent was
accordingly reduced to one mark per annum, and all
arrears remitted, without, however, any subsequent
benefit to the oppressed inhabitants.[2]

The vill of Corsley was, in mediæval times, divided
into several distinct manors, and at the present day
the parish contains no less than seven, four completely, three more only in part.[3] In each manor
a small nucleus of homesteads was naturally formed
round the demesne farm. Then, later, upon the waste
lands which abounded in Corsley new hamlets of
squatters grew up. The names of the hamlets of
Corsley Heath, Whitbourne Moor, and Leighs Green,
seem to imply this origin, and tradition ascribes it
to others, such as Longhedge.

We do not know when squatting on the wastes
commenced in Corsley, but some of these new hamlets
arose not long since, when the development of the
cloth trade in the seventeenth and eighteenth centuries
brought new immigrants. To take an example, the
cluster of houses at Corsley Heath appears to have
sprung up mainly after the enclosure and allotment
of the main part of this common in 1742,[4] though

---

[1] *Ibid.* p. 287.   Inquisition at Longbridge Deverel, Michaelmas,
1322.

[2] *Ibid.*

[3] Great Corsley, Little Corsley, Whitbourne Temple, Huntenhull,
wholly in Corsley parish ; Whitbourne and Bugley, partly in the
parish of Warminster ; Godwell and Chapmanslade, partly in Westbury parish ; and Upton and Norridge, partly in Upton Scudamore.

[4] See map attached to the Enclosure Agreement of 1742, in the
Longleat Estate Office.

a few cottages existed here previously.[1] Most of the houses were probably built on a piece of waste ground left unallotted at the time the inclosure was made, this being at a nodal position where lanes cross the high-road from Frome to Warminster. One small triangle of grass, with a few elms growing on it, still remains unappropriated in the centre of the hamlet, and serves as a playground for the children and a resting-place for the large trees destined to undergo transformation at the hands of the neighbouring wheelwright, or to be hauled to the Radstock coal-pits by the timber merchants. Another strip of turf here has been appropriated and enclosed into some cottage gardens within the last ten years.

Finally, after the enclosure of the common fields, when the land was for a time allotted in large farms, a new colony of labourers clustered round the principal farmhouse, where this was not already the centre of a hamlet. It was in this way that the hamlet of Chips or Landhayes grew suddenly up in a region to the north-west of Cley Hill, now again lonely as in feudal times but for the old house, once the residence of the Kington family, known as Cley Hill Farm. This hamlet sprang up rapidly with the development of corn-growing, and within the memory of living inhabitants formed the busiest centre of agricultural life, disappearing as rapidly as it rose with the agricultural depression of the latter nineteenth century and the changes from arable to pasture-farming.

Thus, while some of the hamlets of recent growth have become well established, and are more populous and important than the older groups, others, owing to the constant ebb of population which has continued since the middle of the nineteenth century, are now deserted, and remain nothing but a name and tradi-

[1] Corsley Survey, 1745, in the Longleat Estate Office.

tion, with, perhaps, a thick bed of nettles to mark where human habitations once stood.

The first description of Corsley which we have at present is found in the Domesday Survey. The vil then had its mill and its wood. There was 1 hide of land, 1 carucate being in demesne,[1] with 4 bordars. The translation of the passage runs as follows :

"Azor holds 1 hide in *Corselie*. The land is 1 carucate, which is there in demesne with 4 bordars. There is a mill, paying 40 pence, and the wood is 1 furlong long and half a furlong broad. It is worth 20 shillings."[2]

We cannot here attempt to unravel the confused threads of manorial, ecclesiastical, and parochial history. Most, if not all, the lands and manors of Corsley passed in pre-Reformation days into the hands of various religious houses, and the lords and tenants of its different component manors shared in the cultivation of the three great common fields of Chedinhanger, Cley Hill, and Bickenham, while holding separate enclosed crofts, probably in the neighbourhood of their homesteads. Sheep-farming and the dairy were important branches of agriculture in mediæval Corsley, and both horses and oxen were used to draw the plough.

In A.D. 1364 the Prior of Maiden Bradley, who was Lord of the Manor of Whitbourne, held $60\frac{1}{2}$ acres of arable and meadow land in the common fields and 34 acres enclosed in crofts ; he had also an acre of wood, which was used for pasture. He might keep 4 farm horses and 12 oxen, 12 cows and 250 sheep.[3]

[1] The expressions ("hide" and "carucate") are not identical, but should both correspond to the plough team. See P. Vinogradoff, "Villainage in England," and other writings.

[2] William H. Jones, "Domesday for Wilts," p. 135.

[3] See extent of Whitbourne in Appendix, p. 293.

The common fields were situated in the north-east and centre of the parish, in districts still almost uninhabited, and common-field cultivation continued until the last quarter of the eighteenth century.

Corsley is in the Hundred of Warminster,[1] and likewise in the Petty Sessional Division to which this town gives its name. It is in the parliamentary constituency of the Westbury Division of Wiltshire. The parish is situated midway on the base of a triangle formed by the market towns of Warminster, Frome, and Westbury, the two former being each about $2\frac{1}{2}$ miles distant from its eastern and western boundaries, while Westbury is $3\frac{1}{2}$ miles from its northern extremity at Chapmanslade.

It has a main line of the Great Western Railway three miles away, with the two important stations of Frome and Westbury, the former just over, the latter just under, 100 miles from Paddington Station. From Warminster it has communication with Salisbury by a branch of the Great Western Railway, which there meets the London and South Western line.

Corsley is traversed by the main road from Frome to Warminster, which passes through or within a mile of nearly all the important hamlets. A main road from Westbury to Frome touches the northern margin of the parish, passing through the village of Chapmanslade. Good roads afford easy means of transit to Bath, Bristol, and Radstock in the west, to Trowbridge and Bradford on the north, to the towns of Somersetshire on the south, and to Salisbury on the east.

[1] In a MS. Register at Longleat it is recorded that " Out of Corsley Manor was paid viii^s yearly to the Sheriff's Turne at *Hundred Oke*." Tradition locates this ancient oak-tree in South-leigh Woods on the far side of Warminster. See *Wilts Archæol. Mag.* xxiii. p. 284.

The parish itself is intersected by an intricate network of lanes and footpaths, which wind about in a manner which is often unintelligible at the present day, but which probably owe some of their unexplained turns to the position of now vanished dwellings. Some are ancient roadways sunk deep below the level of the fields they traverse, and in certain cases another roadway on the higher ground has been formed alongside them. These lanes and pathways connect up all the hamlets and scattered dwellings.

While each hamlet forms a little social group of its own, there are two main nuclei of the parish, the one at Chapmanslade, towards which Huntenhull, Huntley Green, and Gore Lane turn, the other in Corsley itself, which, though it has no definitely located centre, unless we consider the parish church and school as such, yet forms a closely connected whole for social and administrative purposes.

CHAPTER II

SEIGNORIAL UNIFICATION

THE Reformation, which had such a profound and far-reaching influence on agricultural England, marks in Corsley the epoch of its unification and organisation in a form which underwent little change for over two centuries, and which retains some of its principal features at the present day. We may therefore date the modern history of Corsley from this period ; and though there is much in its later life which cannot be fully understood without a reference to that earlier history of the parish which has still to be published, yet the main lines of its social, industrial, and religious development may from this time on be followed by the modern student without serious check.

The manors of Corsley, Whitbourne, and Huntenhull, hitherto held by different religious houses, more or less remotely situated, were after various vicissitudes of grant, sale, and purchase, for the first time collected into the hands of one single lord, Sir John Thynne.[1]

The other manors, partly situated in the present parish of Corsley, namely Godwell and Chapmanslade, Bugley, and Upton and Norridge, do not appear to have been acquired by the Thynne family till a

[1] For list of purchases made by Sir John Thynne in Corsley Parish, see Appendix I. pp. 300, 301.

later date, but Sir John Thynne purchased lands and property in these manors as well as in those where he acquired right of manorial jurisdiction, and thus the main part of the parish was for the first time since the component manors had emerged from the woodlands or had been split up into distinct tenures, brought under the influence and control of a single owner. Again, in ecclesiastical matters, though Corsley, with its adjoining hamlets, had during the preceding centuries gradually acquired parochial rights, other chapels beside the parish church existed within its bounds. Kington Court Chapel, the last of these, ceased to be a place of worship at the time of the Reformation, and Corsley Church became the sole centre of religious life, as it remained till the growth of a dissenting population led to the erection of chapels in the nineteenth century.

The Corsley of Sir John Thynne's day must have differed considerably in outward aspect from Corsley as we know it. It still formed part of the Forest of Selwood, which was not finally disafforested till about 1630 [1] and the wild deer roamed freely over it. In Chapmanslade Wood and Dafford Wood the deer were kept by the foresters of Sir John Thynne. Corsley Woods were unenclosed, and the deer, given mast here in winter, were so tame that they would scarcely move out of the way of passers-by.[2]

Sir John Thynne is reputed to have built the Manor House, now the Manor Farm, adjacent to Corsley Church. He also impaled Corsley Park,[3] whose extent to the south of the old Manor House is still traceable in names such as Parkbarn, near Corsley House, and Deerlip, near Corsley Heath, which was,

---

[1] Depositions as to the extent of Selwood Forest, taken about A.D. 1620–30, printed in the *Wilts Archæol. Mag.* xxiii. p. 289.

[2] *Ibid.*, p. 229.   [3] *Ibid.*

no doubt, one of the boundaries between the park and the forest, a " deer leap " being an arrangement to admit of wild deer entering without affording any mode of egress to them.

Round the park the land lay, for the most part, unenclosed and undivided by hedges or other division.

Near Cley Hill and in the north-easterly districts of the parish were great common fields, divided into irregular strips and patches, cultivated in common, according to ancient custom, by the inhabitants. Besides the three arable common fields the parish had common meadows, where hay was made. The woods of Corsley and the neighbouring manors were at least as extensive and important as at the present day. A great part of the parish was waste land or common, and on the waste lands and in the woods, as well as on the common fields and common meadows, after the harvest was gathered, the flocks and herds of the community pastured together, being watched by the herdsman or shepherd of the manor. But though the main part of the parish was unenclosed till a much later date, some fields or " closes " were already fenced off near the dwellings, and held by separate owners.[1] The main feature of Corsley Heath was the " Coney Warren," which we find mentioned half a century later.[2] Cley Hill then, as now, stood guard over the parish, marked with the lines of ancient encampments, but

[1] See Appendix (Extent of the Manor of Whitbourne, 38 Ed. III.), p. 293.

[2] MS. Bayliffe's Account, Corsley Manor, 1634, preserved in the Longleat Estate Office.

"And for the warren of Connyes uppon Corsley Heath we s. . . . nihil for that the Lord keepeth the same in his owne hande and by his warrenner hath sold the Connyes wch he is to answere for."

as yet maintaining its oval shape, undefaced by quarriers and lime-burners.

The hill in those days not only protected the parish from the east winds, but served as a watch-tower against human enemies. At the time when Spanish invasion was feared Mr. Carr, the elder, of Corsley, with four men from Norridge and Bugley, and others of the " meetest persons," were told off " to look after the watchman, and see that the Beacon was well and orderly watched, and fired only on just cause, nor without making the Justices of the Peace and constables privy thereto." [1] The constables of the Hundred had been instructed to provide that the Beacon " be well and sufficiently furnished with good and dry wood, and a barrel in which pitch hath been, besides 5 or 6 lbs. of pitch." [2]

Wiltshire had long been a centre of cloth-making, but we find no record or trace of the establishment of this industry in Corsley before the Civil Wars. The population was almost entirely agricultural, and the chief inhabitants yeoman farmers. The Lye family, to whom tradition ascribes considerable importance in the parish, who presented to the benefice up to the year 1485 and who have left a permanent mark in the name of one of the most important of the hamlets which constitute the parish, appear to have died out or left the place about this time. The will of William Lye, of Corsley, husbandman, was proved in 1557, and John Lye, of Corsley, was married at Frome in 1597. His administration was granted in 1603, the occupations of the two Corsley men who were his bonds being respectively " husbandman " and " driver." [3]

---

[1] John J. Daniell, " History of Warminster," pp. 63, 64.   [2] *Ibid.*
[3] " The Lyes of Corsley," by J. Henry Lea. To be published in America.

Photo by]

CLEY HILL.

[Whitton, Frome.

To face p. 18.

In the Quarter Sessions' records of the year 1599 we find mention of three inhabitants of Corsley—John Smyth, *alias* Singer, carpenter ; Lambe, husbandman ; and John Holloway, husbandman.[1]

Similarly, whenever we meet with an allusion to a man of Corsley, his occupation, if stated, is one belonging to a farming community, engaged in the main in tilling the soil and the care of animals, with, no doubt, a few subsidiary occupations, such as blacksmith and carpenter, and perhaps also tailor and shoemaker.

An apparent exception occurs in the list of contributors to the Corsley parish stock. These include two vintners, a merchant, an upholsterer, and a victualler. If these people resided and carried on their business in Corsley, the parish was not always purely agricultural in character. But more probably these were men of Corsley abstraction, or men who came to pass their old age in this retired parish, while their working lives were spent, and their fortunes made, in one of the West of England towns.

There were some fairly well-to-do people among the farmers, and probably a certain Welsh, whose house was burgled in 1606, was one of these.

The burglar confessed at Quarter Sessions that he had taken from the house " two wastcotes, a silken scarfe, a gould ringe, a silke apron, a Holland Sheete, a Tynnyn Salte." [2]

One of the leading families of the parish at this time were the Carrs. The head of the family was, as we have seen, appointed to superintend the Beacon in Elizabeth's reign, and a generation later, 1607-8, William Carr was one of the three freeholders of

[1] MS. Wilts Quarter Sessions Minutes, 1599.
[2] *Wilts Archæol. Mag.* xxii. p. 226.

Corsley, the other two being Anthony Raxworthy and Robert Fytchne.[1]

But in 1631, Thomas Carr, in all probability a son of William, or, at any rate, another member of the family, appears to have got into financial difficulties, with the result that Cley Hill Farm, where he resided, became the property of one Hopton Haynes, who endeavoured to take possession of it.[2]

This, however, was strenuously resisted by Carr and his neighbours, " Carr defending his possession with force of arms, and a multitude of base persons assisting him."

Haynes petitioned for ordnance to be obtained from Bristol, and the Privy Council directed the Deputy Lieutenant of the county to assist the Sheriff with such companies of trained bands as he considered necessary. The Sheriff accordingly sent summonses to the inhabitants of Warminster and the neighbourhood, which met, however, with little attention, Sir Edward Baynton, among others, refusing to meet the Sheriff on this business, saying " that he did not much fancy that service." Finally, when Sir John Toppe, the Sheriff, approached the farm, he found that the men who attended him " were totally unprovided with necessaries, and were so disinclined to the work that he felt compelled to withdraw his force, and excuse his departure by reason of the foulness of the weather and nearness of the night." He then endeavoured to obtain gunners from Bristol, and the first gunner with difficulty procured " behaved himself perfidiously by interleaguing with the rioters and letting fall treacherous speeches." The people were all friendly to Carr and against Haynes, and though some of them were taken and committed to gaol,

---

[1] List of Wilts Freeholders, *Wilts Archæol. Mag.* xix. p. 265.
[2] Proc. Court of Chancery, Haynes *v.* Carr, Chas. I. H.H. 69.

this attempt to carry out justice was a failure. Finally a gunner, John Berrow, was appointed, who carried out the service, and the property was delivered over to Haynes.[1]

This episode illustrates the close relation which existed at this time between the land and those settled on it, the rights of the latter being regarded by themselves and their neighbours as something too fundamental to be destroyed by legal enactments. It is also interesting to see what difficulties might be met with by those to whose lot it fell to execute the law, and the amount of persistence and determination which might be necessary in order to carry a decree of the courts into effect. The village community still, for the most part, lived its life in its own way, affected less by outward compulsion than by the ancient customs which it recognised as binding.

This parish does not appear to have given much trouble to the Court of Quarter Sessions. Few entries relating to it are met with in the Minutes, but in July, 1620, we find among the presentments: "Corsley Omnia bene."

The government was doubtless mainly carried on by the Lord of the Manor, or his steward, and the inhabitants themselves in the manorial courts. The manorial fees and rents due to the lord were paid in money or in chickens.

The rent of a cottage appears to have been 8d.; and 1d. a year was the fee exacted from Robert Hooper in 1634 for "setting his pales upon the Lordes wast" of the Manor of Huntenhull.[2]

---

[1] See Cal. State Papers Dom. Chas. I. vol. 1631–33, pp. 157, 168, 170, 192, 193 (3), 194, 251 (2).

[2] The following extracts from the bailiff's account show the rents of this time:

Manor of Great Corsley, 1634. "Y^e rent capons and chicken of

Before the conclusion of the reign of Charles I., Selwood Forest was disafforested. Disafforestations in other parts of Wiltshire and in Dorsetshire were the cause of rebellions and riots among the people of the neighbourhood, but nothing of the kind appears to have been roused in this district, and whether any enclosure affecting the privileges of commoners took place here, or whether all went on as before in Corsley, we do not know.

Corsley possessed a stock of money arising from several charities before 1635.[1] Such stocks of money existed in nearly all parishes, however small, and were administered by churchwardens and overseers, after the creation of these offices. We have, however, no records of the administration of the Corsley stock before the eighteenth century.

Two tablets in the old church at Corsley formerly commemorated the various donations.[2] The donors included two of the ministers, Mr. John Cutlet, who was presented to the living in 1579, and Mr. Richard Jenkins, who was appointed in 1667. Mr. Jeremiah Hollway, merchant, made the munificent gift of £50, two vintners made donations of £5 each, an upholsterer contributed £10, and the second tablet was presented by Robert Hopkins, victualler, in 1688.

this manno^r and ye Capons and chicken paid by John Hill for a coppie of licence ar to be accompted for wth. the rent capons and chicken of Whitborne for all wch. for ye accompt thereof at this audite next to Whitborne."

The Manor of Huntenhull, 1634. "And of Tho. Stephens for the rent of a Cottage wth. in this manno^r neere Whitborne more, viii^d. And of Robert Hooper for setting his pales upon the Lordes wast of this manno^r at 1d. p. annum ij^d . . . . x^d."

[1] Report Charity Commission, 1834, xxviii. p. 389.

[2] For the tablets and other monumental inscriptions, see Sir R. Colt Hoare, "History of Modern Wilts," Hundred of Warminster, p. 66.

But the most numerous class of benefactors were the yeomen, of whom there were five. One of these, Hugh Rogers, died in 1611, bequeathing to the parish £4, a crown of the interest to be added yearly to the stock, and the remainder to be given on the anniversary of his death to the "parson, clark, poore, and bells." We learn from a monumental poem, which formed an acrostic on his name, that this yeoman greatly benefited his poor neighbours during his lifetime by ministering to them as medical adviser, and freely giving them "his salves, his plaisters, and his paynes."

CHAPTER III

CLOTH-MAKING AND ITS EFFECTS IN CORSLEY

(1660—1727)

FROM 1660 till the accession of George II. in 1727 a systematic chronicle of what passed in the parish of Corsley is lacking; but the fragmentary evidence which exists shows plainly that shortly after the Restoration the manufacture of cloth had been introduced, and the main feature of the years which followed was the gradual transformation of a purely agricultural into a semi-industrial population.

The cloth trade had flourished in Wiltshire for at least two centuries, and was established at the neighbouring town of Westbury before the Civil Wars,[1] but in Corsley no trace of its existence before the Restoration is forthcoming, and this evidence, though negative, seems sufficient to show that at least no important industry was carried on in the parish.

At the time of the Civil Wars the Wiltshire cloth trade passed through a great cataclysm. Not only were the manufacturers subject to interference and extortion from the military forces which infested the county, but local government and trade regulations were utterly disorganised, the apprenticeship regula-

---

[1] See Wilts Quarter Sessions Records, in Hist. MS. Com., various collections, vol. i. pp. 74, 114, &c.

tions broke down completely,[1] and probably the Gild regulations fared no better.

Under these circumstances it is not surprising if a capitalist clothier, when peace, but not industrial order, was restored, migrated to this out-of-the-way village, where gilds and industrial regulations had never existed, and here set up his business independently, and this is what seems to have occurred.

The first notice of the cloth trade in Corsley that we have met with is the following tradesman's token :

> George Carey—The Clothworkers' arms
> IN. Corsley, 1666—G.M.C.[2]

We thus find established in the parish a clothier with such a business as to make it worth his while to issue his own tokens. As to where he came from, or when he came, we know nothing. There is nothing to prove that he was not a Corsley man, who had gradually developed his trade in the parish ; but the total absence of any signs of the presence of industry previous to this suggests the probability that he was a capitalist clothier who migrated with his business from some other locality.

However he may have come, he came to stay, and his family remained in the parish, first as clothiers and then as maltsters for about one hundred years. In Corsley Church is a monument with a coat of arms and Latin inscription to—

> GEORGII CARY
> Christiana MDCC.

---

[1] See Wilts Quarter Sessions Records, in Hist. MS. Com., various collections, vol. i. p. 114.

[2] *Wilts Archæol. Mag.* xxvi. p. 396.

In 1712 a tenement with garden, orchard, and meadow in Whitbourne,[1] closes, and 2½ acres of arable in a field near Cley Hill were leased by the Lord of the Manor to Thomas Carey, of Corsley, clothier. In 1734 we find George Carey, of Corsley, clothier, witnessing a deed,[2] and in 1756 the tenement in Whitbourne was renewed to " Geo. Cary of Whitborn, Maltster," and in 1769 to " Geo. Cary of Corsley, Maltster." According to tradition the old house now inhabited by Mr. H. Ball was formerly a malt-house, and this was in all probability the home of the Carey family during their residence in the parish.

To return to the early history of the cloth trade in Corsley. Whenever among the scanty records of the latter half of the seventeenth century allusion is made to the occupation of inhabitants of the parish, the broadweaver and cloth-worker are henceforward found beside the yeoman and husbandman. These handicraftsmen were not, however, very numerous till after the conclusion of George I.'s reign, and were usually immigrants from neighbouring parishes and not of Corsley birth. In 1694 a broadweaver with his family migrated from Freshford,[3] and in 1707 a broadweaver's family from Beckington [4] came

[1] In the survey at the Longleat Estate Office this is noted as Sturford Mead, and the fact that the premises were afterwards leased to a dyer bears out this note, since the dyer, H. A. Fussell, was long a resident at Sturford Mead. It seems probable, however, that the dwelling-house was that now occupied by Mr. H. Ball. The house of Sturford Mead was not built till the nineteenth century.

[2] An indenture between Thos. Wickham, yeoman, and Leonard Humphreys, blacksmith, in the possession of Mr. Seth Sparey.

[3] MS. certificate in Corsley Parish Chest, from the officers of Freshford guaranteeing that Edward Twiney, broadweaver, his wife and family, shall be received back should they become chargeable.

[4] Similar certificate in Corsley Parish Chest, from the officers of

to reside here. Three other families who came from Berkley, Heytesbury, and Buckland Dinham in Somerset during the first twenty years of the eighteenth century [1] were probably likewise attracted to Corsley by opportunities of work in the clothing industry. In 1714 a boy from Frome was apprenticed to a cloth-dresser of Corsley.[2]

By the early years of the eighteenth century George Carey was no longer the only capitalist clothier in the parish. William Elliott, of Boreham, clothier, leased land in Corsley in 1703, and John Hopkins, of Chapmanslade, clothier, rented a piece of ground in the Manor of Huntenhull in 1712.

Some indication of the personnel of Corsley at this time is given by the list of leases in a Survey Book of 1745,[3] but they are not sufficiently numerous before 1730 to afford much clue as to proportion and distribution of occupations.

It is notable that two or three well-to-do men from Warminster or the neighbourhood took land or tenements in the parish towards the end of the seventeenth or early in the eighteenth century. Besides those already mentioned, leases were granted to Edward Halliday, of Warminster, gentleman, in 1677, and to John Barton, of Warminster, mercer, in 1692. The occupations of other tenants are as follows :

From 1690 *to* 1699, *six tenants:*

> 1 yeoman, 1 husbandman, 1 broadweaver, 1 tailor, 1 carpenter, 1 occupation unspecified.

Beckington relating to Jeremiah Jarvis, broadweaver, his wife and children.

[1] Similar MS. certificates from these parishes in Corsley Parish Chest.

[2] See MS. indenture in Corsley Parish Chest.

[3] MS. Corsley Survey, 1745, in the Longleat Estate Office.

From 1700 *to* 1709, *thirteen tenants:*

    3 yeomen, 2 husbandmen, 1 clothworker, 2 tailors, 1 blacksmith, 1 mason, 1 bricklayer, 2 occupation unspecified.

From 1710 *to* 1719, *eight tenants:*

    2 yeomen, 1 labourer, 1 gardener, 1 miller, 1 thatcher, and 2 blacksmiths.

The labourer and the gardener may, perhaps, have owed their occupations to the immigration of the moneyed townsman.

The presence of mason and bricklayer in the first decade of the eighteenth century is an interesting indication that the population had already begun to spurt forward. An investigation of the parish registers leads one to the conclusion that the growth began with the century and continued almost steadily till about 1765. Any estimation of the population at this date must be inconclusive ; but a calculation from the baptisms, deaths, and marriages recorded in the parish register gives an estimated population of seven hundred in 1691, falling to five hundred in 1701, and then rising again steadily to a little over seven hundred in 1731. If the registers were kept regularly throughout these years, there can be no doubt that this fall and rise occurred, though the absolute number must not be regarded as more than a suggestion.

The steady growth of population which went forward from the first decade of the eighteenth century was in all probability due to the development of the cloth trade, which first brought new immigrants, and later, perhaps, stimulated early marriages and a rapid rate of increase. But the records during the reign of George I. are, unfortunately, too slight to permit of very certain conclusions.

We learn from the Longleat Survey Book of 1745 that the payment of rents in kind had never wholly died out or else had been revived in this neighbourhood, and the system lingered on into the eighteenth century. Between 1657 and 1732 the grant of about 120 leases is recorded, some tenants taking out several leases for different holdings. About a quarter of these tenants have to pay capons or chickens as well as a money rent, three have to give one harvest day, one has to give two harvest days, four have to give a day's work with plough or wagon. In only one case is an alternative money payment set down by these payments in kind, where 3s. might be paid instead of two capons. The rents in kind and services are by no means restricted to the leases granted during the earlier years of the period. The following is an example of the leases as recorded in the Survey Book :

CORSLEY SURVEY, 1745

Michael John Dead val 15ll	"Michael Parret holds by Copy from Thoˢ Thynne Esqʳ the 30th of Sepʳ 1679 A Tenement with the Lands Meadows pastures & Appurtenances thereto belonging late Meares's for the lives of the s Michael & of John Parret.	1679. ffine 170ll Rent 7ˢ & a days Carr with a plough & 1ˢ Court Silver Herᵗ in kind.

(1727—1760)

Great changes went forward in Corsley during the reign of George II. At his accession we find a still mainly agricultural community of perhaps seven hundred persons. But in a short space of time industries were extensively developed, and by the end of his reign the population probably numbered twelve or

thirteen hundred, including manufacturers and tradesmen, who, with their workmen, were more important
and numerous than yeoman farmers and the tillers
of the soil.

Much of the wastes and commons had been
enclosed either piecemeal or wholesale by agreement,
and numbers of new cottages had sprung up. With
the rapid increase of population which was taking
place, the housing problem must have been a very
serious one.

The relation between the number of deaths, marriages, and births, as shown by the parish registers,
affords a curious study. Decennial averages between
1715 and 1735 show a rising number of deaths, a
very slightly rising number of marriages, but a falling
number of baptisms. Possibly there was at this
time a considerable overcrowding, and much infant
mortality, which is unrecorded in the registers owing
to the children dying unbaptized. However this may
be, the number of deaths rose enormously, while the
number of baptisms decreased. During the two
decades from 1706 to 1726 the average number of
deaths annually had been 9 and 10 respectively;
during the following ten years (1726-1736) the
average number was 15.2 per annum, and from 1736
to 1746, 21.9 per annum, while during the following
ten years it fell again to 16.4 per annum.

The great rise in the death rate which occurred
between 1726 and 1746 culminated in the five years
1740-45, during which no less than 159 persons died,
or an average of 31.8 per annum. 46 died in each
of the years 1741-42 and 1743-44.

The cause of this mortality is not clear. Smallpox
was a constant visitant from 1730 to 1742, from one
to five families being relieved nearly every year by
the parish officers in this scourge, but it does not

seem to have been heavier in 1742 than in some previous years, and from 1742 to 1748 no cases were relieved. If the deaths in 1743-44 were from small-pox, perhaps the high mortality was the result of neglect on the part of the parish officers, but it seems more probable that the pestilence had for the time being worn itself out, and that the deaths were due to some other and unrecorded cause. Whatever the cause of the mortality, its immediate sequence is striking : from 1743 onwards a great increase in the number of marriages took place, accompanied by a simultaneous, but more gradual, increase in the pro-portional number of births. One can hardly avoid the conclusion that many young people anxious to be married had been debarred by the difficulty of obtain-ing a house, so that the exceptional number of marriages was the direct result of the clearance effected by the high mortality.

To go into the details of these figures : the average number of marriages per annum from 1726 to 1736 was 5, and no increase took place till about 1743-4. During the eighteen years 1743-4 to 1760 the average number is 12, the greatest actual number reached in any one year being 20 in 1755. After 1760 the average falls again, varying between 7 and 11 ; and it is not until the eighties and nineties, when the total population had greatly increased, that a number of marriages per annum slightly in excess of that of the middle of the century is reached.

In 1743, too, the number of baptisms per annum, which since 1725 had been falling, began to rise. The greatest number of births per annum occurred in the early sixties, if the parish registers, which are incomplete for these years, are rightly interpreted. The annual number of births continued high from 1766 to 1775, and then fell off somewhat.

Though the housing problem would seem to have been urgent about 1730, many new cottages had been erected within the memory of man, as we learn from the leases in the Longleat Survey Book. Between 1730 and 1739 leases were granted of cottages "formerly built " by John Bartlet, George Greatwood, and William Singer, two of these men, if not all three, being still alive. They had apparently raised these cottages on the waste lands of the manors, and no doubt other people were doing the same thing. George Greatwood also leased the brickkiln, partly in Corsley and partly in Norton parish, now worked by the Open family, which, perhaps, he had himself built in order to supply materials for the growing demand for houses. John Bartlet's cottage was on the lower side of Corsley Heath, and several cottages seem to have been then recently built on this open ground. A newly-erected cottage on the heath was let in 1733.

In 1736 about two acres of newly enclosed waste land at Whitborne Moor were let to George Prowse, dyer, "with 2 Dyehouses Stove packhouse Stable," and he was excused the usual fine in consideration of his having laid out £400 in building and enclosing.

About this time it was agreed to divide up and enclose the whole of Corsley Heath. Commissioners were appointed, and a deed of distribution, a copy of which is in the Longleat Estate Office, was drawn up and agreed to in 1741. Land was allotted to twenty-seven persons who had common rights, subject to a reserved rent to Lord Weymouth of, roughly speaking, about 1s. an acre. It was stipulated that three of these allottees, Richard Collins, Thomas Rimell, and Robert Meares, or one of them, should buy the new Warren House, lately built and repaired by Lord Weymouth, paying £20 for a lease of three lives and 2s. annually. The holders of land were to " inclose their several proportions and plant the same with Quick Set Thorn plants in a husbandlike manner," and the roads were to be laid out, left, and made according to plan.

We have seen that the population was increasing numerically at a rapid rate ; the mode of living of the community and the character of their occupations appear to have undergone quite as rapid a development. The growing prosperity of the cloth manufacture was the primary cause for all these changes, and the Longleat Survey Book shows conclusively how extensive this had become in the thirties.

Leases were granted to about 40 tenants during the ten years 1730-1739 : of these 40, 2 were clothiers and 14 or 15 manual workers in some branch of the manufacture, including 3 dyers, 4 cloth-workers, 3 broadweavers, 1 shearman, 1 twister, 1 scribbler, 1 shear-grinder, and also a " sievier," who may or may not have had some connection with the industry. Thus of the 40 tenants 16 or 17 were cloth-makers, while only 10 agriculturists took leases, namely, 8 yeomen, a husbandman, and a gardener. This is in striking contrast to the proportions in the earlier decades of the century, when out of 10 or 12 tenants only 1 or 2 would represent the cloth trade, the bulk of the occupations being agricultural.

From 1740 to 1749, again, the proportion of cloth-workers is large, being 5 out of 12. Of these 5, 3 are clothiers, 1 a capitalist dyer, and 1 a twister.

From 1750 to 1759, out of 21 tenants 7 are cloth-workers : these consist of 2 clothiers, 1 cloth-worker, 2 twisters, 1 scribbler, and 1 card-maker.

But though the proportion of agricultural employments falls off during these years, some specialisation seems to have taken place. Between 1740 and 1749

4

we only have four tenants with agricultural pursuits, but one of these is a " drowner," who one presumes was employed by different farmers to supervise the proper flooding of their water-meadows. This may indicate the introduction of some improvement of method in farming. The other three are a yeoman, a miller, and a gardener.

Between 1750 and 1759 we find another occupation subsidiary to agriculture not before met with, that of farrier. During these years leases were also granted to two yeomen, two husbandmen, two gardeners, and a labourer.

During the thirty years the immigration of well-to-do townsmen observed during the reign of George I. continued. Among the newcomers besides the numerous clothiers and Robert Meares, dyer, who probably ranked socially with the yeoman farmer, there was one Thomas Whitaker, of Westbury, gentleman, while the families of Barton, Carey, and others, who had previously come to the parish, continued to renew their leases or take out fresh ones.

Following on the development of the cloth trade we find a set of crafts and trades growing up to provide food, houses, and clothes for this manufacturing population. Between 1730 and 1739 leases were granted to two bakers and a butcher. Bakers may have existed in the parish previously, for negative evidence that no mention of them has been met with is inconclusive, considering the scantiness of the records ; but whether or no these were the first in the parish, their appearance indicates a new demand for ready-baked bread. In most of the old cottages remains of baking ovens are found, and it seems probable that about this time many of the people were growing too busy, and, perhaps, too cramped for house-room, to bake for themselves as they had hitherto done.

Besides these caterers for food supply we find in the thirties a brickmaker and a wheelwright, two carpenters and a blacksmith, and also a shoemaker.

In 1749 an inn was set up at Corsley Heath, and lease granted to William Young. William Young had kept a house where the parish officers could meet and drink previously to this,[1] and tradition relates that the Manor Farm was at one time used as an inn ;[2] but this inn on Corsley Heath is the first of which we have authentic record in the parish.

In the decade 1750-1759 leases were granted to a " victualler " and a tailor, as well as a butcher and a carpenter, so the inhabitants were now able to do practically all their shopping in the parish.

Towards the end of the reign of George II., George Carey, formerly clothier, had developed a malting business, and is specified as " maltster."

The Longleat Survey Book affords material for this sketch of the population of Corsley during the reign of George II. But there is one side of parochial life of which we have a fuller and a fairly continuous record. This is the administration of the Poor Law.

The MS. Overseers' Accounts from 1729 till 1755, and again from 1768 onwards, have been preserved in Corsley Parish Chest.

The first book, which commences in 1729, shows a systematic method of administration, which had, no doubt, been handed down from the days of Elizabeth or the early Stuarts.

It would seem that from 1729 to 1740 with the new industrial openings was a prosperous time in the parish ; nevertheless, a considerable sum of money was expended annually on poor relief, and persons

[1] MS. Overseers' Accounts, May, 1733.
[2] Sir R. Colt Hoare, "History of Modern Wilts," Hundred of Warminster, p. 63.

or families whose number varied through these years from sixteen to thirty-one were relieved regularly. The pensions given in 1729 varied in amount from 1s. to 12s. a month, 2s., 4s., 5s., or 6s. a month being the most common rates.

During the summer half-year in 1729, from May to October, the expenditure on poor relief was £91 18s., so that the annual expenditure can have been little, if at. all, short of £200, though it is not probable that the population at this time much exceeded seven hundred.

In the early forties the number of paupers increased, the regular list in July, 1742, containing forty-five names : this was a year of exceptionally high mortality, as we find by the parish registers. In the year 1748-49 the total expenditure on the poor was £163 1s. 11½d.

Besides distributing regular doles, the parish officers provided exceptional necessaries required by the regular paupers and others. They clothed them ; they housed them, paying their rents, and sometimes repairing the cottages ; when sick they provided medical attendance and nursing, and medicines or extra diet when needed, especially after the smallpox, when allowances of bread, malt, or beer were given. They frequently paid funeral expenses, which usually included beer or drink money. Bedding was sometimes provided, and occasionally fuel.

The overseers occasionally assisted adult inhabitants to earn a livelihood : the rent of a loom for this purpose was several times paid by the overseers, and in 1748 they purchased a broadloom for the parish. They also provided a certain John Haines with a pickaxe and spade costing 2s., and from time to time they purchased " turns " or " spinning turns " for poor women.

We find the parish officers incurring expenses in taking prisoners to the sessions and to gaol, and much trouble was taken by them in dealing with the parents of illegitimate children in order that the burden on the parish funds might be lightened so far as possible. When it became necessary to provide for destitute children the overseers usually boarded them with some woman until they reached the age of seven years, when they were sometimes apprenticed to a master or mistress for a period of not less than seven years. The reputed father of an illegitimate child was required to pay a weekly sum towards its maintenance during infancy and £4 when the child reached the age of seven years for its apprenticeship.[1]

A poor child, Elisabeth Cragg, was bound apprentice by the parish officers in 1743 to a dairyman of Somersetshire till she was twenty-one or married, to be taught " the Art or Business of Housewifry." [2]

Another side of the activities of the parish officers was the jealous guard kept lest strangers should hide themselves in the parish and so gain a settlement ; and expenses, usually a few shillings, are paid from time to time to persons, including Francis Mines, a servant of the parish officers, for " waring " or " warning " out the " outcomers." While thus chasing away any who manifested an inclination to remain without producing a certificate from the place of their legal settlement to hold Corsley " harmless " should they become chargeable to the rates, the parish duly relieved those who were journeying from one place to another with a " pass." Various parties of

---

[1] MS. papers, A D. 1737, in the possession of C. N. Phipps, Esq., relating to bastardy cases in Corsley.

[2] Indenture, A.D. 1743, in Corsley Parish Chest.

sailors were relieved in this way in 1742, 1747, and 1748.

Contributions were regularly made to the county rates, and for prisoners in the King's Bench or Marshalsea, this being frequently entered as the " Jal & Maishel & Vagbun money."

The parish officers appear to have considered that their labours earned them an annual festivity at the public-house, and the expenses on " estertusday," varying from £1 to £1 10s., are an annual charge on the parochial funds till 1751. In one case a puritanical critic has added the comment, " not fit to be allowed." He appends a similar remark to an entry of 16s. expended at the sessions, so it would appear that the burden of holding the compulsory office of overseer or churchwarden was not without its compensations in Corsley.

In 1757 a lease was granted by Lord Weymouth to the churchwardens and overseers of a cottage, garden, and orchard, about 10 lugs of ground, under Gore Hill.[1] The overseers' accounts for this period are missing, but this was probably the first parochial experiment in setting up a poorhouse.

The system of apprenticeship was by no means confined to the children under the care of the parish officers, and any youth would have found it difficult to get a start in his trade or occupation until he had fulfilled his seven years with some master.

An account of the examination of William Chapman in 1739 or 1759, which is found in Corsley parish chest, gives a good illustration of this. He was born thirty-three years before this examination took place, at Rodden. When fourteen years of age his mother bound him apprentice to a chairmaker of Westbury, from whom after four years

[1] MS. Corsley Survey, 1745, in the Longleat Estate Office.

he ran away and for two years wandered the country. At the end of this period he returned to his master and made an agreement with him to serve out the remainder of his time, which he completed in the service of this master, and afterwards of his master's brother. The account concludes, " Soon after he married and has five children—he has lived in Corsley ever since." [1]

William Carpenter, a broadweaver of Corsley, was born in the parish sixty-five years before his examination in 1739 or 1759.[2] He was apprenticed when thirteen to a master at South Brewham, and, after three and a half years, transferred by him, with his assent, to another master at Berkley. Soon after finishing his time with this master he married and had seven children. He declared " that he has continued ever since working at his hands in yᵉ Parish of Great Corsley Aforesᵈ." He was then living in a cottage valued at £8, formerly his father's.

These short biographies illustrate the normal life of the handicraftsman of that day, who still, according to the Statute of Elizabeth, served a long apprenticeship, after which he could reasonably aspire to setting up for himself, marrying a wife, and following his trade until incapacitated by old age [3]

[1] MS account of the examination of William Chapman in 1739 or 1759 (date indistinctly written), in Corsley Parish Chest.

[2] MS. account of the examination of William Carpenter, broadweaver, in 1739 or 1759, in Corsley Parish Chest.

[3] For extracts from Overseers' Accounts see Appendix, pp. 302–5.

CHAPTER IV

INDUSTRY AND AGRICULTURE

(1760—1837)

CORSLEY was now entering upon the period of its fullest life and activity. The estimated population in 1760 was about 1,300, or more than half as much again as at the last census in 1901, when the number returned was 824.[1] This population of 1,300, or thereabouts, continued to grow rapidly, though with fluctuations, till about 1830, reaching its highest recorded figure of 1,729 in 1831, when the census was taken; but it was probably even greater than this a few years previously, as the tide had already begun to ebb, commencing with a number of emigrations to America, in the years which preceded the taking of the census.

Increased vitality in the various departments of life of the community did not fail to accompany the numerical increase. Something like a religious revival in the Church of England seems to have occurred simultaneously with the introduction and growth of Dissent. The continued development of industries in the parish is shown in the new occupations, or new branches of the old industries, which

[1] Census Report, 1901.

were followed by the inhabitants. Parochial administration and methods of Poor Relief, the one side of parish life of which full records remain to us, underwent great changes and development, to meet the needs of the growing population. Lastly, one of the most important events in the whole history of the parish, the enclosure and division of the old common fields, occurred in 1783. Probably in no previous century of its existence as a village community did such vast changes take place, both in the outward aspect of Corsley and in the life of its inhabitants, as between the early years of the eighteenth and those of the nineteenth century.

From 1760 onwards cloth-making continued to flourish and increase. It appears that all stages of the manufacture were carried on in Corsley, including preparing, spinning, dyeing, weaving, shearing and finishing. The work was mainly under the control, direct or indirect, of capitalist clothiers, of whom there were several in the parish. The wool would be purchased by them, either raw, or from the spinners, in the form of yarn, and for each subsequent process they would employ a different set of people ; at some stages giving out the wool to be dealt with at the workers' homes at piecework rates, at others having it handled in their own factories by wage-earning labourers, and finally disposing of the dyed and finished pieces to merchants at Blackwall Hall, or other purchasers.

Some of the old inhabitants remember how the wool, raw as it came from the sheep's back, and sometimes all matted together, would be fetched from Mr. Taunton's factory at the Mill Farm by the women who performed the unsavoury process of " woolpicking " in their own homes. Spinning was doubtless also partly, if not altogether, a home industry.

After being spun into yarn, dyed, and prepared at one of the factories, such as that at the Mill Farm, the wool would be fetched thence by the weavers, in large bags which they carried on their shoulders. Some of the weaving was done in weaving factories, where several looms would be kept at work ; one of these may be seen half-way up Chapmanslade village street. But the greater part of the yarn was woven by independent workers at their own homes. The loom was fitted up in a long weaving-shed at the back of the house, or else in the dwelling itself. Many of the long, low, weavers' windows are yet to be seen in Corsley and Chapmanslade. Both men and women would work at the loom. It took two persons to fix the threads, and then one could work the shuttle, standing with his back to the light and throwing it to and fro.

When the material was woven it was taken back to the factory to undergo the finishing processes. One of these was the raking with " teasels," or thistles, to draw all the threads one way and give a surface.

Shearing, again, was often given out to small independent workers whose homes were fitted up with the necessary appliances. One of these shearers, Down by name, resided at Whitbourne Moor, where he had his apparatus, or mill, with a horse to drive it round.

The very important industry of dyeing the yarn was carried on extensively. The dyers were probably a class of capitalists, distinct from the clothiers, by whom the other processes of manufacture were financed.

Besides Sturford, where extensive dyeworks be-

longing to Mr. H. A. Fussell were in operation
during the first half of the nineteenth century, at
least two dye-houses existed, one belonging, in 1783,
to Thomas Singer,[1] at Dartford or Whitbourne Moor,
the other in the fields near Chapmanslade. In
Corsley Church is a monument to John Carpenter,
" an eminent dyer of this parish," deceased in 1812.
About the year 1770 we learn that dye-stuffs were
stolen from Messrs. James and Nicholas Codell (or
Cockell?), of Chapmanslade.[2] Soapwort, a plant
much used by the dyers, is to be found growing
in a wall near where the lane to Temple branches
from the high-road. Mr. Fussell's dyeworks at Sturford included machinery worked by the stream from
the pond. In the fields near Temple were white
railings or racks, where the yarn was dried under
the supervision of " old Robert Mines." Towards
the middle of the nineteenth century, when the trade
was declining in Corsley, wool used to be fetched
to the dyeworks from Mr. Britten's factory at Colport
Road, Frome.

The total output of cloth from Corsley must have
been considerable, and probably few houses, from
that of the yeoman farmer down to the labourer's
cottage, were at this time without a loom ; for
although the manufacturing handicraftsman was
usually a specialised worker who turned with difficulty to farm labour when the cloth trade deserted
Wiltshire, yet cloth-making and agriculture were not
wholly divorced in Corsley ; and not only was the
capitalist clothier frequently a farmer, but no doubt
weaving was also carried on by the peasants in con-
junction with a little farming or gardening. An

[1] Warminster and Corsley Enclosure Award, with maps, 1783.
[2] *Wiltshire Archæol. Mag.* xvi. p. 325.

example of this is found in the will of James Greatwood, dated 1796,[1] whereby he left to his daughter, Elizabeth White, the east part of the dwelling-houses, with the weaving-shop and broad loom, also the upper part of the garden, the cowbarton or yard, and a close of ground of about two acres. To his son Robert he left the west end of the house, the remainder of the garden, and two acres of the close ; to his son John the remainder of the close and one and a quarter acres of Corsley Heath Warren. The goods, furniture, and residue of his personal estate were to be divided equally between Elizabeth and Robert, who were to pay the funeral expenses. The sum owed on mortgage was to be discharged by his children, and for every £17 owed, Elizabeth and Robert were each to pay £7 and John £3.

This type of small farmer with a second occupation has continued in the parish to the present day, or possibly may have died out and been revived during the last half of the nineteenth century, in a district where the soil is particularly favourable for the success of the small holding.

During the last twenty years of the eighteenth century the expansion of the clothing industry is shown by the immigration of workers in new branches of weaving ; a narrow-weaver, a " casimere " weaver, and a linsey-woolsey weaver took out leases in the parish and settled to work beside the broadweavers, whose predecessors were established there a century earlier.[2]

It seems that even towards the end of the period

---

[1] Loose slip or memorandum in MS. Corsley Survey, 1745, at Longleat Estate Office.

[2] See MS. Corsley Survey, 1745, at Longleat Estate Office.

we are now considering weavers in Corsley could earn a tolerable maintenance by constant work, but, as one of the old inhabitants, Mr. Moses West, remarked, they " had to be always at it." Though women as well as men were engaged in this process, children were not able to assist, and child labour was confined to other branches of the clothing industry, such as spinning.

A silk factory was set up at Whitbourne Moor, probably after the clothing industry had begun to decline, and was working until the middle of the nineteenth century, giving employment to about twenty women and girls.[1]

But while weaving and other home industries were carried on simultaneously with work on the land, the workers in factories were a class apart. An old man states that he can remember when little mites of children, aged seven or eight years, worked at the factories, and all the workers, children and adults, would leave the factories together, stinking of the dye to such an extent that their passing by was a nuisance to the other inhabitants of Corsley. The earnings of the men in the factories were higher than those of agricultural workers, and another old inhabitant remembers hearing that at the Lane End Factory workers got 30s., 20s., or 13s. per week, and a certain George Clements earned 14s. per week in Mr. Taunton's factory, sometimes being kept at work till 7 or 8 p.m. This must have been shortly before the trade left Corsley, towards the middle of the nineteenth century, and wages were probably lower than in the prosperous days of the eighteenth century ; but they still compare very favourably with agri-

---

[1] This is distinctly remembered by many of the older inhabitants of Corsley. Winding silk on to reels appears to have been the particular process carried on.

cultural wages, which at this time seldom exceeded 8s.

Alongside the manufacturing population the tradesman and dealer increased and throve. There were several tradesmen in the parish, and from the old account-book of Mr. Sparey, who kept a store in 1821,[1] we get a glimpse of the way the inhabitants did their shopping. It was probably those living round Sturford and Whitbourne Springs who dealt chiefly at this little shop, where they could purchase bread, butter, cheese, meat, candles, fat, flour, " shugar," salt, biscuits, tobacco, tea, bran, worsted, soap, and paint—red, grey, or brown. The bread was sold by the dozen, but the unit, whether it refers to a weight, or, improbably, to a loaf, must have been quite small.

Credit was granted to many of the customers, and debts amounting to £97 7s. 9½d., due from forty-seven persons, appear to have been owing to Sparey at this time. One of the largest debtors, owing £11 1s. 4d., was Isaac Taylor, or, as entered in the account book, " is taylor," sexton and bellringer at the parish church, a near neighbour, one of a family whose descendants remark that they were " Taylors by name and tailors by trade." Isaac Taylor would sit, cross-legged, stitching, in the large window of his cottage in Sturford Lane, according to tradition, and, doubtless, he found difficulty in getting his accounts settled, so that his neighbour the shopkeeper was obliged to give him long credit till his tailoring bills were paid. Sparey's customers seem to have purchased goods as they wanted them, 7d. or 9d. worth at a time, and to have settled their bills wholly or in part every month or thereabouts. John Moody,

---

[1] MS. Account Book, 1821–23, in possession of Mr. Seth Sparey.

who had about five guineas' worth of goods on credit
during sixteen months, or an average of 1s. 6d. per
week, which goods included bread, butter, cheese,
meat, and fat, paid up his account most promptly
every month or oftener, with the exception of three
months in the summer of 1822, when it ran on, being
paid in full on reaching the sum of 19s. 4½d.

Another customer, Phebe Smith, who was receiving
2s. 9d. per week from the parish as the mother of
two illegitimate children, appears, when credit was
granted her, to have taken goods to the value of about
£1 a month, for which she would then pay a part of
the sum owing. She does not appear ever to have
settled her account in full, and Mr. Sparey seems to
have been naturally reluctant to grant her credit.
Martha Singer, a very regular customer, who had
goods to the value of £7 13s. on credit during sixteen
months, appears likewise to have paid only a portion
of what she owed each month. She continued, however, to receive credit.

With regard to his supplies, Sparey probably purchased them mainly from dealers in Warminster or
the neighbourhood. In March and April, 1822, he
bought ten bags of flour from Mr. Blackmore for
£21 19s., which he paid in instalments. He also
bought from him tea and sugar, tea being apparently
7s. the pound. In February, 1822, he bought teas
to the value of £5 15s. from Mr. Gray, at two months'
credit.

This tradesman was probably William Sparey, who
had migrated from the parish of Boyton, ten miles
distant, the grandfather of Mr. Seth Sparey, who at
present occupies the small farm and house in Sturford
Lane where the shop was kept. His descendants
state that William Sparey was a clothier and farmer,
and we find from the account-book that he had

dealings with London merchants and bankers. On one of the first pages are the addresses of :

> Alex. Buckler,
>> Blackwell Hall Factor,
>>> 74, Basinghall St.
>
> Boyd's Brock Bank,
>> 28, Bucklersbury.
>
> Viçat Draper,
>> 49, Great Surry (?) St.
>>> Blackfrers.

It seems, then, that he followed at once the three separate occupations of farmer, clothier, and retail shopkeeper.

Besides general provision dealers like Sparey there were more specialised tradesmen, such as butchers and bakers, in the parish ;[1] and with agriculture and cloth-making, victuallers and tailors, the parish could have produced most necessary articles of consumption.

But at the same time specialisation and division of labour seem to have led to more extensive dealings with the outside world. It is interesting to note that early in the nineteenth century two poor old men were provided by the parish[2] with a donkey, one also with a cart, to enable them to earn a living, an indication that there was plenty of work for carriers, besides that done by the farmers, who drove every week to the neighbouring markets in their wagons.

A new industry probably had its beginning here

---

[1] See Corsley Survey Book, 1745, &c., in Longleat Estate Office. See also, in various MS. papers relating to the parish, occupations of residents.

[2] Corsley MS. Overseers' Accounts, 7th month, 1828, and 7th and 8th months, 1829–30.

early in the nineteenth century. In a lease of Whitbourne Farm to " James Smith of Corsley, Gentleman," in 1807, besides the usual covenants a special
one was made licensing him to keep and use a limekiln on Cley Hill, and to dig stone and burn
lime, &c. As far as our information goes, this
was the commencement of the operations which now
threaten seriously to deface the chief natural feature
of our parish.

Another new occupation, which was introduced in
the last quarter of the eighteenth century, after the
passing of the Turnpike Act, and which henceforth
filled a prominent place in the manor rolls, parish
accounts, and the private accounts of residents,[1] is
the quarrying of stones. It is not quite clear whether
" quarrying " may not sometimes have meant picking
or collecting the stones off the fields, or whether in
all cases it entailed digging or hewing out. The
work was done to a large extent by paupers, sometimes under supervision of the parish officers.

The stones were collected or quarried in a number
of fields or localities, and even in the roads of the
parish. A presentment of the Court Leet of the
Manor of Great Corsley in October, 1786, runs as
follows :

"Whereas there have frequently been stones quarried by the
sides of the Roads and even into the Roads so as to damage the
said Roads, we present any person offending in this matter in future
(without the leave of the surveyor) to pay five shillings."

It seems also to have been the habit of some of
the inhabitants to dig sandpits in the lanes. This
was forbidden by the Court Leet in 1791, unless
with the leave of the lord and his agents. More
presentments on account of sandpits were, however,

---

[1] See Mr. Barton's MS. Farming Accounts, 1801–11 and 1828–36.

made in 1795, and in 1796 it was necessary for the same Court to present a sandhole at Dodsgate " to be dangerous and to be filled up immediately."

The quarrying of stones would lead us to suppose that an attempt was made to improve the roads, but the method of quarrying in the roads themselves must for the time have rendered them far more dangerous for travellers than before, and throughout the last quarter of the eighteenth century the Manor Courts repeatedly present roads as needing repair. It seems clear that at any rate the lanes and byways of the parish were in a fairly bad state at this time.

We must now consider what was happening in agricultural Corsley.

We saw how in the first half of the eighteenth century the industrial element had begun to preponderate over the agricultural element in the population. An analysis of the people in 1811 shows the extent to which this preponderance had developed by the nineteenth century, and indicates that the number employed in agriculture had remained stationary or had even decreased since the seventeenth century, the surplus of the rapidly increasing population of the parish being entirely absorbed by industries and occupations necessary for the support of the manufacturing community. Of 1,412 persons 698, or about one-half, were employed in trade, manufacture, or handicrafts ; 215, or about two-thirteenths, were employed chiefly in agriculture ; 499, or more than one-third, were unclassified. The unclassified population presumably included all children too young to work, and the main part should probably be estimated as dependent on manufactures and trades and agriculture in the proportion of, roughly speaking, three-fourths to trades and industries and one-fourth to agriculture. This would make the industrial population 1,072, or rather more than three-fourths of the whole. An indefinite number should be subtracted from the 499 unclassified persons for unoccupied adults, domestic servants, and other occupations which do not come under the given headings, so that the actual numbers dependent on agriculture and industries would be somewhat less than the above estimate. We shall not, however, be far wrong in saying that, broadly speaking, three-fourths of the population were dependent on manu-factures and trades and one-fourth on agriculture.[1]

It seems improbable that the total number of persons in the parish in the days when the community was purely agricultural can have been as few as 215, which is the total number employed chiefly in agriculture in 1811. When we add 125, or a quarter of the unclassified persons, we get a total agricultural population of 340, which is not far from the number of the population of Corsley in the earlier part of the seventeenth century, as estimated from the entries in the parish registers preserved in the Diocesan Record Office. It is likely, however, that these registers were incomplete, and the population greater even at that date, when agriculture was pre-sumably the sole occupation and resource of the inhabitants. It appears, then, that the agricultural changes which we must now describe had caused an actual decrease in the number of persons employed, in any capacity, on the land

In Corsley, as in other parts of the country, the growth of an industrial population had reacted on agriculture, and had led to a step being taken which revolutionised the whole agrarian system, setting a term to the ancient communal method of farming,

[1] The above figures are taken from an analysis of the population in "General View of the Agriculture of Wilts," 2nd ed. 1813, p. 238.

effecting a transformation in the outward appearance of the parish, and deeply affecting the lives of the peasant occupiers of the soil.

The common-field enclosure, while it caused profound and not altogether desirable social changes, and reduced the number of persons who obtained a living by cultivation of the land, gave, however, a new birth to agriculture. Large farms in severalty replaced the old distribution in common fields and commons, and corn was produced in large quantities in response to the growing demand and rising prices.

In 1779 the preliminary measures for enclosing Warminster and Corsley were commenced, and the Act was passed in 1783. Hitherto the land of the parish had been divided into great common fields, closes or enclosures round the homesteads, and commons or wastes. The tenants of the Manor of Huntenhull claimed and enjoyed the right of pasturing their cattle on the commons of Westbury, as well as of Corsley.[1] There had been three common fields, namely, Cley Hill Field, Chedlanger Field, adjoining Norridge Wood, and Bickenham Field, adjoining Scudamore parish. Some enclosures had already been made in these.[2] By the Enclosure Award for Warminster and Corsley the whole parish was in 1783 divided up ; strips, patches, and ancient enclosures in the common fields were divided and exchanged among the various persons who had rights ; the commons, too, were divided and allotted, and little was left unenclosed of these pastures and wastes, though some portions remained unappropriated within the memory of old inhabitants, to be absorbed by a slow process of encroachment, till only here a wayside strip and there a triangle of grass at the cross-roads remains.

[1] See Manor of Huntenhull MS. Minutes of Court Baron, 1785.
[2] Warminster and Corsley Enclosure Award, with maps, 1783.

The Enclosure Award map of 1783 shows how the land was allotted among a great number of holders. A large proportion in the centre and other allotments distributed over the parish were assigned to Lord Weymouth, Lord of the Manor. Cley Hill Farm belonged to John Coope, Esq. Land to the west of Cley Hill, where Corsley House now stands, was in the possession of John Barton, some of whose fields are marked as " entailed." A number of detached bits were assigned to Robert Meares, and other owners too numerous to mention had holdings of various sizes in different districts of the parish.

This division and allotment, no doubt, tended to squeeze out the small holder, who lost the advantage of pasturing his cattle on the common, and who could not afford the expenses connected with enclosure and the raising of hedges. It was adjudged by the commissioners that the expense to the Rector of Corsley alone in making fences, barns, &c., which they considered necessary would be £100. Before the enclosure few labourers are to be found among the leaseholders. In 1780 and 1781, the years following the commencement of proceedings, no less than six took out leases, thus leaving evidence that the small holder was being driven to part with his land and become a wage-earning labourer.

The enclosure rendered improved methods of agriculture possible, and the parish became almost wholly arable, so far as farming was concerned. Few cows were kept after the enclosure, though the rich water meadows which border the two small streams of the parish were maintained for pasture and hay crops.[1] In 1828, when a new terrier

[1] See "General View of the Agriculture of Wilts," 1794, by T. Davis, where in the map Corsley is coloured chiefly as arable, with two lines of water meadows running through.

and rate book was drawn up for the parish, a rough calculation of distribution gives :

Arable land ...	...	...	1,511 acres.
Pasture and mead	...	...	466 ,,
Wood and plantation ...		...	194 ,,
Water meadows	...	...	88 ,,
Orchards ...	...	...	49 ,,

the remainder of the parish being occupied by homesteads and a few withy and alder beds.[1]

In 1834 agricultural capital was said to be diminishing owing to the highness of the poor rate,[2] but in 1836, when the Poor Law reform had been carried through, we find that Corsley, unlike some of the neighbouring parishes, was reported as having its people well employed,[3] and though wages were low, no doubt corn-growing afforded amble occupation to the farm labourer.

The Barton family held a large farm in Corsley, partly their own freehold property and partly rented, and their farming accounts between 1801 and 1835 throw light upon the agriculture of Corsley subsequent to the enclosure of the parish.

A valuation of October 18, 1809,[4] and the accounts that follow show clearly that wheat was the main crop, while barley and oats were also cultivated ; peas, beans, clover, and vetches were used as rotation crops. The flock of sheep was an important adjunct of the farm, and no doubt the fold was highly

[1] See MS. Terrier of Corsley, 1828.

[2] Report Poor Law Commission, 1834, vol. xiv. Appendix B1, Part III. p. 571c. Evidence of H. A. Fussell.

[3] Second Annual Report Poor Law Commission, 1836, vol. i. p. 300, Warminster Union. Evidence of John Ravenhill.

[4] See Appendix, MS. Farming Accounts of Mr. Barton, October 18, 1804, at Corsley House, pp. 306, 307.

valued, as in olden days, for manuring the corn lands, while the wool, sold to yeomen of Corsley, may have been worked up in the local woollen industry.   Seven strong horses were kept to draw the plough and drag the heavy corn-wagons into Warminster market.   Pigs and poultry, no doubt, grew fat upon the otherwise wasted products.   Seven cows were kept, but in 1806 their number was reduced to two and in 1809 to one, and for a time the dairy was probably only sufficient to supply Mr. Barton's household.   But in 1828, when the second remaining volume of accounts commences, after an interval of eighteen years, six cows were kept, and some cheese, milk, and butter were being sold.

Women as well as men were employed in agriculture.   During the first decade of the century four were working fairly steadily on this farm at a wage of 4s. for a week, or six days' work.   In 1828 it appears that the size of the farm had been increased. About twelve men were at this time regularly employed.   In January, 1829, their wages were as follows : One 10s., three 9s., one 8s., one 7s., one 5s., one 3s., two 2s. 6d., one 2s.   Probably the earners of two or three shillings a week were paupers.   Besides these regular workers others were employed on miscellaneous jobs, including " bird-keeping."   Allen, the mole-catcher, received large sums on account of moles, besides receiving payment for casual labour.   From 1830 onwards about six women appear to have been retained at farm work.

We learn incidentally from these accounts that potato-ground was leased in 1805 and later years'; the labouring man of Corsley has at least been well provided with allotment land since the enclosure of the parish.

CHAPTER V

THE RELIGIOUS REVIVAL

(1760—1837)

FROM the time of the Reformation till 1742 we have scant information as to the religious life of the inhabitants of Corsley. The volume of Churchwardens' Accounts which has been preserved commences in 1742, but the entries for the first forty years or so relate mainly to the usual payments for the destruction of badgers, hedgehogs, polecats, foxes, moles, and sparrows, or to relief granted to travellers, with occasional payments for repairs to the church or bells.[1]

A new element was, however, introduced after the middle of the eighteenth century, when the preaching of the Methodists, followed a little later by a Baptist mission, brought fresh vitality into the spiritual life of the people, and the enthusiasm of these sects appears to have roused the Church of England to greater activity.

In 1769 Corsley was entered in the Wesleyan annals as a " new place," with thirty-one members.[2] In 1770 it had forty-six members, and in 1777 fifty-

[1] MS. Corsley Churchwardens' Accounts, 1782–83.
[2] Stephen Tuck, " Wesleyan Methodism in Frome," p. 40.

one. Wesley himself preached in the parish in September, 1772, visiting Bath, Frome, Bradford, and Keynsham in the same week.[1]

It seems probable that the Wesleyan community was concentrated mainly round Lane End, where the present chapel stands, the influence extending from Frome.

The Baptist influence appears to have come a few years later from the direction of Westbury. In 1777 a preacher of this denomination began his ministrations at Chapmanslade, and in 1799 a Baptist chapel was nearly completed in this village.[2] The chapel, if it be the same, or on the same site, as the present Chapmanslade Baptist Chapel, was in the parish of Westbury, but there is no reason to suppose that enthusiasm for the new sect was confined to the northern half of the village, and that the inhabitants on the other side of the road in Corsley parish were not equally affected. On the contrary, we know that the Baptist faith soon spread to the south of Corsley, and in 1811 an offshoot of the Chapmanslade community was established at Whitbourne Temple, where a chapel was erected in 1811.[3]

The Congregational Church at Chapmanslade appears from monuments in the present building to have been established by 1771, the leading members being John Turner and John Barter. No history of this establishment has, however, been preserved.

It is interesting to trace the influence of the new religious fervour on the Church. One of its effects was to stimulate the Rector of Corsley to hold an increased number of Church services on Sunday, as

---

[1] Stephen Tuck, "Wesleyan Methodism in Frome," p. 44. Quotation from Wesley's Journal.

[2] W. Doël, "Twenty Golden Candlesticks," p. 173.

[3] *Ibid.* p. 178.

the following entry in the Churchwardens' Account Book indicates :

Easter, 1784. "I, Thomas Huntingford, Rector, do hereby declare that I am not bound by any obligation whatever to serve this church twice on a Sunday, but that I am influenc'd thereto purely upon conscientious motives, and that I think myself at liberty to discontinue it at any time whenever there appears to me cause or reason for so doing.

This entry is elucidated by a further memorandum three years later, when Thomas Huntingford was succeeded as rector by G. I. Huntingford. It was as follows :

Easter, 1787. Memorandum. " That it was customary before the time of the late Mr. Thomas Huntingford to have divine service performed in Corsley Church but once on a Sunday, and the present Rector, the Revd G. I. Huntingford is not bound to any further service than what was required by ancient custom.

(*Signed*) John Knight, Nath : Barton, Jno Cockell, George Marven, James Silcox."

In all probability the second service in the church was continued notwithstanding the anxiety which the innovators of this practice displayed to prevent its becoming a precedent, binding on future rectors. And if they cherished a hope that the new heresies would soon be stamped out, leaving the ministers of the Established Church free to follow their old, easy way, this hope was doomed to disappointment.

Dissent had taken a firm root in the parish, which, from its peculiar distribution in a number of scattered hamlets, was specially adapted for the formation of several small religious communities, collected round the nucleus of their chapel or church. And it is interesting to note that each of these Nonconformist settlements gained a footing in the hamlets most distant from the church, with the exception of Chapman-

slade, whose nearer end is not more than a mile
distant, but which is separated by a hill and valley
from the parish church of St. Margaret. At a later
time, as we shall see, Church people made efforts to
combat Dissent by the erection of Anglican churches
in the vicinity of the two Baptist chapels.

But to return to the end of the eighteenth century.
It is probable that the successor of Mr. Thomas
Huntingford was not less zealous for the religious
orthodoxy of his parishioners than his predecessor
had been, and in 1788 a Sunday School was established, the Easter Sacrament money being applied
for the purpose to purchase eleven spelling-books,
forty-eight catechism books, four horn books, six
testaments, and six coats for six of the poor boys.[1]
Thus the education of the children of the parish,
no less than the ardour of religious life, was stimulated by this rivalry between Church and Noncon-
formists.

We do not know how far the Church service was
a musical one prior to 1817, but the majority of a
vestry meeting in this year directed that a clarionet,
price £2 2s., purchased for the singers, should be
paid for out of the churchwardens' funds.[2] In 1825
Nathaniel Barton's offer of an organ for the use
of the parish church was thankfully accepted at a
vestry meeting. This barrel-organ was played by
the shoemaker, James Cuff, within the memory of
inhabitants now living. Tradition relates that it was
the custom for the ringers and singers to " close up
in the evening " at Mr. Knight's public-house at
Leigh's Green, now the " Cross Keys." The inhabitants of Corsley seldom neglected an opportunity
for convivial gatherings.

[1] MS. Corsley Churchwardens' Accounts, Easter, 1788.
[2] *Ibid.*, April 7, 1817.

Some evidence of the zeal of Church people at this time was given in 1819, when it was decided at a vestry meeting to build a new wall on the south side of the churchyard, and assumed that a donation of bricks from Lord Bath would be granted, and that the carriage would be rendered free of expense by some of the inhabitants.[1]

In 1830, at a vestry meeting, a momentous decision was come to. It was resolved :

"THAT, the parish Church being in a bad state of repair, and its accommodations being insufficient for the Inhabitants of the Parish, it is expedient that the present Church should be taken down and rebuilt on a larger plan.

"Proposed by Mr. Ball, seconded by Mr. Meares," &c.

A sketch of the late parish church, which was in the possession of the late Mr. Moses West, shows a picturesque little building ; and now that the population has again dwindled, while two additional churches have been erected in or near the parish, one cannot help wishing that some other means had been found to provide accommodation for the worship of the population, whose number reached its maximum about the time this resolution was passed. It was, however, during the following years carried into effect, and the present inartistic building was raised in the place of the pretty old parish church which formerly stood on its site.

While the work of destruction and building were in progress, services appear to have been held in Mr. John Ball's malthouse, which was rented by the churchwardens for the purpose.

A new vestry-room was also erected. The votes at vestry were at this time distributed as follows : John Ball and Mrs. Barton each six votes, the Mar-

[1] MS. Corsley Churchwardens' Accounts, March 31, 1819.

THE OLD CHURCH, PULLED DOWN, c. 1830.

(From a sketch in the possession of Mrs. Moses West.)

To face p. 60.

quis of Bath five votes, James Knight five, Mrs. Allard five, J. H. Taunton five ; other inhabitants had four, three, and two votes, and the majority one vote each.[1]

It is interesting to note that Isaac Taylor was appointed sexton in 1837, the post still being filled by members of his family at the present day (1907).

Appended are a few entries in the Churchwardens' Accounts which have not been noticed in the text, referring to events, historical or otherwise, that affected the parish during these years :

	£	s.	d.
1779–80.			
Mr. Bilbie for Casting the Bell	10	7	4
and for adding 198 new Mettle at 14d. ...	11	11	0
Expenses Hanging the Bell	0	6	8
1789–90.			
Four Books for the use of the parish on the Day of Gen. Thanksgiving	0	1	0
Paid the Ringers for Ringing on D°	0	10	6
D° for D° when Lord Weymouth rec^d the Title of Marquess	0	7	6
For a Flag to place on Clay hill when his Majesty Honoured the Marquess of Bath with his Company	0	8	6

March 31, 1807.

it beng agreed on by a Vestry as under :

John Singer to have £1 5s. pr. year for Cleaning the inside of the Church and looking after the Boys Sundays, and furthermor to have £1 for Cleaning the Churchyard, Cutting the Hedges and Cleaning the Walkes, etc., etc.

	£	s.	d.
July 17, 1815.			
T° the Ringers in y° Parrish Acct. on the news of the Battle of Waterloo	0	10	6

---

[1] MS. Corsley Churchwardens' Accounts, April, 1834.

CHAPTER VI

THE HOUSE FAMINE AND ITS RESULTS

(1760—1837)

WE have seen how rapidly the parish was growing and expanding in population, trade, and industry between 1760 and 1837, how the parish was transformed by enclosure, and how new religious elements had quickened the spiritual life of the people. We must now try to discover what was the condition of the population under this somewhat trying process of growth, and especially during those universally terrible years of war and famine which occurred early in the eighteenth century.

One result of the rapid immigration and increase in the population was probably a lack of sufficient house-room. In 1813, 1,412 persons, consisting of 388 families, were residing in 278 houses. This gives an average of 1.395 families, or 5 persons, to each house. Nearly a quarter of the houses in Corsley are now small three-roomed cottages,[1] and it is probable that many of the smaller and worse built houses have been pulled down or allowed to fall into decay during the last eighty years, so that it is not likely that housing accommodation was better, or even so good, a hundred years ago as what remains of it at the

[1] See Part II. p. 133.

present day, and overcrowding must have been a serious evil.

An example of the way in which married people continued to live with their parents is found in the examination of James Durnford in 1821. This young man, aged about twenty-five, was a native of Upton Scudamore; when about twenty-one he became shepherd to Mr. Gane, of Corsley, at a weekly wage of 9s., still returning to his father's house to sleep for the first two years. He then took to staying the night in Corsley. About a year before his examination he had married a Corsley girl, and they had one child, and since his marriage he had slept at his mother-in-law's house at Corsley. He had not apparently gained a settlement in the parish, the custom of hiring servants by the year having fallen out of use a short time previously to this.[1]

The yearly hiring of servants was still the custom at the end of the nineteenth century. The career of John Moody is a good illustration both of the system and of its abandonment. He was born in Corsley about the year 1780. "When I was about 11 years old," he relates, "my father hired me to Farmer Smith at Whitbourne . . . to drive plough and other things." He remained in this service four years, his father receiving his wages, which, when he left at the age of fifteen, amounted to 2s. a week. His father then hired him to Burgess, at Cley Hill, at "2 shillings and 3d. a week, as he told me. I lived with Mr. Burgess a twelvemonth, and after that twelvemonth my father told me he had hired me for half-a-crown a week for a twelvemonth." This seems to leave no doubt that the arrangement was an annual hiring. He remained four years with Mr. Bur-

[1] See MS. account of Examination of James Durnford, Feb. 1821, in Corsley Parish Chest.

gess, getting a rise of 3d. a week for the first three years, and 6d. a week the last year. He probably left in the year 1799, when he must have been about nineteen years of age. He then hired himself to Mr. John Ball, at Chipps Farm, but was drawn for the militia and was out about eleven months. He then hired himself to Mr. Sainsbury as a weekly servant at Corsley Farm, but did not remain in his service twelve months. "I then hired myself again to Mr. Ball at Temple Farm in Corsley before which time I was married to my present wife, Hester Warden."

The cause of this examination, which took place in 1839, then appears : "George Moody, now chargeable to the parish of Corsley, having a broken leg, is my son. I hired him to Mr. James Burgess of Clay Hill when he was about 12 years old at weekly wages, but nothing was said as to time." [1] Clearly, therefore, no agreement for an annual hiring had been entered into, though he lived with Mr. Burgess more than a year, lodging the while at his father's house. The abandonment of the custom of annual hirings, which thus occurred early in the eighteenth century, was probably due, as the above examination suggests, to the war, with its constant demands for recruits for the militia.

Although we find no trace of the custom of the farm labourers living in the houses of the farmers in this parish, nor, indeed, in this district of Wiltshire, it seems that tailors or handicraftsmen would board and lodge their journeymen or workmen. Abraham Doël, about the year 1817, agreed with a tailor, Mr. Edward Pearce, at 3s. per week for

[1] MS. account of the examination of John Moody, A.D. 1839, in Corsley Parish Chest.

the year, with bed and board ; [1] and a similar agreement was entered into about 1827 between John Wheeler and Mr. James Wilkins, the occupation of these men not being stated.[2] These agreements are incidentally mentioned in disputes as to settlements many years later, and there is no reason to suppose that they are isolated instances ; considering the lack of housing accommodation, one may readily suppose that it was usual for the handicraftsman to board and lodge his unmarried workers in his own dwelling.

It is the more remarkable that this practice was not followed by the farmers since there are many roomy farmhouses in Corsley, some of them older than the eighteenth century. But in all the settlement disputes relative to agricultural labourers we find no case in which the labourer was ever boarded in the house of his master ; and in the Report to the Poor Law Commission in 1834 Mr. à Court gives evidence that the custom had not prevailed in this part of Wiltshire, at least since the enclosures were made.[3]

The parsonage-house at Corsley was unreasonably small. William Cobbett, in his " Rural Rides," quotes from the parliamentary returns that it was " too small for an incumbent with a family." [4] It must, if still occupying the same site, have been considerably added to or rebuilt since that time, for though not a large house, the present rectory contains a number of rooms.

In the year 1814 Mr. Barton, who owned land in the eastern half of the parish, began to build

---

[1] MS. paper relating to Abraham Doël, in Corsley Parish Chest.
[2] MS. paper relating to John Wheeler, in Corsley Parish Chest.
[3] Report Poor Law Commission, 1834, Appendix C, p. 472.
[4] William Cobbett, " Rural Rides," 1st ed. 1825, p. 437.

the new part of what is now known as Corsley House.[1]

It was probably owing to the urgency of the housing problem that the parish officers were led in 1769 to abandon the system of maintaining all the poor in their own houses, and to call a meeting for the establishment of a workhouse."[2]   A poor-house seems to have existed near Huntley since 1757,[3] when, no doubt, the population had already begun to outgrow the housing accommodation ; but this proposed workhouse was a much larger and more important enterprise.   Workhouses were not common in this district ; there were never more than forty-one in the whole of Wiltshire, including those in the numerous boroughs and market towns,[4] so that there is ground for believing that exceptional needs led to its establishment in Corsley.

Little seems to have been done for four years, though the churchwardens and overseers took a lease of a messuage and four closes in the Manor of Whitbourne Temple, and some payments for repairs to the poorhouse were incurred during these years.   But in 1773 the matter was again brought forward, and it was agreed at a vestry meeting in April "that there be a Work-house erected as soon as Possible it can be done for the reception of ye Poor of the said Parish."[5]   A committee was at the same time appointed to carry out the work.   Premises

[1] Mr Moses West, son of the carpenter who was imported from a neighbouring parish for this job, on which he was employed for many years, had a slab of wood on which a record of the commencement of the work was cut.

[2] Corsley MS Overseers' Accounts, April, 1769.

[3] MS. Corsley Survey, 1745, at Longleat Estate Office, lease to Churchwardens and Overseers of premises, cottage, garden, and orchard (about 10 lugs of ground) under Gore Hill.

[4] Abstract Poor Returns, 1815, p. 504 (Wiltshire).

[5] Corsley MS. Overseers' Accounts, April 20, 1773.

were leased at Whitbourne Springs,[1] and a thatched workhouse was erected.[2]

This new workhouse was opened in December, 1773, most of the twenty-five persons who disappear from the list of regular pensioners at this date being in all probability moved into the house. These twenty-five included men, women, and children, widows and spinsters, single men, a married couple, and orphaned or deserted children, admitted without their parents. In April, 1774, there were thirty-six inmates,[3] and in June another batch of regular pensioners appears to have been taken in.[4] About twenty-five, however, remained outside the house, and the usual doles and payments for rent, clothing, and funeral expenses for those in receipt of outdoor relief continue in just the same way as before.

Before proceeding to consider the general conditions of the people and of poor relief during the period, it will be well to follow the history of the workhouse from its establishment in 1773. It was, like all workhouses of that date, as its name implies, a place where work was carried on, and its establishment was an effort to lessen the burden on the rate-payers by making the labour of the paupers profitable. Unlike most of these experiments, the Corsley workhouse seems to have been a financial success, and, on the whole, to have rather reduced expenditure, and this without acting as a deterrent, for the number of persons relieved increased, while expenditure per head diminished. Between 1769 and 1772, before the

[1] MS. Corsley Survey, 1745, at Longleat Estate Office, lease taken out in 1773.

[2] Insurance policy, with Bath Fire Office, in Corsley Parish Chest. The house was insured "not exceeding £180," and goods and furniture contained in it "not exceeding £20."

[3] Corsley MS. Workhouse Accounts, April, 1774.

[4] *Ibid.* June, 1774.

workhouse was opened, the number of regular paupers varied from thirty-four to forty-two, and the annual expenditure from £244 to £351. The first four years after the workhouse was opened expenses were rather high, about fifty-five persons being relieved in or out of the house, at an annual cost of from £325 to £460. After this expenditure fell, and during the four years 1776-77 to 1779-80 about twenty people outside the house and about thirty inmates were supported for an annual expenditure of from £242 to £278. From 1783 to 1786 the expenditure was higher without any great increase in the number of paupers. From 1786 onwards the number of poor relieved outside the house increased, but expenditure only once exceeded £350, though the number of persons regularly relieved varied probably from sixty to eighty, or even exceeded that number.[1] It cannot, therefore, be said of the Corsley workhouse, as of many of these institutions, that its maintenance led to an extravagant waste of the ratepayers' money.

We must now see what treatment the inmates received. We have already noticed that persons of both sexes and all ages were sent here. The house received the sick as well as the able-bodied, and at any rate by 1796 it was also an asylum for the insane or feeble-minded. There were several rooms in the building, sometimes as many as four chimneys being swept in the spring, so some classification was possible if desired. The whole was ruled over by a salaried master, whose chief business it was to supervise the work of the inmates. The workhouse never seems to

[1] See Corsley MS. Overseers' Accounts for these years for total annual expenditure on poor relief, and see *ibid.* and Corsley MS. Workhouse Accounts for total number of persons in receipt of regular relief.

have been left without a master from 1774 till 1802, except possibly for a year, in 1794-95. The master's salary was usually £20 per annum, but during part of the period he was paid a smaller sum, receiving in addition a twelfth part of the profits of the work of the paupers. The number of inmates ranged, roughly speaking, between twenty and forty, though there were sometimes more or less than this.

The work to which they were set was very varied. Linsey was manufactured, being sometimes given out for the processes of weaving, milling, and dyeing, and finally sold for the benefit of the parish. Weaving was, however, carried on in the workhouse itself at least during part of these years. Some of the other occupations were spinning and scribbling of wool, knitting, netting, and shoemaking. A garden was kept, and pigs and potatoes were sometimes sold. No doubt the workhouse inmates made their own clothing and grew their own vegetables, pork, and bacon, as well as producing these commodities for sale. The paupers were also employed to quarry stones, and pickaxes, spades, and shovels were sometimes purchased. From 1786 onwards some of the inmates appear to have been hired out regularly to various employers. The age of these workers does not appear, nor the nature of the work performed by them, but the payments to the workhouse account for their labour were small, 1s. 6d. per week being the most common, and it seems probable that they were either children or feeble old men ; 4s. 6d. was received in 1796 for " Yeudles maid 4½ weeks Bird Keeping at 1/P," and 4s. 1½d. was received in 1789 of Mr. Dredge, a regular employer of the paupers, for " Aple Picking."

Each month a few pounds would be received from various sources for sales of the materials manufactured, or for the work of paupers. This amount was deducted from the expenses incurred for maintenance of the workhouse before the account was presented to the parish officers.

The inmates of the workhouse appear to have lived well—wheat, beef, cheese, milk, and malt and hops being purchased in considerable quantities, and no doubt the house brewed its own beer and tobacco was sometimes provided. During the year from April, 1776, to March, 1777, the purchases included :

> 9 cwt. of cheese.
> About 42 sacks of wheat (or its equivalent in flour).
> 12 sacks of malt and 18 lbs. of hops.
> 11 lbs. of tea.
> About 150/- worth of meat, chiefly beef.
> About 4/- worth of milk per month, or 48/- for the year.
> 1 lb. of tobacco.

There was probably an average of at least thirty inmates during this year, besides the master. Other articles of which small quantities were purchased were salt, butter, oatmeal, currants, figs, sugar, treacle, broad beans, cabbage, peas, and barley ; the latter may possibly have been for the pigs, and not for human food. Together with the produce of the workhouse garden and pigstyes, this gives a fair range of variety.

In 1795-96 the provisions for thirty persons are analysed as follows :

	cwt.	qr.	lb.	£	s	d.
Cheese	12	3	1¾	23	3	11
Meat (including 2 pigs killed) ...	19	2	24½	33	18	11¾
Bags flour, 28½	—			75	17	6
Sacks wheat, 22	—			42	8	0
Grinding and baking	—			5	0	0
Coals, 50 qrs. and 2 bushels ...	—			13	16	0
Soap, 103¼ lbs.						

It is stated this year that when earnings were deducted the maintenance cost about 2s. 4d. per head per week, or, with inclusion of the master's salary, about 2s. 7d. per head. In the following year over five pounds' worth of malt and hops were purchased.

The bills for clothing indicate that the paupers were well dressed as well as well fed. Seven pairs of gloves were purchased for them in 1774.[1]

At the beginning of the nineteenth century, when the labouring classes were half starved and corn at a fabulous price, the expense of maintaining the workhouse became very high. Consequently, in 1802 the master was dismissed, and all attempts to set the people to work in the house apparently abandoned ; and it would seem that the workhouse from this time forward became merely a poorhouse, where the destitute could lodge, rent free. The yearly expenses incurred by the parish on account of the workhouse during the next few years amount only to from £10 to £16,[2] and cannot have included food or clothing. Presumably each inmate received a monthly pension from the overseers and catered for him or herself.[3]

In 1812 a woman was paid 8s. for looking after the old people in the workhouse,[4] and with this exception the inmates were left to their own devices to look after themselves or each other.

[1] For all particulars of workhouse receipts and expenditure, number of inmates, &c., see MS. Workhouse Accounts.

[2] See Corsley MS. Overseers' Accounts.

[3] This is borne out by the recollections of an old inhabitant who remembers the years previous to the Poor Law Reform. Another old inhabitant states that the workhouse "seemed to be everybody's house, for any one to go in and out as they liked." So far as he remembers there was no supervision.

[4] Corsley MS. Overseers' Accounts, September, 1812.

It cannot be supposed that the withdrawal of all
authority over this community of thirty persons or so,
of every age, sex, and condition, who were thus left
to live as they could or pleased, would conduce to
good order.   In 1819 a committee was appointed
to make regulations for the governance of the workhouse and its inmates, and one of the parish officers
or the assistant overseer were desired to attend once a
week to see that the orders were duly observed.[1]
This seems rather insufficient, especially as we find
that the insane were still housed here, expenses being
incurred in bringing a lunatic hither in 1822.[2]
Nothing further, however, appears to have been done.

In 1830-31 the workhouse or poorhouse was
paved [3] and newly thatched,[4] and it lingered on as
an institution until the erection of the Warminster
Union workhouse, after the Poor Law Reform, in
1836.

[1] Corsley MS. Overseers' Accounts, Lady-day, 1819.
[2] *Ibid.* February, 1822.
[3] *Ibid.* 12th month, 1830–31.
[4] *Ibid.* 13th month, 1830–31.

CHAPTER VII

CORSLEY UNDER THE OLD POOR LAW

(1760—1837)

THE general administration of poor relief outside the workhouse continued from 1768 on the same lines as during the first half of the century,[1] with gradual changes which naturally followed on the increase of poverty on the one hand, and on the other the growth of knowledge and of new ideas, whether true or false. House rents and repairs were paid by the parish, and relief in money or kind was distributed, the poor, when not too infirm, attending at the vestry to receive their portions. Medical relief was freely given, three or more different doctors often receiving an annual settlement of their accounts. Sometimes a contract was entered into with some doctor to attend all the poor for a fixed sum per annum, but further expenses were always added before the year was out. In 1772 the parish began to subscribe to the Salisbury Infirmary, and occasionally to send its sick thither. In 1779 it became usual to send poor people to Bath Hospital, and from 1782 onwards subscriptions were paid regularly to the hospitals at these cities, both more than twenty miles distant.

[1] See Corsley MS. Overseers' Accounts for the administration of poor relief prior to 1836. The accounts are missing for the years 1742–47 and 1756–68.

The small-pox was still a frequent visitant, and in 1773 the practice of inoculation was begun, the patients being brought to the church porch for treatment, as tradition relates. Whole families would be inoculated with small-pox by order of the parish. In 1779 a number of families, comprising thirty-six persons, were inoculated wholly or partly at the parish expense. In 1798, again, £13 13s. was paid to a doctor for inoculation alone. Probably this inoculation often caused serious illness, and necessitated relief to the sick. We sometimes find it noted early in the nineteenth century that a case relieved was "natural small-pox," which still seems to have found victims throughout these years in spite of the wholesale inoculations.

After 1753 the parish incurred law expenses from time to time in disputes relating to settlements. The most serious of these was settled in 1776, the lawyer's bill amounting to £207 3s. 2½d., of which, however, Warminster parish paid £74.[1]

The moderate sum of £1 was charged to the parish account for the Easter dinner in the seventies, but in the nineteenth century the custom was kept up with unnecessary expense, the bill for this social gathering in 1824 amounting to nearly £5. The parish, too, bore the expense of the "possessioning," presumably beating the bounds, which took place at intervals of eighteen to twenty years. These expenses included a bountiful supply of beer and stronger drinks, besides some meat and cheese. But the official expenses at sessions, and for "signing the book," which, no doubt, included refreshments, during the first half of the eighteenth century, became much smaller, and also less frequent, during this period.

[1] See Corsley MS Overseers' Accounts for the administration of poor relief, April, 1776.

The parish officers continued to show a readiness in helping poor parishioners to earn a living, and besides from time to time providing tools or stock-in-trade of some description, they would now and then assist a needy family to repair their loom or twisting mill. But the great standby from 1774 onwards, after the passing of the Turnpike Act, was the quarrying of stones. Any unemployed who applied for relief could be set to this occupation, and the parish paid for the work accomplished, apparently on a piecework system.

It is noticeable that between 1774 and 1791 no expense for premiums was incurred for the poor children apprenticed, their labour being, perhaps, of sufficient value in the clothing industry to induce employers to take them free. Between 1792 and 1799, however, premiums were paid with most of the seven children apprenticed by the parish. After 1830 it became usual to send the children out to service instead of apprenticing them, the only expense to the parish in this case being a clothing outfit.

From 1778 to 1784, and again between 1793 and 1815, the parish had to provide for all the various expenses connected with finding recruits for the militia, and providing for the families of the absent men. A large part of this outlay was, however, received back from the county treasurer.

We have in the Overseers' Accounts in 1787 a curious memorandum, which indicates that destitution was not the test for granting relief. A woman in receipt of relief, Jane Lumberd, received special indulgence and commendation on account of her honesty in giving up her house for the benefit of the parish, it being sold for £28. It was evidently considered that she was fully entitled to relief without sacrificing her property had she desired it. After

the new Poor Law of 1834, the one grievance of
the poor people of Warminster Union, we are told,
was the demand of the guardians that an applicant
for relief who possessed a cottage should sell or
mortgage the latter. It was not usual under the old
system to make such demands, though the parish
officers were ready to make a bargain with a cottage
owner when occasion offered. In 1796 the house of
Uriah Gritt was repaired, in return for which it was
to become the property of the parish. Another
cottage was "signed to the parish" in 1804 when
expenses on account of this cottage were met by
the parish officers. It was thus only when relief was
granted on account of the house itself that it was the
custom to appropriate it under the old system.

Some light on parish customs and manners is
thrown by the following undated slip found in one
of the parish books. Gane was overseer in the
year 1808, so it may have been drawn up at this date :

"In consequence of a report of there being Mad-dogs in the
Parish of Corsley, the paymasters are determined to lessen the
number kept, and the following resolutions ordered, and entered
into, this day at a Vestry Meeting.

"Resolved whoever keeps a Dog after this time shall have
no relief of the Parish, whatever. They shall not be permitted
to live in any House, belonging to the Parish. To have no part
of the Gift at Christmas, or be entitled to either of the Half-
Crowns given by the will of the late Mr. Adlam.

"(Signed) W. GANE, Overseer.
EB\u02b3· COOMBS.
JOHN BALL.
JO\u02e2 JONES."

It would seem that, besides participation in the
charitable bequests with which Corsley is rather
richly endowed, to live rent free and receive poor
relief were advantages widely enjoyed at this

time. One or two curious entries having some relation to this may be quoted. In February, 1775, the parish paid 6d. for "catching rats at Widow Hainses." In 1790, 3s. was given to Thomas Pewsy "to begin housekeeping." A generous conception of the province of poor relief was thus in existence prior to the commencement of wholesale pauperisation in the early years of the nineteenth century.

As a rule, relief was ordered to the poor by the Vestry Meeting, but now and then, when refused help here, the applicant would refer to the magistrates, and relief was given, as the entries record, "by order of ye Justices."

Towards the end of the eighteenth century, probably marked by the year 1795 in Corsley, began a period the darkest since the time of the Black Death in the fourteenth century for the English labourer. War abroad and famine at home rendered the means of a decent livelihood practically unattainable for the labouring classes. An old inhabitant of Chapmanslade would relate with horror the tales which his father had told him of the terrible years about 1801, when he resided on the border of Wilts and Somerset. Men would go about with a piece of sacking tied round their necks, with holes for their arms and legs, as sole clothing. The people would feed on acorns, or anything they could obtain. So high was the price of corn that a man could carry a guinea's worth of bread on his head.

Another old inhabitant tells how his aunts could remember the "barley times," and when "their supper was lack of food." Clothing, too, was very expensive; his father, born in 1790, had to pay £5 for his first Sunday coat, and though the winters were very severe, people could not afford to buy warm clothes.

A third relates that his father, who was born about 1790, never ate meat as a young man ; the poor could not buy bread, but ate barley bannocks ; and flour was in those days £7 7s. the bag.

The Poor Law accounts bear out the tales as to the hardness of the times. In June, 1801, no less than 236 cases were relieved in Corsley in a population of 1,412, and, as a large proportion of these doubtless represented a family, the total number dependent on relief must have been far greater. This number, too, does not probably include any of the inmates of the workhouse.

In 1802, as we have seen, the main part of the workhouse organisation was abandoned, supervision of the work in the house being no longer kept up, and the inmates being no longer catered for. About the same time a paid assistant overseer was appointed to perform the work of paying the poor of the parish.

The custom of hiring out the inmates of the workhouse to employers in the parish continued, and a new practice first made its appearance, payments being made to an employer on account of a certain labourer, Shadrach Singer. This has every appearance of being the first definite rate in aid of wages made in Corsley. The practice was continued, though it never seems to have become a very prominent evil in the parish. At the time of the Poor Law Commission in 1834 it was reported by Mr. Fussell that there were four or five able-bodied labourers in the employment of private individuals in receipt of relief to make up their earnings to the scale allowed by the Warminster magistrates.[1]

In 1802, £1,640 3s. 5¼d. was expended on poor relief by the parish of Corsley. But things soon,

[1] Report Poor Law Commission, A.D. 1834, vol. xiii. Appendix (B1) II. p. 571b. Evidence of Mr. H. A. Fussell.

began to improve here, if expenditure may be taken as a test, this not again exceeding £1,000 till seventeen years later.

The rise of the rates in 1827 marks the beginning of a time when the prospect was again looking black for the labourer of this district, owing principally to a decline in the cloth trade, which threw numbers of unemployed weavers upon the hands of the farmers, who took on inefficient workers rather than leave them entirely a burden on the rates. This was detrimental to the farmers and disastrous to the genuine agricultural labourers, these being often crowded out by inferior workers, whose competition also lowered the standard of wages.

Hard as were the times, it is probable that Corsley suffered rather less than many of the neighbouring parishes. Industry was still in a fairly thriving state here, and we do not learn that any Corsley men joined in the agricultural riots of the district in 1830.

Some of the women and children, as well as the men, worked for wages in those days, but the united earnings of the whole family were very small. From the report to the Poor Law Commission [1] we learn that there was employment for the women in hay-harvest and in the silk factory which was being worked at this time at Whitbourne Moor. Many of the boys were employed in agriculture, probably beginning work at seven or eight years of age.[2] The girls were employed in woollen and silk manufacture.

---

[1] Report Poor Law Commission, A.D. 1834, vol. xii. Appendix (B1), I. p. 571a. Evidence of Mr. H. A. Fussell.

[2] An old inhabitant, Mr. Alfred Down, born about 1820, states that he and his brother went out to work at the age of seven. Probably the employment of children of this age continued in the parish till the passing of the Education Act, in 1871.

Mr. Fussell, in his report, states that women and children under sixteen could probably earn £10 per annum, "when the domestic duties of the woman will permit her to do anything, which, I think, must seldom be the case." [1] It does not appear, therefore, to have been a universal custom in Corsley for the women to go out to work.   The wages of men in the district were 7s. or 8s. per week.[2] Mr. Fussell reported that it was possible for families to subsist on these earnings, but only on a diet composed almost wholly of vegetables, with bread occasionally.[3]

Corsley may have been slightly better off than its neighbours, owing to the extensive emigrations to Canada which took place from the parish in 1828 and the following years.

In 1830 the parish shipped off at its own cost sixty-six of the least desirable of its inhabitants, about half being adults and half children, or "under age."   This was only following the example set by natives of Corsley who had previously emigrated on their own account.[4] Emigration became the fashion, and this means of drafting off the surplus population must have helped to mitigate the misery which followed on the decay of the clothing industry in the neighbourhood, with the consequent pressure on agriculture, which thus became

[1] Report Poor Law Commission, A.D. 1834, vol. xii. Appendix (B1), i. p. 571a.   Evidence of Mr. H. A. Fussell.

[2] Second Annual Report Poor Law Commission, 1836, vol. i., p. 300, Warminster Union.   Evidence of John Ravenhill.

[3] Report Poor Law Commission, 1834, vol. xiii. Appendix (B1), ii. p. 571b.

[4] 1831. About two hundred persons are stated to have emigrated within the last three years. "Accounts and Papers," 1852–3, vol. lxxxv. Population of England and Wales—Corsley. Numbers of the inhabitants 1801-51.

the sole occupation of many formerly busy cloth-making parishes.

To raise money for shipping off these sixty-six persons, some houses belonging to the parish were sold, and a considerable sum was raised by subscriptions. Clothing as well as money was contributed. These emigrants consisted of " several families of the very class one would wish to remove—men of suspected bad habits, and bringing up their children to wickedness " l There were several poachers among them, and other reputed bad characters. The captain of the ship came up to arrange as to taking them on board his vessel at Bristol for Newport, whence the ship of Quebec would sail. Finally it was arranged that the whole party were to leave Corsley on a certain day in wagons, accompanied by the assistant overseer and some of the ratepayers, who, avoiding the towns on their route, were to deliver the party safely to the vessel in the river below Bristol.¹

This was probably the largest party which left Corsley in a body, but other families were helped to emigrate by the parish in subsequent years,² and doubtless some of the people who owned a little property sold it and sailed for America at their own cost. Thus the congestion of unoccupied population caused by decaying industries was relieved, and we learn, after the Poor Law Reform of 1834 had been carried out, and conditions possibly improved thereby, that the people in the Corsley district were " well employed," ³ although there was

---

¹ See paper *re* Corsley emigration at the Longleat Estate Office, and Corsley MS. Overseers' Accounts for this year.

² Corsley MS. Overseers' Accounts.

³ Second Annual Report, Poor Law Commission, 1836, vol. p. 300, Warminster Union. Evidence of John Ravenhill.

still much able-bodied pauperism in neighbouring districts, and fifty labourers out of work in other parts of the Warminster Union. Other parishes in the vicinity soon followed the example set by Corsley,[1] in emigrating some of their surplus population.

We must not leave the history of the people of Corsley under the old Poor Law without alluding to the Corsley Walking Club, which was founded about 1798, or perhaps earlier.[2] This club, which had a large roll of members during part of the nineteenth century, has recently come to an end, being practically superseded by larger societies, such as the Shepherds, Wiltshire Conservative Benefit, and Hearts of Oak.

[1] See pamphlets by Paulet Scrope, relating to emigrations in Wiltshire, in the Devizes Museum.

[2] In an article in the *Warminster and Westbury Journal*, June 17, 1905, it is stated that the club was founded 107 years before this date Allusions to a club are found in the Corsley MS. Overseers' Accounts in 1789 and 1794. Whether or no this was the Corsley Walking Club does not appear.

CHAPTER VIII

CORSLEY IN THE NINETEENTH CENTURY

At the accession of Queen Victoria an era of steady decline and depopulation had already set in for Corsley ; and its story during her reign is one of the constant mutual adjustment, on the one hand of population to the changes and decreasing requirements of industry and agriculture, and on the other of agricultural methods to the variations in the supply of labour. At the census of 1841 the population numbered 1,621 persons, in 1901 it was reduced to 824.[1] The parish was therefore about twice as populous at the Queen's accession as it was when she died. The decrease was most rapid between 1841 and 1861, the term when Corsley was finally deserted by the cloth trade and other manufactures. Since then the population has declined at an average rate of about one hundred every ten years, the movement being greatest during the seventies, when agricultural changes were going forward.

By 1837 the new Poor Law, and a more stringent system of relief, was established. The old workhouse premises were sold in 1838,[2] and indoor relief was thenceforth administered in the newly-erected War-

---

[1] For census returns of Corsley, 1801 to 1901, see Appendix I. p. 305.

[2] MS. Corsley Vestry Minutes, August, 1838.

83

minster Union, other cottages belonging to the parish being disposed of in subsequent years.[1] Some confusion and difficulty was met with at first by the Corsley people in administering the new law. At Lady Day, 1843, it appears to have been formally discussed at a Vestry Meeting whether or no the old custom of the parish should be maintained in preference to adopting the new modes of procedure, and the decision come to is entered in the minutes, " that at this and all future Meetings the Law should be the Guide." [2]

The year 1844 was a hard time in Corsley. This was very probably owing to the closing of a large cloth factory, which we learn from the Census Report [3] occurred between 1841 and 1851. Though several families migrated elsewhere in search of employment, many persons became a burden upon the rates. A resolution passed at a Vestry Meeting in January that rates levied upon cottages and gardens should be paid by the tenants, allowance being made to them by the proprietors in the rents,[4] was presumably an attempt to make the bulk of the population realise the incidence of the burden of pauperism. Later in the year the Vestry decided that the unemployed paupers should be divided among the " paymasters " according to the number of acres in their occupation. A committee was appointed to investigate the matter. From their report we learn incidentally that 7s. a week was considered the minimum wage in Corsley for an able-bodied man, and in computing the number already employed, two women were to count as one

---

[1] MS. Corsley Vestry Minutes, November, 1839, and February 6, 1840.

[2] *Ibid.*, March 25, 1843.

[3] See Appendix I. p. 305.

[4] MS. Corsley Vestry minutes, January 15, 1844.

COTTAGE WITH WEAVER'S WINDOW, INHABITED BY JOHN MINES, THE LAST WEAVER IN CORSLEY.

man.[1] How the scheme worked, or whether, indeed, it was ever carried into effect, is not recorded.

In 1854 a salaried assistant overseer was appointed for Corsley.[2]

In December, 1856, the Vestry, anticipating lack of employment during the winter months, agreed that persons seeking work were to be referred to the Waywardens, who were promised an additional way rate, when necessary, to defray the expense of providing employment.[3]

In 1889, and again in 1893, the Corsley Vestry pressed for greater publicity of the proceedings of the Warminster Board of Guardians, and demanded that copies of the financial statement should be distributed among all the larger ratepayers.[4]

Having briefly surveyed the action of the Corsley Vestry in regard to pauperism, under the new law, we must turn our attention to the chief cause which aggravated poverty, namely the decline in the cloth trade Within the memory of the older inhabitants now living there were three manufacturers who employed a considerable number of workpeople. These were Mr. Fussell, the dyer, at Sturford ; Mr. Taunton, clothier, miller, and farmer, at the Mill Farm ; and Mr. Coombs, who had a silk factory at Whitbourne Moor. The factories were situated on the small streams of water which flow through Corsley. By the middle of the century, or shortly after, all these works were closed.

The last factory which is remembered was just without the parish at Lane End. This was burnt

---

[1] Papers in Corsley Parish Chest. Minute of Vestry Meeting, October, 1844, &c.

[2] MS, Corsley Vestry Minutes, September 14, 1854.

[3] *Ibid.* December 2, 1856.

[4] *Ibid.* March 25, 1889, and March 25, 1893.

down and never rebuilt, but was made into a logwood mill, in connection with the dyeing factories. The loss of this factory was keenly felt. After its destruction many Corsley people went to work in the factories at Rodden, or Frome, from which also spinning and other home work was fetched by Corsley women. We have already seen that some of the men thrown out of work were billeted upon agriculture, while the majority probably migrated to other parts of England or to the colonies.

The agriculture of Corsley was in a prosperous state in the earlier part of the reign. Since the enclosure, nearly the whole parish had been converted to arable, and wheat was the principal crop. The land was mainly in the hands of large farmers, and the big farmhouses were the scene of busy life and activity, especially Cley Hill Farm, with the neighbouring hamlet of Chipps, then belonging to Mr. Barton, which the people say seemed like a little town. Very few cows were kept, and milk was not easily obtainable by the poor, but the farmers would always allow the labourer to rent potato ground at 1s. [1] a pole.

But the prosperous days for the English producer of corn were drawing to a close. The agriculture of the New World was developing, means of transport were improved, and the competition of American wheat brought down prices in the English market to such an extent that its cultivation became unprofitable in most districts of England, and after much loss, and even ruin to some farmers and landlords, the country has for the most part been turned down to grass, acre by acre, and converted into dairy and cattle-rearing farms or broken up into market gardens.

[1] This rent is given on the authority of one old lady's recollection. Probably the price varied as in the allotments at present.

Between 1871 and 1881 a marked increase in the movement of depopulation occurred in Corsley, and this corresponds with the crisis of the change in agriculture, which in less than thirty years converted Corsley from a wheat-growing to a dairy-farming parish. The conversion of arable to pasture was mainly effected between about 1870 and 1885,[1] though it continued on into the twentieth century.

The difficulty of letting large farms at this time led to some of them, such as that at Whitbourne Temple, being broken up, and leased in small holdings. This reversion to something more nearly resembling the old system of distribution in Corsley was ultimately a great boon to those of the inhabitants who remained. The rich sandy soil is peculiarly favourable for the success of the small holding, and there are probably at least thirty families in Corsley at the present day with less than twenty acres, who as market gardeners or dairy farmers make their living mainly from the land. Dairy farming is also a reliable and satisfactory form of agriculture for the larger farmer, though the small amount of labour it demands, and the consequent lack of encouragement which it gives to the labouring lad to remain on the land, is to be deplored.

When the land was laid down to grass, women, too, ceased to be employed in agriculture Forty years ago women worked in the fields of Corsley gathering stones off the plough-lands, planting beans, tying corn, hoeing roots and corn, and cleaning up the fields at a wage of 10d. per day, and four women were employed by Mrs. Barton in her garden.[2] But with the conversion of arable to pasture, and a further reduction in the demand for agricultural labour

[1] When questioned in 1905, most of the inhabitants stated that the change occurred mainly twenty to thirty-five years previously.

[2] These details are related by an old inhabitant of the parish.

caused by the use of machinery, women ceased altogether to be employed as agricultural wage-earners,
though at the present day the wives of small holders,
and many cottagers, work on their own land or
gardens. The demand for women's work in industry
having failed, and the demand for women's work in
agriculture having failed, the young women naturally
took to migrating elsewhere, and for the most part
entered domestic service in the towns. The migration of the female population of Corsley is at the
present day greater than that of the male. It has
been suggested that this departure of the young
women has contributed to make the young men unwilling to remain on the land, and undoubtedly the
parish is far duller for the few young people who stay
here than it was a couple of generations ago, before
most of the youth had departed.

Owing to the gradual adjustment between population and the demand for labour, together with the
revival of the small holding, the reign of Victoria,
which began with painful and violent cataclysms,
sudden loss of employment, the breaking up of homes,
and departures from Corsley, drew to a peaceful
conclusion in this village.

The only industries now carried on in the parish
besides a few to supply local needs, such as shoemaking, tailoring, dressmaking, baking, and the like,
and the domestic industry of gloving, are building
and cart-building. Mr. Eyers at Chapmanslade
carried on a considerable business, and in the winter
of 1905-6 employed about twenty hands in building
and plumbing. Mr. John Pearce employs some
twenty-five carpenters, wheelwrights, painters, &c.
at Corsley Heath, besides about twenty masons and
others elsewhere. The largest shop remaining in
the parish is that of Mr. Henry White, at Lane End,

who supplies bread, groceries, and general provisions. Several smaller bakeries and shops are yet to be found scattered over the parish.

Notwithstanding the steady decline in the population since 1830, considerable additions have been made to the accommodation for religious services in Corsley. In 1849 the Wesleyan Methodist chapel at Lane End was rebuilt, at a cost of £244 12s. 4½d.[1]

In 1867, on the far side of the road at Chapmanslade, just outside the parish of Corsley, an Episcopal church was built,[2] and a few years after the period we are considering, in 1903, the new Episcopal church at Temple was completed, according to the will of the late Mrs. Barton. Nonconformist chapels already existed at Chapmanslade and near Temple, which are, however, a mile or so distant from the parish church, and a missionary zeal for religious orthodoxy was probably the motive which led to the establishment of churches in these districts.

Among the events which have most profoundly influenced the life of Corsley in the Victorian era we must count the establishment of the National School in 1848, and the law which enforced compulsory school attendance in 1871. Previous to 1848 there were private schools in the parish, such as the " Ranters' shop," belonging to the Primitive Methodists at Whitbourne Moor, kept by Thomas Ansford, and the school kept by Miss Mines at Longhedge, who is remembered as a very old woman, with a long stick with which she could reach all the children from where she sat. At Leighs Green, Mrs. Haines, a " turrble strict woman," had a small school where she taught five to eight children to read and write. Another school is said to have been

[1] Corsley Wesleyan Methodist Chapel MS. Baptismal Register, note on flyleaf.

[2] W. Doël, " Twenty Golden Candlesticks," p. 172.

kept by the Gutch family at Temple.[1] There is no reason to suppose that this is an exhaustive list. Any man or woman who could read was in those days considered qualified to keep school, and probably many such small institutions were distributed over the parish.

In 1846 a collection was set on foot for the establishment of a National School, and £678 16s. 6d. was raised. By 1848 the work of building appears to have been complete.[2]

In 1861 Lord Bath made a gift to the parish of the site of the National School House. It was stated at this time that 535 children had passed through the school since its establishment, and the number on the books in this year was 105.[3]

In 1870 statistics in the matter of education in Corsley were collected,[4] which show that of 175

[1] These schools are remembered by old inhabitants.
[2] MS. Papers relating to Corsley National School.   [3] Ibid.
[4] Ibid. Population 1,235.

"*Present Supply.*

" National School, on the books	83
National School. provided for in Dilton's Marsh of Chapslade	11
	94

"*Adventure Schools.*

" Not recognised by the Government	Ann Morgan			17
	Ann Hyatt, Lane End			6
	Jane Watts, Long Edge			16
	George Stevens, Dartford			26
	Miss White, Temple			5
				70

Total	164

" Census of children from one year to twelve years :

Result	290
Those under five years	115
	175 "

children between the ages of five and twelve years, 94 were being educated in the National School and 70 in "adventure schools," leaving only 11 who were receiving no education. As, however, a large proportion of the population at the present day, of forty years old and upwards, are unable to write, and read only with difficulty, there is reason to doubt whether in all cases the education was very efficient. A proposal was made at this time for the erection of a "Chapel" school at Temple, the National School premises being inadequate, but the scheme seems to have been dropped.

In 1873 the Rector stated that the attendance at the National School had increased, funds being needed to provide a more adequate teaching staff.

Some of the "adventure schools" continued. George Stevens, a one-legged man, kept a school, attended chiefly by the sons of farmers and tradesmen, whom he taught reading, writing, arithmetic, and book-keeping, until in 1891 free education gave the death-blow to his institution. One or two of the small schools for infants yet remain in the parish.

The last great influence, which has perhaps done more to change the habits and mode of living of country people than any other single factor, was the introduction of railways. In 1850 the Great Western Railway opened the line to Frome, and this line has since undergone improvements and extensions. In 1856 the G. W. R. line from Warminster to Salisbury was opened.

The railway development further encouraged the movement of population to the towns. It also brought about a strong reaction of town life on country life. The youth or maiden who left his or her native village could easily return, and within living memory urban habits and fashions in dress and amusements have come down and overset the ancient customs of nearly every village in England   We shall conclude this chapter with a description of the early Victorian personnel of Corsley, with their distinctive characteristics, habits, and amusements, as remembered by the older people of the parish, before this last disturbing influence was brought to bear.

The principal family in the parish were the Bartons, of Corsley House, who lived in a homely way, farming their own land and taking part in the incidents of rural life, whilst occasionally entertaining the neighbouring gentlemen at a large dinner or banquet, commencing at an early hour. Residing continually in the parish, they lived in close relations with their humbler neighbours, especially their own employees, and many tales are told of the chaff, repartee, and practical jokes which passed between them. Harvest was the great festival of the year, when, the work being concluded, all partook of a generous feast, neither meat nor beer being stinted.

Mr. H. A. Fussell, the dyer, was residing in the house he had built at Sturford Mead, with his family of twelve sons and daughters. They likewise lived quietly, going in very little for show, and walking to church, instead of driving as was the habit of well-to-do people in those days. Mr. Fussell made it a rule that all the men employed in his dye-works should attend a place of worship on Sundays, but they were free to choose among the church and chapels of the parish.

Mr. Taunton, the clothier, of the Mill Farm, is always spoken of as a great benefactor to the parish. He employed probably forty hands, and if any man went to him wanting work he would find him a job if possible. He also ground corn, killed pigs, made cheese and bars of soap, and he would let his poorer workmen have bacon, flour, cheese, and soap at cheap rates, this system of " truck " being much appreciated by the receivers. But this Mr. Taunton, who was a kind and a businesslike man, had children who turned out wild. One was accused of the murder of a Corsley man, and he fled to America, though the crime was never brought home to him.

Mr. Coombs, the silk manufacturer, had daughters, who, when the factory was broken up, went to live with their uncle, Mr. James Sainsbury, at Sturford Cottage. This Mr. Sainsbury is said to have been a self-made man. He began by buying a sack of corn and dealing with it. He then took to riding to Salisbury market every week, and eventually accumulated a considerable fortune, which he left to his nieces. He was a very reserved man, holding conversation with no one if he could avoid it. He " kept no company," except that once every month he gave a dinner to all the people in the parish who had only one leg, one arm, or one eye.

Near by, at Whitbourne Springs, in the house now occupied by Mr. Harry Ball, and formerly in all probability the residence of the Carey family, Mr. Dredge, a very stout man, carried on his malting business.

Somewhere in the neighbourhood of Leighs Green lived Mrs. Eyers, who kept an old-fashioned gig, in which she was driven every Sunday to the Whitbourne Baptist Chapel, taking the preacher back to dinner with her. This lady bequeathed to the chapel £500.

Among the larger farmers were Mr. Bailey, of Pool Farm, and Mr. Ball, of Church Farm.

Big farmers in those days, say some of the old people, did not live as well as working people do now. These two farmers would drive or ride to Warminster market every week, always attired in a smock frock. When driving they would have wagons with four horses and bells. Warminster market must have presented a very different appearance to the markets of to-day, when every small farmer, and many market gardeners and others, drive in small carts, dressed in the conventional ready-made great coat and bowler hat.

At Corsley Heath there lived a blacksmith, who with his wife saved £1,000 in twenty years. These people would fatten a pig from time to time, and eat salt bacon. They never ate fresh meat more than once a week, though they had no children to save for. One old lady relates that it was the custom for working men to take out with them half a small loaf and a large onion for their dinner, never meat or cheese. Breakfast and supper generally consisted of home-grown potatoes, with a little of something to flavour it. Very little meat was eaten. The period of famine appears to have taught a hard lesson in thrift, which was not forgotten for more than a generation, either by the labourer whose wage was still not more than 8s. a week, or by the more well-to-do country people.

Among the notable characters we must not omit to mention John Moody, a labourer, who early in the nineteenth century brought up a family of six sons and one daughter, who is still living, without receiving any assistance from the parish. He was afterwards presented with a sum of money in recognition of this remarkable independence, together with a book for " religious and moral conduct." One of his sons, John, worked as a labourer for Farmer Ball's family for over forty years. Another son, Robert, became butler to the Bartons, and on his death left the Moody Charity, including the church clock, to the parish. Some of the descendants of the first John Moody, yet living in Corsley, display the same extremely independent spirit manifested by their ancestor.

There were plenty of people with horses and carts and a great deal of trade going on in Corsley in early Victorian times. An elderly couple were able in a few minutes to recollect about ten men besides the farmers who kept traps in their young days, and they say that there were many more, though whether as many as there are to-day it is not possible to guess.

There were many gipsies about, who camped on the remaining bits of waste land. These men would fight among themselves or with the inhabitants for money, and murder was sometimes done. A certain old Jack Youdall, who is said to have killed a man, was a "vagabond upon the earth." He was allowed to dig up a bit of the waste land at the lower side of Corsley Heath and plant potatoes. He used to make up people's "banks" for them, and when his daughter, a housekeeper, married her master, she was said in a local newspaper to be a "banker's" daughter.

At Norton Common lived an old lady mysteriously clever in curing wounds, bruises, and sores, who was visited by patients from far and near.

The inhabitants of Corsley had several amusements early in the century, which are now obsolete. 'A' skittle-ground used to exist at Longhedge, the gipsy fights have already been noticed, and the great events of the year were the Corsley Fairs. There had been one at Whitsuntide, and one on July 27th from ancient times. This latter used to be held fairly recently at Corsley Heath on "Cock Heap," a large artificial mound which has now disappeared. Cheese was pitched here, and teams of horses were brought to be sold. There were stalls where gingerbread and fancy things could be bought. There were ponies for telling fortunes, cheap jacks, and other shows and amusements. The Corsley fairs have now been entirely dropped.

One old amusement, which probably dates from time immemorial, yet remains. This is a game played up Cley Hill with a ball and sticks on Palm Sunday.

But though we still find many old people, with the old ideas and old tales of the past, though many ancient superstitions yet linger on half-concealed among the population, though many of the young people who remain are true children of their parents, conservative in ideas and habits, yet the youth of Corsley as it grows up tends more and more to assimilate to the modes of thought and habit of the dweller in towns, and the more energetic, unless withheld by the prospect of becoming the master of a small farm or gardening business, continue to migrate to districts where their urbanised tastes may be gratified.

What, however, Corsley has lost in picturesqueness it has undoubtedly gained in solid comfort ; and with an extension of educational methods better adapted to foster a taste for rural life, with fuller prospects in the future for those who remain on the land, and with ever increasing facilities for bringing the more varied, more exciting, or more intellectual life of the towns into the country districts, a reaction against emigration to the towns, or a counter current of emigration into the country, some indications of which are already discernible, may set in, and an increasing number of people may find that this parish, with its healthy climate and its singularly beautiful scenery, is, after all, a good place to live in.

PART II

CORSLEY IN THE PRESENT

CHAPTER IX

INTRODUCTION—METHOD OF INQUIRY

THE following description of life in Corsley is based
on the results of systematic inquiries, addressed to
the inhabitants, and others who were able to furnish
the desired information. Before giving the conclusions, it will be well to describe the nature and
method of the investigation. The bulk of the information was collected by a house-to-house inquiry
in November and December, 1905, and the first weeks
of January, 1906. During these visits the following
form was filled up, so far as possible, for nearly
every household, from information given by the
householder, his wife, or one of his children.

1. Name.

2. Age.

3. Place of birth.

4. Occupation.

5. Name of employer (or state if on own account).

6. Wife's name.

7. Wife's place of birth.

8. Father's name.

9. Father's occupation.

10. Father's place of birth.

11. Paternal grandfather's name.

12. Paternal grandfather's occupation.

13. Paternal grandfather's place of birth.

14. Maternal grandfather's name.

15. Maternal grandfather's occupation.

16. Maternal grandfather's place of birth.

17. Names and sex of all children born, and date of birth; marking those which are still living; and trade or occupation of those who have left school.

18. Have any of your children left the parish? and if so, state where they went to, and what occupation they are following.

19. How many rooms are there in the house that you occupy?

20. Does any one else, and if so, who, dwell in the house?

21. If occupying land state the number of acres.

22. If employer, state occupation and number of persons employed, men, women, and young people.

Towards the end of 1905 a second inquiry was made as to the characteristics of the various households. Several reports were obtained for most of the families, care being taken in each case to question persons likely to be well acquainted with the characters of the persons concerned, and to have no personal interest in concealing or exaggerating the facts. The inquiry as to earnings was somewhat difficult, and this investigation was spread over a whole year, from the winter of 1905—6 to the winter of 1906—7. Information was obtained in three ways. In the first instance, employers were usually approached. When willing to give information at all, some of these stated fully the wages and all extras which they gave , others stated only a sum, without explanation as to whether this was money wage, or the real wage including all extras, and, in the latter case, what estimation they made for a cottage, beer, or other extras given ; some, again, refused definite information, but stated that they paid "about" so much. Further inquiry revealed a strong tendency amongst some of the employers to estimate the extras given at a rather liberal rate. When, therefore, an employer stated that a man was paid "about" so much, it has been assumed that this was not the exact wage given, but that, taking into consideration the observed tendency, it was probable that the man received a little less.

Secondly, in a large number of cases, earnings have been ascertained from labourers or their wives. These were not, as a rule, directly questioned, but in many cases the information was volunteered, and persons keeping a diary of their food were paid a small sum, in return for which they were usually quite willing to answer any inquiries. Two tendencies were noticed among wage-earners in regard to giving information as to their incomes. Firstly, some of the more independent were unwilling to reveal their income at all. Secondly, those people, especially the women and housekeepers, who were anxious to participate in public or private charities, were sometimes inclined to understate it, either by omitting some of the extras given by employers, or by mis-stating the money wage. It is quite possible that in the latter case the women were sometimes ignorant of the exact weekly sum received by their husbands, though the amount retained as pocket-money by married men in Corsley is not usually large, and is generally kept with the approval of the wife.

Thirdly, in addition to these two sources, valuable help was given by a person who knew the parish intimately, and could give information as to the wages, in money and kind, of the large majority of wage-earners in Corsley.

All these sources of information were liable to more or less error, and at first sight the results appeared to be in disagreement. A closer scrutiny, however, showed that this was not the case. The apparent discrepancies were usually fully accounted for by the omission or over-estimation of the extras given. These have been generally ascertained, and allowed for at the rate as given in the section on Labourers, in Chapter X., so that, with a few exceptions, it has been possible to estimate the real wage and money wage of nearly all the workers with a considerable degree of accuracy, the margin of doubt in most cases being *nil* or very small. In a very few cases hopelessly contradictory information has been received, owing mainly to confusion of names in a parish where most of the people are related to one another, and possibly in one or two instances in consequence of a wish to mislead. But the earnings of these men have been assumed to be the same as other workers of the same class and about the same ability in the parish. These doubtful instances are in any case too few to appreciably affect statistical results, though if wrongly estimated the family may not have been placed in the right economic class in the chapters on Poverty.

The family budgets were collected at various dates during 1906 and 1907, and notes as to diet were also taken while the other inquiries were being carried on. The diaries of food were kept in prepared copy-books by some member of the family, usually one of the children, or the mother. The person keeping the diary was requested to write down after each meal what had been put on the table, and a small sum was paid for the trouble. Frequent calls were usually paid to the houses to see that particulars were being carefully entered at the time. In most cases the mother also gave an account of her receipts and expenditure for each week.

Inquiries were made in the winter of 1905-6 as to religion, friendly societies, insurance, amusements, and many other things. In the autumn of 1907 supplementary information was sought on various points, including women's earnings, medical attendance, and rents.

Though the investigation has been spread over a period of two years, the result may be considered a picture of Corsley in 1905-6, when the bulk of the information was obtained. It is not probable that any appreciable change has taken place in the particular departments on which information was obtained later, for such changes, had they recently occurred, would undoubtedly have been remarked on. To obviate confusion, when necessarily omitting all names, each household in the parish was allotted a number. Care was taken to avoid any sort of order in numbering which could assist in establishing the identification of any particular household. In the section on Character, in the diaries of food, and other parts where separate households are referred to, this index number is given, each household being always identified by the same number.

In order to avoid identification and to obtain statistical results the households have been divided into groups under the heading of their occupations.

Some arbitrary classification was, however, necessary, to include people such as the lime-burner and the road-mender. Where, as in the case of these men, there were only one or two of a class they have been included in a group earning similar wages, and it is stated that they are so included.

The whole inquiry was greatly facilitated by the willingness which most of the inhabitants displayed to give the desired information, as soon as it was made clear to them that the names of present inhabitants would be treated confidentially and that the inquiry was only being undertaken with the object of describing their parish as an example of rural life.

CHAPTER X

WHO THE CORSLEY PEOPLE ARE AND HOW THEY GET A LIVING

THE geographical position of Corsley has been described in the opening chapter of Part I., and we have seen that the population is scattered over the area of 3,056 acres in a number of hamlets and scattered homesteads, being most thickly congregated in the westerly and southerly districts. We must now consider the people who inhabit these lonely houses or more sociable hamlets. When the last census was taken in 1901 there were 824 persons in Corsley. In the winter of 1905-6 the population was distributed in 220 households. The occupations of the heads of these households may be roughly classified as follows :

	Per cent
Agriculture	57'7
Trades...	4'5
Artisans	11'3
Miscellaneous	15'7
Women living without a male relation ...	10'8
Total	100'0

Any accurate analysis is rendered wellnigh impossible by the fact that in Corsley it is the exception rather than the rule for each man to depend on one source of income alone. To take an example, one inhabitants hold three public offices under the central government and local governing bodies, besides following the occupations of farmer and also of timber-haulier and coal-merchant. The public-house keepers are all either farmers or artisans. Artisans are sometimes also small farmers. Lastly, gardening is a source of income in Corsley which is difficult to estimate for individual cases. Most labourers add to their earnings by selling garden produce, and the market gardeners range between people having no other source of income and the labourer working regularly at full time for another employer, with such imperceptible gradations that it is often impossible to guess whether the living is made principally from the garden or from the wage. The following is an attempt at classification, including each man under what appears to be his most important occupation. All working as artisans are included as such. All farmers, not artisans, are grouped under this heading. In this classification, therefore, the publicans, of whom there are five, are not mentioned, but are included as artisans or farmers. There are in reality a few more farmers included among the unoccupied or the artisans, a few coal-haulers and traders classed as farmers, and many more market gardeners who have some other source of income, regular or occasional.

With these qualifications the occupations of the householders are as follows : The rector (Church of England), 1 Congregational minister ; 3 private gentlemen (migrated to parish since 1890) ; 1 retired estate agent ; 1 schoolmaster ; 32 farmers, including all grades ; 10 market gardeners, marketers or gardeners, with no other occupation ; 7 head gardeners, coachmen, and grooms ; 1 thatcher ; 1 woodman with high earnings ; 2 dairymen earning over £1 ; 72 labourers (including carters, agricultural or other, cowmen and dairymen earning less than £1, a shepherd, woodman, under-gamekeepers, a roadman, a mason's labourer, under-gardeners, a worker at the limekiln, and men who work at malting in winter and do casual labour in summer) ; 1 warrener ; 3 shopkeepers ; 1 coal and timber merchant, having no other occupation ; 2 shoemakers ; 1 "naturalist" ; 1 builder and wheelwright, large employer of labour ; 1 plumber and builder, large employer of labour ; 9 wheelwrights or carpenters ; 1 sawyer ; 2 plumbers ; 4 masons ; 1 plasterer and tiler ; 2 painters or glaziers ; 3 blacksmiths ; 3 brickmakers ; 1 commercial traveller ; 1 assistant clerk of works ; 1 police-constable ; 1 platelayer, Great Western Railway ; 1 worker in Westbury Iron-works ; 1 worker in cloth factory, Frome ; 12 persons retired with means (including a house decorator, a 'bus-driver, an engineer and publican, a shopkeeper, 2 farmers, a head gardener, a shoemaker and factory hand, a shoemaker, a policeman, and a signalman ; these, with the exception of 1 farmer and 1 shoemaker, spent their working lives elsewhere) ; 5 labourers retired ; 1 labourer ill ; 1 retired schoolmaster ; 1 retired mole-catcher ; 2 retired market-gardeners ; 1 plasterer out of work ; 24 women householders who have no male wage-earner living with them. There are in all 38 households whose head is a woman ; but 14 of these women having a son or other male wage-earning relative residing with them, their households have been included under the heading of the male relations' occupation in the above classification.

The occupations of the 24 women without male relations living with them are as follows : Seven living on private means, 1 farmer and coal-haulier, 3 laundresses, 2 who keep a shop and also take in sewing or other work of some description, 2 charing and washing, 2 widows kept by children, 7 occasional jobs and miscellaneous, including 4 who have poor relief.

Farmers.

The main part of the land of Corsley is now laid down to grass, and the majority of farms are chiefly or entirely dairy farms.

In 1904 out of 3,056 acres only 512 were returned to the Inland Revenue Office as arable, viz. :

Under crops and bare fallow... ...	361	acres.
Under clover and rotation grasses ...	151	,,
Total arable land	512	,,

But as returns are made in each case under the parish where the farmer resides, though his land may lie partly in an adjoining parish, and as no returns are made by holders of less than one acre, the actual area of arable may be estimated at anywhere between 500 and 550 acres.[1]

This is, roughly speaking, one-sixth of the total area. An indefinite area is covered by homesteads, 280 acres or upwards by woods, and the remainder is pasture or grass.

A considerable amount of milk is sent from the dairy farms to London all the year round. Some is sold to the United Dairies Factory in Frome. Milk is also sold in small quantities and is easily obtainable in the parish, but it is said that good butter is now hard to get locally. On some of the

[1] I am indebted for this information to Mr. Lewis P. Bunn, Inland Revenue officer.

farms cheeses are made in summer and butter in winter.

There is some cattle-rearing. Pigs and poultry are frequently kept.

The size of farms varies from 454 acres down to 3 acres, the smaller farmers merging sometimes into market gardeners. The market gardeners often have a second occupation, and most of the cottagers do a little market gardening ; it is therefore impossible to draw distinct lines between the different sections of people who rent or own land for productive purposes, though under the heading of farmers and market gardeners we have to include people at opposite ends of the social scale, some being among the most important of the parishioners and employers and others being actually in receipt of poor relief.

Again, some of the farmers, both large and small, have a second occupation ; among them are publicans, coal-hauliers, artisans, a carrier, a postmaster, a postman, a man who undertakes miscellaneous jobs such as pig-killing, a sexton, a small baker, and a pensioner.

It is thought that thirty-four who call themselves farmers may fairly be classified under this heading,[1] at least twelve of these have a second occupation or source of income.

> Five of these have over 100 acres of land.
> Four between 50 and 100 acres.
> Seven between 25 and 50 acres, twelve between 10 and 25 acres.
> Four under 10 acres.
> Of three particulars have not been ascertained.

Some particulars of each of these farms will give the best idea of the agriculture of Corsley. No farmer not residing in Corsley has been included, and gentlemen who do a little farming are also omitted.

[1] On p. 106 only 32 have been classified as farmers, but in this list we include 2 who are there classed as artisans.

No.	No. Acres	Nature of Farm.	No Men and Boys employed, including Sons or other Relatives.
102	454	Arable and grass. Wheat, oats, beans, sold Frome and Warminster markets. Calves reared. Sheep. Butter-making. Sometimes milk sold	10 regular.
74[1]	327	Dairy	—
93	255	25 acres arable, the rest grass Dairy. Milk sold in London. Grow enough wheat to supply own straw, and roots for own supply	7
75	224	80 acres arable, the rest grass. Dairy. Cheese-making, summer, Milk sold in London in winter. Wheat, barley, peas, and beans sold Warminster and Frome Markets	7
87	195	70 acres arable, the rest grass. Cows, horses, pigs, poultry. Milk sold to United Dairies Factory, Frome, and in the parish. Wheat, barley, oats, swedes, &c., sold Frome and Warminster markets . .	5
86	90	5 acres arable, rest pasture. Dairy. Cheese-making summer. Butter-making winter Both sold at Frome. Pigs and chickens.	1
85	83	... .	2
101	80	Dairy, &c.	3
89	48	Dairy. Cheese-making summer Sometimes make butter. Sometimes sell milk Poultry, especially turkeys	2
82	47	Chiefly arable, but also dairy	—
76	45	Dairy. Cheese-making summer. Butter-making winter. Poultry and pigs ...	1
79[1]	77		3
103	39	Dairy. Cheese - making — cheeses sold to dealers	1
78	28	Dairy	None.
98[2]	26	Dairy. Butter-making. Milk sold in parish	2
90	19+?[3]	Dairy. Milk sold to Frome factory. Pigs and poultry. Some arable, where corn and roots for the cattle are grown ...	1 regularly.
95[4]	18		None.

[1] Also publican.   [2] Also postmaster, coal and timber merchant, &c.
[3] Unknown amount in another parish.   [4] Also carrier, &c.

No	No Acres.	Nature of Farm.	No Men and Boys employed, including Sons or other Relatives
8₄	17	Dairy. About 12 cows kept in summer and 10 in winter. Poultry and turkeys. Rear upwards of 200 chickens and 50 turkeys, besides ducks and geese. Butter and eggs sent to London. Dealer in calves and pigs	
77¹	17	Dairy	1 Man 2 hours daily.
92²	—	Dairy, &c.	2 regularly.
97	13+?³	Dairy	2
169⁴	14	... ...	None.
96⁵	13	Dairy	None.
81⁶	13	Arable. Corn and vegetables, sold to market gardeners locally, who carry it to Frome. Pigs and poultry	1
112	13	Dairy. Poultry. Butter merchant (buys butter in the market and sells in Corsley) ...	None.
83	13	Dairy	1
88	11	Dairy. Poultry and market garden ...	None regularly.
91	11	Market garden. Two or three cows. Poultry	None regularly.
80	9¾	A few cows. Butter-making. Poultry Butter fetched by Frome purchaser. Eggs sold to local marketer ...	None.
99	8	... ...	None.
195⁷	7½	Two or three cows. ½ acre arable	None.
150⁸	3	Cows. Poultry	None.
94⁹	—	Dairy (50 cows). Cheese-making — cheeses sold to dealer at Yeovil. Winter, milk sold in London	1
184¹⁰	47	Dairy	2 (no male in family.)

¹ Also does odd jobs, such as pig-killing.
² Also coal haulier and timber merchant.
³ Unknown quantity in another parish.
⁴ Also artisan.   ⁵ Pensioner.   ⁶ Sub-postman and sexton.
⁷ Also baker.   ⁸ Also brickmaker and labourer.
⁹ Dairyman, rents the cows.   ¹⁰ Also coal and timber hauliers

Coal Hauliers and Timber Merchants.

Four of the farmers are also coal hauliers and timber merchants. There are besides these at least two other coal and timber merchants in Corsley. These people are the successors of the wagoners who in the olden times carried the corn from the renowned Warminster market to Bath and Bristol, and returned, *via* Radstock, where they loaded up with coal.

They now carry timber from the Longleat estate to the collieries and return with coal.

One of these people hauls the Longleat coal supply, another carries coal to Warminster, a third supplies Corsley House, a fourth supplies the villagers, going round with small quantities, a fifth resides in Chapmanslade, and probably supplies the inhabitants of that part of the parish.

Market Gardeners and Marketers.

Many of the cottagers do some market gardening to supplement their wage-earnings, but besides these and two or three who have been counted among the farmers there are ten or more men, not always heads of households, who make a living mainly by market gardening or marketing.

These include men with a few acres and some capital and people who have fallen back on this occupation owing to the failure of other sources of income. If a man loses an arm, becomes rheumatic, or in any way is so disabled as to have difficulty in finding an employer as an agricultural labourer, he cultivates his garden, perhaps manages to obtain a horse and cart, builds himself a rough stable of corrugated iron and some pigstyes, and, working with his wife, manages to make a hard living, probably being reduced to dependence in his old age.

On the other hand, a small capitalist, often a labourer who has saved money, invests it in a market garden or small farm, and makes a good thing of it, thereby raising himself in the social scale.

The most important of these people, and such as have no other source of income, are included in the following table, which, however, is not exhaustive. Some of the lesser people, not sole earners in the family, are picked at random as examples.

No	Size of Holding.	Remarks	Men Employed
113	6 acres.	Vegetables. Pigs and poultry. Business has been in family fifty years. Horse and cart to take produce to market.	1
118	Big garden and allotment.	Has horse and cart and goes to market Saturdays. Occasional labourer for other people. Wife takes in washing	None.
114	—	Horse and cart. Does some carrier's work as well as market gardening.	None.
117	Two gardens.	Wife nurse.	None. Son [sometimes.
116	Garden and ½ acre.	Market garden. Pigs. Poultry. Horse and cart, does some carrier's work, but no marketing for others.	None.
115	6 acres (?)	Horse and cart. Market gardener and carrier.	None.
111	Large garden.	Market gardeners and marketers for other people. Walk in with basket. Poor relief.	None.
72	About 1 acre.	Market gardening. Pony and cart. Living with father, who is pensioner.	None.
24	About 50 poles.	Market gardening. Mainly marketers—collect eggs, butter, &c., from farmers, &c., and sell in Frome. Horse and cart. Head of household a wage-earning labourer.	

[Continued on next page]

No	Size of Holding	Remarks.	Men Employed.
190	Allotment and garden.	Old woman. Grows fruit. Son a labourer.	None.
207	10 acres (?).	Market gardener. Horse and cart.	Occasionally a man.
109	3½ acres.	Horse and cart. Also blacksmith.	Occasionally a man.

The business of marketing is frequently carried on with that of market gardening, but there are also people, mostly women, who follow this business solely. The marketers range from capitalists with a horse and cart, or wagon, to old women who walk to Frome with a basket and hawk the produce from door to door. The marketers collect butter and eggs, fruit and vegetables from farmers and others, paying a little less than market price, and carry these goods to customers or the markets in Frome or Warminster.

In Warminster these people are allowed to hawk without a licence. In Frome they pay, with baskets, 2s. 6d., with a donkey 5s., and with a horse and cart 7s. 6d. per annum for the right to hawk from door to door.

Marketers, besides taking Corsley produce to market, bring in supplies for Corsley people. One marketer, included in the list of farmers, buys butter at the market and sells it in this parish, for though a considerable amount of butter is made in Corsley, it is difficult to obtain locally.

It may be noted here that besides well-to-do people who keep a carriage or pony-cart, and about thirty farmers with holdings of three acres upwards, who keep a horse or pony, there are at least twenty men with a pony or horse and cart. These include a few tradesmen, such as builders, coal hauliers, and shopkeepers, but are mainly cottagers. Probably fifty-five is an under-estimate of the number of persons keeping a horse or pony and cart, and there can be no doubt that at least one-quarter of the Corsley households have a " trap " of some description to drive about the country.

Labourers.

The majority of labourers are employed in agriculture, and include carters, cowmen, woodmen, a shepherd, and under-gardeners, as well as general labourers ; and for convenience a few others, such as under-keepers, road labourers, a lime-burner, and a mason's labourer, have been included in the group.

The money wages of the majority of wage-earners in the parish, whether householders or subsidiary earners, have been carefully ascertained, every effort being made to check inaccuracies, either accidental or intentional, in information given, by supplementary evidence.

The extra payments given to agricultural labourers in money or kind have also been inquired into. These consist mainly of house and garden rent free, harvest money, and beer or ale daily ; also in a few cases milk or meals are given.

These have been estimated at fixed rates as follows :

	s.	d.	
House and garden	1	6	per week
Beer	1	0	,, ,,
Harvest money, where amount given is not stated, £2 12s. or	1	0	,, ,,

Some of the cottages and gardens are, no doubt,

worth more than 1s. 6d., but a special assessment in each case was not found practicable.

In certain cases farmers give 1s. a week extra above the usual wage instead of beer ; this seems, therefore, to be the commonly accepted value, and 1s. has been taken for beer in all cases where it is given, though in fact the amount given by different employers varies.

In many cases the amount of harvest money given has been ascertained. Where this has not been done £2 12s., or 1s. per week, has been taken, this being a mean between sums given in ascertained cases.

In the case of milk the market value of the amount given, or 3d. per quart, is allowed.

Carters.

There are eighteen carters, sixteen of whom may be considered to be earning full men's wages.

The normal carter's wage is 15s.

No of Men.	Money Wage s d.	No of Men.	Real Wage. s d.
2	18 0	1	20 6
1	16 0	1	19 0
7	15 0	1	17 6
4	14 0	4	17 0
2	13 0	2	16 6
2	10 0	5	16 0
		1	15 6
		1	15 0
		1	10 6
		1	10 0

Omitting the two who earn 10s., which is not the wage of a full-grown, able-bodied man, the average money wage for the sixteen men is 15s. ; the average real wage for the sixteen men is 16s. 9d.

Dairymen.

Two dairymen who receive more than £1 a week real wages are not counted among labourers.

A third included below receives rather more than the average cowman.

Cowmen.

There are 10 cowmen. Their normal money wage is 13s. or 14s., 6 out of 10 receiving this amount.

No. of Men	Money Wage. s.	d.	No. of Men.	Real Wage s.	d.
1	16	0	1	18	0
2	15	0	1	17	6
3	14	0	2	17	0
3	13	0	1	16	0
1	12	0	1	15	0
			1	14	6
			2	14	0
			1	13	0

The average money wage is nearly 13s. 11d., the average real wage 15s. 7d.

Agricultural Labourers.

(1 road labourer, 1 worker at the limekiln, and 1 keeper's labourer are included.)

The parish contains 37 agricultural labourers regularly employed, 1 road labourer, 1 keeper's labourer, 1 labourer at the limekiln, and 6 boys or lads employed in agriculture.

The normal labourer's wage is 14s. or 15s.

Out of 27 labourers whose earnings have been ascertained, two-thirds receive one of these sums— i.e., 11 get 15s. and 7 get 14s. More than half the labourers in receipt of 15s. are given beer as well ; in the other cases the wage is nominally 14s. and 1s. extra in lieu of beer.

No of Men.	Money Wage	No of Men.	Real Wage.
	s. d.		s d.
11	15 0	2	17 0
7	14 0	6	16 6
5	13 0	6	16 0
3	12s. to 13s.	2	15 6
	according to season	2	15 0
1	10 0	1	14 6
13	unknown	3	14 0
		1	13 6
		1	13 0
		3	12 6
		13	unknown

The average money wage of the 27 men is nearly 13s. 11d. ; the average real wage is 15s. $3\frac{1}{2}$d.

If we divide the 27 into 2 groups, the first including the 18 men with a wage of 14s. or 15s., the second the 9 men with lower wages, we get the following results :

	s	d
GROUP 1.—Average money wage	14	7
Average real wage	16	1·2

These 18 men are working for farmers or employers resident in the parish.

	s.	d.
GROUP 2.—Average money wage	12	6
Average real wage	13	$4\frac{1}{2}$

The striking fact of this group is that though the money wage is exceptionally low they receive very little addition in kind. This appears still more forcibly if we omit the ninth, an old man working for a farmer at 10s. a week, who receives considerable additions, such as a roomy house which shelters a large adult wage-earning family. The rule has been followed of reckoning this at 1s. 6d., though it is worth more, but even so this man brings down the average of the money wage, and raises that of real earnings in the group.

The other eight men receive 13s. in the summer, but three of them probably have their wage reduced to 12s. in winter.

This group includes the road-mender and other workers for employers not resident in the parish, who, so far as can be ascertained, receive no extras whatsoever.

About half are in an employment which offers some advantages over that of small farmers, such as less supervision and easiness of work. In certain cases, too, a pension may be gained after twenty-five years' continuous service.

This group remains, however, the lowest paid in the parish.

Taking the whole 27 labourers together, it is not probable that if particulars had been obtained respecting the remaining 13 the result would be materially affected. Their omission is due to accidental causes, which do not seem likely to give any particular bias ; 3 are working for employers likely to give the highest customary wage, 3 for very small employers, who labour on their own land. In 1 of these cases the wage is likely to be very low. Four are omitted owing to confusion of names which prevents proper identification, and one or two of them are working for farmers in other parishes. One was out of work at the time the investigation was made.

The following is a table of the earnings of boys and lads employed in agriculture in Corsley.

Boys and Lads.

No.	Money Wage s. d		No.	Real Wage. s. d.	
1 (aged 18)	12	0	1	12	0
3	9	0	1	10	6
1	7	0	1	10	0
1	6	6	1	9	0
			1	8	0
			1	7	6

Under-gardeners.

Ten men have been classified as under-gardeners ; normal wage 14s.

No of Men.	Money Wage. s. d.		No of Men.	Real Wage. s. d.	
1	16	0	1	16	0
1	15	0	1	15	6
4	14	0	1	15	0
2	13	0	3	14	0
2	unknown		2	13	0
			2	unknown	

The average money wage of the 8 men is 14s. 1½d. ; the average real wage, 14s. 3¾d.

Under-gardeners might be counted with agricultural labourers without materially affecting the average money wage, which is 13s. 11d. for agricultural labourers. Their real wages, however, are greatly less than those of farm labourers, since they seldom receive a cottage, harvest money, or beer.

Possibly perquisites of some description are given in certain cases, but these have not been discovered or estimated.

Day Labourers and Woodmen.

There are eighteen men in the parish who do not work regularly for any employer at a fixed wage, but work by the day, or at piecework, as farm labourers, woodmen, drainers, hedgers and ditchers, mowers, &c. There is also a woodman working regularly for a low wage who can probably supplement his earnings considerably by doing piecework jobs.

The normal rate for an able-bodied man with no special skill such as that possessed by woodmen is 2s. 6d. per day.

No of Men.	Rate per Day Summer.	Winter	Average Weekly Wage.	Weekly Wage when in full Employment
1 (wood-cutter) —		—	25 0	—
1	—	—	18 0	—
1	3 0	3 0	—	18 0
4	3 0	2 6	—	15s. to 18s.
1	—	—	15 0	—
9	2 6	2 6	—	15 0
1	2 0	2 0	—	12 0

The general idea in the parish is that the day-labourer can earn more than the regular labourer.

His money earnings when in work are, no doubt, higher than the average, but besides the uncertainty of employment he probably receives less payment in kind, such as house and garden rent free, than the regular farm labourer, and his real earnings are probably considerably lower.

Gardeners.

There are two head gardeners and one foreman gardener in the parish, all in receipt of good wages and earnings.

Groom-gardeners.

There are three groom-gardeners, whose earnings are probably equal to or higher than those of labourers.

Thatcher.

There is one thatcher in Corsley, who works with the assistance of a lad who lives in his house. He probably gets constant employment either in Corsley or in neighbouring parishes. He is paid on a piecework system.

The Building Trades and Artisans.

With a declining population there is no great scope for the speculative builder in Corsley. There are, however, two builders resident here, who are the chief employers of labour in the parish.

Mr. Pearce, wheelwright and builder, living at Corsley Heath, employs over twenty inhabitants, besides about twenty workmen who are not resident in Corsley.

Mr. Eyers, builder and plumber, at Chapmanslade, employs fifteen to twenty men resident in the parish.

The work carried out by Mr. Pearce at his Corsley workshop is mainly that of cart-building ; he also undertakes house carpentering, painting, &c.

There are some good cottages in the parish built by Mr. Eyers, though his business consists more in executing repairs than in the construction of new buildings.

The greater number of artisans living in Corsley find employment at the workshops of one of these tradesmen, while the remainder, or most of them, work for employers residing in other parishes.

In considering the earnings of artisans it will be convenient to include under this heading wheelwrights, carpenters, masons, plumbers, plasterers and tilers, blacksmiths, some brickmakers, and a sawyer.

[Hudson, Frome.

CORSLEY HEATH WAGON WORKS

Photo by]

To face p. 155

Artisans' Earnings.

The earnings in this group usually run from 20s. to 25s. per week. A few get less than this and a few get more ; none, however, receive more than 30s. per week.

Information given as to the earnings of plumbers, carpenters, and masons is somewhat conflicting.

One informant states that the best men in these trades can earn 5d. to 6d. an hour ; but though this is true for wheelwrights and carpenters, no case has been found where plumbers or masons resident in the parish receive more than 4½d. per hour. Individual earnings have not, however, been ascertained in every case.

Masons.

There are six masons, two mason's labourers, and one plasterer and tiler (out of work) in the parish.

Masons' wages are 4d. to 4½d. per hour. For a week of 56 hours this amounts to 18s. 8d. or 21s.

Plumbers.

There are 4 plumbers and 1 lad learning the trade. Earnings appear to be similar to those of masons.

Painters.

There are 5 painters (1 out of work), also 2 lads and 1 apprentice in the trade.

Wages have not been satisfactorily ascertained, but the average is probably 21s. per week.

Carpenters and Wheelwrights.

There are 5 wheelwrights and carpenters and 6 carpenters in Corsley.

Wheelwrights, working full time, can earn 24s. to 25s. per week. One worker is said to be able to earn 27s. per week. The rates are 5d. and $5\frac{1}{2}$d. per hour, for a week of 59 hours. But some workers do not work full time.

Carpenters usually receive 20s. per week. One is said to receive not much short of 30s.

Brickmakers.

One or two Corsley men work at the Rodden Brickyard, where it is said men can earn £2 to £2 10s. a week in the summer.

The brickyard at Dartford, on the borders of the parish, is worked by the tenant, with the help of his own sons.

Blacksmiths, Sawyer.

There are one or two wage-earning blacksmiths and one sawyer in the parish.

WOMEN'S WORK

It remains to consider the work and the earnings of women in Corsley. The chief occupations followed by women are laundry-work, charing, gloving, nursing and midwifery, dressmaking, sewing, marketing, shopkeeping, and baking.

Laundry-work.

Several women in Corsley take in sufficient washing to oblige them to employ other women to help them, and many more take in a small amount regularly, or occasionally, earning from a few pence to a shilling or two weekly. There are four laundresses living at Longhedge, one at Temple, and one at Corsley Heath. These do the washing of the larger houses in the parish, and also take in some from Warminster. The prices charged for washing are not uniform, but most charge at a low rate, leaving a very small margin of profit. A laundress whose gross earnings are 12s. weekly has to pay a woman for two days' work and provide her food. She must provide materials such as soap, and extra firing, which amounts to something considerable in damp weather. If 3s. be allowed for the extra labour and 1s. 6d. for firing and materials, her nett earnings are 7s. 6d. For this she has to work hard. Whatever the weather may be, the washing has to be finished by a certain time. Should wet weather set in on drying day, she must often remain up all night drying the linen before the fire. There are few washerwomen in Corsley who have attained middle-age without being seriously affected by the trying conditions of their occupation, rheumatism in many forms being prevalent among them. It is absolutely necessary that they should feed well, and with the strictest economy most of them can save little towards a provision for old age, notwithstanding the fact that to end their days without coming upon the parish often appears to be the chief anxiety of their hard-working lives.

One or two Corsley laundresses charge rather higher prices than their neighbours, and, no doubt, make larger profits; one takes in a large amount of washing and by hard work probably makes a fairly good income; in two other cases the laundress is not the only supporter of the family. The fact remains, however, that the remuneration for laundry-work is in most cases unreasonably low.

The women employed by the laundresses receive 1s. per day and their food. They expect good food ; probably meat is provided every day. This may be estimated in money as a total of 1s. 6d. per day. Many women go out for the day washing, but they cannot as a rule get employment for more than two days a week at this work. They are sometimes able, however, to get charing work on other days.

Charing.

Many women say that they do occasional charing, and some have regular employment at this occupation. The customary wage appears to be the same as for laundry-work—1s. per day, and food. Some, however, are able to obtain 2s. per day without food or 1s. 6d. with food, and it is to be hoped that this rate may become more general.

Gloving.

A large proportion of the married women and girls in Chapmanslade, and a few in other parts of Corsley, take in " gloving " from the two glove factories at Westbury and Westbury Leigh. They have to fetch the work from the factories, three or four miles distant. They bring home the leather ready cut into shape, stitch the seams by hand, and return the gloves to be finished in the factories.

The work is poorly paid. The women have to provide their own needles and thread and they receive $4\frac{1}{2}$d. or 5d. per pair according to the quality of the glove. Each pair takes four hours' steady work, so that three pairs are considered a good day's work.

This at six full days a week only yields eighteen pairs at 7s. 6d. for the better class of glove, and means toiling at high pressure for an excessive number of hours, the work being very trying to the eyesight ; and even by the most skilled workers this output is only accomplished now and then as a record, although occasionally a small pair of ladies' gloves may be done in less than the four hours. Married women with a household to look after probably seldom earn more than 2s. 6d. or 2s. per week at gloving, and girls living at home with their relations, and working regularly, but not at high pressure, probably earn about 4s. per week. No case has been found where a single woman or widow is able to support herself by this work, though several women in receipt of poor relief add a little to their incomes by gloving. It must, therefore, be considered entirely a parasitic industry.

Sewing.

A few women try to support themselves by taking in sewing. This, like gloving, is usually badly paid. One single woman said that she could make 4s. to 5s. per week at sewing, sitting at it all the time.

Nursing and Midwifery.

We now come to an occupation where women have been able to raise their standard of earnings somewhat. Three of the five nurses or midwives residing in Corsley parish were questioned, with the following results :

No. 206 serves the very poor. In the case of confinements in the near neighbourhood she charges 5s., not staying in the house of her patient but making occasional visits for one week. If the patient is more than a mile or so distant, she charges 7s. 6d. She is not, she says, able at this price to provide herself with all that is required by the inspector.

No. 1 seldom nurses the very poor. When she does so she says that she charges 5s. or 6s. for a confinement, her usual rate being 7s. 6d. for the week. A labourer's wife recently attended by her paid 10s. per week, no doctor being called in, and this is probably her customary charge.

No. 180 seldom nursed the inhabitants of Corsley. She usually attended farmers' wives, &c. in other parishes. Her charge was 10s. per week.

The fourth midwife residing in Corsley does not practise in the parish.

The fifth woman, who goes out nursing occasionally, is said to be a very capable attendant. Her scale of charges was not ascertained.

Since the winter of 1905-6 a Benefit Nursing Association has been established, which enables the cottagers, by subscribing, to obtain attendance in sickness or confinements at a much cheaper rate.

Dressmakers.

There were in the winter of 1905-6 at least three dressmakers in Corsley. The rates of payment are low, being about 3s. 6d. for making a skirt or a blouse, and probably less is charged in some cases. Nevertheless, a clever dressmaker, working alone, is able to make as much as £1 a week, or, allowing for slack seasons, holidays, and illness, over £40 per annum. Those who have to assist in housework, who are slower workers, or who do not get fairly regular employment, cannot, of course, make so much. Probably the actual takings of the dressmakers vary from 7s. to £1 per week.

Girls going out to work for the day as dressmakers, having received a training, get 1s. per day and food, like laundresses and charwomen. Apprentices taken by village dressmakers receive no remuneration or food during the first year. During the second year they are paid 1s. a week.

Marketing.

This business, which is largely followed by women, has already been dealt with in the section on market gardeners and marketers. It is not possible to discover the nett earnings of such people, these being made up of a number of small and miscellaneous items.

Shopkeeping.

At least three women keep shop, in addition to other occupations, or to supplement the earnings of their menkind. One of these does a good business, but little is done by the others, the people of Corsley now buying their provisions mainly from the towns, or from people who hawk round from door to door.

Baking.

At least two women earn a little by baking. They usually bake twice a week, and send a child round to their customers with the bread. It has not been ascertained what profits they are able to make in this way.

This exhausts the principal remunerative occupations followed by women in Corsley, as far as can be ascertained.

Speaking broadly, the wage of a woman, be

10

she laundry-worker, charwoman, or dressmaker's assistant, is 1s. per day and food. Few women, however, can get more than four days' employment in a week, unless in regular service. This, calculating food as 6d. per day, gives a maximum of 6s. per week, which may be sufficient for a single woman, but cannot allow her to provide for children or other dependants, nor to save much towards a provision for her old age. When, however, a woman is supported by her husband or son, and works only for pocket money, she is able to make a good thing of it. One woman, the wife of a labourer, was able to save £70 out of her earnings working at farmhouses, and has set up with her capital as market gardener and marketer.

Women's work is to a large extent parasitic, those women who are able-bodied and without dependants or family naturally preferring to enter domestic service or migrate to districts where remuneration is higher. It is to be feared, therefore, that women's wages will not easily be raised, those who are solely dependent on their own earnings being too few and too isolated to fight effectively against a rate of payment which usually forces them in the end to seek relief from the Board of Guardians. It is, as might be expected, from the more well-to-do, those who have substantial savings or are being kept by their male relatives, that the only efforts to raise the rates of pay have come. These can refuse the work as not worth their while to undertake should the reward be too small, and in a few cases such women have succeeded in obtaining a higher scale of payment than their less fortunate sisters.

CHAPTER XI

HOUSES AND GARDENS IN CORSLEY

THE parish of Corsley boasts of no great house, the lord of its manor for the past three hundred and fifty years having been the owner of Longleat, in the neighbouring parish of Horningsham. It is, however, well provided with houses of a moderate size. There are, firstly, Corsley House and Sturford Mead, and the small house of Sandhayes, occupied by the households of the three gentlemen mentioned in the last chapter. These houses were built, or received considerable additions and alterations, during the nineteenth century. Next we find two old houses, now used as farmhouses, the one the Manor Farm, an Elizabethan house built by Sir John Thynne, and the other Cley Hill Farm, probably in part of more ancient date, and the dwelling of the Kington family prior to the Reformation.

Another picturesque old farmhouse at Whitbourne Springs was in all probability the home of the Carey family in the seventeenth century.

In addition to these there are a number of comfortable-looking houses studded all over the parish, most of them not much more than a century old, and some of quite recent erection. These are chiefly occupied as farmhouses.

There are about 165 inhabited cottages in Corsley, in addition to the farmhouses and other substantial dwellings. It is not, however, possible to draw any very firm line of division between houses and cottages.

The cottages appear on the whole to be neither specially good nor specially bad. It is a grievance that few have a parlour as well as a kitchen, and this is asserted to be a reason why young married people often refuse to set up house in the parish, but the influence of this demand for a newly-coveted mark of social distinction is probably much exaggerated.

There is a fair proportion of really good cottages, mainly owned by residents in the parish.

Cottage property in Corsley is owned by a number of different persons, including builders and tradesmen, private gentlemen and farmers, besides cottagers who own their own dwelling, but the majority of the houses belong to the principal landlord, Lord Bath.

Peasant owners of one or two cottages are fairly numerous, and are sometimes the successors of squatters on the once extensive commons of Corsley.

Some of the cottages are still let on a lease of lives, but ordinary yearly or weekly tenancies have during the last forty years been gradually substituted for this old system as the lives fall in.

The population of the parish is declining, being now less than half what it was in 1831, and numbers of cottages have been pulled down or allowed to fall into disrepair since that date.

At the present day if a cottage stands empty, it is usually allowed to fall into ruin, while its garden can generally be let at a good rent.

The 165 cottages contain 689 rooms and are inhabited by 624 persons.

The size of the cottages is as follows :

No. of Cottages							
8	...	...	...	...	with	2	rooms.
51	...	...	...	...	„	3	„
45	...	...	...	...	„	4	„
33	...	...	...	...	„	5	„
18	...	...	...	...	„	6	„
4	...	...	...	...	„	7	„
5	...	...	...	...	„	8	„
1	...	...	...	...	„	9	„
165							

It will be seen from this table that nearly one-third of the whole are three-roomed cottages, though four or five roomed dwellings are also numerous. The larger dwellings of six rooms and upwards are frequently two small cottages rented by one tenant.

As there are 689 rooms, or thereabouts, in these cottages, and only 624 persons, including children, there is more than one room per head for the cottage population.

An examination of the distribution of population among these cottages shows only three cases of over-crowding according to the Registrar-General's definition, of more than two persons to a room.[1] Forty-two cottages have more than one person, but not more than two to a room. The remaining 120 have one or more rooms for each inmate.

[1] See "Poverty : a Study of Town Life," by B. Seebohm Rowntree, p. 145.

Occupations of Householders.	Total No. of Cottages.	No Rooms.	No Inhabitants.	No Cottages with		
				1 or more rooms per head	Less than 1, not less than 2 rooms per head	Less than 2 rooms per head
Small farmers and market gardeners	14	69	58	13	41	
Brickmakers, shoemakers, &c.	5	20	17	4	1	
Carters	13	51	66	5	7	1
Cowmen	7	30	31	5	2	
Labourers	33	136	148	20	13	
Miscellaneous agricultural ...	14	56	60	9	3	2
Miscellaneous gardeners, retired labourers, and others, and persons working outside parish...	25	89	75	20	5	
Artisans	20	104	85	14	6	
Women householders ...	34[1]	134	84	30	4	
	165	689	624	120	42	3

Rents for cottages in Corsley run from about £3 to £6 a year. Probably the two-roomed houses are less, and a few of the best cottages are more.

Practically every cottage in Corsley has a garden, which is included in this rent.

The rent for an ordinary cottage with three rooms and a pantry, and a good garden of 20 to 40 poles, is £4 a year. A cottage of better type with about four rooms and a garden is £5. If the garden be very large, or the cottage larger or better built than the average, rents are naturally higher, amounting

[1] This number includes all women householders living in cottages, some having sons or other male relatives living with them.

to as much as £8 in one case for a good house of eight rooms and garden. Whilst some of the inhabitants, including those who own their cottages, and also many of the tenant occupiers, have resided in the same house for a number of years, a constant movement is going on among another section of the population. In the autumn of 1906 it was found that besides a few families who had left the parish, and a few who had newly settled there, many had changed from one cottage to another in Corsley or Chapmanslade since the preceding winter. There are families who have moved their house three or more times within the last ten years. The reason for change is not always apparent, though it is sometimes accounted for by the growing up of the children, the need for more accommodation, and an increased income which makes it possible to rent a larger house.

One or two of the smaller farmers, a few of the widows or single women, and some of the tenants of the large and well-built cottages take lodgers. Orphans from the Union workhouse are occasionally boarded out with women in Corsley.

Besides the regular lodgers, who are usually working lads or men employed in the parish, " visitors " from the towns find accommodation here in the summer, when many strange faces may be seen about the parish. These visitors are sometimes put up in the smaller cottages, and the crowding must be great.

Allotments.

There is a considerable amount of land available for allotments in Corsley, viz., about 30 acres in Corsley and 15 acres at Broadpath, Chapmanslade.

Rents are reasonable, being from 3d. to 6d. per

lug or pole, or £2 to £4 the acre. It is let in 20-pole holdings, one man often getting three or four into his hands, though, nominally, this is forbidden ; the holders, too, will sometimes sublet to other villagers. The actual amount held by any individual is, therefore, not easy to ascertain.

The rents for grass land are high, and cause grumbling, nevertheless, when any grass land is to be let, people " tumble over each other " to get it. There are a number of people in the parish renting small plots of land which they use either as gardens or dairy farms. The soil is particularly favourable for the success of small holdings and these people usually thrive.

Some of the cottagers also keep pigs or poultry, and the majority add to their income by selling garden produce, even when not holding an allotment.

The garden is, of course, usually cultivated as an additional source of income, but there are, or have recently been, several persons in the parish who, cut off from other means of earning a livelihood, contrive to make one from the garden alone, either with or without a small preliminary capital invested in a horse and cart.

These people probably work very hard, and have a struggle at first, but they seldom come upon the parish until extreme old age.

This proves what a valuable asset the labourer's plot of land is to him, under favourable conditions, and the following account from the wife of No. 131 is an example of what can be done with an ordinary cottage garden in Corsley.

"I have a patch of the garden to myself ; in this I have a strawberry bed, raspberry bed, gooseberry-trees, currant-trees (black and red), apple-trees and a fowl pen. I have to look after this myself and keep it clean; the fowls enjoy all the weeds which I hoe off and throw into the pen.

"Below is what I sold:

	£	s.	d.
Gooseberries	0	11	4
Strawberries	1	11	5
Raspberries	1	14	8
Black and red currants	0	9	2
Apples	0	19	5
Poultry	1	5	0
From other parts of the garden:			
Young potatoes...	0	8	6
French beans and peas	0	6	5
Flowers	1	2	6
Total during year	8	8	5

"When I am selling my fruit in the summer, I sell the finest fruit, and boil down into jam all the small fruit, which makes quite as good jam, but does not command so good a price at the market. The jam I find very useful in the winter when butter is dear."

The man in this case had no time to work in the garden, so that a woman, working alone, and having her household duties and cooking to attend to, was able to supply all the fruit and vegetables and some eggs and poultry for home consumption, and in addition to make a profit of over £8 from garden produce and poultry out of a garden of 50 poles, rented, with a five-roomed cottage, for £5 5s. per annum.

the minimum cost at which food, fuel, dress, household sundries, and house-room, sufficient for efficiency, can be obtained in the parish, and it has then been seen how many families were below this standard, or in primary poverty.

Mr. Rowntree, in his " Poverty : A Study of Town Life " (pp. 88-106), enters into a scientific inquiry as to the nutritive value of various dietaries, and adopts a certain standard, less generous than that of the Local Government Board dietaries for workhouses, since it omits meat, as the cheapest upon which efficiency is obtainable. He then calculates on a scientific basis the amount required for men and women, and for children of different ages, and from this deduces an average of 3s. for a man or woman and 2s. 3d. for a child as the minimum necessary cost of food, though ignorance and prejudice would prevent the poor from actually selecting any such scientifically economical diet.

To estimate the necessary cost of food per head in Corsley, comparison has been made between the prices paid here and those given for York by Mr. Rowntree.[1]   From this we find that provisions as bought by the poor are dearer in Corsley than in York.   On the other hand, the inhabitants of Corsley obtain potatoes, vegetables, and fruit from their gardens cheaper than could be obtained by the inhabitants of York.   Mr. Rowntree's minimum, based on the cheapest diet sufficient for efficiency, has therefore been adopted, viz., 3s. for an adult ; 2s. 3d. for a child.

This standard has likewise been taken by Mr. Mann in his study of the village of Ridgemont, in

[1] See " Poverty : a Study of Town Life," by Seebohm Rowntree, p. 104.

Bedfordshire, published in "Sociological Papers," vol. i.

Rent is omitted, since practically every cottage in Corsley has a good garden, and the value of garden produce in some cases more than equals the rent. Probably, in an average case, rent and value of produce (including that consumed by the family) about balance. An old person unable to work his garden would, no doubt, have to pay more in rent than he could get back by the lease of his garden, and in such cases the minimum will therefore be placed a little too low, while in the instances where a man is able to earn more than the total rent from his garden produce it will be placed a little too high.

Mr. Mann estimates that, allowing for wood, &c., picked up, 1s. per week per household would probably be sufficient for fuel, irrespective of the number of persons. He allows 2d. per week per head for household sundries. For dress he has followed Mr. Rowntree's standard of 6d. per week for a man or woman and 5d. for boy or girl under sixteen.

As there seems no reason to suppose that conditions are materially different in Corsley, I take these figures as the minimum necessary. The table then stands as follows, these figures being estimated as the very lowest on which, with the most judicious and economical expenditure, efficiency is possible.

> Food, 3s. per adult.
>   „ 2s. 3d. per child.
> Rent, none, as garden produce equals rent.
> Firing, 1s. per household.
> Sundries, 2d. per head.
> Dress, adult, 6d. per week.
>   „ child, 5d. per week.

The following table gives the minimum necessary income for families of various sizes.

			Food.		Dress, Fuel, and Household Sundries.		Total	
			s.	d.	s.	d.	s.	d.
1 adult	...	...	3	o	1	8	4	8
2 adults	...	...	6	o	2	4	8	4
3 ,,	...	...	9	o	3	o	12	o
4 ,,	...	...	12	o	3	8	15	8
5 ,,	...	...	15	o	4	4	19	4
2 ,,	1 child	...	8	3	2	11	11	2
2 ,,	2 children	...	10	6	3	6	14	o
2 ,,	3 ,,	...	12	9	4	1	16	10
2 ,,	4 ,,	...	15	o	4	8	19	8
2 ,,	5 ,,	...	17	3	5	3	22	6
2 ,,	6 ,,	...	19	6	5	10	25	4
2 ,,	7 ,,	...	21	9	6	5	28	2

For every child 2s. 10d. is added.
For every adult 3s. 8d. is added.

This corresponds with the table given by Mr. Mann, except that rent is here omitted.

Having thus discovered the minimum upon which efficiency is possible, we find that 28 families, comprising 144 persons (57 adults, 87 children under sixteen), are living in primary poverty in Corsley.

These may be divided into three groups :

(a) Where there is at least one A.B. male wage-earner, but where, through largeness of family or smallness of wage, earnings are insufficient.

(b) Where the wage-earner is incapacitated through old age or illness.

(c) Households without a male wage-earner.

(a) The first of these groups is largest. It contains 17 families, 40 adults and 82 children. If one family of 9, whose earnings are unknown, be omitted, this gives 113 persons with a total weekly income of 297s. and a weekly deficit on what is required for efficiency of 70s.

(*b*) The second group contains 7 families, 12 adults, and 3 children. Some of these families are in receipt of poor relief and some are not.

Five are persons or families of good character who, through some misfortune, such as illness or accident, were unable to earn good wages in their younger days, and hence have been unable to provide for old age and sickness, or else they have been defrauded of the fruits of their thrift, by the recent breaking up of the old Corsley Walking Club. The other two are of more doubtful character, and may owe their poverty to wasteful expenditure, or drink.

(*c*) The third group consists of 4 households containing 5 adults and 2 children, being women with or without children or other dependants, who, through old age or illness, are unable to earn and do not obtain from any other source sufficient for efficiency for themselves, or for themselves and dependants, as the case may be.

The occupations of the heads of the 28 households in primary poverty are as follows :

A.B. labourers	16
Retired market gardeners	2
Labourers retired from old age or sickness ...	5
Warrener	1
Women householders	4

The following tables show the economic position of each family :

(*A*) HOUSEHOLDERS IN PRIMARY POVERTY OWING TO LARGENESS OF FAMILY AND LOWNESS OF WAGE.

Index No.	Adults.	Children.	Income. s. d.	Deficit. s. d.
5	2	3	13 0	3 10
11	3	5	25 0	1 2
12	2	4	16 6	3 2
28	2	7	17 3	10 11
29	2	3	16 0	0 10
32	2	6	17 0	8 4
36	4	4	23 6	3 6
37	2	6	24 0	1 4
42	2	6	20 6	4 10
44	2	5	15 0	7 6
45	2	4	17 3	2 5
49	3	5	15 0	11 2
51	2	4	16 0	3 8
54	2	3	15 6	1 4
58	3	5	25 6	0 8
62	2	6	20 0	5 4
63	3	6	unknown	unknown deficit.
	40	82	297 0	70 0

(*B*) HOUSEHOLDS IN PRIMARY POVERTY OWING TO OLD AGE OR ILLNESS OF WAGE-EARNER.

Index No	Adults.	Children.	Income s. d.	Deficit. s. d.
65	1	0	4 0	0 8
66	3	0	unknown	prob. deficit.
67	2	3	12 0	4 10
68	1	0	3 6	1 2
70	1	0	4 6	0 2
73	2	0	unknown.	deficit.
111	2	0	unknown.	deficit.
	13	3		

(C) HOUSEHOLDS WITHOUT MALE WAGE-EARNER IN PRIMARY
POVERTY.

Index No.	Adults	Children.	Income.	Deficit.
183	2	0	unknown	prob. deficit.
179	1	0	unknown	certainly deficit.
205	1	1	6 0	1 6
212	1	1	unknown	prob. deficit.
	5	2		

Total number of persons in primary poverty: 57 adults, 87 children.

Secondary Poverty.

It will have been noticed that in estimating the minimum income necessary, nothing is allowed for clubs, insurance, and provision against old age and sickness generally, though it is the practice even of the poorest labourers of Corsley to make such provision. Nor is anything allowed for waste owing to ignorance of the most nourishing and economical foods, or accident of any kind.

It does not appear, therefore, that a family has a secure position above the line of primary poverty, unless it has a surplus of at least 1s. per head per week.

It is usual in an analysis of this kind to take a section who are described as in secondary poverty.

Under this heading we shall include all households whose income does not give this margin of 1s. per head above primary poverty, as well as those households where the income should be sufficient, but where it is squandered and the members are obviously living in want. Probably a few families who might be included for this reason are omitted, since an appearance of dirt and untidiness has not been taken by

11

itself as a proof that a sufficient diet was not provided, though this is likely to be the case.

There are 37 households which, for one or other of the causes mentioned, come under this definition of secondary poverty. These contain 80 adults and 48 children. Thirteen are labourers, 3 being included on account of drink or other wasteful expenditure, or bad management, though the incomes should be sufficient. The other 10, including a carter, cowman, underkeeper, and road labourer, have not the margin of 1s. per head.

A small farmer, a small shopkeeper, and four market-gardeners are included. It is not possible to do more than make a guess at the income of these people, but they appear to have a struggle to keep going, and their incomes do not probably exceed the limit to secondary poverty.

Four are families where the head of the household is aged and the margin of the income over the primary poverty line is small. Nine are women householders.

Five are carpenters, masons, or blacksmiths, with five or six in family, but no supplementary earners. In one case grown-up daughters are kept at home idle. Another case, owing to want of work, drink, and extravagance, is probably in primary poverty, in spite of substantial help from relations and others.

The total number of households in the parish is 220 ; of these, therefore, 155 are above the margin of secondary poverty, though it must be remembered that even artisans and others, well above this line, are liable to be plunged into extreme poverty, by misfortune, such as serious sickness in the family.

About five-sevenths of the households are above poverty, rather less than one-sixth in secondary poverty, about one-eighth in primary poverty.

But as poverty is mainly due to the presence of non-productive members, we find that numerically the group of primary poverty with 144 persons is greater than that of secondary poverty with 128 persons. Similarly these two groups, which form about two-sevenths of the households, in all probability contain more than two-sevenths of the population. If the decline of the population has continued since the last census, this is certainly the case, although the higher group contains many well-to-do households swelled by the presence of domestic servants and grown-up children.

	Adults	Children	Total Population.	No Families
Primary poverty ...	57	87	144	28
Secondary poverty ...	80	48	128	37
Over line of secondary poverty	—	—	—	155

Having defined poverty, it will be interesting to investigate its incidence in the households of labourers and artisans.

Out of 70 households [1] whose head is a labourer only 16 are in primary and 13 in secondary poverty; the remaining 41 are, therefore, above this line.

Of these 41, only 13 have a child or children in the household.

We will take first the group of 28 households having no children below fourteen years old.

(A) These contain 78 adult persons.

Nearly all the male wage-earners are labourers (as defined above) ; but among the subsidiary earners are found one coal merchant, one mason, one labourer

---

[1] On p. 107 (Chapter X.) the number of labourers is given as 72, but two sons of widows, who are usually away malting in winter, which were included there, are here omitted.

in iron-works, and one employee in gas-works. An electrician is also included in this group as a lodger.

(*B*) The second group of 13 is similar to the above, except that each household contains one or more child. These families are composed of 47 adults and 20 children. The number of adults and of wage-earners is, therefore, preponderant over that of children, many of the women in this group being wage-earners.

Like the first group, the male earners are labourers with the exception of a market gardener, a blacksmith, a worker in Frome foundry, and an engine-driver.

The households in Groups A and B are all well above the line of primary poverty, having a margin of at least 1s. per head.

(*C*) Group C consists of 13 families in secondary poverty, containing 29 adults and 25 children.

Ten of these are households where there are not more than two children, or where a second male member of the family has just reached an age to contribute to the family income, and has thus enabled the family to rise above primary poverty.

The other three are families where, owing to laziness or drink, the household appears to be sunk in poverty, but where earnings should be sufficient if work was regularly undertaken and the money properly expended.

There are few subsidiary earners in this group. All are labourers. No household in this group has more than 1s. per head over the minimum required for efficiency.

(*D*) Group D has 16 families in primary poverty, containing 37 adults and 76 children. There are about 6 subsidiary earners in this group, 2 being wives with large young families. In all cases but one the poverty is entirely due to the wage of the man being insufficient to provide efficiently for his family. The one exception is where poverty is due to illness of adult members of the family, and in this case probably help is received from private charity.

The most striking fact that emerges from this analysis is that, though only 16 out of 70 households in which the head of the family is a labourer are in primary poverty, yet 76 out of 121 of their children are being brought up in this condition, which precludes a sufficient supply of nourishing food or good clothing ; and of the other 45 children the great majority have either passed their infancy, or will pass their later childhood should more children be born to their parents, in a condition of primary poverty.

It would appear that only in households where adults outnumber the children can these be brought up under conditions which give scope to full development of their faculties.

Turning to the artisans, we find 25 families whose head has been classified in this group. These 25 householders contain altogether 69 adults and 41 children.

Among the supplementary earners, besides artisans and brickmakers, are several labourers.

The wage-earner in this group very frequently has a second occupation, and among the 25 artisans and brickmakers are 3 publicans, 2 small farmers, and a small shopkeeper. The public-houses and the shop are carried on partly or mainly by the wife. This, of course, raises the income of these households above what it would be were the craft the sole source of earnings.

But among those who have no second occupation we find four families who have not a margin of 1s.

per head above primary poverty. Two of these have each 4 children, one 3, and in one adults are kept at home idle. Twelve of the 41 children in the whole group belong to these four families.

There are no artisans in primary poverty, none having more than four children under fourteen. A fifth child would frequently reduce a family in this group, having no additional source of income, to primary poverty. But none of the younger married people have had more than four children, and the majority have only one or two, in this contrasting with market gardeners, and other independent workers, who, when they have any children at all, usually have a long family. There are two large families, however, among the older artisans, some of their children being already grown up and themselves wage-earners.

CHAPTER XIII

CHARACTER AND ITS RELATION TO POVERTY

Relation of Poverty to Character and Ability.

FULL reports have been obtained from various sources as to the characters of parents and children in the majority of families in the parish. The households omitted are those of most of the larger farmers and publicans, and most of the gardeners, coachmen, and grooms in private service, except in cases where the man is practically a labourer, and has been born and bred in the parish. Tradesmen and dealers are omitted with the exception of one or two cottage shopkeepers. The inhabitants of the larger houses, professional people, and clerks or agents are omitted, and also about ten respectable poorer households, mostly of men retired from work. Many of the respectable women householders have been omitted, these being both comfortably off and of good character.

But where any of these households have children attending the parish schools, reports of the children have been obtained. Full reports have been obtained of 162 households, and school reports of 7 more. These are printed, together with particulars of the circumstances of the families, on pp. 156-184. The authorities at Corsley and Chapmanslade schools have reported on the children belonging to 66 families, resident in Corsley parish and attending one of these schools. The circumstances of each family were ascertained from other sources, and a comparison made of the results.

Primary and secondary poverty are taken in the senses defined in the chapter on Poverty. In each division all the families have been marked with an asterisk where one or more children show character-istics which might be the result of poverty and insufficient feeding. These marks of *deficiency* are dulness, nervousness, laziness, " strangeness " or " peculiarity " of disposition, dirtiness of disposition. Signs of neglect on the part of the parents, resulting in untidiness or dirtiness of the person, for which the child itself is not responsible, are omitted. The inclusion of these would emphasise the facts which are brought out by the former, as an examination of the reports will show.

1. We have, first, seven respectable families, who, owing to the uniqueness of their position in the parish, cannot be reported on separately. These include three farmers, a policeman, a head gardener, and a groom, and a cook in a private house. There are no deficient children in this group.

2. There are children of school age in ten families of artisans, three being in secondary poverty. Only two of these families have children who can be included under our definition of deficiency, the first being a " neglected, strange " family of naughty children, in secondary poverty, and the second a large family where the eldest child, still of school age, is rather dull. It is noteworthy that during the earlier childhood of this boy the family was probably in primary or secondary poverty, though the united

earnings of the family are probably now quite sufficient.

3. There are 16 households other than artisans' above secondary poverty, whose full characters are given in the tables on pp. 169-184. The children of five out of these sixteen have characteristics which might, were their home conditions unknown, be put down to malnutrition. Of these five, one is the family of a respectable and prosperous carter, one is a batch of boarded-out workhouse children, one is the family of a labourer, who was probably in primary poverty till recently, when his elder children became wage-earners, one is an illegitimate child living with its grandparents, and the fifth a farmer's child who is characterised as "lazy."

4. Fifteen families with school children are in secondary poverty, either from the small margin of the income over primary poverty, or from the bad character of the parents.

Six or seven of these fifteen families have deficient children ; in regard to one of the seven the teachers remark that the children would be all right but for the bad home, so this should, perhaps, be excepted.

5. There are 18 families with children of school age in primary poverty. No less than 10 of these have deficient children. In only 4 of these 10 cases is any fault found with the parents and homes, as an examination of the tables will show, and of these four, one is a case where poverty appears to have had a lethargic effect on parents as well as children.

These facts show emphatically that the dulness and deficiency of the children, even in a rural district where every advantage of good air and healthy surroundings is obtained, is mainly due to malnutrition ; for though a certain proportion of dulness is found in all or most classes, whether well fed or otherwise, the greatly larger percentage among the children of the very poor, even where the parents are in every respect satisfactory, can hardly be due to any other cause.

Circumstances of Family			No. of Families	No. where there are Deficient Children.
Well-to-do ...	...	...	30	6
Secondary poverty	...	...	18	7 or 8
Primary poverty	...	...	18	10

Full particulars have been obtained from various persons likely to be well informed as to the characters of 162 households, including all the poorer and practically all the less respectable families. In about eighteen of these we find that there is one or more member who drinks either more than he or she can afford or sufficient to make him drunk. The following table gives the proportion in each economic group :

Circumstances of Family.			No of Families	No where one or more Members drink too much
Well-to-do ...	...	...	101	8
Secondary poverty	...	...	33	6
Primary poverty	...	...	28	5

The larger proportion who drink too much, among those in primary poverty, is due to the inclusion under our definition of those who drink more than they can afford ; the proportion of drunkards is greater among the people in secondary poverty.

Honesty, Promptness in paying Debts, and Thrift.

Nearly every working man in Corsley belongs to a friendly society ; these will be dealt with in a later section.

Some of the cottagers insure their children or themselves. There are two kinds of insurance, death insurance and life insurance ; in the latter case payment is made by the Company if the persons insured live to a certain age. No statistics have been obtained as to insurance, but the custom is not general, and the sum insured for, as death insurance, is not usually more than 30s. or 40s., 1d. per week being collected from the person insuring. There are indications that the insurance of children has been lessened since the opening of the Corsley School savings bank. About twenty-three children pay money into this, and in some cases at least this plan has been substituted by the parents for insurance.

Besides the very universal thriftiness and foresight displayed by the working classes in joining friendly societies, to which they make regular and prompt payments for fear of sacrificing the benefits which they hope to derive, a very large amount of honesty and careful management is displayed in the regular and prompt payment of debts to tradesmen. The characteristics of the various households in this respect have been ascertained from people with whom they have dealings, and the results are given in the tables on pages 156-184. A summary of the results, classified according to the circumstances of the families, is as follows :

Circumstances of Family.		No. of Families.	No. where one or more Members are bad at Paying or Thriftless.
Well-to-do	... ...	101	6
Secondary poverty	...	33	5 (also 1 where sons have spent parents' savings)
Primary poverty	...	28	6

Of the six families in primary poverty who are " bad at paying," five have each five or more young children ; the sixth is an extravagant aged couple.

REPORTS ON CORSLEY HOUSEHOLDS.

PRIMARY POVERTY :

Households are marked, if having a member who drinks † ; who is unthrifty * ; a deficient child ‡.

No	Family.	Probable Income in Money or Kind	Amount above + or below − Primary Poverty	General Character.	Promptness in Paying Debts and Thrift Generally.	School Report.
5.	Labourer, wife, 3 children (eldest 8).	13s.	− 3s. 10d.	Quite respectable.		Very nice child.
11.	Labourer, wife, son (15), 5 younger children.	25s. (irregular).	− 1s. 2d.	†Rather rough family. Convicted once or twice for drunkenness.	*Shocking one to pay. Has owed one tradesman money for four or five years. Earns plenty of money in summer, and spends it on drink.	Three children fair; n o t h i n g special about them. One boy mischievous.
29.	Labourer, wife, 3 children.	16s.	− 10d.	Very respectable. Wife respectable since marriage. "Quiet, steady young fellow."	Nothing against them.	Nice children. One boy bright.
28.	Labourer, wife, 6 children.	17s. 3d.	− 8s. 1d.	Respectable man.	Nothing against them.	Nice children. Very clean.
12.	Labourer, wife, 4 children.	16s. 6d.	− 3s. 2d.	†Man best of the two Wife very free with the drink, like her mother.	Pays very well. Nothing against them.	‡Not particularly tidy or bright. Not satisfied with eldest (aged 11) School-attendance poor.

32.	Cowman, wife, 6 children (eldest 8).	17s.	— 8s. 4d.	Never seen out, so does not go to public-house Gives no trouble.		†Very tidy. Inclined to be dull.
36.	Cowman, wife, 1 daughter (invalid), 1 son (agricultural wage-earner), 4 children (youngest of family of 10).	23s. 6d.	— 3s. 6d.	Respectable man and family.	Always pay their way. Has always been a lot of sickness in the family.	‡Extraordinary family. Very untidy. Can't afford to keep the children very well. Parents very ignorant.
37.	Labourer, wife, son (agricultural wage-earner), 4 children.	24s. (estimate).	— 1s. 4d.	"Bad party; no good to anybody." Poacher by trade, but can't be caught, as he has leave to catch his employer's rabbits, &c.	Not long in parish.	Good character, but rough. Very untidy. Have not much clothes, but mother tries to keep them clean.
42.	Carter, wife, 6 children (eldest 9).	20s. 6d.	— 4s 10d	Can't say much for them, but man does not get into trouble. Neither of parents have any energy.	*Shocking at paying debts. Cannot get anything out of them. Can't say much for them.	‡Several very bad children. Worst family in the school. "Haven't a good word for them in any way. They swear, &c. Are neglected at home, untidy, dirty."
65.	Retired stone-breaker, afterwards marketer (has lost one leg), over 80 years old.	4s.	— 8d.	Respectable.	"Has always been a straightforward, hard-working man, so long as I can remember." He has not been on the parish long.	

¹ In these tables "labourer" has been substituted for lime-burner and warrener, to prevent identification of these families

No.	Family	Probable Income in Money or Kind.	Amount above + or below − Primary Poverty.	General Character.	Promptness in Paying Debts and Thrift Generally.	School Report.
66.	Retired labourer and market gardener, wife, daughter.	Unknown and irregular.	Probably inadequate.	Very respectable old man.		Children rather clever, but very much neglected. Inclined to be untidy. Mother not at all a nice woman.
67.	Retired labourer (aged 80), wife, 3 children.	Say 12s.	− 4s. 10d.	(1) Nothing to say about him. Present wife used to bear a bad character, but appears clean and hard-working (2) First wife was "a brute of a woman and tried to make him the same. Don't know anything against his present wife —very hard-working."		
68.	Retired labourer.	3s. 6d.	− 1s. 2d.	"Poor old man—respectable old chap."	Nothing against him. Was farm labourer as long as he was able. Belonged to local club, which has come to an end, therefore destitute.	
70.	Retired labourer (aged 87).	Say 4s. 6d.	− 2d.	Very old man. Know nothing about him.	Has always been a very good man to pay. Is over 80, and has only just come on the parish owing to break-up of local club.	

No.	Family					
73.	Labourer (retired on account of ill-health), wife.	Unknown.	Probably inadequate.	"Nothing for nor against."	All right. Always paid very well. Not doing much work now.	‡Peculiar boy. Dirty little rascal. Sharp at lessons.
212.	Widow, child (grandson, illegitimate child of daughter).	3s. 6d. poor relief and something from daughter.	Probably inadequate.	Respectable.	Not long in the parish.	
183.	Widow (aged), daughter. Baking, &c.	Unknown.	Probably inadequate.	"Very nice old lady."	Always paid up. Daughter very hard-working.	
44.	Carter, wife, 5 children (eldest 11).	15s.	— 7s. 6d	(1) Respectable. *Employer.* "Has rather a hard family." (2)	*Got a "little hard family," and bad manager in his wife. A bad one to pay."	‡Eldest boy not very satisfactory. Bad attendance. Only fairly clean and tidy.
45.	Carter, wife, 4 children (eldest 11).	17s. 3d.	— 2s. 5d	(1) Respectable. *Employer.* Very nice man; wife dirty and untidy. (2)	Nothing against him.	‡Dull children. Tidy.
49.	Carter, wife, 5 children, son.	15s.	— 11s. 2d.	†Man gives no trouble. Wife inclined to drink; respectable otherwise. Son out of work; was bad at getting up in the morning some time back.	*None of the briskest to pay. Does not earn high wages and has a large family."	†"Don't think much of parents." Eldest child slow, second dull, fourth *very* sharp.

No.	Family.	Probable Income in Money or Kind	Amount above + or below − Primary Poverty	General Character.	Promptness in Paying Debts and Thrift Generally	School Report
54.	Odd jobs (labourer), wife, 3 children (eldest 7).	15s. 6d.	− 1s. 4d.	(1) Quite respectable. (2) *Employer*: "Very satisfactory."	Satisfactory to deal with.	
58.	Agricultural engineer, wife, 1 daughter, 5 children.	25s. 6d.	− 3s. 6d.	(1) Man best of two. Wife often in debt. Children all right. (2) Wife not up to much. Nice man, quiet and steady.	*Don't know much about him *School*: "Spend all they get as they get it; live very extravagantly."	†Extraordinary tribe. Children inclined to be tidy, but mother very thriftless, &c. Fairly sharp.
62.	Labourer, wife, 5 children (youngest of family of 9). One son apprenticed to trade.	20s.	− 5s. 4d.	Very respectable. Wife one of most contented women in the parish.	"Never heard anything against him."	Very good attendance. Inclined to be sharp. Clean. Nice little children.
51.	Carter, wife, 4 children (eldest 8).	16s	− 3s. 8d.	A steady, industrious fellow.	They always pay cash.	†Two children, rather strange children. Nervous disposition. One has chorea.
63.	Casual labourer, wife, daughter (afflicted), 6 children (youngest of family of 9).	Earnings unknown.	Inadequate.	†"Likes a drop of drink sometimes," but not seen drunk. "Wife poor, helpless creature."	Not long in the parish.	

179	Widow. Does a little washing— not strong enough to do much.		Certainly deficit.	Respectable old lady.	"Don't know how she gets a living; she goes out to work." She has a son in London who is very good to her." She will not apply for poor relief. Can earn very little. Son can only help a little. She sometimes has a meal from a neighbour.	
205	Widow (charwoman), niece (aged 12)	? 6s.	– 1s. 6d.	Very decent woman— hard-working	Very honest woman.	"Nice little maiden." Clean, fairly intelligent.
111.	Market gardener, wife.	Probably 2s. 6d. + earnings marketing and garden.	Deficient.	†Market people Seem fairly broken down now.	*First labourer. Has been market gardener, but has given it up now. Both on parish. Had always worked hard. Drank a good deal of their profits. Wife got so drunk she could hardly sit in the cart. Seen one day in public at Frome having glass of port— more than such people could afford.	

12

SECONDARY POVERTY.

No	Family	Probable Income in Money or Kind	Amount above + or below − Primary Poverty	General Character.	Promptness in Paying Debts and Thrift Generally	School Report.
116	Market gardener and carrier, wife, daughter (dress-making), 2 children.	Say 16s. 10d.	+ 0 (on − margin of primary poverty).	"I think he and his family are all right."	"Maimed and got no compensation. Just manages to make a living. Could not do much else (*i.e.*, other kind of work). Know nothing against him."	†Very nice children. Very clean. One very dull.
118.	Market gardener and labourer, wife (takes in washing).			(1) "Don't know how he lives—hard to say. Has pony and trap and does a bit of greengrocery. Drives to market on Saturdays. Wife does some washing. Quarrelsome man; drinks a lot of beer at home and at Frome Market. Not often seen in public-houses, except to fetch some in jar. Never knew anything against wife." (2) *Employer* "Fairly satisfactory."		

No.	Family	Earnings	Poverty	Character	Quote	Notes
135.	Labourer (in brick-yard), wife, 4 children	Say 30s. (earnings unknown).	+ 10s. 4d (secondary poverty owing to character).	†Can't say much for them. Wife hard-working woman, but bad manager.	"Not much of it. A poor lot. Drink too much and don't pay much and Dirty lot Inspector has been down on them once or twice—woman keeps house so dirty."	†Dirty children. Noted family. Have been on point of reporting parents to Officer of Society for Prevention of Cruelty to Children Yet children wouldn't be so bad with careful training. Attendance bad; they take turns to come
109	Market - gardener, wife, 4 children		Probably sufficient.	Very respectable		Cantankerous parents. Chapel people. *Very* sharp children. Very clean and tidy.
191	Widow (char - woman), nephew (out of work), niece (12).	6s. and probably income from some undis- covered source.	Probably not below poverty line.	Very respectable woman and nephew.	Very nice woman; very hard-working and industrious.	Nice child; good-tempered, very clean, &c
200.	Widow. Kept by children.		Probably sufficient.		"Never heard anything against her. She pays all right."	

No.	Family	Probable Income in Money or Kind.	Amount above + or below − Primary Poverty.	General Character.	Promptness in Paying Debts and Thrift Generally.	School Report.
203.	Two spinsters.		Probably sufficient		In reduced circumstances.	
204.	Widow (charing and washing), lodger (male), 2 children. Poor relief.	Say 19s.	+ 5s.	†(1) Drinks. Accused of being a prostitute. (2) House bare, dirty, and neglected. Appear to feed well.	* "Better not put her down at the top of the tree."	†Clean and tidy as far as she can keep them. Very poor. Lazy, difficult to manage, sulky. One of poorest houses.
209.	Spinster. Takes in a little washing and has poor relief.	Say 4s. 8d.	Say + − 0.		Appears to pay up all right.	
195.	Widow (baker and farmer), son (labourer, &c.), daughter.		Have struggle to keep going	Respectable. Son rather rough (bad language). As much as they can do to make both ends meet.	Very good, straightforward, hard-working people, "so far as I know."	
127.	Retired schoolmaster.	Poor relief and help from neighbours.	Probably sufficient.	Respectable.		

No.						
148.	Shopkeeper and wife.	Owns cottages and small shop.	Probably sufficient.	Very respectable man and wife.	Belonged to a building society, so got his cottages.	
69.	Retired labourer, daughter (washerwoman).		Probably just sufficient.	Very respectable, all of them.	"They keep themselves—are not beholden to any one."	
71.	Retired agricultural worker, wife, son (agricultural earner).	Say 12s.	+ o. −	Respectable man and wife; latter a gossip. Son would be all right if he left the drink alone.	"Has always been a straightforward sort of man. I know nothing good about the son. He could do any sort of skilled work, such as grafting trees, if he liked, but does not work more than about two days a week."	
208.	Widow, 2 sons (agricultural wage-earners), 3 children.	21s. 6d.	+ 1s. 8d.	†Don't know much about her; used not to bear good character. "Eldest son lazy, drunken, little beggar." Those young men generally in any mischief going.		‡Clean and lazy children. Bigger boy slow and plodding. Mother clean and hard-working; very poor. Husband was very lazy; she always bad to keep the children.

No	Family	Probable Income in Money or Kind	Amount above + or below − Primary Poverty.	General Character	Promptness in Paying Debts and Thrift Generally	School Report.
176.	Widow (laundress), daughter.		Probably sufficient.	Quite respectable.	"Ought to have been pensioned years ago—is 85 years of age Husband spent a good deal She had nearly to keep the house going when he was alive"	
185.	Widow, son (artisan learning trade).	10s.	+ 1s. 8d.	(1) "Not a woman of best character at one time. Know nothing about her now." (2) "Has had 1 or 2 illegitimate children."		†Child (now left school) was lazy and slow; not very intelligent. Clean and tidy.
187.	Widow (laundress), daughter, grandson.		Probably sufficient.	Very hard-working woman.	Always made her living by washing. "I never knew anything against her. Always found her all right to deal with."	Nice boy; rather smart. Clean and tidy.
6.	Labourer, wife, boy (16), 2 younger children.	20s. 6d	+ 2s. 4d.	Very respectable people. Wife very hard-working woman He occasionally goes to the public-house.		Very nice children. Learn very quickly. Are clever with their hands. "Want to be kept in their places."

7.	Labourer, wife, 1 child at home and pay 1s. per week for a child away.	14s.	+ 1s. 10d.	Very steady man. Have had much trouble with delicate children.	Pays all right.	
10.	Labourer, wife, 2 young children.	17s. 9d.	+ 3s. 9d.	Respectable man.	Satisfactory.	
13.	Labourer, wife, 2 young children.	16s.	+ 2s.	†Hard-working people, Man "not one of the best of them, rather free with the drink and foul-tongued sometimes." Wife respectable.		Eldest child (aged 4) attends school 1 mile distant in summer.
21.	Labourer, wife, 2 young children.	17s.	+ 3s.	"Don't think you could say very much for them."	"Nothing against them."	Eldest (5). Very nice and tidy.
25.	Labourer and wife.	Could earn 12s.	+ 3s. 8d. (secondary poverty owing to character).	"No good. Was compositor and tailor. Would not work at either. Has deserted his wife time after time. Used to go on the tramp. Has stopped at work now nearly six years."	*"Too lazy to do anything. Spends all he earns. Does not pay up."	
30	Labourer, wife, 2 young children.	16s.	+ 2s.	(1) "Very decent young fellow—not often at the public-house" (2) "Steady man."		Very nice children.

No	Family.	Probable Income in Money or Kind	Amount above + or below − Primary Poverty.	General Character	Promptness in Paying Debts and Thrift Generally	School Report
33.	Labourer, wife, niece (mentally deficient).	19s.	+ 7s	†(1) "He is a man who works all the time, but you always see him in the public-house Gives no trouble. Quiet man, and never saw him the worse for drink. (2) "Don't know much as he might have been better."	Wife hard-working woman.	
53.	Labourer, wife, child.	13s.	+ 1s. 10d.	Very decent man now. Some years ago was one of worst drunkards in village, now a teetotaler. "In my opinion an underminded man—won't stick to his opinions"	Straightforward man.	†Nervous child, not very sharp; fragile. Nice and clean.
64.	Underkeeper, wife, son (agricultural wage - earner), 4 children (youngest of family of 10).	25s. 6d.	+ 2s. 2d.	Nothing known of him in parish.		†Two elder boys very sharp, one a strange boy. Third child dull. Youngest "can't make anything of." Clean and tidy.

No.	Family	Probable Income in Money or Kind	Amount above + or below – Primary Poverty	General Character.	Promptness in Paying Debts and Thrift Generally.	School Report
100	Retired farmer, &c., wife.			"All right; used to be tidy old nut (swore) in his time. Got over it now."	Had a little money together. Sons have spent it.	
78.	Farmer, wife.	? Sufficient.			Doesn't allow himself enough to eat, and takes very small amount of coal. Always letting dealers get the upper hand of him He had a few hundred pounds to start with, but probably has nothing left but his stock.	

ABOVE LINE OF SECONDARY POVERTY.

No.	Family	Probable Income in Money or Kind	Amount above + or below – Primary Poverty	General Character.	Promptness in Paying Debts and Thrift Generally.	School Report
48	Carter, wife, 2 children, 3 sons wage-earners (labourers or artisans).	58s.	+ 33s.	Respectable. Sons good at athletic games.	Very good, straightforward people. Pay their way. "I don't know a man who works harder in Corsley—he is working day and night, always willing, never tired."	†Extraordinary children. One girl with all the ideas of a lady. The other very dull. Fairly clean; not very tidy.

No	Family.	Probable Income in Money or Kind	Amount above + or below – Primary Poverty	General Character.	Promptness in Paying Debts and Thrift Generally.	School Report
52.	Carter, wife, 1 young child.	16s.	+ 4s. 10d.	Fairly respectable Wife rather loose character at one time.	Appears to pay all right "Know nothing against him."	
72	Labourer (retired), married daughter with children, son (market-gardener).	Pension 6s. and earnings of others.	Probably quite sufficient.	Man respectable. Daughter "has not been any too respectable."	Son satisfactory to deal with.	
206	Widow (midwife), 1 child, 2 sons (agricultural wage-earners).	37s. (Poor relief for child).	+ 12s. 2d.	Passable. Lads fairly respectable, but room for improvement.	"Always paid up very well, so far as I know."	"Very nice, most sensible boy," Plenty of common sense.
181.	Widow, 2 sons (mainly agricultural wage-earners), widowed daughter, 1 child.	32s.	+ 13s. 6d.	†Husband killed in drunken brawl Children have not been very respectable.		
199.	Widow (aged), granddaughter (14).	Private means.	Probably ample.			

No.	Family	Earnings		Character	Character	Remarks
174.	Widow, 2 sons (artisan and agricultural wage-earner).	Say 22s.	+ 7s. 10d.	Owns her own house. She bought it.	Nice sort of woman and son.	
2	Labourer, wife, 2 daughters, 4 sons (agricultural wage-earners), 1 child.	72s. 6d.	+ 39s. 4d.	"Agricultural people. Can't say anything against them, nor very much for them. Rather rough family"	Nothing to say against them. Have always been straightforward and pay very well.	
3.	Labourer, wife, 1 child, wife's brother.	30s (half irregular).	+ 15s. 2d.			
15.	Labourer, wife, 2 sons (agricultural wage-earners), 5 children.	41s. (irregular).	+ 11s. 2d.	Very hard-working man. Man and family "respectable so far as I know." Have had a "long family."	Pays very well "for aught I know of."	Four children. A year or two since very untidy. Now most clean and tidy, also reformation as to attendance.
20.	Labourer, wife, 3 children (boarded-out orphans).	17s. 6d.	+ 6s. 4d.	Hardly ever goes to a public-house. Seldom seen about.	Hard-working man.	*Very nervous children (from Warminster Union) "Want some one with strong will to look after them"
22.	Labourer, wife (invalid), daughter, son (agricultural wage-earner), 1 grandchild.	30s.	+ 11s. 6d.	Respectable man.	Nothing against him.	*Tidy, rather dull

No	Family	Probable Income in Money or Kind	Amount above + or below − Primary Poverty	General Character.	Promptness in Paying Debts and Thrift Generally.	School Report
24	Labourer, wife, and son (market-gardening), 1 grandchild.	15s. + market garden earnings.	+ earnings of garden, &c.	†Respectable man, except when he goes on the drink for a week or fortnight. Son respectable young fellow. Wife hard-working woman.	Very good to pay Wife earns a lot of money, and has saved money.	
31	Labourer(crippled), son (18), daughter, 2 children.	22s.	+ 6s. 4d.	Fair.	Know nothing against him.	Very nice. Very clean. Not very sharp.
35.	Cowman, wife, aged mother, lodger, 1 child.	25s. 3d.	+ 6s. 7d.	Respectable.	They pay up all right.	Very nice little child.
40	Dairyman, wife, 1 young child.	23s.	+ 11s. 10d.	Very steady man.		
60	Woodman, wife, child.	25s.	+ 13s. 10d.	(1) Satisfactory. (2) Husband and wife said to quarrel.		Cleverest boy in school.
34.	Cowman, wife, 1 young child.	17s.	+ 5s. 10d.	Respectable.	Very industrious young man.	

No.						
46.	Carter, wife, aged mother-in-law, son (blacksmith), 2 children.	36s.	+ 14s. 8d.	All right.	Always pay their way very well. Thrifty parents. Saved up money to provide children with costumes for school concert.	Very nice. Very clean and tidy.
96.	Farmer, wife.		Ample.			
81.	Farmer and other occupations, wife, son (helping father), daughter (gloving).	15s. 6d. and profits of small farm.	Probably ample.	†"Very respectable man and wife, but she is not particular about running into debt. He visits public-house pretty well. Has plenty, but have never seen him the worse. Very quiet man and son."		
92.	Farmer and coal-haulier, wife, 2 sons, daughter.			All right, sons and father.	Very fair man; hard-working.	†When at school was nice boy, but lazy.
77.	Farmer, wife.			Respectable man.	"Don't know much about him. He never would push on and go away from home."	
84.	Farmer, wife.			He is all right.	Was farmer's son. Earned a bit of money, and so got on. Has always paid his way so far as I know.	

No.	Family.	Probable Income in Money or Kind	Amount above + or below − Primary Poverty	General Character.	Promptness in Paying Debts and Thrift Generally.	School Report
90.	Farmer, wife, aged mother			Very respectable. Used to attend public-house years ago, but now not more than once or twice a week, perhaps. Used to be bad drinker years gone by. Reformed		
95	Farmer, carrier, &c., wife, son (agricultural wage-earner), 1 child.		Very ample.	Hard-working man.	Pays all right. Has saved a bit of money Was only a working man. Very industrious.	Very nice child.
114.	Market gardener, wife, 3 sons (agricultural wage-earners or mechanics), grand-daughter (a child).	64s.		Respectable.	Has always been a very good man at paying	Always very clean and tidy.
83	Farmer, wife, son.		Ample.	Very respectable family.	Pension Quite straight.	
113.	Market gardener, wife, 4 children.			Very respectable people.	Hard-working. Always at work.	

112.	Farmer and poulterer, two daughters.			(1) Respectable. (2) Daughters are very kind when people are ill in neighbourhood.	Dealings very satisfactory and straight.	When at school very nice and clean.
88	Farmer, wife.			No trouble with him. Always been a respectable man	Used to work at brick-making, and saved money.	
117	Market gardener, wife (midwife), two sons (artisans out of work), daughter (gloving).	19s. 6d	Ample	(1) Man that visits public-house very little. Very respectable family. Three sons have been in army. (2) "Satisfactory family."		
91	Farmer, wife, 2 daughters (teaching and dressmaking).			Respectable man.		
80.	Small farmer, wife.				Always very industrious man; tree-feller. Had money left him by his mother. Saved up a bit of money and went into farm Kept both jobs up for some time Old employer wanted to keep him.	

No.	Family	Probable Income in Money or Kind.	Amount above + or below – Primary Poverty.	General Character.	Promptness in Paying Debts and Thrift Generally	School Report
99	Farmer			Respectable young fellow.		
97	Farmer, wife, son, and daughter.			Very respectable people.	Hard-working.	Girl of 16 still at school. Sharp at music, not sharp at lessons.
110	Retired labourer, wife, 2 sons (agricultural wage-earners).	29s. +indefinite amount.	Ample.	(1) All very respectable, steady, quiet young fellows (2) *Employer*: "Very respectable family."	Must have saved money when young. Has not done anything for nearly 20 years. Quite straight with money.	
108	Brickmaker, wife, 2 daughters, 2 sons (helping father), 2 children.		Ample	Respectable people.	They pay very well.	
150	Farmer and brickmaker (wage-earning), wife, daughter (servant), son (labourer), 1 child.	Say 58s.	+ 37s 6d.	Hard-working people. Boys respectable.	Has saved up. He goes out to work, and wife has worked nearly all her life.	Very clean and tidy. Smart-looking. Average at work.

105.	Shoemaker, daughter, 2 sons (artisan and agricultural wage-earner).	Say 30s (Difficult to ascertain earnings.)	+ 14s. 4d.	Respectable man and family.	Pay up very well.
106.	Labourer, nephew (artisan).	30s. (probably)	+ 21s. 8d.	†Addicted to drink, but doesn't get drunk. Not very energetic man.	†Can't say much for him. Wife helped with business when she was alive. He drinks more than he can afford, but does not get drunk. Has not paid rent for about 12 months. Formerly had little farm as well as business Now labourer.
134.	Worker in factory (Frome), wife.	19s.	+ 10s. 8d.	Very respectable man.	
133.	Labourer in iron-works, wife.	15s.	+ 6s. 8d.	"Husband and wife quarrel. Has been summoned several times for filthy language She governs him a bit now."	Recently married. Hard-working, steady man Honest, I should say.
132	Gardener, wife, 2 sons (agricultural wage-earners).	37s.	+ 21s. 4d.	(1) Very respectable. Boys remarkably steady, quiet lads, (2) *Employer*. "Very respectable."	(1) Always very good people; steady and industrious (2) A very honest woman.

No	Family	Probable Income in Money or Kind	Amount above + or below − Primary Poverty.	General Character.	Promptness in Paying Debts and Thrift Generally.	School Report.
189.	Widow.	Private means.	Probably ample.	"Should think she is a very respectable woman. Should think she has a little income."	Some arrangement by which she lives rent free. "I think her two children are good to her."	
182.	Widow.		Probably ample.	Very straight woman.	All right.	
177.	Spinster (takes in sewing and keeps small shop), lodger (female).		Probably sufficient.	Very respectable.	Owns house where she lives. Pays up all right.	
188.	Deserted wife (laundress).		Probably ample.	Fairly respectable, but "gift of the tongue."	Always very good at paying.	
193.	Widow (aged; kept by children).		Sufficient.	Very respectable woman.		
210.	Spinster (washerwoman).	Say 6s.	+ 1s. 4d.	Very respectable.		
180.	Widow (midwife), son (artisan), daughter.	Say 23s.	+ 11s.	Nothing against woman. Son up to all the mischief he can get into. A sly one—ringleader. Don't know that there is any harm in him.	Deserted by husband. Son satisfactory.	Children before they left school very, very clean. Rather nice children. Not *very* much intelligence.

No.	Family	Children	Income	Sufficiency	Character	Remarks
142.	Retired railwayman, wife.		Savings.	Sufficient.	Very respectable.	Has saved enough money to keep him the rest of his days.
136.	Retired tradesman (London), wife, daughter.			Probably ample.	Quite respectable.	†Often had bailiffs in house when he was in business in London. "He does not trouble."
143	Retired weaver in factory, wife.		Savings and garden.	Sufficient.	Very respectable; rumoured that years ago he used to be a poacher.	Know nothing against him. A man who has always kept himself, though he has done no work for some time.
41.	Carter, wife, daughter.	1	20s. 6d.	+ 8s. 6d.	(1) Very decent man. Wife a bad woman; would do any one harm if she got the chance. (2) Very nice, hard-working man; wife not so good as he is (tongue).	
38	Cowman, daughter (laundress), son-in-law (labourer).		35s. or more.	+ 21s.	(1) All very respectable. (2) *Employer*: "A very good servant."	Steady old man.
190.	Widow (grows fruit), son (agricultural wage-earner).		Unknown.	Probably quite sufficient.	†Always full of complaints; "comic old customer as a neighbour." Son inclined to drink, but gives no trouble.	(1) "Very honest woman. Always pays up for what she has." (2) Son not up to much. Likes to go rabbiting or do odd jobs; will not stick to a constant job.

No	Family.	Probable Income in Money or Kind	Amount above + or below — Primary Poverty.	General Character	Promptness in Paying Debts and Thrift Generally	School Report.
194.	Widow, 2 daughters (one "afflicted," mother and other do needlework and charing), son (agricultural wage-earner).	24s 6d.	+ 8s. 10d.	Respectable.	Has maintained herself since death of husband. Has poor relief for daughter	
211.	Widow (infirm), son (agricultural wage-earner or malting).	Poor relief 2s. 6d. + help from son.	Probably ample.	"Son a little rowdy."		
196.	Widow, daughter (laundress), son (market gardener, marketer and odd jobs).		Probably quite sufficient	Very respectable.	Very old. Has been doing washing till quite recently. Son was tailor by trade, but didn't much care for it. Now does odd jobs.	
207.	Widow (midwife), 2 sons (market gardener and agricultural wage-earner), daughter.		Ample.	Very respectable woman. Very quiet young men		

No.	Family	Wages	Deficit	Character	Notes
1.	Labourer, wife (midwife).	19s	+ 10s. 8d.	Quite respectable. Man constitutionally delicate. Wife supposed to drink formerly.	*Both hard-working, but though both earning money, and no family, very difficult to get money from if allowed credit.
8.	Labourer, wife, 3 sons (2 agricultural wage-earners, 1 artisan).	63s. 6d	+ 44s. 2d.	"Fairly respectable. Don't get drunk, but like their drink." One son sent to reformatory as a boy for stealing flowers.	Always paid very well.
9.	Labourer (old soldier), wife, son (agricultural wage-earner), daughter (gloving).	36s.	+ 20s. 4d.	Very respectable people.	Very straightforward.
14.	Labourer, wife.	14s. 6d.	+ 6s. 2d.	Not long in parish.	
16.	Labourer, wife, daughter (dressmaker).	25s.	+ 13s	(1) Very respectable people. Informant had once seen him with "a little beer" and then very quarrelsome. A man scarcely ever seen at public-house. (2) "Hard-working, steady man."	

No	Family.	Probable Income in Money or Kind	Amount above + or below − Primary Poverty.	General Character.	Promptness in Paying Debts and Thrift Generally.	School Report.
18.	Labourer, wife.	15s.	+ 6s. 8d.	(1) "Goes on better than formerly." Used to be very fond of drink. His family rather rough. (2) Doesn't care for constant employment. Works in woods on piecework jobs.		
19.	Labourer, wife, son (agricultural wage-earner).	40s.	+ 28s.	†Fairly respectable. Son a "drunken sot," not his own fault—father always in the habit of going to public-house, but does not get drunk.	*"None too extra well to pay." All wage-earners; man and wife get a lot of money, but they "tipple" and live above their income and only just "keep the wheels going." He always stands out for foreman's work with high pay, but is no better off on Saturday night than other people.	
23.	Labourer, son (miner, iron-works).	30s.	+ 21s. 8d.	Respectable father and son.	Very good to pay up.	

26.	Labourer, daughter, 3 sons (agricultural wage-earners).	37s. 6d.	+ 18s. 2d.	†Man better than his wife (now dead). She was very fond of drink. Can't say much for the children — nearly all inclined to drink.	Nothing against him. Belonged to local club which recently came to an end.
27.	Labourer, wife.	16s. 6d.	+ 8s. 2d.	All right. Very steady man.	Nothing against him. Belonged to Shepherds' Friendly Society.
4.	Labourer, wife, daughter.	18s.	+ 6s.	(1) All right. Has stayed at same place long time (2) Employer: "Very satisfactory."	Always a good man to pay.
61.	Woodman, daughter, son (coal merchant).	13s. + son's earnings.	Ample.	Respectable. Has been offered pension but will not give up work.	All right with money. Very steady man. Has probably saved.
59.	Tree-feller.	13s. to 15s.	+ 9s. 4d.	Respectable.	All right.
57.	Shepherd, wife.	15s.	+ 6s. 8d.	Respectable. Not long in parish.	All right.
56.	Agricultural worker, wife, daughter (dressmaker), lad (assistant to householder).	Say 30s. to 40s.	+ 20s. 4d.	Very respectable man	All right.
55.	Labourer, wife.	14s. 6d.	+ 6s. 2d.	†Respectable man. Wife rather fond of drink.	Used not to pay up formerly Do not know at present.

No	Family	Probable Income in Money or Kind	Amount above + or below − Primary Poverty.	General Character.	Promptness in Paying Debts and Thrift Generally	School Report.
50	Carter, wife.	17s.	+ 8s. 8d	Respectable man.	Nothing against him. Have always paid their way very well.	
47	Labourer, wife, 2 sons (agricultural wage-earners).	43s.	+ 27s. 4d.	Respectable.	Nothing against him. Wife was a bad one to pay in years gone by. [probably while 7 children were not above school age].	
43	Carter, wife.	15s.	+ 6s. 8d.	Very respectable man.	Very steady man. Belongs to benefit society of a village where they formerly resided.	
17	Piecework labourer, wife, daughter, grandchild (illegitimate).	Savings and odd jobs.	Probably sufficient.	Respectable, hard-working people. Have allotment and keep pigs. Wife does "marketing."	Very good man to pay. Only goes out to work occasionally, has saved a bit of money. Wife goes marketing—carries basket.	
115	Market gardener and carrier, wife.		Sufficient	Respectable. Newly married.	†Is not much of a one to pay, before he was married, at any rate. Don't know how he and his mother managed to live. They were supposed to do market gardening, but didn't do much.	Mischievous. Clean and tidy.

Artisans.

The artisans, 22 in number, are so uniformly reported as respectable and prompt in payment that they have been omitted from the foregoing tables and only the few exceptions need be noted.

No. 159.   A very respectable man, but has a bad wife, who drinks, squanders all money, including any capital which comes into her hands, and spends her time writing begging letters. The home is in a squalid condition.

No. 156.   Very decent people—too grand to visit public-house much, but extravagant and frequently in debt.

No. 168.   With a large family, is reported as fairly respectable, but "none too bright to pay."

No. 166.   Thoroughly respectable in every way, is having a struggle owing to much serious illness in the household.

All except possibly No. 159 are above primary poverty and have good homes, but when there are children the margin is frequently small.

School reports on all who have children of school age are given below.

SCHOOL REPORTS ON ARTISANS' CHILDREN.

No.	Family.	Circumstances	School Report
154	Man, wife, 4 children	Secondary poverty	Very nice children. Very clean and tidy. Fairly sharp. Seem to have very good home from appearance in school.
155	Man, wife, 4 (or more) children.		"Exceedingly nice children, nice manners. Brain power all right, but not clever with hands."

No.	Family.	Circumstances	School Report.
163	Man, wife, 2 children, son (agricultural wage-earner).		Very clean and tidy. Not very bright.
162	Man, wife, daughter, 2 children.	Secondary poverty	Good family
158	Man, wife, 4 children, maid-servant.		All right.
157	Man, wife, 1 child.		Nice little child and quick at learning.
171	Man, wife, 4 children	Secondary poverty.	Neglected. Strange family. One girl most innocent-looking child, very naughty. Bad little boy, not truthful.
170	Man, wife, 4 children		Very nice children. Two of boys very clever. Always very clean and tidy.
168	Man, wife, 4 children, 3 sons (agricultural wage-earners, 2 out of work).		Clean and tidy, but eldest rather dull. Little ones fairly sharp.
166	Man, wife, 2 children		One a nice child. These two boys would be better if parents at home more. Rather neglected. One rather wilful.

SCHOOL REPORTS ON CHILDREN OF FARMERS, GARDENER, GROOM, COOK, AND POLICEMAN.

No.				School Report
128	...	...	...	Very nice children indeed. Some of best in school and very clean and tidy.

No.				School Report.
121	...	...	...	Very good family.
76	...	...	...	Children all right. Fair— tidy. Not specially bright.
93	...	...	...	Boy—very regular. Very good family, sharp, plenty of common-sense.
75	...	...	...	Very clean and tidy. Spoilt children.
216	...	...	...	Sharp—common-sense. Spoilt. Very nice boy in school.
214	...	...	...	Sharp—very clever little girl. Sweet little child. Has good home.

State of Education.

Before leaving the subject of character it may be remarked that a large proportion of the adults in the parish are unable to write and some are unable to read. This fact was discovered partly from statements of the people themselves, and also from secretaries to friendly societies, who assert that men of forty years of age and upwards are often unable to sign their names.

Pauperism in Corsley.

The paupers have already been included in the preceding lists, but it will be convenient to give a table of these separately .

In addition to the fifteen families or persons in receipt of relief during the year 1904-5 who were still residing in the parish in the winter of 1905-6, relief was granted in 1904-5 to five aged persons, since dead, and to the family of one man in prison.

Two of the cases of widows with family afford striking examples of the futility, if not the actual harmfulness, of granting in such cases small and inadequate doles, unconditionally, and in these instances apparently without inquiry as to the character of mother or home.[1]

No. 206 was receiving relief on the understanding that she had two children at home, though as a matter of fact the elder had been out in service for a year or two. She was herself earning good money as a midwife, her receipts being, however, irregular. Her two sons were earning probably 30s. a week between them, and her boy, still at school, was able to contribute to the family purse by running errands or doing garden work after school hours. The income of the family was therefore considerably in excess of that of the average labourer. Since that date her boy has left school, and relief has been stopped. She has quarrelled with her elder sons, and is now solely dependent on the earnings of her boy of fourteen and her own, which are less than formerly. Her health has improved with this reduction of her income to 7s. or 8s. per week.

No. 204 works at charing during the day, neglecting her home and children. She is said to bear a very bad character, and to earn money by prostitution. The children struck the school teachers as coming from an exceedingly poor home, but were clean and tidy as far, they said, " as the mother can

[1] For the unsatisfactory condition of homes and families of widows in receipt of outdoor relief found in all parts of England as a result of this system see Minority Report of Poor Law Commission 1909 Cd. 4499 p. 753.

Index No.	Sex	Status re marriage	Age	Actual Earnings	Normal earnings when in work	Present or last Occupation	Health	Club	Savings	Character	Family	He
211	F	Widow	58	None		At one time had small farm	Cripple			Nothing against her	1 son at home, mal'm'n in winte 1 son name Wales 2 daughters in service	3 roo
210	F	Spinster	67	None	14s per week	Laundress	" Afflicted "		Some	Very respectable	Living alone	3 roo pai
209	F	Spinster	63	6d per week		Occasionally does a little washing	Afflicted		? None	Honest	Living alone	5 roo
191	F	Spinster	26	A few pence knitting			Cripple			Mother (widow) and sister needlework charing and laundry. Be her lab'urer.	4 roo
206	F	Widow	50	Say 5s		Midwife	Moderate		None	' Passable	2 sons in regular work 1 boy aged 11	8 roo
67	M	Married	85	None		Labourer (retired)	All right			Formerly not good	Wife charing and laundry work 6s 3 children boy of 15 in War ministr.	2 roo
65	M	Widower	77	None		Stonebreaker then marketer with donkey cart	Poor			Always very hard working. Respectable	Living alone Stepson sends money to 1 nightly and pays more 6d per week to look after him	2 roo
212	F	Widow	66	None			All right			Respectable	Illegitimate grandson Daughter away did not keep up payments, so P.R. to be reduced	3 roo
68	M	Widower	72	Probably none	12s	Labourer (retired)	All right but feeble	Belonged to Corsley Club now broken up		Respectable	None	3 roo
11	M	Married	72	Something from garden and marketing	?	Market gardener	Rheumatic			Hardworking, but drank more than could afford	Wife 3 sons in Wales who send money 1 daughter married	3 roo
208	F	Widow	50	Probably none			All right			Clean and hard working	2 sons labourers at home 3 children at home 2 sons away	4 roo
214	F	Widow	43	Unknown		Charing. Takes M lodger and said to earn money by prostitution	All right			Very bad character said to be prostitute and drinks	3 children M lodger	3 roo pai
70	M	Widower	85	None		Labourer (retired)	All right but feeble	Belonged to Corsley Club now broken up		Honest Has only just come on the parish over 80 years old	Living alone 2 sons and 3 daughters who help him	22 ro
127	M	Single	74	None		Schoolmaster (retired) now helps tradesman with accountkeeping and receives food &c in return	All right, only one leg			Respectable	Living alone	?3 ro
140	F	Spinster	17	?		Servant to tradesman's	Ill				Residing with employers	

keep them.'' The small dole given in this case is quite insufficient to enable the woman to stay at home and look after her children, or to encourage her to take to a more respectable mode of living.

These cases may be compared with those of two old men dependent on poor relief through no fault of their own.

No. 68, in receipt of relief, has no relations who can help him. His next-door neighbour does his washing and odd jobs which he cannot do for himself, and in return he helps to work her garden, lights her fire when she is out, and has promised to leave her his '' few traps '' when he dies. This old man, with no other source of income, who worked hard all his life, and is deprived of the results of his thrift in belonging to a club by the break-up of the latter, receives only the inadequate sum of 3s. per week.

No. 70, a very old man in receipt of poor relief, has worked hard as a labourer all his life. He gets about 3s. 6d. per week from the parish, part being contributed by a daughter. His children may, perhaps, give him a little further help.

Probably the majority of aged paupers receive some little additional help from relatives, and their case is at least not harder than that of some others who receive no parish relief.

Provision for the Aged. Non-paupers.

There are many more poor old people in Corsley who refuse to apply for parochial relief. There is a very independent spirit among the majority of the inhabitants, and sons and daughters often pinch themselves in order to prevent their old parents from '' coming upon the parish.''

One old man, No. 66, started life as a farm

labourer, but after twenty-eight years was crippled with rheumatism. Since then, with the help of his wife and children, he supported himself as a " market gardener." Now that the old couple are past work, their children keep them, though most of them are married, with families, and have a struggle themselves to make both ends meet. It is the children rather than the parents who are averse to application for poor relief in this case.

Another old labourer, No. 22, now in poor health, has an invalid wife, a daughter, and a son living with him. He receives much kindness from the farmer who employed him, and is sent money by a daughter living away from home. One of his sons would also send him money if necessary.

An old woman at Chapmanslade, No. 193, widow of a small farmer, is supported by her children, mainly by a married daughter.

Provision has been made for No. 167, the widow of a carpenter who earned £1 per week, as follows :

Two sons each pay 2s. per week ; married daughter makes a home for her mother, taking 3s. 6d. of the money for her keep, while the other 6d. goes towards clothing, and collection in church on Sundays. In the summer the old lady helps her daughter with the housework, while the latter is busy in her garden, and in return the daughter gives her a share of the profits, amounting to 12s. or 13s., as pocket-money. The family live and feed very well (see Budget 131 on p. 235).

Another old widow, No. 179, is too feeble to work, and her sons, having families and inadequate incomes, can help her very little. She refuses to apply to the parish, though accepting a little private charity, and consequently is more than half starved and always in bad health.

Similar cases occur from time to time, considerable privation being undergone in preference to application for outdoor relief ; and, in case of illness, those who have once been in a better position will firmly refuse to enter the workhouse, though lacking the most necessary attendance.[1]

Though the amount of poverty in Corsley is not great, the proportion of pauperism is still further reduced by the existence of this spirit among a section of the people.

[1] Since the above was written most of these old people have been granted an old-age pension.

CHAPTER XIV

THERE is in Corsley no lack of competition for the custom of the labouring classes. The housewife may purchase her groceries either from one of the village shops or from the stores and shops in Frome and Warminster. Various butchers and bakers drive round the parish with their carts, delivering goods to their regular customers. Milk she can obtain from most of the numerous small farms. Beer and ale are supplied by at least eight brewers from Frome and Warminster, whose carmen deliver the casks at the houses. Coal and wood appear to be mainly supplied by one local coal-haulier and timber merchant, and a competitor setting up a few years ago failed to get any custom.

Most of the cottages do the main part of their weekly shopping on Saturday at Frome or Warminster, according to whether they live on the eastern or western side of the parish. During the week they supplement their Saturday's purchases from the nearest village shop, where credit is usually granted them if desired.

It is not, however, necessary for any one to go out to shop. One old man in January, 1906, got most of the necessaries of life from the baker, who brought him bread, butter, and sugar regularly, and sometimes tea. Coal was brought round to him once a fortnight, and so he got all his provisions without leaving the house.

Milk is easily obtainable in all parts of the parish. Nearly all the farmers will sell it to the poor in small quantities. Some send it round to the cottages, but it usually has to be fetched, this being no hardship where the dairy farm-houses are near together and widely distributed over the parish. The usual price of new milk is 3d. per quart, or 1½d. per pint all the year round. In certain cases, in summer, or by special favour, it is sold cheaper, at 1d. per pint. In the winter it is sometimes scarce locally, and the cottagers may then have difficulty in obtaining it, or may have to send farther for it, and perhaps get short quantity for their money. This is, however, the exception.

The greater number of households, irrespective of the number of persons, take 1d. worth of new milk per day. A few of the more well-to-do families take more than 1d. worth, or taking 1d. worth regularly, supplement it by frequently buying more in the afternoon. A few families take separated or skim milk instead of new, or to supplement it.

The produce of the garden furnishes a large proportion of the food of the people. Potatoes, onions, greens, and other vegetables figure largely in the menu of the poorest households, especially those with many children. Bacon is almost universally eaten. Meat is eaten in all but the very poorest houses at least once or twice a week, and it is an article of daily consumption in the majority of cottages.

At the mid-day dinner-hour in winter the wife or mother is very frequently found preparing a stew with meat, potatoes, and vegetables, if well off, or if poor, of potatoes and cabbage, or potatoes and

14

onions alone. The well-to-do sometimes have hot
or cold roast meat, meat pies, chicken, where fowls
are kept, &c., by way of variety. They will also
have a second course of tarts, pancakes, or other
sweets. If poor they will vary the stew of potatoes
and vegetables by having bread with bacon, dripping,
or pickles, children being sometimes fed on the latter.
School-children who cannot return home to dinner
take bread with butter, jam, or dripping. The
mothers find that meat sent with the children is
too often thrown away and wasted. On their return
some mothers give the children hot vegetables or
meat with their tea, or let them share in an early
supper after a tea of bread and butter with jam or
cake. Other mothers give nothing further but a
plain tea, an inadequate diet for growing children
who have a long walk in addition to their school
work, and it must be remembered that little milk is
taken per head in a large family.

The time and constitution of the meals taken subsequent to the mid-day dinner vary from one household
to another. Most of the well-to-do have a good
meal of bread and butter, cake, and jam about 4.30,
followed by supper later. In some poorer families
one meal takes the place of tea and supper. At
tea-time one sometimes finds prepared a meal of hot
meat or stew, kippers and other fish, jam-tarts, &c.,
besides jam and cake, and in one very poor family
where the mother was out working the tea appeared
to consist of bread and jam and the contents of
innumerable jars and pots. There has been a great
increase in the quantity of groceries consumed by
cottagers within the last forty years, since the rise
of wages. People dealing with a certain shop would,
some thirty years ago, buy 1 oz. of tea or of coffee
to last a whole week, and 1 lb. of sugar. Fifteen

years later the same families would take $\frac{1}{4}$ lb. of tea and 3 lbs. of sugar per week.

In the budgets which follow the daily menu shows the form and variety of food eaten in thirteen households taken as examples. The list of articles purchased indicates the amount of the various commodities besides home produce which are available for division among the members of the family, whose number is given. The preliminary remarks should be consulted to see how much cooking is done, in cases where it is not stated whether meals are hot or cold. Nos. 44, 51, 62, and 36 are families where the income is insufficient. Not only is the quantity of nourishing food obtainable by these families inadequate, but the inevitable monotony of the diet is extremely trying, especially when any member of the family is in poor health and not enjoying a good appetite.

It will be seen that some women are much better managers than others. No. 62, for instance, gives a more varied and appetising diet than No. 51, though the poorer of the two.

Nos. 29, 116, and 193 are near the margin of primary poverty. No. 29 is 2d. per head per week below the minimum of efficiency by the regular wage, but this is, no doubt, made up by Mrs. T.'s occasional earnings, and by extra money which T., being a strong and industrious man, can make out of his garden over and above the rent. This diet is an excellent one for the income, owing to Mrs. T.'s cleverness as manager and cook. No. 116, too, yields a fairly varied diet. No. 193 is an old woman who is provided by her children with what they deem necessary, and who depends for cooking, &c., upon relatives residing near. It may here be remarked that probably a few of the very poorest old people, paupers, and others, live almost entirely on bread and butter and tea.

Nos. 46, 20, 206, 117, 105, and 131 are all well above the margin of poverty, having more than 2s. per head over the necessary minimum. The quality of the menu in these cases varies with the competency of the housekeeper. The menu of No. 206, where the manager is not in good health, and possibly given to drink, is very poor when the income of the family is considered. That of No. 105 would probably be more regularly appetising if there were an experienced woman to manage the housekeeping, which is now done jointly by the father and a young daughter. On the whole, however, these diaries show a fairly generous diet, and if the section on poverty be compared, it will be found that the majority of households in the parish can afford to feed in this manner, the exceptions being labourers with several children, and others who for one reason or another are in primary poverty.

The budgets have been arranged as far as can be ascertained in order of poverty, beginning with those with the largest deficit, and proceeding to the family with the largest surplus per head.

BUDGET No. 44.

Deficiency of Income, 7s. 6d.

Labourer, wife, five children. Wage 15s. All the man's wages are given to the wife.

Regular Expenses.—House-rent, 1s. 6d. per week. Allotment (20 poles), 5s. per annum. Man's Friendly Society, 2s. 5d. per month.

The family take 1d. worth of new milk (less than 1 pint) per day, or when occasionally no new milk is to be had, 1 quart of skim milk.

"Broth" is made of butter, milk, and water.

At the time the diary was being kept the mother was nursing her youngest child, and therefore usually had a supper of quaker oats.

The father and school-children usually carry their dinner with them.

Tea is taken at about 4.15, when the children return.

The children share supper at 6 p.m.

Things Purchased.

January, 1906. First week.

	s.	d.		s.	d.
½ lb. tea	0	8	Forward	7	0
3 lb. sugar	0	5½	Coal	1	2½
1½ lb. butter	1	6	Loaf	0	2¼
Bacon	1	4	Milk	0	6½
Quaker oats	0	5½	Butter	0	4
2 oz. tobacco	0	6	Sugar	0	2¼
Cheese	0	9	Loaf	0	2¼
½ lb. lard	0	2½	Oil	0	2½
¼ lb. suet	0	2	Stockings	0	6½
Baking powder ...	0	1			
Papers	0	2		10	4¾
1 lb. soap	0	3	Bread bill	3	0
Oranges	0	2			
½ lb. currants ...	0	1½	Expenditure during week	13	4¾
1 pt. beer	0	2			
	*7	0			

January, 1906. Second week.

	s.	d.		s.	d.
Bread	2	6	Forward	11	2¾
Oil	0	2½	Matches	0	1½
Beef	1	0	¼ lb. sweets	0	1
Milk	0	7	Oranges	0	3
Coal, 1 cwt.	1	2½	Tobacco	0	6
Flannelette	1	4¼	Pepper	0	1½
½ lb. tea	0	8	Quaker oats	0	5½
3 lb. sugar	0	5½	Biscuits	0	1
3 lb bacon	1	6	Lard	0	2½
2 lb. butter [?] ...	1	0	F. fish	0	4
1½ lb. cheese ...	0	9	2 lb. sprats	0	2
	11	2¾		13	6¾

* This store was probably purchased on Saturday at Warminster, and the other groceries bought during the following week.

	Breakfast.	Dinner.	Tea.	Supper.
SATURDAY...	Father.—Fried potato, bacon, tea. Mother and Children.—Potatoes and bacon and tea.	Bread, fresh butter, tea.	Bread and butter, tea.	
SUNDAY	Parents.—Bacon and tea. Children.—Porridge.	Potatoes, cabbage, boiled bacon, currant and suet pudding.	Bread and butter and cake, tea.	Mother.—Porridge.
MONDAY	Father.—Fried potato, bacon, tea. Mother and Children.—Toast and tea.	Father.—Bread and cheese. School Children.—Bread and butter, tea. At home.—Fried potato, bacon, tea.	Toast and tea.	Potatoes, greens, bacon
TUESDAY	Father.—Fried potato and bacon. Others.—Porridge.	Father.—Bread and cheese. School Children.—Bread and butter. At home.—Porridge.	Toast and tea.	Potatoes, greens, bacon, suet pudding.
WEDNESDAY	Father.—Fried potato, bacon, tea. Others.—Toast and tea.	Father.—Bread and cheese. Others.—Bread and butter, suet pudding. Potatoes and bacon.	Toast and tea.	Potatoes, greens, bacon, tea.
THURSDAY...	Father.—Fried potato, bacon, tea. Others.—Broth.		Toast and tea.	Potatoes, greens, tea.
FRIDAY	Father.—Fried potato, bacon, tea. Others.—Toast and tea.	Father.—Bread and cheese. School Children.—Bread and lard. At home.—Soup (a present).	Toast and tea.	Potatoes and greens.

SATURDAY...	Father.—Potato, bacon, tea / Others.—Broth.	Father.—Bread and bacon. / Others.—Soup (a present).	Sprats and tea.	Mother.—Porridge.
SUNDAY ...	Fried fish and tea.	Potatoes, greens, beef, suet pudding.	Bread and butter, tea.	Potatoes and fried onions.
MONDAY ...	Father.—Fried potato, bacon, tea. / Others.—Toast and tea.	Father.—Bread and cheese / School Children.—Bread and butter and tea / At home.—Fried potato, bacon, tea	Toast and tea.	
TUESDAY ...	Father.—Fried potato, bacon, tea.	Father.—Bread and cheese / Children at home.— Fried potato, bacon, tea.	Toast and tea.	6 p.m.: Potatoes and fried onions.
WEDNESDAY	Father.—Fried potato, bacon, tea. / Others.—Toast and tea.	Father.—Bread and cheese. / School Children.—Bread and butter. / Others.—Fried onions, bacon, bread.	Toast and tea.	Potatoes, greens, bacon, tea.
THURSDAY...	Father.—Fried potato, bacon, tea. / Others.—Toast and tea.	Father.—Bread and cheese. / School Children.—Bread and butter. / Others.—Potatoes, bacon, tea.	Toast and tea.	Potatoes, greens, bacon, tea, bread.
FRIDAY ...	Father.—Fried potato, bacon, tea. / Others.—Toast and tea	Father.—Bread and cheese. / School Children.—Bread and butter. / Others.—Milk broth.	Tea, bread.	Rabbit soup, potatoes, bread.

BUDGET No. 62.

Deficiency of Income, 5s. 4d.

Labourer, wife, six children (eldest boy of 14, youngest an infant). Two older children have left the parish, one child (the second out of nine), died as an infant.

The family of eight live in a three-roomed cottage, which they get rent free, with small garden, from employer.

	s.	d.
Man's wage	13	0
Boy's wage	3	6
	16	6 per week.

The man gets £3 over-money at Christmas, and now and then a rabbit. In summer they are allowed to collect some firewood free.

All earnings are given to the wife. They have no beer, and man keeps no pocket-money. They are better off than a few months ago, before boy began to earn.

EXPENDITURE.

January 6–12, 1906.

	s.	d.			s.	d.
Bread	3	11½	Forward	12	5
Flour	0	5	Mr. N.'s Club	0	3½
Tea	0	8	Mrs. N.'s Clothing Club	0	3
Sugar	0	8	Ellen's „	0	2
Bacon	1	6	Eva's „	0	2
Cheese	1	2	Cwt. coal	1	1½
Fresh butter	0	7¼	Lamp oil	0	4½
Salt butter	0	6	Milk	0	3½
Best lard	0	4	Salt	0	0½
Soap	0	1½	1 doz. boot laces ...	0	2
Fresh pork	1	5	1 reel black cotton ...	0	1
Candles	0	1½	1 card angola	0	1
Pepper	0	1	Wool for mending ...	0	2
Mustard	0	1			
Starch	0	1½	Total expenditure ...	15	7½
Cocoa	0	3½			
Currants	0	2			
Shoe blacking	0	1	The rest was put by for boots.		
Grate polish	0	1			
	12	5			

January 13–19, 1906.

		s.	d.			s.	d.
Bread		3	11½	Forward		13	5
Flour		0	5	Mr. N.'s Club		0	3½
Tea		0	8	Mrs. N.'s Clothing Club		0	3
Sugar		0	8	Ellen's „		0	2
Bacon		2	0	Eva's „		0	2
Cheese		1	2	1 cwt. coal		1	1½
Fresh butter		0	7½	Milk		0	3½
Salt butter		0	6	Lamp oil		0	4½
Best lard		0	4½	1 reel of thread ...		0	1
Soap		0	1½	2 pieces tape		0	1½
Candles		0	1½	2 yards calico		0	5½
Soda		0	1½	Boots mended		0	7
Coffee		0	5				
Salt		0	1	Total expenditure ...		17	4
Beef		2	0				
Fish		0	2				
		13	5				

January 20–27, 1906.

		s.	d.			s.	d.
Bread		3	11½	Forward		11	2
Flour		0	5	Mr. N.'s Club		0	3½
Tea		0	8	Mrs. N.'s Clothing Club		0	3
Sugar		0	8	Ellen's „		0	2
Cheese		1	1	Eva's „		0	2
Pork		1	4	1 cwt. coal		1	1½
Butter		0	7½	Lamp oil		0	4½
Salt butter		0	6	Milk		0	4½
Lard		0	4½	3 yds. flannelette at 3½d.		0	10½
Rice		0	4	Cake		0	4
Baked faggots		0	2	Fish		0	2
Blue		0	1				
Candles		0	1½	Total expenditure ...		15	3½
Suet		0	2				
Cocoa		0	3½				
Soap		0	1½				
Starch		0	1	The rest was put by for boots.			
Pepper		1	1				
Sweets		0	1				
		11	2				

This budget was carefully kept by the wife, and is probably accurate.

Three or four of the children are of an age to attend school, and though they live two miles away the attendance of the three elder ones is very regular. These and the father must take their dinners out with them.

Only ½d. of milk is taken each day, and as this makes bread and milk twice a day no doubt it is skim milk.

Most of the marketing is done in Warminster. The only store in the house worth consideration was potatoes. The man has to work hard for his over-money at Christmas, and sometimes is not in till 8 or 12 p.m. It is probably on these nights only that supper is taken.

	Breakfast.	Dinner.	Tea.	Supper.
SUNDAY ...	Bread and fresh butter, tea, sugar, milk, bread and milk.	Boiled potatoes, pork, cabbage, bread, gravy, currant pudding.	Bread and butter, bread, jam, tea, sugar, milk.	Bread and cheese, cocoa, sugar, milk, bread and milk.
MONDAY ...	Bread and butter toasted, tea, sugar, milk, bread and milk.	Bread and meat, cold pork, tea, sugar, milk, bread and milk.	Boiled potatoes, bacon, cocoa, sugar, milk.	
TUESDAY ...	Bread and fried bacon, tea, sugar, milk, bread and milk.	Bread and cheese, cocoa, sugar, milk.	Bread and fried bacon, fried potatoes, tea, sugar, milk, bread and milk, pepper, salt.	
WEDNESDAY	Bread and butter toasted, tea, sugar, milk, bread and milk.	Boiled potatoes, bacon, bread, cocoa, milk, pepper, salt.	Bread and butter, bread, jam, tea, sugar, milk, bread and milk.	
THURSDAY...	Bread and fried bacon, fried bread, tea, sugar, milk, bread and milk.	Boiled potatoes, boiled bacon, bread, suet pudding, cocoa, milk, sugar.	Bread and butter, bread, jam, tea, sugar, milk, bread and milk.	
FRIDAY ...	Bread and salt butter toasted, bread, dripping, tea, sugar, milk, bread and milk.	Bread and cheese, bread and cold pork, cocoa, sugar, milk.	Boiled potatoes, fried bacon and bread, pepper, salt, tea, sugar, milk, bread and milk.	
SATURDAY...	Bread and fried bacon, tea, sugar, milk, bread and milk.	Boiled bacon, potatoes, with suet dumplings, pepper, salt, onions, cocoa, sugar, milk.	Bread and butter, bread and dripping, tea, sugar, milk, bread and milk.	Bread and fish, cocoa, sugar, milk.

	Breakfast.	Dinner.	Tea.	Supper.
SUNDAY	Bread and fried bacon, tea, sugar, milk, bread and milk.	Potatoes, cabbage, beef, bread, gravy pepper, salt, plain suet pudding.	Bread and butter, bread, jam, tea, sugar, milk, bread and milk.	Bread and cold beef, mustard, salt, coffee, sugar, milk.
MONDAY	Bread and butter toasted, bread and dripping, salt, tea, sugar, milk, bread and milk.	Bread and cheese, coffee, sugar, milk.	Cooked potatoes, bacon, pepper, bread, salt, tea, sugar, milk, bread and milk.	
TUESDAY	Bread and fried bacon, fried bread, tea, sugar, milk, bread and milk.	Bread and cold beef, mustard, tea, sugar, milk	Bread and fresh butter, rice pudding, tea, sugar, milk, bread and milk.	Bread and cheese, coffee, sugar, milk.
WEDNESDAY	Bread and salt butter toasted, tea, sugar, milk, bread and milk.	Bread and cheese, tea, sugar, milk.	Boiled potatoes, bacon, bread, pepper, salt, tea, sugar, milk, bread and milk.	
THURSDAY	Bread and bacon, potatoes (fried), pepper, salt, tea, sugar, milk, bread and milk	Bread and cold beef, mustard, coffee, sugar, milk.	Boiled potatoes, bacon, pepper, salt, plain suet dumplings, bread, tea, sugar, milk, bread and milk.	Bread and meat, fish, coffee, sugar, milk.
FRIDAY	Bread and salt butter toasted, tea, sugar, milk, bread and milk.	Bread and cheese, mustard, coffee, sugar, milk.	Bread and fresh butter, bread and jam, tea, sugar, milk, bread and milk.	
SATURDAY	Bread and butter toasted, bread and dripping, salt, tea, sugar, milk.	Bread and cheese, mustard, tea, sugar, milk.	Boiled potatoes, fried bacon, bread, pepper, salt, tea, sugar, milk, rice pudding.	

SUNDAY ...	Bread and butter and dripping, tea, sugar, milk, bread and milk.	Boiled potatoes, cabbage, roast pork and gravy, plum suet pudding, bread, pepper, salt.	Bread and butter, cake, tea, sugar, milk, bread and milk.	Bread and cold pork, mustard, cocoa, sugar, milk.
MONDAY ...	Bread and fried bacon, bread and fried bread, tea, sugar, milk, bread and milk.	Bread and cheese, cocoa, milk, sugar.	Bread and butter, rice pudding, tea, sugar, milk, bread and milk.	
TUESDAY ...	Bread and fried bacon, bread and fried bread, tea, sugar, milk, bread and milk.	Bread and cold pork, mustard, cocoa, sugar, milk.	Boiled potatoes, boiled bacon, bread, pepper, salt, tea, sugar, milk, bread and milk.	
WEDNESDAY	Bread and butter, bread and dripping toasted, tea, sugar, milk, bread and milk.	Bread and cheese, cocoa, sugar, milk.	Bread and butter, bread and jam, tea, sugar, milk, bread and milk.	Bread and fried fish, cocoa, sugar, milk.
THURSDAY...	Bread and fried bacon, fried potatoes, tea, sugar, milk, bread and milk.	Bread and cold pork, cocoa, sugar, mustard, salt.	Boiled potatoes and bacon, bread, rice pudding with milk, tea, sugar, milk, bread and milk.	
FRIDAY ...	Bread and butter, tea, sugar, milk, bread and milk.	Bread and cheese, cocoa, sugar, milk	Bread and butter, bread and jam, tea, sugar, milk, bread and milk.	Bread and cheese, cocoa, sugar, milk
SATURDAY...	Bread and fried bacon, bread and dripping, tea, sugar, milk, bread and milk.	Boiled potatoes, bacon fried, bread, pepper, salt, cocoa, sugar, milk.	Bread and butter, bread and jam, tea, sugar, milk, bread and milk.	Bread and cheese, cocoa, sugar, milk.

BUDGET No. 51.

Deficiency of Income, 3s. 8d.

Family : Labourer, wife, four children. They live in a three-roomed cottage, and have about 40 poles of potato-ground. The man belongs to a good club. Mother and children belong to a medical club. They belong to a clothing club. The children are all insured.

The mother was expecting her confinement, for which she was saving. One of children at school suffers from chorea.

There is considerable discrepancy in the statement as to the earnings of this man from his employer, his wife, and a third source of information. The wife states that the employer gives 12s. 6d. and pays half the rent. This seems to be an under-statement. Probably the man receives 13s. to 14s. and house and garden rent free, paying rent for his extra land.

The wife states that her husband keeps 1s. for boots, &c., and gives her 11s. 6d. for housekeeping.

They, no doubt, supplement this from sale of garden produce and occasionally they fatten a pig.

They are said always to pay cash for their purchases.

They have about 1 quart of skim milk daily from the employer.

The diary was kept by the wife. It may err by omissions.

EXPENDITURE.

January 12–18, 1907.   *First week.*

	s.	d.
3 large loaves	1	1½
½ lb. salt butter	0	6¼
¼ lb. lard...	0	3
Bacon	0	6
Clothing club	1	0
3 large loaves	1	1½
4 lb. sugar	0	8
¼ lb. tea	0	5
2 lb. rice...	0	4
Suet	0	3
Lamp oil	0	4
Soap	0	3
	6	9½

January 19-25, 1907. *Second week.*

			s.	d.
3 large loaves	...	... ...	1	1½
½ lb. salt butter	...	... ...	0	6½
Ox cheek	...	... ...	1	0
3 large loaves	...	... ...	1	1½
Suet	...	... ...	0	3
4 lb. of sugar	...	... ...	0	8
¼ lb. of tea	...	... ...	0	4½
Flour	...	... ...	1	0
Lamp oil	...	... ...	0	4
Soap	...	... ...	0	3
Soda	...	... ...	0	2
			6	10

	Breakfast.	Dinner.	Tea.	Supper.
SATURDAY...	Bread and butter, bread and milk, tea.	At home. — Potatoes, parsnips, bread.	Bread and jam, tea, milk.	Bread and lard, milk and water.
SUNDAY ,,	Tea, toast with lard.	At home. — Potatoes, cabbage, bacon	Bread and butter, tea, milk.	Bread and milk.
MONDAY ...	Bread and butter, tea.	At home.—Bread and bacon (husband). Children's (carried) — Bread and jam.	Toast with lard, tea, milk.	Bread and milk.
TUESDAY ...	Fried potatoes, bread.	At home. — Potatoes, cabbage, bacon. Children's (carried).— Bread and lard.	Bread and butter, tea, milk.	Bread and milk.
WEDNESDAY	Bread and butter, tea, milk.	Baked potatoes, boiled rice. Children's (carried).— Bread and lard.	Bread and jam, tea, milk.	Boiled rice, milk and water.
THURSDAY .	Toast with lard, tea, milk.	Potatoes, boiled onions. Children's (carried).— Bread and jam.	Bread and butter, tea, milk.	Bread and milk.
FRIDAY ...	Fried potatoes, bread, tea, milk.	Potatoes, cabbage, fried suet. Children's (carried).— Bread and butter.	Dry toast, tea, milk.	Bread and milk.

SATURDAY...	Dry toast, tea, milk.	At home. — Potatoes, onion soup.	Bread and butter, tea, milk.	Bread and butter, milk and water.
SUNDAY ..	Dry toast, tea.	At home. — Potatoes, cabbage, ox cheek.	Bread and jam, tea, milk.	Husband out.
MONDAY ...	Fried potatoes, bread, tea.	At home.— Bread and meat Children's (carried).— Bread and jam.	Bread and lard, tea, milk.	Bread and milk.
TUESDAY ...	Dry toast, tea, milk.	At home. — Potatoes, onion soup. Children's (carried).— Bread and jam.	Dry toast, tea, milk.	Onion soup.
WEDNESDAY	Fried potatoes, bread, tea.	At home. — Potatoes, boiled rice. Children's (carried).— Bread and butter.	Toast, butter, tea, milk.	Bread and meat, milk and water.
THURSDAY...	Butter and toast, tea.	At home. — Potatoes, pea soup. Children's (carried).— Bread and jam.	Bread and butter, tea, milk.	Bread and milk.
FRIDAY ...	Fried potatoes, bread, tea.	At home — Potatoes, pea soup. Children's (carried) — Bread and dripping.	Bread and butter, tea, milk.	Pea soup, bread.

15

BUDGET No. 36.

Deficiency of Income, 3s. 6d.

Family : Labourer, wife, son, three children. Some of the family are very delicate. They reside in a five-roomed cottage with a garden.

The man belongs to the Corsley Gathering Club. The son belongs to a good Friendly Society. They insure some of the children, and belong to a medical club and a clothing club.

The father earns 14s., the son 7s. 6d., per week. Of this the father gives 13s., the son 4s., towards housekeeping expenses.

EXPENDITURE.

The regular weekly expenses are stated as follows :

	s.	d.
Insurance : son...	0	3
„ Jack	0	2
„ Tom	0	1
Club (Jack, 7d. per month)	0	1¾
Clothing club	0	3
Father's club	0	3
Doctor's money...	0	2½
House-rent	3	4*
	4	8¼

THINGS BOUGHT.

January, 1907. First week.

	s.	d.		s.	d.
4 loaves	1	6	Forward	8	8½
2 loaves	0	9	½ oz. pepper	0	0½
2 lb. of liver	0	4	¼ lb. tea	0	4½
½ lb. fat	0	2	2 loaves	0	9
Milk for week	0	7	Bag of flour	0	6
Beef	2	2	A small loaf	0	6
2 lb. cheese	1	4	1 pint of lamp oil ...	0	1
Bloaters...	0	3	Matches...	0	0½
½ lb. butter	0	6½	Coal	1	0
2½ lb. sugar	0	5	3 lb. bacon	1	9
¼-lb. tin Fry's cocoa ...	0	7½	Candles	0	1½
1 lb. salt...	0	0½		13	10½
	8	8½			

* This is probably given erroneously. Two shillings a week is a more likely figure, but, as the house is two cottages knocked into one, the rent may be somewhat higher than customary.

THINGS BOUGHT.

January, 1907. *Second week.*

	s.	d.		s.	d.
2 loaves	o	9	Forward	8	5
½ lb. butter	o	7½	Milk for week	o	7
¼ lb. tea	o	4½	4 loaves	1	6
Pork	2	0	¼-lb. tin of Fry's cocoa	o	7½
2 lb cheese	1	4	2 lb. pigs' liver	o	8
3 lb. bacon at 7d. ...	1	9	½ lb. fat	o	2
Coal	1	0	3 loaves	1	1½
Lamp oil	o	2			
2½ lb. sugar	o	5		13	1
	8	5			

The wife cooks only once or twice a week during the winter. She cooks oftener in summer when potatoes are more plentiful.

The children always take bread and jam or bread and butter to school for their dinner.

The diary was kept by one of the children, and is not perfectly clear and accurate.

	Breakfast.	Dinner.	Tea.	Supper.
SATURDAY...	Bacon, fried potatoes, tea, cocoa, bread.	Pickled cabbage, cocoa, meat, bread.	Bread and butter, tea, bloaters, cake.	Bread and cheese, cocoa.
SUNDAY ...	Bread, bacon, toast, tea, cocoa.	Beef, potatoes, greens, gravy, cocoa.	Bread and butter, tea, cake.	Cocoa, bread and meat.
MONDAY ...	Bread, bacon, potatoes, tea, cocoa.	Pudding, bread, meat, cocoa.	Bread and butter, cake, tea.	Bread and cheese, cocoa.
TUESDAY ...	Bread, bacon, potatoes, tea, cocoa.	Potatoes, greens, beef, cocoa.	Bread and butter, cake.	Bread and cheese, cocoa.
WEDNESDAY	Bread, bacon, potatoes, tea, cocoa.	Bread, beef, pickled cabbage, cocoa.	Bread and butter, cheese, tea, cocoa.	Bread and meat, cocoa.
THURSDAY...	Bacon, vinegar, tea, cocoa.	Fried onions, cocoa.	Bread and butter, jam, tea.	Bread and cheese, tea.
FRIDAY ..	Bread, liver, tea, cocoa.	Boiled beef, soup, potatoes, turnip, onions.	Bread and butter, tea.	Bread and cheese, cocoa.

SATURDAY...	Bread, bacon, potatoes, tea, cocoa.	Bacon, cocoa, bread.	Bread and butter, jam, tea.	Bread and cheese, tea.
SUNDAY ...	Bacon, fried potatoes, tea, cocoa, bread and butter, bread.	Bacon, cocoa, potatoes, greens.	Bread and butter, jam, tea.	Bread and cheese, tea.
MONDAY ...	Bread, bacon, potatoes, tea, cocoa.	Pork, bread, cocoa.	Bread and butter, tea, cocoa.	Bread and butter, tea.
TUESDAY ...	Bread, bacon, potatoes, tea, cocoa	Pork, tea, bread, apple-dumpling.	Bread and butter, tea.	Bread and cheese, cocoa.
WEDNESDAY	Bread, fried bacon, fried potatoes, tea, cocoa.	Onion soup, tea, bread. Bread and butter, cake, for Willie. Bread and meat for Fred.	Bread, toast, with dripping on it, tea, cocoa	Bread and cheese, tea.
THURSDAY...	Bread, fried bacon, fried potatoes, tea, cocoa.	Fried liver, onions, bread, cocoa. Bread and meat for Fred. Bread and butter, cake, for Willie	Bread, toast, with dripping on it, tea.	Bread and cheese, tea.
FRIDAY ...	Bread, bacon, potatoes, tea, cocoa.	Bread, onion soup. Bread and butter for Willie. Bread and meat for Fred.	Bread and butter, cake, tea, cocoa.	Bread and cheese, tea.

BUDGET No. 29

Deficiency of Income, 10*d.*

Family : Labourer, wife, three children, also girl of eleven years for some meals.

They reside in a three-roomed cottage with large garden (¾ acre) for which they pay £6 per annum.   Rent for water, 10s. per annum.

The man belongs to a good club.   Mrs. T. pays 3d. a week for each child into savings bank at Corsley School.

Mr. T.'s wage is 15s.   He keeps 5s., out of which he pays his club, firewood (buying 40 faggots at a time for 10s.), coal (half ton for 9s. 8d.), ale (5s. per month), and all outdoor expenses, such as food for pigs and fowls.   He pays for the clothing of the family out of the profits of garden, pigs, &c.

Mrs. T. receives 10s. per week from her husband for the house-keeping, and she occasionally makes 6d. for washing.   During the fortnight the budget was kept she had a present of some liver from their butcher.

Mrs. T. has been a cook and takes pride in her cooking and housekeeping   She cooks every day.   Potatoes for breakfast, and meat, potatoes, and pudding for dinner.   The children do not like milk puddings so she usually makes tarts, &c.   They have cold food in the evening.

They take 1d. worth of milk per day at 1½d. per pint.

All the family are home for the midday dinner.   The children do not take supper.

The budget was kept very carefully by Mrs. T. and is probably quite accurate.

December 30, 1905.

STORE IN HOUSE.

Sugar, tea, ½ lb. cheese, ¾ lb. butter, 1½ lb. bacon, a large loaf, five eggs, two bloaters, flour, currants, jam, pickles, store of potatoes.

EXPENDITURE.

December 30, 1905—*January* 12, 1906.

	s.	d.		s.	d.
12 large loaves	5	0	Forward	13	2
[2 have not been put			¼ lb. tea	0	4½
down, but bread bill			¼ lb. currants	1	0½
was 5s.]			Tin mustard	0	1
3 lb. beef	1	9	Soap	0	3
1 lb. butter	1	1½	Rabbit	0	6
1 lb. mutton	0	8	Beef	1	3
Bloaters	0	3	Lamp oil	0	4
7 lb. sugar	1	2	Flour	0	6
1 lb. lard	0	6	1 lb. mutton	0	8
1 lb. sultanas	0	4	Fish	0	3
Egg powder	0	2	Lamp oil	0	4
¼ lb peel	1	0½	Butter	1	1½
1 lb. 14 oz. cheese ...	1	1	14 days' milk	1	2
Salt	0	1	Bacon	1	2½
			½ lb. tea	0	9
	13	2		1	3	0

	Breakfast.	Dinner.	Tea.	Supper.
SATURDAY...	8 a.m.: Tea with milk and sugar, fish, fried potatoes, bread, toast, butter.	1 p.m.: Bacon, potatoes, parsnips, cabbage.	5 p.m.: Tea, milk and sugar, bread butter, jam.	9 p.m.: Bread and cheese, ale, celery.
SUNDAY ...	8 30. a.m.: Meat, hot potatoes, bread and butter, tea, milk, sugar.	12 30.: Roast beef, cabbage, potatoes, plum pudding.	5 p.m.: Tea, milk, and bread butter, cake.	8.30 p.m.: Bread, meat, cheese, pickles, ale.
MONDAY ...	8 a.m.: Tea, milk, sugar, fried bacon, fried potatoes, bread and butter.	1 p.m.: Cold beef, potatoes, cabbage, plum pudding.	5 p.m.: Tea, milk, and sugar, bread butter, cake.	9 p.m.: Bread and cheese, pickle, cabbage, ale.
TUESDAY ...	8 a.m.: Tea, milk, sugar, fried bacon, potatoes, bread and butter.	Stew beef, potatoes, cabbage, turnips.	Tea, sugar, milk, bread and butter, jam.	Bread and cheese, beet-root, ale.
WEDNESDAY	8 a.m.: Tea, sugar, milk, fried bacon, bread and butter, toast.	1 p.m.: Roast mutton, potatoes, cabbage.	5 p.m.: Tea, sugar, milk, bread and butter, cake, toast.	8.45 p.m.: Fried liver, bread, ale.
THURSDAY...	8 a.m.: Tea, sugar, milk, bread and butter, bread and milk.	1 p.m.: Roast mutton, potatoes, parsnips, turnip, boiled apple dumplings.	5 p.m.: Tea, milk, sugar, toast, bread and butter.	9 p.m.: Fish, bread and cheese, ale.
FRIDAY ..	8 a.m.: Tea, milk, sugar, fried fish, potatoes, bread and butter.	1 p.m.: Fried liver, potatoes, cabbage, boiled rice.	5 p.m.: Tea, milk, and sugar, bread butter, toast.	9 p.m., Cold mutton, bread, pickle onions, ale

SATURDAY...	8 a.m.: Tea, milk, sugar, bread fried bacon, and butter.	1 p.m.: Hash mutton, potatoes, cabbage.	Tea, milk, sugar, bread and butter, toast, jam.	8.30 p.m.: Bread and cheese, celery, ale.
SUNDAY ...	8 a.m.: Tea, milk, sugar, fried bacon, bread and butter.	1 p.m.: Roast rabbit, potatoes, parsnips, turnips, apple pudding.	5 p.m.: Tea, milk, sugar, cake, bread and butter.	8.30 p.m.: Cold rabbit, celery, bread, ale.
MONDAY ...	8 a.m.: Tea, milk, sugar, fish, bread and butter.	1 p.m. Roast beef, potatoes, cabbage.	5 p m.: Tea, milk, sugar, bread and butter, cake, jam.	8.30 p.m.: Bread and cheese, celery, ale.
TUESDAY ...	8 a.m.: Tea, milk, sugar, fried bacon, bread and butter.	1 p.m.: Hash beef, potatoes, cabbage.	5 p.m.: Tea, milk, sugar, bread and butter, toast.	8.30 p.m.: Bread and cheese, pickle onions, ale.
WEDNESDAY	8 a.m.: Tea, milk, sugar, fried bacon, bread and butter.	1 p.m.: Cold beef, potatoes, cabbage, jam tart.	5 p.m.: Tea, milk, sugar, bread and butter toast.	8.30 p.m.: Cold beef, beetroot, bread, ale.
THURSDAY...	8 a.m.: Tea, milk, sugar, bread and butter, bread and milk.	1 p.m.: Roast mutton, potatoes, parsnip.	5 p.m.: Tea, milk, sugar, bread and butter, buns, jam.	8 p.m.: Fish, bread, ale.
FRIDAY ...	8 a.m.: Tea, milk, sugar, bread and butter, fried bacon, potatoes.	1 p.m.: Mutton, potatoes, cabbage.	5 p.m.: Tea, milk, sugar, bread and butter, toast.	9 p.m. Bread and cheese, pickle onions, ale.

BUDGET No. 193.

Aged widow of small farmer supported by her children.   A daughter pays her rent (£5), and sends her bacon, butter, potatoes, or a load of wood, if her own do not last out.

Her children send her money, but not regularly.

One of her nieces and family live near, and look after her.

January 14–21, 1906.

						s.	d.
1½ lbs. cooked ham	...	...	...	from daughter.			
1 lb. bacon ...	...	...	...	,,			
⅛ lb. fresh butter	...	...	...	,,			
½ lb. salt butter ...	...	...	...	,,			
2 eggs ...	...	...	...	,,			
1 lb. sugar ...	...	...	...	...	...	0	2
¼ lb. tea ...	...	...	...	...	...	0	5
½ lb. candles ...	...	...	...	...	...		
1 lb. pork ...	...	...	...	...	...	0	8
Beer for two nights ...	...	...	...	...	0	2½
Two small loaves ...	...	...	...	...	0	4½

January 22–28, 1906.

						s.	d.
1½ lbs. pork ...	...	...	...	from daughter.			
4 lbs. bacon ...	...	...	...	,,			
½ lb. fresh butter	...	...	...	,,			
¼ lb. salt butter ...	...	...	...	,,			
2 small loaves ...	...	...	...	...	...	0	4½
¼ lb. tea ...	...	...	...	...	...	0	5
1 lb. sugar ...	...	...	...	...	...	0	2

This budget was kept by great-niece, who lives near, and is probably quite accurate.

	Breakfast.	Dinner.	Tea.	Supper.
MONDAY ...	9 a.m. : Bread and butter, tea.	1 p.m. : Fried bacon, potatoes.	4 p.m. : Toast, buttered, tea.	8.30. p.m. : Bread and cheese, glass of beer.
TUESDAY ...	9 a.m. : Bacon, fried potatoes; tea.	1 p.m. : Potatoes, boiled bacon, cabbage	4 p.m. : Bread and butter, tea.	8.30. p.m : Bread and cheese, glass of beer.
WEDNESDAY	9 a.m. : Buttered toast, tea.	1 p.m. : Bread and butter, boiled eggs.	4 p.m. : Bread and butter, cake, tea.	8.30. p.m. : Bread and cheese, glass of beer.
THURSDAY...	9 a.m. : Buttered toast, tea.	1 p.m. : Cold ham, bread.	4 p.m. : Bread and butter, tea.	8.30. p.m. : Bread and cheese, glass of beer.
FRIDAY ...	9 a.m. : Fried bacon, potatoes, tea.	1 p.m. : Boiled potatoes, cold ham.	4 p.m. : Bread and butter, tea.	8.30. p.m. : Cold ham, bread, glass of beer.
SATURDAY...	9 a.m. : Buttered toast, tea.	1 p.m. : Fried bacon, potatoes.	4 p.m. : Bread and butter, tea.	8.30. p.m. : Bread and cheese, glass of beer.
SUNDAY ...	9 a.m. : Buttered toast, tea.	1 p.m. : Roast pork, potatoes, cabbage.	4 p.m. : Bread and butter, tea	8.30. p.m. : Bread, cold meat, glass of beer.

	Breakfast.	Dinner.	Tea	Supper.
MONDAY ...	9 a.m.: Bacon, fried potatoes, tea.	1 p.m.: Cold pork, boiled potatoes.	4 p m: Bread and butter, tea.	8.30 p.m.: Bread and cheese, glass of beer.
TUESDAY ...	9 a.m: Buttered toast, tea.	1 p.m.: Boiled bacon, cabbage, potatoes.	4 p.m.: Bread and butter, jam, tea.	8.30 p.m.: Bread, cold bacon, glass of beer.
WEDNESDAY	9 a.m.: Fried bacon, bread, tea.	1 p m.: Fried bacon, potatoes, cabbage.	4 p m.: Buttered toast, tea.	8.30 p.m.: Bread, cold meat, glass of beer
THURSDAY...	9 a.m.: Buttered toast, tea	1 p m.: Boiled bacon, cabbage, potatoes	4 p m.: Bread and butter, tea.	8.30 p.m.: Bread and cheese, glass of beer.
FRIDAY ...	9 a.m.: Fried bacon, potatoes, tea.	1 p.m.: Fried bacon, boiled potatoes.	4 p.m.: Buttered toast, tea.	8.30 p.m.: Bread and cheese, glass of beer
SATURDAY...	9 a m.: Fried bacon, bread, tea.	1 p.m: Cold meat, bread.	4 p.m.: Buttered toast, tea.	8.30 p.m.: Bread and meat, glass of beer.
SUNDAY ...	9 a.m.: Fried bacon, egg, tea.	1 p.m.: Roast pork, potatoes, Brussels sprouts.	4 p.m.: Buttered toast, tea.	8.30 p.m.: Bread and meat, glass of beer.

BUDGET No. 116.

Income Sufficient—on margin of primary poverty.

Family : Market gardener and carrier, wife, two children. Other sons and daughters sometimes at home.

Mr. H. belongs to a good friendly society, paying 3s. 9½d. per month to it.

The receipts vary considerably ; 16s. per week is perhaps an average sum.

The school-children come home for their dinner, and there are usually about five persons present for meals.

They take 1d. worth of milk, or about 1 pint, per day from Mrs. H.'s brother. They have meat or soup for dinner most days.

The budget was kept by one of the children, and is not very complete. For instance, it was found that coffee or cocoa is usually taken for supper, and sometimes the parents have porter. This has been omitted in the diary.

EXPENDITURE.

January 7-13, 1907. First week.

	s.	d.
Butter	1	3
Milk	0	1
Sugar	0	4
Starch	0	4
Blacklead	0	2
Flour	0	6
Meat (fresh beef for stewing)	1	6
Club	1	9½
Bread	1	3½
Milk	0	2
Butter	1	3
*Baking [?]	4	0
Oil	0	6
Soap	0	6
Coals	2	6
Paper	0	4
Oranges	0	6
Sugar	1	0
	18	0

* Possibly bacon.

January 14–20, 1907. Second week.

							s.	d.
Sugar	...	...	...	...	...	...	1	0
Cheese	...	...	...	...	...	...	2	0
Butter	...	...	...	...	...	...	1	0
Lard	...	...	...	...	...	...	0	6
Mutton	...	...	...	...	...	...	2	6
Steak	...	...	...	...	...	...	1	0
Suet	...	...	...	...	...	...	0	8
Candles	...	...	...	...	...	...	0	4
Soda	...	...	...	...	...	...	0	3
Bread	...	...	...	...	...	...	1	6
Flour	...	...	...	...	...	...	0	6
Corn for fowls	...	...	...	...	...	...	1	6
							12	9

January 21–27, 1907. Third week.

				s.	d.					s.	d.
Bread	...	...	...	2	8	Forward	...	...		7	11½
3 lb. beef		...	...	1	9	Oil	...	...	...	0	4
1 lb. butter		...	...	1	2	Powder for washing	...		0	3
Coals	...	...	...	1	3	Corn for fowls	...	...		1	6
Wool	...	...	...	1	1½	Milk	...	...	...	0	8
				7	11½					10	8½

	Breakfast.	Dinner.	Tea.	Supper.
MONDAY ...	8 a.m.: Tea, bacon, potatoes, bread and butter, milk, sugar.	1 p.m.: Bread, cold meat, pickles, milk.	4 p m.: Bread and butter, cake, tea, milk, sugar.	Bread, cold meat, celery.
TUESDAY ..	8 a m.: Toast, bread and butter, tea.	1 p.m: Stewed rabbit, carrots, potatoes.	Bread and butter, cake, tea, milk, sugar	Bread and cheese, butter.
WEDNESDAY	Bread, bacon, porridge, tea, milk, sugar.	Potatoes, cabbage, meat	Bread and butter, jam, cake, tea, milk, sugar.	Bread and cheese, butter, coffee.
THURSDAY..	8 a m.: Mutton chops, butter, toast, tea, milk, sugar.	1 p.m.: Soup, carrots, onions, meat, potatoes.	5 p m : Bread and butter, fish, tea, milk, sugar.	8 p.m.: Bread, meat, cheese.
FRIDAY ...	8 a.m. . Bread and butter, toast, milk, quaker oats.	1 p.m.: Potatoes, greens, pork, Christmas plum-pudding.	5 p.m.: Bread and butter, jam, apple-tart, tea, milk, sugar.	Bread and cheese, butter, pickles.
SATURDAY...	8 a m : Bread, toast, butter, bacon, tea, milk, sugar.	1 p.m.: Potatoes, bread, roast pork.	5 p.m.: Bread and butter, jam-tart, tea, milk, sugar.	8 p.m.: Bread and butter, cheese, cocoa.
SUNDAY ...	Steak, bread and butter, tea, milk, sugar.	Potatoes, sprats, roast mutton, plum-pudding.	Bread and butter, jam, plum-cake, scones.	Bread, cold meat, cheese, butter.

	Breakfast.	Dinner.	Tea.	Supper.
MONDAY ...	8 a.m.: Tea, bread and milk, sausages, bread and butter.	1 p m : Potatoes, cold meat, mince-pie.	5 p m.: Bread and butter, cake, tea, jam, milk, sugar.	8 p.m.: Bread and milk.
TUESDAY ...	8 a.m. : Bread, bacon, fried potatoes, tea, milk, sugar.	Potatoes, parsnips, boiled bacon.	Bread and butter, jam, tea, toast, milk, sugar.	Bread and cheese, celery.
WEDNESDAY	Bread and butter, bacon, fried potatoes.	Potatoes, meat.	Bread and butter, tea, milk, sugar.	Bread and cheese.
THURSDAY...	8 a.m.: Bread, bacon, fried potatoes, tea, milk, sugar.	Potatoes, greens, fried bacon.	5 p.m. : Bread and butter, rice - pudding, tea, milk, sugar.	Bread and cheese, butter, coffee.
FRIDAY ...	8 a m. : Bread and butter, toast, tea, milk, sugar.	1 p.m. : Soup, potatoes, suet-pudding.	5 p m. · Bread and butter, jam, tea, milk, sugar.	Bread, cold meat, coffee.
SATURDAY...	8 a.m : Bread and butter, cold meat, tea, milk, sugar.	1 p.m.: Hot potatoes, steak, bread.	5 p m : Bread and butter, jam, tea, milk, sugar.	8 p m : Soup, bread, meat.
SUNDAY ...	8 a.m. Bread, meat, butter, tea, milk, sugar.	1 p m : Potatoes, greens, roast beef, plum-pudding.	5 p.m.: Bread and butter, apple-tart, tea, milk, sugar.	8 p.m. : Cold meat, cheese, pickles.

BUDGET No. 20.

Income Sufficient + 6s. 4d.

Family : Labourer, wife, one boarded out orphan.

They reside in a six-roomed cottage, rent £4, and rent some land at £2 per annum.   They keep pigs.

The husband belongs to a good club.   Both man and wife have insured their lives so that if they live to a certain age a sum of money will be paid them.

They take 1 quart of milk, price 3d., daily all the year round.

Weekly receipts for housekeeping :

	s.	d.
From husband	10	6
For orphan	3	6
	14	0

EXPENDITURE.

January, 1907.   First week.

	s.	d.		s.	d.
Bread	0	9	Forward	4	7
1 lb. fresh butter ...	1	3	2 lb. bacon	1	4
½ lb. tea	0	10	Beef (brisket, English)	2	6
3 lb. sugar	0	6	Bread	0	7
2 lb. flour	0	4	Bread	0	7
½ lb. lard	0	4	Mutton (at 7d. lb.) ...	1	7
1 lb. currants	0	4	Camp coffee	0	6
Pepper	0	1	2 cwt. coals	2	6
Salt	0	1	4 sheep's hearts ...	0	10
Mustard	0	1	1 lb. mixed jam ...	0	6
	4	7		15	6

January, 1907. *Second week.*

	s.	d.			s.	d.
1 lb. fresh butter ...	1	3	Forward		8	1½
Bread	0	9	¼ lb. starch		0	2
½ lb. tea	0	10	2 lb. soda		0	1
3 lb. sugar	0	6	Ball blue		0	1
2 lb. flour	0	4	2 cwt. coals		2	6
½ lb. lard	0	4	Lamp oil, 2 pts. ...		0	3
1 lb. currants	0	4	2 lb. cheese		1	5
2 lb. bacon	1	4	1 lb. candles		0	6
4 lb. beef (brisket) ...	2	2				
1 lb. soap	0	3½			13	2
	8	1½				

This budget was kept by the wife, and appears to have been very carefully kept in every respect.

	Breakfast.	Dinner.	Tea.	Supper.
SATURDAY...	At 7 o'clock. Bacon, bread and butter, tea.	At 12 o'clock: Cold ham, beetroot, bread, coffee	At 5 o'clock: Bread and butter, tea.	At 8 o'clock: Bread and butter, cheese, coffee
SUNDAY ...	At 7 o'clock: Bacon, bread and butter, tea.	At 12 o'clock: Roast mutton, cabbage, potatoes.	At 5 o'clock: Bread and butter, cake, tea.	At 8 o'clock: Cold mutton, bread and butter, coffee.
MONDAY ...	At 7 o'clock: Bacon, bread and butter	At 12 o'clock: Cold mutton, winter greens, potatoes.	At 5 o'clock: Bread and butter, cake, tea.	At 8 o'clock: Bread and cheese, butter, coffee.
TUESDAY ...	At 7 o'clock: Bacon, bread and butter	At 12 o'clock: Cold beef, cabbages, potatoes, apple-pudding	At 5 o'clock: Bread and butter, tea, seed cake.	At 8 o'clock: Bread and cheese, coffee.
WEDNESDAY	At 7 o'clock: Bread and butter, tea.	At 12 o'clock: Sheep's hearts, cabbage, potatoes	At 5 o'clock: Brea and butter, jam, tea	At 8 o'clock: Bread and cheese, coffee.
THURSDAY...	At 7 o'clock. Cold beef, bread butter, tea.	At 12 o'clock: Cold and hearts, bread cheese, milk rice pudding.	At 5 o'clock: Bread and butter, tea.	At 8 o'clock: Bread and cheese, beetroot, coffee.
FRIDAY ...	At 7 o'clock. Bread and butter, tea.	At 12 o'clock: Fried bacon, potatoes, greens, coffee	At 5 o'clock: Bread and butter.	At 8 o'clock: Sheep's hearts, bread, coffee

	Breakfast.	Dinner.	Tea.	Supper.
SATURDAY...	At 7 o'clock: Bread and butter, tea.	At 12 o'clock: Bread and cheese, beetroot.	At 5 o'clock: Bread and butter, jam.	At 8 o'clock: Bread and butter, cheese, coffee.
SUNDAY ,,	At 7 o'clock: Fried bacon, bread and butter, tea.	At 12 o'clock: Roast beef, cabbage, potatoes	At 5 o'clock: Bread and butter, currant cake.	At 8 o'clock: Cold beef, bread, coffee.
MONDAY ...	At 7 o'clock: Bread and butter, tea.	At 12 o'clock: Cold beef, potatoes, greens.	At 5 o'clock: Bread and butter, tea.	At 8 o'clock: Bread and cheese, beetroot, coffee
TUESDAY ...	At 7 o'clock: Fried bacon, bread butter, tea	At 12 o'clock: Fried fish (cod), bread, cocoa.	At 5 o'clock: Bread and butter, tea.	At 8 o'clock: Bread and cheese, cocoa.
WEDNESDAY	Bread and butter, tea.	At 12 o'clock: Cold beef, cabbage, potatoes.	At 5 o'clock: Bread and butter, currant cake, tea.	At 8 o'clock: Bread and cheese, cocoa
THURSDAY...	At 7 o'clock: Fried bacon, bread, tea.	At 12 o'clock: Fried bacon, fried potatoes, bread, cocoa, apple pudding.	At 5 o'clock: Bread and butter, tea	At 8 o'clock: Bread and cheese, coffee.
FRIDAY	At 7 o'clock: Fried bacon, bread and butter, tea	At 12 o'clock: Cold beef, fried potatoes, tea, rice milk pudding.	At 5 o'clock: Bread and butter, tea.	At 8 o'clock: Bread and cheese, beetroot, coffee.

BUDGET No 206.

Income Sufficient + 12s. 2d.

Family : Widow, midwife, only goes out occasionally for the day ; two sons, agricultural wage-earner and carter ; boy of 12.

The family resides in a double cottage of eight rooms, one of the sons paying half the rent, and contributing 4s. per week towards household expenses when away from home. The mother receives 1s. 6d. per week poor relief for her boy, who also earns something running errands, &c., after school hours. The total family income must average more than 30s. per week, but this is not all contributed to the housekeeping expenses.

The budget was kept by the boy of 12, and the diary of food is probably quite accurate.

The mother has a poor appetite and eats little.

Saturday, December 30, 1905.

STORE IN HOUSE.

2 lb. cheese, butter, 2 lb. bacon, cocoa, store of potatoes.

EXPENDITURE.

First week, December 30, 1905, to January 5, 1907.

Saturday :
    ½ lb. tea.
    ¼ lb cocoa.
    ½ lb. salt butter.
    4 lb. sugar.
    3 large loaves.
    3 lb. mutton.
    2 lb. salt fish.
    Milk, 1d.
Sunday :
    Milk, 1d.
Monday :
    1 large loaf.
    Milk, 1d.

Tuesday :
    Chole of bacon, 1s.
    Milk, 1d.
    3 large loaves.
Wednesday :
    Milk, 1d.
    ¼ lb butter.
    2 lb. sugar.
Thursday :
    3 large loaves.
    Milk, 1d.
    1½ lb. bacon.
    ¾ lb cheese.
Friday :
    Milk, 1d.

Second week, January 6–12, 1906.

Saturday :
  Milk, 1d.
  2 lb. bacon.
  3 lb. cheese.
  ½ lb. butter.
  Pot of jam.
  1 lb. dripping.
  ½ lb. bongalia tea.
  4 lb. sugar.
  3 lb. beef.
  3 loaves.
  1 lb. meat cuttings.
  3d. fresh herrings.
  Cake, 4d.
Sunday :
  Milk, 1d.

Monday :
  Milk, 1d.
  2 large loaves.
Tuesday :
  Milk, 1d.
  3 large loaves.
Wednesday :
  Milk, 1d.
  ½ lb. cocoa.
  2 lb. sugar.
  2½ lb beef.
  3d. bloaters.
Thursday :
  Milk, 1d.
  3 large loaves.
Friday :
  1 lb. sugar.
  ½ lb. butter.

	Breakfast.	Dinner.	Tea.	Supper
SATURDAY...	Taken out.—Toast with butter, cold tea.	Taken out —Bread and cheese, cold tea.	At 6 o'clock: Fish, tea, bread.	At 9 o'clock (mother and myself): Bread and milk. At 10 o'clock (two brothers): Bread and cheese, cocoa.
SUNDAY ...	At 8 o'clock (all together): Fish, tea.	At 1 o'clock (all together): Potatoes, greens, mutton, pudding.	At 5 o'clock (all together): Bread and butter, tea, cake.	At 9 o'clock (all together): Bread and cheese, celery, cocoa.
MONDAY ...	At 7 o'clock (two brothers): Fried bacon, bread, tea. At 8 o'clock (mother and myself): Toast, tea.	Taken away.—Bread and cheese, cold tea. Mother and myself.—Bacon and potatoes at 1 o'clock.	At 5 o'clock (mother and myself): Bread and butter, tea At 6 o'clock (two brothers) Bacon and fried potatoes, tea.	At 10 o'clock (two brothers): Bread and cheese, cocoa At 8 o'clock (mother and myself): Bread and butter, tea.
TUESDAY ...	Two brothers (taken away): Bread and meat, cold tea. At 8 o'clock (mother and myself): Dry toast, tea, bread and butter, tea.	Two brothers (taken away): Bread and cheese, cold tea. At 1 o'clock (mother and myself): Fried bacon, bread.	At 5 o'clock (mother and myself): Bread and butter, tea. At 6 o'clock (two brothers): Stewed meat, onions, turnips, parsnips, potatoes.	At 9 o'clock (mother and myself): Cup of tea. At 10 o'clock (two brothers): Bread and cheese, cocoa.
WEDNESDAY	At 8 o'clock (mother and myself): Fried bacon, bread. At 7 o'clock (two brothers): Fried bacon and potatoes, tea.	At 1 o'clock (mother and myself): Stewed meat, bread. Two brothers (taken away): Bread and cheese, cold tea.	At 5 o'clock (mother): Bread and butter, tea. At 6 o'clock (two brothers): Potatoes, greens, pig-meat, tea.	At 9 o'clock (mother and myself): Bread, soup, cow-heel.[1] Two brothers supper out.

[Continued on next page.]

[1] Brought home by one of the sons as a delicacy for his mother, who was ill

	Breakfast.	Dinner.	Tea.	Supper.
THURSDAY...	At 8 o'clock (mother and myself): Dry toast and tea, bloaters, bread, tea. At 7 o'clock (two brothers): Fried bloaters, tea.	At 1 o'clock (Mother and myself): Soup and bread. Two brothers (taken away): Bread, meat, cold tea.	At 4 o'clock (mother and myself). Bread and butter, tea. At 6 o'clock (two brothers) · Fried potatoes and bacon, tea.	At 8 o'clock (mother and myself): Soup. At 9 o'clock (two brothers) · Bread and cheese, cocoa.
FRIDAY ...	At 8 o'clock (mother and myself): Bread and butter, tea. Two brothers (taken away): Cold meat with cold tea.	Mother and myself: Fried bacon, potatoes, cocoa. Two brothers (taken away). Bread and cheese, cold tea.	At 4 o'clock (mother) · Bread and butter. Myself away. At 6 o'clock (two brothers): Bacon, potatoes, tea.	At 8 o'clock (mother and myself). Bread and milk. At 9 o'clock (two brothers): Bread and cheese, cocoa.
SATURDAY...	At 8 o'clock (mother and myself): Dry toast, tea, potatoes, bacon. At 7 o'clock (two brothers): Bacon, eggs, bread, tea.	Two brothers (taken away): Bread and cheese, cold tea.	At 4 o'clock (mother and myself): Bread and butter, tea. At 6 o'clock (two brothers): Bread, fried meat, tea.	At 9 o'clock (mother and myself): Fish, bread, cocoa. At 10 o'clock (two brothers): Bread and cheese, cocoa.
SUNDAY ...	At 8 o'clock (all together): Bread, fish, tea.	At 1 o'clock (all together): Potatoes, greens, beef.	At 5 o'clock (all together)· Bread and butter, cake, tea.	At 9 o'clock. Bread, meat, cocoa, for us all.

MONDAY ...	Two brothers (taken away): Meat and bread, cold tea. At 8 o'clock (mother and myself): Bacon, bread, tea.	Two brothers (taken away): Bread and cheese, cold tea. Myself: Bread and jam at school. Mother: Fried potatoes, bread, cocoa.	At 6 o'clock (all together): Tea, toast.	At 9 o'clock (mother and myself): Bread and milk. At 10 o'clock (two brothers): Bread and cheese, cocoa.
TUESDAY .	Two brothers: Bread, meat, cold tea. At 8 o'clock (mother and myself): Fried bacon, bread.	At 1 o'clock (myself): Bread and dripping. Mother: Bread, meat, cocoa. Two brothers (taken away): Bread and cheese, cold tea.	At 5 o'clock (mother): Bread and butter, tea. Myself out. At 6 o'clock (two brothers): Potatoes, stew.	At 9 o'clock (mother): Bread and butter, cocoa. At 10 o'clock (two brothers): Bread and cheese, cocoa.
WEDNESDAY	At 8 o'clock (mother): Bacon, fried potatoes. At 7 o'clock (two brothers): Bacon, potatoes, tea.	Brother: Bread, meat, cheese, cold tea. Mother: Soup. Myself: Bread and jam at school.	At 4.30 (mother): Bread, fish. At 6 o'clock (myself and two brothers): Potatoes, cabbage, meat, bread, tea.	Mother and myself: Beef, bread. At 10 o'clock (two brothers): Bread and cheese, cocoa.
THURSDAY...	Mother and myself: Bread and butter, tea. Two brothers (taken away): Bread and butter, cold tea.	Mother: Soup. Myself: Bread and dripping at school. Two brothers (taken away): Bread and meat.	At 5.30 (all together): Fried bacon, onions, bread.	Mother: Bread, meat, cocoa. Myself: Bread and cheese.
FRIDAY ...	Two brothers (taken out): Bread, meat, cold tea. Mother and myself: Bread and butter, tea.	Two brothers: Bread and cheese, cold tea. Mother: Bread and soup. Myself: Bread and jam.	Mother: Bread and butter, tea. Myself away. Two brothers: Vegetables, bacon.	Myself away. At 9 o'clock (mother and two brothers): Onion broth.

BUDGET No. 46.

Income Sufficient + 14s. 8d.

Family: Labourer, wife, son (artisan), two children, aged mother-in-law.

The family live in a four-roomed cottage and have a garden and allotment. They pay £5 per annum rent.

Father and son belong to good friendly societies. Man and wife are insured, the money to be paid to survivor on death of either. The children pay money into Corsley School savings bank.

The man's wage is 14s., out of which he keeps 1s. "Sunday money," paying 13s. to his wife for housekeeping. The son, who is earning good wages, pays 8s. 6d , or less than half, to his mother. Total available for housekeeping, 21s. 6d.

The wife and other children do not go out to work, but some garden produce is sold.

Expenditure.

Mrs. J. pays ready money for everything. She pays the baker one week and the grocer the next.

She usually buys per week seven or eight 4-lb. loaves, and two joints of meat, about 6 lb. and 4 lb., and takes 1d. worth of milk per day.

The family do not as a rule take their meals all together.

They eat meat every day, and eat more meat now than they did before the eldest son began to earn money. The children always have a little meat for tea or supper.

Mrs. J. gives the following account of their usual menu:

Breakfast.—Bacon or toast. Son sometimes has porridge. Children occasionally bread and milk. Formerly they always had bacon for breakfast, but they are now tired of it and often have toast instead.

Dinner.—Father and son take dinner out with them—always bread, meat, and cheese. The children take dinner to school, bread and butter or bread and jam. Mrs. J. sometimes keeps some vegetables hot for the children when they come home from school.

Tea.—All except the two men take tea, with cake, bread, butter, and jam.

Supper.—Father and son, and sometimes the children, "if they fancy it," take supper. Meat and vegetables, bread and cheese.

BUDGET No. 131.

Income Sufficient + 10s. 8d.

Family : Labourer in Frome, wife, wife's mother (three adults). Five-roomed cottage with large garden.

Mrs. J. is a careful manager, buying her groceries monthly at a Working Men's Co-operative Store, and receiving a half-yearly dividend on the money expended. She is careful not to waste any of the fat from the meat, which can be utilised for making cakes or stock for soup. She buys in a small cask of beer, so that her husband may have his pint for supper without going to the public-house. When the couple married they had a little capital left after furnishing their cottage, and they have made it a rule always to pay ready money for all purchases, thus getting them cheaper.

The following is an average of the amount of food-stuffs used weekly :

20 lb. bread.	2¾ lb. sugar.
5½ lb. fresh meat.	6 oz. tea.
1 lb. salt meat.	2 lb. flour.
1½ lb. butter.	8 pints milk.
¾ lb. cheese.	8 pints ale.

Blacking, blacklead, ink, &c., cost about one farthing per fortnight.

Other expenses are collection at church, 3d. per week; newspapers, 2d. per week; magazine, 1d. per month; 1s. annually to Home Missions and 1s. 6d. to the Bell-ringers.

Mr. J.'s ordinary wage is 17s. He keeps 1s. 6d. of this for the Amalgamated Weekly Club, tobacco, and pocket-money.

Mrs. J. pays £2 per annum into the Oddfellows Club, which ensures a weekly sum during illness, with medical attendance and medicine.

The following diary of purchases and food was kept by Mrs. J. herself during January, 1907, and is, no doubt, quite accurate. They live, she says, much more cheaply in the summer, requiring less meat and hot soup, and saving coal by the use of an oil-stove.

				s.	d.
Money received from husband	...	...	...	15	6
„ „ „ mother	...	...	...	3	6
				19	0

EXPENDITURE.

January 14–21, 1907. *First week.*

	s.	d.		s.	d.
Monday :			Forward	8	9
1 cwt. coal	1	3	Saturday :		
Soap 3d., soda 1d.,			6 oz. tea	0	7½
starch and blue 1d.	0	5	2¾ lb. sugar	0	6
2½ lb. collar of beef...	1	3	1 lb. bacon	0	9
3 2-lb. loaves... ...	0	6¾	¾ lb. cheese	0	6
Tuesday :			1 oz. pepper ½ lb. salt	0	1½
Clothing club ...	1	0	2 lb. flour	0	4
Wednesday :			8 pts. milk	0	8
6 kippers	0	6	8 pts. dinner ale ...	0	10
1 lb. pork	0	8	Biscuits 1d., ¼ lb. cur-		
Thursday :			rants 1d.	0	2
3 2-lb. loaves... ...	0	6¾	Rice 1d., 3 eggs 3d.	0	4
Friday :			Whiskey	0	3
1½ lb. fresh butter ...	1	10½	Peppermint	0	0½
½ gal. lamp oil and			4 2-lb. loaves ...	0	9
1 lb. candles ...	0	8	2 lb. 2 oz. pork ...	1	4
	8	9		15	11¼

In hand for collection, papers, rent, club, clothing, 3s. 0¾d.

January 22–28, 1907. Second week.

	s.	d.		s.	d.
Monday :			Forward	11	0
2 cwt. coal	2	6	Saturday :		
Soap 3d., soda 1d.,			1 oz. peppermint and		
starch and blue 1d.	0	5	½ lb. salt	0	1¼
3 2-lb. loaves... ...	0	6¾	2 lb. flour	0	4
Tuesday :			8 pts. milk	0	8
2 lb. pork, salted ...	1	4	8 pts. dinner ale ...	0	10
Thursday .			Suet 1d., carroway		
4 2-lb. loaves... ...	0	9	seeds ¼d.	0	1¼
¼ bullock's cheek ...	0	7½	Gin and peppermints	0	1½
Friday :			7 eggs...	0	6
1½ lb. fresh butter ...	1	10½	3 lb. roasting beef for		
Saturday			Sunday	2	0
3 2-lb. loaves ...	0	6¾			
6 oz. tea	0	7½		15	8
2¾ lb. sugar	0	6			
1 lb. bacon	0	9			
¾ lb. cheese	0	6			
	11	0			

In hand for collection, papers, rent, club, and clothing, 3s. 4d.

	Breakfast.	Dinner.	Tea.	Supper.
MONDAY ...	Husband—6 a.m.: Hot tea with milk and sugar, bread and butter. 8.30 a.m.: Cold tea, bread and butter. Mother and myself—6 a.m.: Hot tea. 8 a.m.: Hot tea, bread and butter	Husband.—12.30 p.m.: Cold roast pork, mince-pies, bread, cold tea, cheese. Mother and myself—12.30 p.m.: Hot stewed beef and onions, boiled celery, parsnips, potatoes, apple-tart	Husband.—6 p.m.: Hot stewed beef and onions, boiled celery and potatoes, hot tea with milk and sugar. Mother and myself—4 p.m.: Hot tea with milk and sugar, bread and butter, cake.	Husband.—8 p.m.: One pint of beer, three thin lunch biscuits. Mother and myself—8 p.m.: half pint of beer, six biscuits.
TUESDAY ...	Husband—6 a.m.: Hot tea, bread and butter. 8.30 a.m.: Hot bacon, one egg, bread, cold tea. Mother and myself.—Hot tea with milk and sugar. 8 30 a.m: Hot bacon, bread, hot tea with milk and sugar.	Husband.—12.30 p.m: Cold roast pork, bread, mince - pie, cheese, cold tea. Mother and myself.—12 30 p.m.: Hot stewed pork, onions, boiled celery, potatoes, bread, apple-tart.	Husband—6 p.m : Hot stewed pork, boiled onions, turnips, potatoes, hot tea with milk and sugar. Mother and myself.—4 p.m. Hot tea with milk and sugar, bread and butter, cake.	Husband.—8 p.m.: One pint of beer, two biscuits. Mother and myself.—8 p.m.: Two glasses hot peppermint, bread and butter.
WEDNESDAY	Husband.—6 a.m : Hot tea with milk and sugar, bread and butter. 8 30 a.m.: Hot fried bacon, and bread, cold tea Mother and myself—6 a.m. Hot tea with milk and sugar. 8 30 a.m.: Bread and butter, strawberry jam, hot tea with milk and sugar.	Husband.—12.30 p.m.: Cold stewed beef, bread, mince-pie, cold tea. Mother and myself.—Hot roast pork, boiled greens, potatoes.	Husband—6 p.m.: Hot roast pork, boiled greens and potatoes, hot tea with milk and sugar. Mother and myself.—bread and butter, cake, hot tea with milk and sugar.	Husband.—8 p.m.: One pint of beer. Mother and myself.—8 p m : One glass of beer, one wineglass of whiskey and water, bread and butter.

THURSDAY...	Husband.—6 a.m : Hot tea, bread and butter, 8.30 a.m : Bread and butter, toasted kipper, cold tea. Mother and myself.— 6 a.m : Hot tea. 8.30 a.m.. Bread and butter, two kippers, toasted, hot tea with milk and sugar.	Husband.—12.30 p.m.: Cold pork, bread, cheese, cold tea. Mother and myself.— 12.30 p m.: Cold beef, pickled onions, bread, rice-pudding, baked and stewed apples.	Husband.—6 p.m.: stewed beef and onions, boiled turnips and potatoes, baked rice-pudding, stewed apples. Mother and myself.— 4 p.m.. Bread and butter, cake, hot tea with milk and sugar.	Husband.—8 p.m.: One pint of beer. Mother and myself.— 8 p.m.: Two small glasses of beer (or ½ pint), bread and butter, cheese (The above means one piece of bread and butter for mother, one piece of bread and cheese for myself.)
FRIDAY ...	Husband.—6 a.m.: Hot tea, bread and butter. 8.30 a.m . Toasted kipper, bread and butter, cold tea Mother and myself.— 6 a m : Hot tea. 8.30 a.m.: Toasted kipper, bread and butter, hot tea.	Husband.—12.30 p.m.: Bread and cheese, pickled onions, cold tea. Mother and myself.— 12.30 p m.: Boiled bacon, greens, potatoes, boiled apple-dumplings.	Husband —6 p.m.: Boiled bacon and greens, boiled potatoes, boiled apple dumpling, hot tea. Mother and myself.— 4 p.m.: Bread and butter, cake, hot tea.	Husband —8 p.m.: One pint of beer.
SATURDAY...	Husband.—6 a.m.: Hot tea, bread and butter. 8.30 a.m : Hot fried bacon, one egg, and bread, cold tea. Mother and myself.— 6 a m Hot tea 8.30 a.m : One boiled egg, bread and butter, cold boiled bacon, bread, hot tea.	Husband.—1.40 p.m.: Hot roast pork, potatoes, greens, stewed apples. Mother and myself : Hot roast 1.40 p.m.. pork, potatoes, greens, stewed apples.	Husband —5.15 p m ; Bread and butter, cake, jam-tarts, hot tea, milk, sugar. Mother and myself.— 5 15 p.m.. Bread and butter, celery, cake, jam-tarts. Hot tea, milk, sugar.	Mother and myself— 8 p.m.: One glass of beer, wineglass of whiskey and water, two pieces of bread and butter.
SUNDAY ...	Husband.—5.30 a.m.: Hot tea, bread and butter 8 30 a.m . Bread and butter, cold tea. Mother and myself.— 5.30 a.m.: Hot tea. 8.30 a.m.: Bread and butter, hot tea.	Husband.—12.30 p.m.: Cold roast pork, bread, jam turnover. Mother and myself.— 1 p.m : Cold roast pork, bread, hot apple-tart.	Husband.—6 15 p.m.: Hot fried bacon, two eggs, bread, one pint of beer. Mother and myself.— 4 p.m.: Bread and butter, cake, hot tea.	Husband. — 8.15 p.m.: One pint of beer. Mother and myself.— 8.15 p m : One small glass of beer, one wine-glass of whiskey and water.

	Breakfast.	Dinner.	Tea.	Supper.
MONDAY ...	Husband.—6 a.m.: Hot tea, bread and butter. 8.30 a.m. Bread and butter, cold tea. Mother and myself.—6 a.m. Hot tea, 8.30. a.m.: Fried bacon, bread, hot tea.	Husband.—12.30 p.m.: Cold roast pork and bread, jam turnover, cold tea. Mother and myself—12.30 p.m.: One poached eggs, bread and butter, bread and cheese, one glass of beer, apple-tart.	Husband.—6 p.m.: Hot pork, greens, potatoes, apple-tart, hot tea. Mother and myself.—4 p.m.: Bread and butter, cake, celery, hot tea.	Husband.—8 p.m. : One pint of beer Mother and myself.—8 p.m.: Two glasses of hot peppermint, two pieces of bread and butter.
TUESDAY ...	Husband.—6 a.m.: Hot tea, bread and butter, 8.30 a.m.: Fried bacon, one egg, bread, cold tea. Mother and myself.—6 a.m. Hot tea. 8.30 a.m. Bread and butter, hot tea.	Husband.—12.30 p.m.: Cold roast pork and bread, jam turnover. Mother and myself.—12.30 p.m. Hot stewed pork, and onions, boiled celery and potatoes, stewed apples	Husband.—6 p.m.: Hot stewed pork, onions, boiled celery and potatoes, hot tea Mother and myself.— 4 p.m.: Bread and butter, cake, hot tea.	Husband.—8 p.m.: One pint of beer. Mother and myself—8 p.m.: Two glasses of peppermint, bread and butter.
WEDNESDAY	Husband.—6 a.m.: Hot tea, bread and butter. 8.30 a.m.: Hot fried bacon, one egg, bread, cold tea. Mother and myself.—6 a.m.: Hot tea. 8.30 a.m.: Fried bacon and bread, hot tea.	Husband.—12.30 p.m. Cold stewed pork and bread, jam turnover, cold tea Mother and myself.—12.30 p.m.: Cold stewed pork, bread, boiled apple-dumplings.	Husband.—6 p.m.: Boiled vegetable marrow, potatoes, fried bacon, boiled apple-dumpling, hot tea. Mother and myself.—4 p.m.: Bread and butter, cake, hot tea.	Husband.—8 p.m.: One pint of beer. Mother and myself.—8 p.m.: Two glass of beer (or ½ pint), two pieces of bread and butter.

THURSDAY...	Husband.—6 a.m.: Hot tea, bread and butter. 8.30 a.m.: Bread and butter, cold tea.—Mother and myself.—6 a.m.: Hot tea. 8.30 a m : Bread and butter, hot tea.	Husband.—12,30 p.m.: Cold stewed pork, bread and cheese, one pint of beer.—Mother and myself.—12.30. p.m.: Hot stewed bullock's cheek, onions, parsnips, potatoes, and suet-dumpling.	Husband.—6 p.m.: Hot stewed bullock's cheek, onions, parsnips, potatoes, suet-dumpling and large cup of hot soup—Mother and myself—4 p.m.: Bread and butter, blackberry jam, hot tea	Husband —9 p.m.· One glass hot beer. Mother and myself.—8 p.m : Two glasses of hot peppermint, one piece of bread and cheese, one piece of bread and butter.
FRIDAY ...	Husband —8 a.m · Ho fried bacon, two eggs, bread and hot tea—Mother and myself.—8 a m.: Hot fried bacon and bread, hot tea.	Husband —12.30 p.m.: Hot stewed bullock's cheek, bread and half a pint of hot soup.—Mother and myself.—12.30 p.m.: Hot stewed bullock's cheek, onions, parsnips, potatoes, and suet-dumplings.	Husband.—6 p.m.: Hot stewed bullock's cheek, onions, parsnips, potatoes and suet-dumpling.—Mother and myself —4 p.m.: Bread and butter, blackberry jam, hot tea.	Husband —9 p m One glass of hot beer. Mother and myself.—8 p.m.: One breakfast cup of bread and milk, one glass of hot peppermint, one piece of bread and butter.
SATURDAY...	Husband.—8.30 a.m.: Hot fried bacon, one egg, bread, hot tea.—Mother and myself.—8 30. a.m.: One boiled egg, bread and butter, hot tea.	1.40 p.m.: Hot stewed bullock's cheek, onions, parsnips, and potatoes, with hot suet-dumplings.	5.30 p m : Bread and butter, cake and jam, hot tea.	8.30 p.m Two glasses of beer, one glass of gin and water, one piece of bread and butter and two pieces of bread and cheese.
SUNDAY ...	8 30 a m : Fried bacon and bread, two eggs, bread and butter, hot tea.	1 p.m.: Hot roast rib of beef, greens, potatoes hot apple-tart, two glasses of beer.	4 p.m.: Bread and butter, cake and blackberry jam, hot tea.	8 30 p.m.: Cold roast rib of beef, bread, and pickled onions, cold apple-tart, two glasses of beer, one wineglass of gin and water.

17

BUDGET No. 105.

Income sufficient + 14s. 4d.

Shoemaker, daughter, two sons (artisan and labourer), one out of work. Earnings uncertain, but do not average " anything like " 10s. per week. Pig-keeping helps, and one son contributes 7s. per week to the housekeeping The father usually does the family marketing as the daughter is inexperienced, and does not buy so economically. The family appears to be in quite comfortable circumstances. The father does not belong to a club. One son belongs to a good friendly society. The daughter insures her father.

1d. worth of milk is purchased every day ; amount obtained varies with the season.

The daughter cooks every day—sometimes twice a day.

EXPENDITURE.

January 7–13, 1906.   *January 14–20, 1906.*

	s.	d.		s.	d.
Milk	0	7	Sugar	0	6
Mutton chops	0	10	Pepper...	0	3
Pork	2	0	Butter	0	7½
Cheese	1	0	Cheese...	1	10
Fish	0	8	Bacon	2	0
Sugar	0	8	Fish	0	9
Tea	1	0	Loin of mutton and		
1 lb. butter	1	3	mutton chops ...	4	0
Ham	3	0	Milk	0	7
	11	0	Tea	1	7
			Bread	0	4½
				12	6
			Bread bill " bonfire		
			night " (Nov. 5th) to		
			Jan. 14th 1	0	0½
			£1 12	6½	

This budget was nominally kept by the daughter, but she was absent part of the time, so it is possible that strict accuracy was not observed in filling in from memory.   The father estimated that over 17s. worth of provisions were consumed during each week, though the amount purchased (omitting the bread bill) does not appear so large.

	Breakfast.	Dinner.	Tea.	Supper.
MONDAY ...	8.30 a.m.: Tea, milk, bread, boiled bacon.	None.	4 p.m.: Toast, bread and butter, honey.	8 p.m.: Potatoes, cabbage, boiled bacon
TUESDAY ...	8 a.m.: Tea, milk, bread and butter, boiled bacon.	12 o'clock. Potatoes, sprouts, roast mutton.	5 p.m.: Bread and butter, tea, milk.	9 p.m.: Bread and cheese, Father, brandy and water.
WEDNESDAY	8 a.m.: Tea, milk, bread, bacon.	1.30 p.m.: Mashed potato, beef, bread.	5 p.m.: Bread and butter, cake, tea, milk.	9 p.m.: Bread and cheese, cocoa, milk, mutton.
THURSDAY...	8.30 a.m.: Tea, milk, bread, bacon, egg.	1.30 p.m.: Potatoes, sprouts, bread, mutton.	5 p.m.: Tea, milk, butter, bread, jam.	9 p.m.: Bread and cheese, beef, pickled cabbage, cocoa, milk.
FRIDAY ...	8.45 a.m.: Tea, beef, marmalade, milk.	2 p.m.: Tea, bread and butter, milk.	None	Potatoes, stew, bread, soup.
SATURDAY...	8.15 am.: Tea milk, bread, bacon.	1.45 p.m.: Bacon fried potatoes, bread, tea, milk.	6 p.m.: Milk, tea, toast, honey.	9.30 p.m.: Bread and cheese, pickles, butter, cocoa, milk.
SUNDAY ...	8.45 a.m: Tea, milk, bread, fish, vinegar.	12.30 p.m.: Potatoes, sprouts, bread, pork.	4.30 p.m.: Tea milk, bread and butter, toast, jam.	9 p.m.: Bread and cheese, pickles, glass of beer.

MONDAY ...	8.30 a.m.: Tea, milk, bread, toast, bacon.	1 p.m.: Potatoes, cabbage, pork, bread.	5 p.m.: Tea, milk, bread and butter.	9.15 p.m.: Bread and cheese, glass of beer.
TUESDAY ...	8 a.m.: Tea, milk, bread, ham, fried potatoes.	12.30 p.m.: Bread and cheese, pickles, coffee, milk.	4.30 p.m.: Tea, milk, bread and butter, honey.	8 p.m.: Potatoes, cabbage, bread, ham.
WEDNESDAY	8 a.m.: Tea, milk, bread, bacon.	1 p.m.: Potatoes, cabbage, bread, ham.	4 p.m.: Tea, milk, bread and butter.	9.15 p.m.: Bread and cheese, beer.
THURSDAY..	8 a.m.: Coffee, milk, bread, fried bacon.	1 p.m.: Mashed Potatoes, bread, boiled bacon.	5.30 p.m.: Tea, milk, bread and butter, toast.	9 p.m.: Bread and cheese, butter, cocoa, milk.
FRIDAY ...	7.45 a.m.: Tea, milk, bread, butter, ham.	12.30 p.m.: Bread and cheese, butter, roast onions.	4.30 p.m.: Tea, milk, bread and butter.	7.30 p.m.: Potatoes, cabbage, bread, bacon.
SATURDAY...	8 p.m.: Tea, milk, bread and butter, toast.	1.30 p.m.: Potatoes, cabbage, bread, bacon.	6 p.m.: Milk, tea, bread and butter, honey.	9.15 p.m.: Cocoa, milk, bread, fish.
SUNDAY ...	8.45 a.m.: Tea, milk, bread and butter, fish	1 p.m.: Potatoes, sprouts, mutton, bread.	4.30 p.m.: Tea, milk, bread and butter, honey, cake.	9.15 p.m.: Bread and cheese, milk, cocoa, beer.

BUDGET No. 117.

Income ample.

Family : Father (retired artisan), mother (midwife), two sons (artisans, but when out of work, market-gardeners jointly with father), daughter (does housework and earns some money gloving).

Total income of family not given, and was, no doubt, uncertain, as sons were out of regular work, but the family were probably quite comfortably off.

The father and eldest brother belonged to a good club, but father was resigning his membership. The youngest brother was not in a club.

Rent for cottage, large garden, and common for fowls and pigs, £10 per annum.

Milk taken :—½d. one day, 1d. the next, delivered at door, and sometimes a 1d. worth from another farmer during the day. Average 1d. per day. Price 1¼d. per pint.

January, 1907. *First week.*

		s.	d.
Money received from son		8	0
„ „ „ „		8	0
„ „ „ daughter		5	0
		21	0

EXPENDITURE.

	s.	d.			s.	d.
2¼ lbs. 2 oz. beef ...	1	9	Forward		10	7
1½ lbs. mutton	1	1½	Soap		0	3
1½ lbs. cheese	1	0	Starch		0	2
1½ lbs. butter	1	10½	Blue		0	0¼
Bacon	0	10	Coal		2	6
3 lbs. sugar	0	6	12 small loaves... ...		2	3
¾ lb. tea	1	6	Flour		0	3
Cocoa	1	3	Rabbit		0	8
Oil	0	6				
Candles	0	3			16	8½
	10	7				

Second week.

	s.	d.
Beef...	3	3
Fresh herrings	0	6
Kippers and haddock	1	3
Extract of beef	1	3
Biscuits	0	6
1 lb. butter...	1	3
	8	0

The regular weekly expenses of the family, besides food, clothing, &c., were as follows :

	s.	d.
Doctor (club)	0	2½
Club	0	9½
Insurance...	0	4
*Rent (?)	0	6
Garden (?)	0	3
Coal (paid fortnightly)	1	10½

This budget was kept by the daughter, and probably the diary of meals is fairly accurate, though the list of things bought appears to be very incomplete, and there is some confusion in the statements as to expenses.

* Possibly these sums were put by weekly towards rent paid quarterly. The total rent cannot have been less than 3s 6d. to 7s. weekly, and the statement that it was £10 per annum is probably accurate.

	Breakfast.	Dinner.	Tea.	Supper.
SATURDAY ...	8 30 (No. of persons to breakfast, five): Bacon, bread and butter, tea. 9 30 (Father's breakfast): Cold mutton, cocoa.	1 o'clock: Bread and cheese, cocoa. Father's dinner: Bread and butter, boiled egg.	4 o'clock: Buttered toast, tea.	9 o'clock: Bread and cheese, quaker oats, cocoa.
SUNDAY ...	8.30 Bacon, toast, tea. 9.30 (Father's breakfast). Bread and butter, boiled egg, cocoa.	1 o'clock: Boiled rabbit, ham, potatoes, turnip, carrots, jam tart, tea.	4 o'clock · Bread and butter, toast, tea.	9 o'clock: Bread and cheese, pickles, cocoa, beer.
MONDAY ...	8.30 Bacon and eggs, tea, bread and butter. 9.30 (Father's breakfast): Cocoa, bread and butter, boiled eggs.	1 o'clock: Cold rabbit, ham, bread, cup of tea, jam tart. Father had cocoa, and one cup before dinner.	4 o'clock: Bread and butter, cake, tea.	9 o'clock: Bread and cheese, tea. Father had mutton chop, cocoa, and had two cups of cocoa in the afternoon.
TUESDAY ...	8.30 Bacon and fried potatoes, bread and butter, tea. 9.30 (Father's breakfast): Mutton, cocoa.	1 o'clock: Roast beef, Brusselssprouts, potatoes.	Bread and butter, jam, tea.	Bread and cheese, pickles, cocoa. Father had three cups of cocoa between meals to-day.
WEDNESDAY	8.30 Bacon and fried potatoes, tea 9.30 (Father's breakfast): Cold mutton, cocoa	1 o'clock. Cold beef, bread, tea Father had cold mutton, cocoa.	4 o'clock: Bread and butter, jam, tea.	9 o'clock: Bread and cheese, pickles, cocoa.
THURSDAY...	8.30 Bacon and fried bread, tea 9.30 (Father's breakfast): Bread and butter, boiled egg, cocoa.	1 o'clock: Potatoes and stew, beef, carrots, onions, tea, biscuits.	4 o'clock: Bread and butter, toast, tea.	9 o'clock · Bread and cheese, tea Father had cold mutton, cocoa
FRIDAY ...	8.30 Bacon and fried potatoes, tea. 9.30 (Father's breakfast): Bread and butter, boiled egg, cocoa.	1 o'clock: Fried bacon, eggs, bread, tea.	4 o'clock: Bread and butter, jam, tea.	9 o'clock: Rabbit, potatoes, turnip.

	8.30	1 o'clock	4 o'clock	9 o'clock
SATURDAY...	8.30: Fried bacon, bread and butter, tea. 9.30 (Father's breakfast): Bread and butter, boiled eggs, cocoa.	1 o'clock: Fried bacon, bread and cheese, cocoa. Father's dinner: A mutton chop, cocoa.	4 o'clock: Bread and butter, toast, tea.	9 o'clock: Fresh herrings, bread and cheese, beer, cocoa.
SUNDAY ...	8.30: Bacon, bread and butter, tea. 9.30 (Father's breakfast): Mutton chop, cocoa.	1 o'clock: Roast beef, Brussels sprouts, potatoes.	4 o'clock: Bread and butter, jam.	9 o'clock: Cold meat, cocoa.
MONDAY ...	8.30: Bacon, fried potatoes, tea. 9.30 (Father's breakfast): Cold mutton, cocoa.	1 o'clock: Potatoes, cold meat, tea.	4 o'clock: Bread and butter, toast, tea.	9 o'clock: Bread and cheese, beer, cocoa.
TUESDAY ...	8.30: Bacon, fried potatoes, tea. 9.30 (Father's breakfast): Cold mutton, cocoa.	1 o'clock: Potatoes, stew, beef, carrots, onions. 2 o'clock: Cup of tea.	4 o'clock: Bread and butter, jam, tea.	9 o'clock: Bread and cheese, cocoa.
WEDNESDAY	8.30: Buttered toast, tea. 9.30 (Father's breakfast): Cold mutton, cocoa.	1 o'clock: Bread, cold meat, pea-soup.	4 o'clock: Bread and butter, jam, tea.	9 o'clock: Bread and cheese, cocoa.
THURSDAY...	8.30: Bacon, fried potatoes, tea. 9.30 (Father's breakfast): Bread and butter, boiled eggs, cocoa.	Bread and butter, boiled eggs, tea.	4 o'clock: Buttered toast, tea.	9 o'clock: Bread and butter, kippers, tea.
FRIDAY ...	8.30: Bacon, fried potatoes, tea. 9.30 (Father's breakfast): Bread and butter, kipper, cocoa.	1 o'clock: Bread and butter, haddock, tea.	4 o'clock: Buttered toast, bread and butter, tea.	9 o'clock: Bread and cheese, cocoa.

Friendly Societies or Sick Benefit Clubs.

It will have been noticed in the family budgets that club money is often put aside every week. Nearly every working-class householder and most of the young men belong to a benefit society, to secure medical attendance and a weekly allowance in case of their own illness, and burial money on the death of themselves or their wives. Thirty-two families were specially questioned as to membership of clubs. In only three cases was it found that the head or principal male wage-earner of the family had no club. The first case was that of a man in receipt of a good pension, who therefore did not need it ; the second was a shoemaker, his life being insured by his daughter. The sons of these two men belonged to clubs. The third exception was a man who for some reason in the history of his character or health was refused admittance to the better clubs, and thought the local public-house clubs not worth joining.

In two cases one or more sons living at home with their parents had not joined a club, though their fathers belonged to one. In most families all adult males belonged to a friendly society. These thirty-two families give a total of 39 men in clubs and 7 men without a club. The 32 householders or principal male wage-earners were 18 labourers, 7 artisans, 4 market gardeners, 1 shopkeeper, 1 brickmaker (on own account), and 1 shoemaker.

A more complete census would probably give much the same results, it being a rare thing to find a Corsley man who does not belong to a sick benefit society.

For more than a century village clubs have existed in Corsley, and these were in a thriving condition at the middle of the nineteenth century. During the last fifteen years branches of the Ancient Shepherds and of the Wilts Working Men's Conservative Benefit Society have been established here ; and the old local dividing clubs, being unrenewed by young blood, have fallen more or less into decay. The oldest of these clubs, which lingered on into the twentieth century, was the Corsley Walking Club, broken up in June, 1905.[1] If, as alleged, this club had been founded 107 years before, it was not the first to exist in Corsley.[2] It derived its name from the practice of the members walking round the parish in procession at Whitsuntide, headed by their banner and with a band. Forty years ago there would be 200 men in the procession. They first attended service at the church, then they walked to Corsley House, proceeding thence to Corsley Heath, where the fair was still held at this time. They dined at the public-house and then marched to Lane End and back, after which they were supposed to spend £1 at the public-house. The club-room was built on to the house opposite the Cross Keys Inn, with a separate outside stairway. The club box was stolen or broken into once or twice, and some fifty years ago the members purchased a strong one, bearing the date of 1817, and an inscription stating that it was the property of the Broad and Narrow Weavers' Society, this Society in connection with Shepherds' cloth mills at Frome being broken up at that time.

In about the year 1855 the membership was 230, the practice of belonging to a club being evidently fairly general even in those days of low wages. In 1905, when the club was broken up, only about twelve members remained, most of them being aged men, some of whom were forced to come upon the

---

[1] See *Warminster and Westbury Journal*, June 17, 1905.
[2] See MS. Corsley Parish Accounts, April, 1789.

parish in consequence. About 1 os. per head remained to be divided up.

The Corsley Gathering Club, another of the old dividing societies, is still in existence, having about 22 members in the winter of 1905-6. It provides medical attendance and an allowance for twelve weeks in sickness ; 1s. is paid on the death of a member by each of the others to the widow. The money is divided up every three years. Most of the members of this club are old men.

The Corsley Mutual Provident Society, or Baptists' Club, founded in 1891, is on much the same lines. It throve at first, but has been reduced lately by the competition of the branches of larger clubs lately established in Corsley. In the winter of 1905-6 it had a membership of 22.

Another old parish club, the Working Men's Benefit Society, meets at the "Three Horse Shoes," Chapmanslade. Particulars of membership have not been ascertained.

This concludes the list of the local parish clubs, so far as can be discovered, though it is not beyond the bounds of possibility that another similar institution may linger in some nook or corner of the parish.

We now come to the new clubs, on county or national basis and established on sound financial principles. The first of these to set up a branch in Corsley was the Loyal Order of Ancient Shepherds, established here in 1893. This branch now has 23 adult and 15 juvenile members resident in Corsley. It aims at providing for its members in sickness and death, and paying old age pensions to those who live to require them.[1] The other new club is the Wiltshire Working Men's Conservative

[1] See manifesto of the Society.

Benefit Society, a non-political club. The Corsley branch was started in 1900. The Society aims at providing for members in sickness and death, and acts as a savings fund. In December, 1905, it had 40 adult members, 3 being women, and 2 juveniles. Only the members of these branch clubs actually residing in Corsley have been enumerated. They also have members residing in other parishes.

The hundred or more persons who constitute the membership of these various clubs by no means include all the men who belong to a friendly society. Many Corsley men belong to the Hearts of Oak, the Oddfellows, and the Foresters, these having no local branch in the parish. Most of the men who have migrated from some other parish or district belong to the branch of some club in the locality from which they have come. The exact number belonging to clubs is therefore unknown, but undoubtedly a large estimate should be allowed for members of clubs or branches outside Corsley. Out of 30 men who gave particulars of the club or branch they belonged to, 21 belonged to a Corsley club or branch, 9 to clubs or branches not in Corsley. These were : Hearts of Oak, 1 ; Foresters, 3 ; Oddfellows, 3 ; Warminster branch of Shepherds, 1 ; the local club of a neighbouring parish, 1. These figures are not, however, sufficient for any statistical conclusions.

Some of the people of Corsley insure themselves, their children, or their parents, but the practice is not very general and amount of insurance is usually very small.

Twenty-three children belonged to the Corsley School Savings Bank in January, 1906, some of whom brought their money regularly, some irregularly. The younger children usually draw it out at intervals. The elder girls keep it in till they leave school, when, no doubt, it helps to provide a clothing outfit for going out to service.

Medical Attendance.

Most of the men of Corsley are provided with medical attendance and medicines free by their clubs. Twenty-seven families of labourers, artisans, and market gardeners and women householders, taken at random, were questioned as to medical attendance in case of illness of the women or children.   Seven of these, including three laundresses and four families of labourers, belonged to the Medical Club of a Warminster doctor, who, for the payment of 4s. 4d. a year per head for each adult and less for a child, attends in case of illness and provides medicines free.   All members of the Medical Club spoke of the kindness and attention which they receive from their doctor.

Four widows were attended and received medicines free from the parish doctor.   One of these had belonged to his club, but, on becoming a widow was told that she was no longer to pay a subscription. The only extra expense to members of the Medical Club, and the only charge to those receiving attention free, is any incurred in sending for medicines.

The remaining families were 7 labourers, 3 artisans, and 4 women (laundress, baker, charwoman, and needlewoman with a small property).   In these cases the women and children of the family made no provision for medical attendance, but when requiring it paid the usual doctor's fees ; 5s. per visit and medicines extra appears to be the customary charge when a doctor is sent for specially, he usually having to drive three or four miles to see a patient in Corsley.

Less is charged when the patient attends at the doctor's house. One woman owed £12 after her mother's illness and death. A man had to pay 13s. for three visits and medicine in the illness of his wife.

There are many doctors in Frome and Warminster who attend the poor. They usually allow some time to elapse before asking for settlement of their accounts, and these appear to be often paid in instalments.

In the summer of 1906 it became possible, by the establishment of the Cley Hill Nursing Association, for the people of Corsley to make provision for good nursing in case of sickness. By paying an annual subscription, beginning at 2s. for a labourer, 3s. for an artisan, and rising to 10s. for a large farmer, subscribers are provided with a trained nurse at the same rate per week during sickness. Much of the nursing is still done by local midwives, of whom some account has been given in the section on Women's Work.

CHAPTER XV

ANCESTRY AND CHILDREN OF CORSLEY

THE reader, if he refers to the form of inquiry given on p. 99, will see that information was asked from every householder as to the birthplace and occupation of himself, his father, and his two grandfathers, his wife's birthplace, the total number of children born to him, distinguishing those still living from those since dead, and finally the present place of abode of his living children. Particulars as to the occupations of all his children over school age were also noted on the forms.

In the present chapter the information thus collected is analysed. In the great majority of cases information was duly obtained respecting the man, his wife, and children. In a fair number the birthplace and occupation of the father, and sometimes one grandfather, was also stated, and in a comparatively few instances particulars for father and both grandfathers were remembered, and the form fully filled up.

All this information is, of course, liable to natural errors from inaccuracy of memory, and from the tendency which many people have to magnify the social position of their family, especially that of their ancestors. The history of some of the present inhabitants shows it to be a common thing for a man to follow many occupations in succession or simultaneously, and in such a case his descendant naturally elects to think of, and dwell on, that one which affords him the most satisfaction ; thus, while in a few instances a man has stated that his father started as a labourer, and after a time became a shop-keeper, or acquired a small farm, the majority in such a case have probably simply returned their ancestor as shopkeeper or farmer ; and, while some have stated that the father or grandfather " kept a few cows," which suggests that this was only one of two or more occupations, others, descendants of such small holders, have no doubt set down " farmer " without qualification.

The result of this is that the number of farmers among the ancestry is probably exaggeratedly large— or at least many of the farms were extremely small, and the farming rather a bye-industry than a main occupation.

Again, in tabulating results, it has usually been necessary, where two or more occupations are set down for one person, to select one of these. In such cases the occupation which seemed the more im-portant has been chosen, so that throughout the tendency is in the direction of calling a man an independent worker, or employer, rather than a wage-earner, when, in fact, simultaneously or in succession he has been both.

With regard to the children, there are a few omissions, and perhaps also some mis-statements. It is likely that some of the children who died in infancy were omitted, and though in nearly all cases the parents appear to have been very frank in giving information, one or two in lunatic asylums or in prison may have been left out. Memory also some-times failed with regard to the children. One man, for instance, with a long family, after consulting his wife as to the total number, was unable for some

18

time to recall the names and account for them all. It was often necessary to consult the family Bible before a list of the children could be made out, and where this was not kept posted up, sometimes neither wife nor husband could remember the age or year of birth of their children. In stating occupations of children the present occupation only is given, and no account is therefore taken of the fact that some of the men residing here have previously served in the Army. While the following figures do not therefore claim perfect accuracy, they are, taken altogether, a fairly good indication of the origin and migrations of the people, and the degree in which children tend to follow the occupations of their parents among the inhabitants of Corsley.

Average Size of Families in Corsley.

We have particulars of the children born, and now living or dead, in 195 out of the 220 households of Corsley.

No papers were filled up for the gentlemen's houses, the clergyman, Congregational minister, nor schoolmaster ; the police-constable has also been omitted in this classification ; particulars are missing for two or three farmers, and one artisan and publican ; and a few other papers were not filled up owing to illness or absence.

The 195 householders are of all ages, and some are sons of other householders, and thus come twice into the classification as both parents and children.

The total number of children stated to have been born to these 195 householders is 742, and of these 660 are still living and 92 dead. Many of the latter died in middle age, being children of the oldest living inhabitants of Corsley.

The following is a summary of those born to householders of various occupations :

Occupation	No for which Particulars	No unmarried	No married without Children	No with Children	Total No Children born.	No. still living.	No dead	Average No of Children born per Family where any.	Percentage of Total dead
Farmers	28	3	8	17	68	65	3	4	4·6
Market gardeners and marketers ...	9	—	2	7	47	46	1	6·7	2·1
Labourers	32	—	5	27	126	112	24	4·6	21·4
Carters	12	—	2	10	53	50	3	5·3	6·0
Dairymen or cowmen	8	—	1	7	37	34	3	5·3	8·8
Miscellaneous agricultural ...	8	—	1	7	33	27	6	4·7	22·2
Retired labourers, &c.	9	—	2	7	40	31	9	5·7	29·0
Head gardeners, coachmen, groom-gardeners	7	—	1	6	27	24	3	4·5	12·5
Keepers, &c.	3	—	—	3	28	27	1	9·3	3·7
Manual workers residing in Corsley, but working elsewhere ...	3	—	1	2	14	9	5	7·0	55·5
Miscellaneous, residing in Corsley, retired from work elsewhere ...	8	1	2	5	18	15	3	3·6	20·0
Tradesmen and dealers	5	—	—	5	28	23	5	5·6	21·7
Independent workers (brickmaker, saddler, and 2 shoemakers)	4	—	2	2	21	21	—	10·5	0·0
Artisans	22	—	2	20	79	70	9	4·0	8·86
Women householders	37	7	3	27	123	106	17	4·5	16·0
	195	11	32	142	742	660	92	5·2	12·3

In the following table the last two columns of the preceding are arranged in order according to the average number of births per family to each occupation.

	Average No of Children born per family, where any	Percentage of Total dead.
Miscellaneous, retired from work, not in Corsley	[1] 3·6	[2] 20·0
Farmers	4·0	4·6
Artisans	4·0	8·86
Servants (head gardeners, coachmen, grooms)	4·5	12·5
Women householders ...	4·5	[2] 16·0
Labourers	4 6	21·4
Miscellaneous—agriculture ...	4·7	22·2
Carters	5·3	6·0
Dairymen or cowmen... ...	5·3	8 8
Tradesmen and dealers ...	5 6	21·7
Retired labourers	5·7	[2] 29·0
Market gardeners	6·7	2·1
Persons working elsewhere ...	7·0	55·5
Keepers	9·3	3 7
Independent workers	10·5	0·0

All the 195 householders with the exception of 4 farmers, one being retired from another parish, and 7 women are, or have been, married. One or two other unmarried male householders are omitted, since particulars were not obtained. A large proportion of the married farmers are childless, because the class includes several labourers who, having no children, were able to save sufficient capital to take a small farm. The average number of children born in each farmer's family is small, being 4, but the number of these surviving is large, only 4 6 per cent. having since died, though some middle-aged and a few old

---

[1] Possibly the small number of children returned for this group is due to some of the forms being incompletely filled up.

[2] These groups contain many old persons and therefore have an abnormally large percentage dead.

people are included in the class. Among the artisans there are only two childless couples. The average number of births per family is 4, like that of farmers, and the percentage of deaths is also not large. Gardeners and coachmen have slightly larger families and also more deaths. But when we come to labourers and miscellaneous agricultural workers, we find only a slightly larger average of births per family, but a greatly increased number of deaths, and since the retired labourers, including most of the aged, are given separately this indicates an unnecessarily high infantile mortality rate and a wastage of human life. Carters and dairymen show a higher percentage of births and a low rate of deaths, the latter being probably mainly due to a lower average age among carters and cowmen than among labourers ; it might also be partly the result of the higher rate of wages among the former, and facilities for obtaining milk among the latter, producing a lower death rate for the young children.

But the most remarkable fact that comes out of these figures is the high number of births and very small proportion of deaths in the seven market gardeners' families, there being 6.7, as compared with 4.0 children born on the average, and less than half as many dying as in the farmers' families, while there are 6.7 as compared with 4.6 born, and only about one-tenth as many dying as in labourers' families.

It must be borne in mind that the number of families in most of these groups is too small to afford reliable statistical results, since one or two exceptional cases are sufficient to alter the whole, and these figures must only be taken for what they are worth. The average number of children born per family to the total of 142 families with children is 5.2.

Birthplace and Migrations of Corsley People.

Some particulars as to birthplace have been obtained from 198 householders, and the results are given in a table. Out of 198 householders, including 36 women, 107 were born in Corsley and 58 in the neighbourhood, while 33, or 16.6 per cent., were born more than twenty miles from the parish.[1] Particulars are given of 167 grandfathers. Of these, 76 were born in Corsley, 63 in the neighbourhood, and 28, or 16.6, not in the neighbourhood. Presumably a large proportion of those, either grandfathers or fathers, of whom their descendants could tell nothing, were of Corsley descent, migration being an event which would probably be remembered in the family. Out of 159 fathers of whom particulars were given, 90 were Corsley born, and 45 were born in the neighbourhood, while 24, or nearly 15.1 per cent. were strangers.

Of the male householders 12 gave no particulars as to the birthplace of their wives, a few of them being unmarried. We have particulars therefore respecting the wives of 150 ; 65 had married women of Corsley birth, 50 had married wives from the neighbourhood, and 35, or 23.3 per cent., had married strangers. Some of the men, not of Corsley birth, residing here are married to women born in the parish, there being frequently a family connection which induced persons born elsewhere to migrate here.

The 198 householders, including widows, have 456 living sons and daughters over school age. Of these,

[1] Known places within a radius of twenty miles have been included as "near Corsley," but as many of the localities were unknown these may have been wrongly grouped ; the error in this case will generally be in the direction of making too many "strangers."

200 are residing in Corsley and 256 are residing elsewhere. The latter include many who, though their parents are now inhabitants of Corsley, were born before they came here, and who therefore may never have been in the parish. We shall see presently what proportion of males and females have left the place, and what kind of occupations they are following.

GRANDFATHERS				FATHERS.				PRESENT
Born in Corsley	Born near Corsley	Not born in Neighbourhood.	Unstated	Born in Corsley.	Born near Corsley.	Not born in Neighbourhood	Unstated.	Occupation.
9	21	5	21	11	9	3	5	Farmers... ...
6	2	—	10	7	—	1	1	Market gardeners and marketers...
10	7	4	43	22	5	2	3	Labourers ...
7	4	—	13	7	4	—	1	Carters ... ...
—	2	3	11	1	4	2	1	Dairymen or cowmen .. ...
—	2	4	10	1	2	2	3	Miscellaneous agricultural ...
5	4	—	9	5	3	—	1	Retired labourers...
2	3	—	9	2	2	1	2	Head-gardeners, coachman, grooms, groom-gardeners..
—	—	—	6	—	1	2	—	Keepers, &c. ...
2	—	—	8	1	3	—	1	Manual workers residing in Corsley, but working outside parish ...
7	5	2	4	5	2	1	1	Miscellaneous residing in Corsley —retired from work outside parish... ...
4	1	—	5	3	—	—	2	Tradesmen and dealers ...
2	—	2	6	2	1	2	—	Independent workers (brickmaker, saddler, naturalist, 2 shoemakers) ...
7	4	5	28	9	3	7	3	Artisans... ...
14	8	3	47	14	6	1	15	Women householders ...
76	63	28	230	90	45	24	39	

	HOUSEHOLDERS.				WIVES.				ADULT CHILDREN	
Total Number.	Born in Corsley	Born near Corsley	Not born in Neighbourhood	Unstated	Born in Corsley	Born near Corsley	Not born in Neighbourhood	Unstated, or Man not married	Residing in Corsley.	Migrated elsewhere
28	14	10	4	—	5	11	3	9	24	16
9	7	2	—	—	7	2	—	—	16	20
32	24	6	2	—	21	7	4	—	33	34
12	7	5	—	—	6	5	1	—	12	9
8	2	4	2	—	3	4	1	—	5	13
8	1	2	5	—	1	3	4	—	5	11
9	6	2	1	—	6	2	—	1	12	16
7	2	2	3	—	—	2	5	—	5	13
3	—	1	2	—	—	1	2	—	3	9
5	3	2	—	—	1	3	1	—	3	2
9	5	3	1	—	2	2	3	2	3	12
5	3	1	—	1	5	—	—	—	10	12
5	2	1	2	—	1	2	2	—	9	10
22	9	6	7	—	7	6	9	—	16	22
36	21	11	4	—	—	—	—	—	44	57
198	107	58	33	1	65	50	35	12	200	256

are : 1 dairyman and 2 labourers.   The females are : 5 married and 1 at-home, an invalid.

Employed in Agriculture with higher Wages.—There are 4 men, 2 being dairymen, 1 a woodman, and 1 a thatcher, who receive higher wages or rates of payment than other agricultural workers.   These have given particulars of 7 grandfathers, viz.: 3 farmers, 1 woodman, 1 thatcher and innkeeper, 1 weaver and 1 woodman, 1 "independent." Their fathers were : 1 dairyman, 1 woodman, 1 thatcher, and 1 worker in Frome iron-works.

These 4 families have 5 male and 11 female children over school age.   The occupations of the males are: 1 gardener, 1 soldier, 1 sailor, 1 apprentice in outfitter's shop, and 1 clerk.   The females are : 2 married, 2 at home (one learning dressmaking), and 7 in service.

Miscellaneous Agricultural.—There are 8 miscellaneous agricultural workers for whom we have particulars.   These give the occupation of 3 grandfathers as 1 gardener, 1 carpenter, and 1 dyer.   The fathers of 5 were 2 labourers, 1 woodman, 1 timber-merchant and 1 market gardener.

There are among these 8 families 4 male and 5 female children over school age.   The occupations of the males are : 1 farmer in America, 1 coal-merchant, 1 in police-force, 1 cowman.   The females are: 2 married, 2 at home, 1 in domestic service.

Gamekeepers.—There are 3 gamekeepers or keepers' labourers ; 1 of these, however, was out of work at the time the inquiry was made.   The fathers of these 3 men were : 1 gamekeeper, 1 dairyman, and 1 labourer.

They have 4 male and 7 female children over school age.   The occupations of the males are : 1 gamekeeper, 2 labourers, 1 baker's assistant.   The 7 females are: 2 married, 4 in service, and 1 living with a sister.

Retired Labourers.—We have particulars for 9 retired labourers, including a mole-catcher, a stone-breaker and two who became respectively a small farmer and a market gardener.   These give the occupations of 7 grandfathers as 5 labourers (two with a query), 1 weaver, and 1 who rented the limekiln on Cley Hill.   The fathers of 8 were : 3 labourers, 1 shepherd, 1 sawyer, 1 worker at limekiln, 1 market gardener, and 1 soldier.

Among the families of these 9 labourers are 13 male and 14 female grown-up children still living.   The occupations of the males are very various, viz.: 1 labourer, 1 market gardener, 1 market gardener and blacksmith, 1 gamekeeper, 1 brickmaker, 1 worker in malthouse, 1 coal-miner, 1 engine-driver, 1 mason, 1 plumber, 1 messenger in country town, 1 doing odd jobs, 1 unknown. The 14 females are : 9 married, 2 living at home (1 a laundress), 3 unstated.

Head Gardeners, Coachmen, and Grooms.—We have particulars for 6 head gardeners, coachmen, grooms, or groom-gardeners. Four grandfathers of these men were : 1 employed in iron-works at Frome, 1 in dye-works, 1 a tailor, 1 a groom. The fathers of 5 were : 1 foreman in woollen factory, 1 farmer, 1 shoemaker, 1 labourer or thatcher, 1 labourer.

There are among these 6 families 12 male and 5 female children over school age. The occupations of the males are : 1 gardener, 1 market gardener, 1 labourer, 1 in motor works, 2 on railway, 2 in glove factory, 1 grocer, 1 grocer's assistant, 1 caretaker, 1 wheel-wright's apprentice. The females are : 2 married, 1 at home, 2 in domestic service.

Miscellaneous working elsewhere.—There are 5 miscellaneous manual workers employed outside the parish. Six grandfathers of these men were · 3 labourers, 2 carters, 1 shepherd. Their fathers were : 3 labourers, 1 carpenter and odd man, 1 platelayer G. W. R.

One family has 2 male, another 3 female children over school age. The occupations of the males are : 1 gardener and 1 labourer. The 3 females are in domestic service.

Miscellaneous retired from Work elsewhere.—There are particulars for 8 men who are retired and living in Corsley, having worked elsewhere. The occupations which were followed by these men are 1 farmer, 1 baker and grocer, 1 house decorator, 1 engineer and publican, 2 factory workers, 1 policeman, 1 signalman. They state the occupations of 11 grandfathers to have been . 4 farmers, 1 market gardener, 1 pig-butcher, 1 "business," 2 weavers, 2 labourers. The fathers of 7 were . 2 farmers and 1 who helped his sister with her farm, 1 baker and grocer, 1 card-spinner in factory, 1 lime-burner, 1 labourer.

The occupations of children are in one case unstated. Among the remaining families are 6 male and 8 female children still living. The occupations of males are ; 3 colliers, 1 quarrier, 1 assistant in co-operative warehouse, 1 in post-office. The 8 females are all married. Probably none of the sons and daughters of this group were born or brought up in Corsley.

Tradesmen and Dealers.—There are particulars for 5 tradesmen or dealers, including a builder and wheelwright, a grocer and baker, a coal and timber merchant, a shopkeeper and a plumber and builder, who gives no particulars of ancestry. The tradesmen return 4 grandfathers as 1 butcher, 1 woodman, 1 gardener, and

1 labourer. The fathers of 4 were; 1 gardener, 1 grocer and baker, 1 labourer, and 1 blacksmith.

The 5 families have 9 male and 12 female children over school age. The occupations of the males are: 1 plumber, 1 helping father, 1 farmer, 1 assistant schoolmaster, 3 coachmen, 1 carter, 1 unstated. The females are: 8 married, 2 at home, 2 keeping shop, 1 unstated.

Independent Workers and Miscellaneous.—There are particulars for 8 families, 5 being independent workers, viz : 1 brickmaker on own account, 1 saddler, 1 naturalist or bird-stuffer, 2 shoemakers, and 3 miscellaneous, viz : 1 assistant clerk of works, 1 police-constable, 1 brickmaker and small farmer. These return 7 grandfathers as 1 coal-hauler, 1 head gamekeeper, 1 brick and tile maker, 1 mason and builder, 1 shoemaker, 1 shepherd, and 1 soldier. The fathers of 6 were : 1 brick and tile maker, 1 brickmaker, 1 shoemaker, 1 woodman and engine-driver, 2 labourers.

One of these men has not stated what his children are doing. The 7 families have 14 male and 16 female grown-up children. The occupations of the males are : 3 brickmakers, helping father, 1 collier, 1 plumber, 1 painter, 1 gasfitter, 1 engine-fitter, 1 estate carpenter, 1 carter, 4 labourers. The females are : 4 married, 5 at home, including one who goes out as a daily servant, and 7 in domestic service.

Artisans.—We have particulars for 21 artisans. These give information about 18 grandfathers, whose occupations were : 1 farmer, 1 kept a cow or two, 1 rented limekiln, 1 publican, 2 blacksmiths, 1 sawyer, 1 plasterer and tiler, 2 boot or shoemakers, 1 butcher, 1 dyer, 1 carter, 1 cowman, 1 woodman, 2 labourers, 1 emigrated to America. The fathers of 19 were as follows : 2 blacksmiths, 1 mason, 1 plasterer and tiler, 2 carpenters, 2 wheelwrights, 2 sawyers, 1 shoemaker, 1 butcher, 1 publican, 1 woodman and afterwards farmer, 2 carters, 1 cowman, 2 labourers.

Among the 21 families are 20 male and 17 female children over school age. The occupations of the males are · 2 carpenters, 1 carpenter-builder, 1 blacksmith, 1 painter, 1 bricklayer, 1 apprentice painting, 2 engineers, 1 working in malthouse, 1 coachman, 1 groom, 1 baker, 1 carter, 6 labourers. The females are . 5 married, 2 at home, including a laundry-worker and an imbecile, 8 in domestic service.

Women Householders.—The remaining section, "Women Householders," contains the widows and children of so miscellaneous an assortment of workers that it is not worth while to analyse here the occupations pursued by their children, sufficient indication of these being given by the table on p. 272.

The following is a summary of occupations pursued by the children of male householders in Corsley, which may be compared with those of their fathers in Chapter X. ; 166 male householders are included in this inquiry, but a large number have no adult children.

OCCUPATIONS OF SONS OF MALE HOUSEHOLDERS OF CORSLEY.

Farmers	12[1]
Market gardeners	3
Labourers, inclusive	55[2]
Gardeners, coachmen, and grooms	14
Tradesmen or tradesmen's assistants	14[3]
Artisans	26[4]
Engineers	8[5]
Railway clerks	3
Miners	10[6]
Soldiers	3
Sailors	2
Abroad or emigrated	2
Domestic service	2
Assistant-schoolmaster	1
Clerk	1
Post-office	1
School attendance officer	1
Working in malthouse	2
Glove factory	2
Police force	1
Barman	1
Wood-carver	1
Caretaker	1
Messenger, country town	1
Odd jobs	1
Out of work	2
Unknown or unstated	2
Total	172

[1] Including several sons helping their fathers.

[2] This includes all the agricultural employments.

[3] Including three timber-hauliers, one helping father, one coal-merchant, one grocer, one baker, the rest being assistants.

[4] Including three brickmakers helping their father and two apprentices.

[5] These are either in motor or cycle works, or motor or engine drivers.

[6] Including colliers, quarriers, miners, and employees in iron-works.

OCCUPATIONS OF DAUGHTERS OF MALE HOUSEHOLDERS
OF CORSLEY.

Married	74
Living at home	42[1]
In domestic service	66
Barmaid	1
Unstated	4
Total	187

The following is a summary of the occupations of
the children of 36 women householders.

OCCUPATIONS OF SONS OF WOMEN HOUSEHOLDERS OF CORSLEY.

Farmers	3
Market gardeners	3[2]
Labourers	17
Gardeners, coachmen, and grooms	5
Artisans	7
Miners	1
Soldiers	2
Abroad or emigrated	3
Odd man	1
Signalman	1
Inspector of water-works	1
Labourer, gas-works	1
Malting	3
	48

OCCUPATIONS OF DAUGHTERS OF WOMEN HOUSEHOLDERS OF
CORSLEY.

Married	25
Domestic service	16
At home	11
Shop-assistant	1
	53

[1] Ten of these follow some occupation, such as dressmaking or
laundry-work.

[2] One of these is helping his mother.

This gives a total of 460 adult children from 202 families, 4 being included which were omitted from the table of ancestry on p. 265.

That table shows that of 456 children over school age and still living, born to 198 of the householders of Corsley, 200 are now residing in the parish, while 256 are living elsewhere. Having viewed in detail the occupations which these persons are following, it will be interesting to consider more generally what becomes of Corsley's sons and daughters. From the appended table on p. 264 it will be seen that more than half the 219 males have remained in the parish, 121 being still in Corsley, while 98 have left. These 121 are many of them married and themselves householders. Of the 98 who have left, 51, or about half, are living in a town, mining districts and moderate-sized market towns being both included. 34 have migrated to other country districts, and are chiefly working in agriculture, or in the service of country gentlemen. 7 are in the Army or Navy, and it may be noted that many of the present residents of Corsley have previously passed some period in the Army. 6 are abroad or in the Colonies. It will be noticed that it is the sons of people of a higher social status than that of agricultural labourer who chiefly find their way to the towns ; gentlemen's servants, artisans, and market gardeners furnishing a larger proportion than the labourers, carters, and cowmen. The sons of these latter, when they leave the parish, migrate more to other country districts, or enlist in the Army. Of the 237 females, only 79 remain in Corsley, while 158 are residing elsewhere. About 26 of those still living in Corsley are married, while over 70 of those living elsewhere in town or country are married. 53 are living at home, many of these being laundresses, dressmakers, or glovers.

19

82 are in domestic service, ranging from " generals "
to housekeepers in large houses. Most Corsley girls
on leaving school go out as general servant or nurse-
maid to a farmer's wife, or to a tradesman in one of
the neighbouring small towns. After a year or two
they usually migrate to the larger towns, still as
general servants, or else they enter a gentleman's
house as scullery-maid or between-girl. Sooner or
later the majority find their way into a middle or
upper class household, and they remain in domestic
service until they marry. It will be seen from the
table that the exodus of females is much greater
than that of males, there being exceedingly few
well-paid occupations available for women in the
parish, as was shown in the section on Women's
Work (pp. 124—130).

The following table shows the migrations of the
adult children belonging to the 198 households re-
referred to in the table of ancestry on p. 264.

MIGRATION OF CHILDREN OVER SCHOOL AGE.

Occupation of Father	Adult Children residing in Corsley.		Adult Children migrated to a Town[1]		Adult Children migrated to other Parts of Country		In Army or Navy.	Abroad, or emigrated.	
	M	F	M.	F.	M.	F.		M.	F
Farmers	12	12	4	4	2	5	—	1	—
Market gardeners, or marketers	11	5	5	6	2	6	—	—	1
Labourers	22	11	4	14	6	7	3	—	—
Carters	12	—	—	6	1	2	—	—	—
Dairymen or cowmen	2	3	1	7	2	2	1	—	—
Miscellaneous agricultural	2	3	—	6	1	2	1	—	1
Retired labourers	7	5	5	9	1	—	—	1[2]	—
Head gardeners, coachmen, grooms	4	1	6	2	2	2	—	1	—
Keepers, &c.	2	1	—	7	2	—	—	—	—
Miscellaneous, working outside parish	2	1	—	2	—	—	—	—	—
Miscellaneous, retired from work, not in Corsley	—	3	6	6	—	—	—	—	—
Tradesmen and dealers	5	5	—	3	4	5	—	—	—
Independent workers (brickmaker, saddler, shoemaker)	6	3	—	2	2	6	—	—	—
Artisans	9	7	7	3	4	8	—	—	—
Women-householders	25	19	13	24	5	10	2	3	—
	121	79	51	101	34	55	7	6	2

[1] Under the heading of Town are included market towns and mining districts as well as the Metropolis and other large cities.

[2] Unknown

CHAPTER XVI

SOCIAL LIFE IN CORSLEY

SOCIAL life in Corsley centres round the family or household, round clubs for games and recreation, and the public-houses, and round the churches or chapels of the various religious denominations. Family life has already been considered from an economic point of view ; we may now regard it in its purely social aspect, together with various forms of recreation, and with the religious life of the community.

In a scattered parish, such as Corsley, where many of the houses are situated in lonely lanes, the family is naturally inclined to live a more isolated life than in villages where even on a dark winter's night the street forms a sociable meeting-place ; and although Corsley is well provided with public-houses—and it cannot be said that these are unattended—yet most of the married men prefer to have their cask of beer at home, taking a glass after supper with their wives, rather than turn out habitually into the dark muddy lanes which have to be traversed before they reach the haunts of men.

The reading-room at Corsley Heath is very little frequented except by those living in its near vicinity. The total number of members in the winter of 1905-6 was thirty.

When inquiries as to the population were being

made during the winter of 1905-6, many of the visits
were paid between 6 and 7.30 p.m. At this time
the whole family would almost invariably be found
at home, grouped round the fire, or where there
were children they might be seated round the table
playing some game. At Christmas-time not uncom-
monly a small Christmas-tree for the children would
be standing in the corner of the room. A large
proportion of the young people of Corsley quit the
parish on leaving school ; but the young men who
remain very frequently take up some hobby, such
as fretwork, photography, or music, with which they
employ their evenings quite happily at home. The
few young girls who stay with their parents usually
complain that it is " dull," especially in the winter,
when they often go out very little. These remarks
naturally apply more to the smaller hamlets of
Corsley than to Chapmanslade, where a real village
exists, with a somewhat different type of social life,
and where the parishioners of Corsley join with those
of Westbury, on the other side of the way, in getting
up concerts, dances, and other festivities during the
winter months. Music is the fashion here, too, and
Chapmanslade has its own brass band, composed of
local musicians.

But even in other parts of Corsley a few occasions
for social gathering occur in the course of the winter.
Of late years most successful and popular dramatic
entertainments have been given at the school by the
children of the parish, under the tuition of the master
and mistress. Occasionally, too, a concert is got up
at the reading-room. Such entertainments are always
largely attended.

Evening services at the chapels take out some of
the older people, and there is probably a little visiting of each other in the evening among the more
well-to-do.

But while part of the people appear to be almost puritanical in their lives, it must be admitted that there are some families who regularly frequent the public-house. It is not the custom for sons living at home to pay more than 7s. or 8s. per week to their parents, unless in exceptional cases. A few sons living with parents consequently get into the habit of working only part time, and thus take to loafing ways, working on odd jobs not more than two or three days a week, much to the distress of the parents. Those young men who, working regularly, occupy their leisure with performance on a musical instrument, or some such hobby, usually save a good deal of money. Others, though spending a considerable part of their earnings on beer and tobacco, yet manage to save something. A remaining section spend all they get on food and drink, or dissipation in the neighbouring towns, to the neglect sometimes of their recognised liabilities to relatives. These people, mostly unmarried men, described by a native of Corsley as " sillylike," thinking, she says, of nothing but what they eat and drink, and going to the public-house in the evening for a " lark," form the chief clientele of the public-houses. It was not found possible to ascertain the amount of beer consumed in Corsley, for while some keepers of public-houses were good enough to furnish particulars, others declined to do so, and a large amount of beer is also taken direct from the brewers by the cottagers and others. It cannot, however, be doubted that the average consumption per head is somewhat large. At Christmas-time, 1905, notes were made of persons in the six public-houses of Corsley, including one situated a few yards outside the parish, with the following results :

		December 25th.		Present.
No. 1	...	9 p.m.	...	8 men, 2 wives.
No. 2	...	9.30 p.m.	...	11 men, 4 strange women. Singing.
No. 3	...	9.50 p.m.	...	13 men, 1 wife, also 10 strangers, male and female. Gramaphone and singing.

		December 26th.		
No. 1	...	7.30 p.m.	...	15 men.
No. 2	...	8 p.m.	...	17 men.
No 3	...	8 30 p.m.	...	17 men, with 5 wives or daughters, 4 strangers, male and female. Gramaphone.

		December 27th		
No. 1	...	9 p.m.	...	10 men.
No. 2	...	10 p.m.	...	5 men, one with wife and daughter from Frome.
No. 3	...	9.30 p.m.	...	14 men. Concertina and tambourine playing.
No. 4	...	8.15 p.m.	...	6 persons. Talking of coming election.
No. 5	...	9 p.m.	...	4 persons. Talking about Ireland, one of the company being bound there.
No. 6	...	7.45 p.m.	...	4 persons. Playing bagatelle.

		December 28th		
No. 1	...	9.30 p.m.	...	8 men.
No. 2	...	9.30 p.m.	...	8 men.
No. 3	...	6 p.m.	...	9 men.
No. 4	...	8 p.m.	...	7 persons. Talking of agriculture.
No. 5	...	7 p.m.	...	2 persons. Playing darts.
No. 6	...	9 p.m.	...	6 persons. Playing bagatelle.

		December 29th.		
No. 4	...	9 p.m.	...	5 persons. Playing darts.
No. 5	...	9.30 p.m.	...	1 person. Drinking.
No. 6	...	9 p.m.	...	6 persons. Playing bagatelle.

		December 30th.		
No. 1	...	7 p m.	...	4 men.
No. 2	...	7.30 p.m.	...	2 men. The landlord gave free drinks, 8.30 to 10 p.m., to finish up the Christmas holidays
No. 3	...	8 p.m.	...	5 men.

December 31st.

No. 1 ... 9 p m. ... 8 men.
No. 2 ... 8 p.m. ... 9 men.
No. 3 ... 9.40 p.m. ... 6 men.

January 1st

No. 4 ... 9 30 p.m. ... 3 persons. Playing darts.
No. 5 ... 8 p.m. ... 8 persons. Playing darts.
No. 6 ... 8.30 p.m. ... 2 persons. Drinking only.

January 2nd.

No. 4 ... 9 p.m. ... 1 person. Drinking
No. 5 ... 9.45 p m. ... 2 persons. Playing darts.
No. 6 ... 9.15 p.m. ... 4 persons. Playing bagatelle.

January 3rd.

No. 4 ... 8 45 p.m. ... 10 persons. Talking of the coming election.
No. 5 ... 8 p m. ... 4 persons. Playing dominoes.
No. 6 ... 9.15 p.m. ... 8 persons. Playing bagatelle and talking of the coming election.

January 6th

No. 4 ... 8.30 p m. ... 5 persons. Talking of shooting pigeons, there being a shooting match in the village.
No. 5 ... 8 p.m. ... 10 persons. Playing darts and talking of coming election.
No. 6 ... 9 p.m. ... 9 persons. Playing bagatelle—some only drinking.

It is not to be supposed that this census, taken at Christmas-time, and when also an election was looming in the near future, is in any way typical of the ordinary attendance, which is probably considerably smaller at a less festive season. Moreover, besides the number of persons noted as " strangers," many names are included of persons not residing in Corsley, though well known to some of the inhabitants. An investigation at this time, however, showed the kind of amusement which was sought in these houses, games such as " darts " or bagatelle prob-

TEMPLE AND THE LONGLEAT WOODS.

ably taking an even more prominent place at a season when exceptional entertainments such as gramaphones and singing were unprovided. But no doubt, though the number who go merely to " soak " may not be numerous, a considerable amount of liquor is consumed by the players, or conversationalists, as well as by the less sociable drinkers.

The main amusement at Corsley on holidays during the winter is football, in which many of the men take part, while the women and girls, and older men, will often go to watch. In the winter of 1905-6 there were 48 members of the Corsley Football Club. The talk at public-houses, &c., during the winter months is mainly of football, unless an election or some such exceptional excitement should claim a share of attention. After a match men of all ages may be found going up, when the day's work is over, to learn the result.

For the mothers of Corsley a weekly recreation is provided in the mothers' meeting, held at the Reading Room by a lady of the parish.

So much for the winter. In summer the inhabitants and visitors, or lodgers are to be seen about in the roads and lanes till after dusk, and the household is no longer so isolated and self-contained as during the winter months. Cricket forms the chief occupation and amusement of the men, after their work is over. In 1906 there were 42 members of the Corsley Cricket Club.

While most of the natives of Corsley are known to each other, and display a friendly interest in one another's concerns, especially when united by the bond of mutual religious sect, it appears to be difficult for a newcomer to make friends or even acquaintances. A young farmer's sister after being over a year in the parish had made acquaintance with no farmers' daughters, or other young girls, and cottagers' wives who have been only a year or two in the place usually tell one that they have made no acquaintances. The Corsley people, on the other hand, will tell you that these newcomers have only recently arrived and that they know nothing of them.

The distinction between the inhabitant of Corsley descent and the stranger in the land, in the minds of the former, is probably something far deeper than the outsider has any notion of. Nevertheless, memory does not go back very far. Many inhabitants could not tell whether their own grandfathers were natives of the place, and a couple of generations is therefore sufficient to establish an old family.

The religious groups into which the people of Corsley assort themselves have already been alluded to. There is firstly the Church of England, with the parish church of St. Margaret and the smaller church of St. Mary at Temple. Two services are usually held at each on Sunday by the Rector, in addition to occasional week-day services, and Sunday School is held at St. Margaret in the afternoon. A good attendance at the morning service at the parish church would number about 100 persons, including children and the choir. The evening services are more fully attended.

The Wesleyan community at Lane End has on Sunday preaching services, morning and evening. These are usually taken by lay preachers from the neighbourhood, and occasionally a travelling preacher attends. The congregation numbers as a rule about 70 at each service. Prayer-meetings or preaching services are also held on Tuesday evenings. Sunday School is held twice on Sundays, and the Wesleyan community give their children a school treat from time to time.

The Baptists at Whitbourne have their chapel, with an organ, and an adjoining room where Sunday School and prayer-meetings are held. The chapel is surrounded by a burial-ground, and beyond that is a deep tank for use in the rite of baptism. The Baptists, like the Wesleyans, give treats to the children attending their school.

At Chapmanslade members of the Church of England, Congregationalists, and Baptists are provided with churches and chapels within the parish of Westbury or Diltons Marsh.

The bond of union between members of each Nonconformist community appears to be close, the members taking a keen interest in one another, and the more well-to-do exercising much kindness toward the poorer members when these are ill or in trouble.

On Sundays, when the holiday cannot be devoted to cricket or football, many of the parishioners take walks about the lanes, and groups of young men are usually found standing at the cross-roads, dressed usually in black coats and bowler hats. The people of both sexes usually go out carefully dressed on a Sunday, and all who are seen on the roads appear to possess good clothes.

It remains to notice the execution of public business in Corsley. The Parish Council, having eleven members, besides the Rector as Chairman and the Clerk, meets four times a year. The members are mainly farmers and tradesmen, with one or two artisans. The proceedings are conducted with a fair degree of formality, but a good deal of conversation in undertones goes on between the farmers during the meetings. Keenness is shown by some of the members in the detection of possible flaws in the modes of procedure adopted, and all, or nearly all, are alert to find means to avoid expenditure of the ratepayers' money. On the whole the Council appears anxious to carry out conscientiously the work entrusted to it. Since the first formation of a Corsley Parish Council under the Act of 1894 the matters which have been chiefly dealt with by this body are the formalities and necessary arrangements for conducting the business of the meetings, the parochial charities, the repair, &c., of footpaths, the state of the roads, the establishment of a postal-telegraph office and second delivery of letters in Corsley, Chapmanslade water supply, arrangements for celebration of the Diamond Jubilee, and the expression of congratulation or condolence with important persons connected with the parish, or members of the Council.

CHAPTER XVII

CONCLUSION

HAVING endeavoured to give a faithful description of Corsley as it was in 1905-6, perhaps the writer may be allowed to summarise briefly the conclusions to which she was forced during the course of her investigations, and the subsequent analysis of their results—conclusions some of which were entirely at variance with the preconceived notions she had formed from twelve years' superficial acquaintance with the parish and its inhabitants.

One is accustomed to think of the labourers of Wilts and Dorset as the worst paid and most poverty-stricken class in rural England. Looking therefore to find poverty in a Wiltshire village, it was no small surprise to the investigator to discover that the majority of the inhabitants were in quite affluent circumstances, and that only about one-eighth of the households had an income insufficient, with wise and careful management, to procure food and clothing adequate in quantity and quality to keep all the members in full health and vigour, or, as Mr. Rowntree expresses it, to maintain efficiency.

This prosperity of the majority of the families was found to be due to two main causes, the one highly satisfactory and promising for the future, the other of a more dubious nature.

First and foremost, this prosperity results from the distribution of land in the parish, from the good gardens attached to each cottage, the abundance of allotment land, the number of small holdings and the ease with which these are newly formed and obtained by any, one in a position to rent them from the principal landlord of the parish.

The advantage resulting from this easy access to the land cannot be overrated. Not only do many families derive a living entirely from gardening or farming on their own account, but nearly all have one or other of these occupations as a bye-industry. The wage-earning labourers and artisans are nearly all market gardeners, and a few of them farmers ; the publicans and the various functionaries of the parish are likewise in most instances farmers or gardeners. Moreover, the land is quite elastic in its fertility, and a family left with no other resource can by concentrating all their efforts on one cottage garden make a hard living from this alone.

The second cause of prosperity is a negative one, namely absence of children. Many, of the farmers are childless couples, who were able to save out of a low labourer's wage, and thus become small capitalists. There are market gardeners, too, who come under this category, though not so shown in the table on p. 259 (Chapter XV.) as a man often remains nominally a labourer, while a considerable part of his time and the whole of his wife's is in reality devoted to gardening.

The reverse side of the prosperity which appears so striking when the household is taken as the unit is, however, discovered when we examine more minutely into the various data collected and tabulated in Chapters XIV. and XV.

We find in the first place that from the insignificant one-eighth of the households in primary poverty, two-fifths, or nearly half, of all the children in the parish are drawn, and that only one-third of all the children are in households above the line of secondary poverty.

In the second place it becomes clear when the mortality figures are compared that a huge wastage of human life occurs among the descendants of agricultural labourers, this being the class that passes through periods of primary poverty. This wastage would seem to be mainly due to infantile mortality or deaths during later childhood.

In the third instance it was plainly shown when the school reports were compared that the children from homes in primary poverty often reveal evident marks of insufficient nutrition of brain and body, most of the children characterised by the teachers as dull and lazy coming from these homes, or from those in secondary poverty, and be it noted that the comparison is largely with similar labouring families where either because the elder children are already at work, or the family is comparatively small, the income per head is larger, for with very few exceptions all agricultural wage-earners who have several children pass in turn through a period of primary poverty, and the condition is characteristic of the class in Corsley, and not due to any avoidable fault of any particular family.

In striking contrast to the agricultural wage-earning families is the extraordinary vitality displayed by the children of market gardeners. It is shown by the table on p. 259 [Chapter XV.] that the total number of children born to 27 labourers was 126, or an average of 4.6 per family, and that of these 24, or 21.4 per cent., were since dead, although the children of aged retired labourers were not included.

The same table shows that 7 market gardeners' families had produced 47 children, or an average of 6.7 per family, and that of these 47 of all ages, only one, or 2.1 per cent., had since died.

There were, therefore, 2.1 less children born on the average in the family of a labourer than in that of a market gardener, and in these smaller families the death rate was just ten times as great.

It has often been pointed out by writers on infantile mortality that the true gravity of a high rate lies not so much in the numerical loss of population as in the fact that when conditions are such as to produce a large proportion of deaths among infants, these conditions also inflict an unmeasured injury on the constitution of those infants who succeed in surviving.

It may, therefore, be surmised that not only do these children of market gardeners live, while the children of labourers die, but that if a careful examination could be made into the life history of these children, they would be found on the average more vigorous, healthy, and intelligent than those men and women who, born in labourers' households, had passed through the ordeal of " survival of the fittest." An examination of the occupations being followed by the children of various groups given on pp. 266—270 shows at least that the sons of market gardeners are in the main following skilled trades and those of labourers unskilled occupations.

The greatest vitality of all is shown in the families of a brickmaker on his own account, and a shoemaker, who with a total of 21 children born have lost not one.

The true cause of this difference is obscure. Does the independent worker, gardener or handicraftsman, succeed by some means in avoiding the deadly grip of poverty at the period when his numerous young family are all dependent on him, or is he merely more skilful in averting its pressure upon his offspring? These questions the present writer cannot attempt to answer; she can merely state such facts as the inquiry brought to light.

Besides the families containing 122 persons where want was caused by the presence of a number of children too young to earn a living, there were 11 households in Corsley, comprising in all only 22 persons, in primary poverty, owing to old age or widowhood. Some of this poverty will have been alleviated by the granting of old age pensions, and nearly the whole of it would have been abolished had not several old people been forced to seek relief from the guardians a few years since when the old Corsley Walking Club broke up, thereby becoming disqualified under the present law for receiving State pensions.

Notwithstanding the peculiar gravity of the incidence of poverty in Corsley, which falls, as we have seen, mainly upon the children, there is much hopefulness in the fact that the machinery already exists for its alleviation when local authorities awake to the fact that the conditions of child life need special care and supervision in the country districts of England as well as in the towns.

By exercising the care for school children, which Acts of Parliament have made a duty in part compulsory, in part optional, of the local education authority, and by extending various municipal and charitable experiments which aim at reducing infant mortality, successfully at work in certain urban districts, to country places such as Corsley, the greater part, if not all, of the child poverty might be prevented, and with finer results here than in the

20

towns where mere poverty is only one of many
evil conditions to be contended with.

When these unsatisfactory conditions of child life
shall have been abolished it may confidently be expected that Corsley, in common with other rural
parishes, will bring up an increased number of sons
and daughters, more healthy, vigorous, and efficient
than their elder brothers and sisters of the past, and
ready to renew the less generous blood of the towns,
or to recruit the Army and Navy ; perhaps, too, more
attractive occupation may be provided for the girls
as well as the boys, and with a well-adapted education there seems no reason why women should not
again take a share in agriculture, and so we may
find a larger number of natives remaining in the
parish, applying an intensive cultivation, which its
soil can well bear, and in their turn bringing up the
healthy and vigorous sons and daughters who were
regarded by Elizabethan statesmen as the mainstay
of national wellbeing.

APPENDICES

APPENDIX I

RECORDS RELATING TO CORSLEY

(A) MEDIEVAL AND STUART RECORDS.

Grant of the Manor of Corsley to the House of Studley.

"*Inspeximus* and confirmation of a charter of Godfrey de Craw-
cumb giving to St. Mary and the house of Stodleg and the nuns
there, in frank almoin, the manor of Corsleg, saving the King's
service, and the advowson of the chapel of the manor, which was
already given to William de Hydemuston ; and the said prioress
and house shall support two chaplains celebrating divine service
daily for the souls of the said Godfrey and Joan his wife, one
chaplain to celebrate daily a mass of St. Mary (celebrabit singulis
diebus de Sancta Maria) and the other for the faithful departed.
Witnesses, Sir Robert de Muscegros, Henry de Capella, Hugh
Giffard, Godfrey de Skydemor, William Bastard, Richard de Ansy,
Nicholas de Haveresham, John de Elsefeld, Roger de Craunford,
John de Esses, and William de Hydemeston, steward of the said
Godfrey.

April 12, 1245, Westminster."[1]

The manor remained the property of this religious house until its
dissolution in the reign of Henry VIII.[2]

---

[1] Cal. Charter Rolls Hen. III. vol. i. p. 283.

[2] See William H. Jones, " Domesday for Wilts," p. 209, quotation
from "Nomina Villarum" A.D. 1316, Harl. MS. 6281, p. 231 ; and
Gairdner, " Letters and Papers of the Reign of Hen. VIII." A.D. 1536,
vol. x. p. 526, and A.D. 1537, vol. xii. 1, p. 143.

An inquisition made in the Hundred of Warminster in the reign of King Edward III. declared that—

"Item the hamlet of Corsley used to be in the hands of the King's predecessors of the (present) King, belonging to the manor of Warminster, until the King Henry aforesaid gave it to one Henry Dodeman, Norman ; which hamlet the Prioress of Studley now holds of the gift of Godfrey Cracumbe in alms.

"Item the Prioress of Studley holds half a Knight's fee of the King in chief in Corsley in demesne.

"Item the Prioress of Studley has gallows (&) assize of bread and beer in Corsley by charter of King Henry father of the present King.

"Item the Prioress of Studley has warren at Corsley by Charter of King Henry father of the present King."[1]

The origin and ownership of the other manors which now form part of the parish remain in obscurity pending the publication of the Victoria County History, but the greater part appear to have been in the hands of various religious houses. Thus the manor of Godwell and Chapmanslade belonged to the Abbey of St. Mary, Stanley, Wilts,[2] prior to the Dissolution, when it was granted to Sir Edward Bainton.[3]

In 1337 William de Littleton bequeathed eighty-one acres of land in Great Corsley, Warminster, and Smalebrook to the Convent of the House of Lepers of St. Mary, Maiden Bradley.

"Licence for the alienation in mortmain to the prior and convent of the house of lepers of St. Mary, Maydenbradelegh, in satisfaction of 60ˢ of the 10ˡ yearly of land and rent which they have the king's licence to acquire, of the following, which are of the yearly value of 43ˢ· 10ᵈ ⁱ as appears by the inquisition ; by Master William de Littleton, a messuage, 76 acres of land, 5 acres of meadow and 6ˢ of rent, in Great Corselegh, Wermenstre, and Smalebrook, and by John Danyel, chaplain, and Reginald le Palmere, six messuages, 12 acres of land and 5 acres of wood, in Maydenbradlegh and Hulle Deverel."   Oct. 9, 1337.   Tower of London."[4]

---

[1] Extracts from Rotuli Hundredorum, vol. ii. 276 (Record Commission), translated from the Latin.

[2] See Wilts Archæological Magazine, vol. xv. p. 25.

[3] Gairdner, "Letters and Papers of the Reign of Hen. VIII." A.D. 1537, vol. xii. part 1. p. 143.

[4] Cal. Patent Rolls, Oct. 9, 1337, vol. 1334–1338, p. 540.

The manor of Whitbourne was sold in 1544, on the dissolution of the Monastery of Maiden Bradley, together with lands in Bugley, Corsley, and Whitbourne, also belonging to the Monastery, to Ric: Andrewes and John Howe for the sum of £1,094. 3. 2.,[1] and it was probably the prior of this house who is mentioned in the following extent of the fourteenth century.

"*Whyteborne. Extent of the same.* [*Sept.* 30, 1364.]

"Extent of the Manor made on Monday after the festival of St. Michael, in the 38th year of the reign of King Edward III.

"A court with a small piece of land (or garden *Curtilagium*) is worth yearly after deductions [value not given].

"And at Whitborn a court with curtilage.

"There are 34 acres of land in 7 crofts.

"Also in the field of (?) Chadinhangre are 25 acres of land.

"Also on the Lygh 3½ acres.

"Also in the field of Cly 28 acres.

"Also at Bykenham a half-acre.

"Also there are 3½ acres of meadow.

"Also one acre of wood, which is worth in pasture . . .

"Also the lord prior can have and hold there 4 farm-horses and 12 oxen, 12 cows, 250 sheep.

"John de Vake holds in fee two messuages at the rent of 18d. And must do suit at the court of the lord, and must do homage and all other services.

"Henry de Frenshe holds in fee 1 messuage and 3 acres of land at the yearly rent of 6s., and must do all services as the aforesaid John Vake does.

"*Tenants in villenage (bondagio).* Thomas Pykenet holds at the will of the lord one messuage and 7 acres of land at the rent of 3s.

"Adam Frenshe [holds] one messuage and 2 acres of land.

"J Forester [holds] 2 messuages and 4 acres of land.

"Edwardus Carpenter holds land and a tenement in Whiteborn for the term of his life, at a yearly rent of 40s., to be paid at the 4 terms of the year.

"Walter [Deye][2] holds manor land and a tenement of Grendon for the term of his life. Rent, 53/4." [3]

---

[1] Gairdner, "Letters and Papers of the Reign of Hen. VIII." A D. 1544, vol. xix. Part I. p. 629.

[2] Name supplied from p. 2 of MS.

[3] MS. Extent of the Manor of Whyteborne 38 Ed. III. at Long-

In 1415 a papal bull was obtained granting licence for burial in the Corsley churchyard and full parochial rights. This is translated in Hoare's "Modern Wilts" as follows :[1]

"From the Register of Bishop Hallam 1415. License for sepulture to Corsley, which before that time buried at Warminster, by a papal bull.

"'Johannes Episcopus servus servorum Dei' to his beloved children of both sexes dwelling in Corsley and the hamlets adjoining. 'Whereas the church of Corsley before this time was parochial in all respects except only the above right, the Pope, on account of the distance and bad roads in winter, now permits them to bury in the Church-yard of Corsley, and delegates John Cosham, Prior of Bruton, to carry his bull into execution.'

"WILLIAM FOVENT, then Vicar of Warminster."

Although the Pope had granted his licence, distinct parochial rights do not appear to have been actually and fully obtained for Corsley until the incumbency of William Woolfe, who was appointed to the benefice in 1505.

The following account of the church is found in the record of the Corsley Perambulation of 1754.

"*An Abstract of the Church Book of Corsley, wherein are set down and recorded divers Things appertaining to the s^d. Church and Parish.*

"1636

"First the Church of Corsley was sometime a Chappell called S^t. James's but by a Composition made between Dr. Bennett Vicar of Warminster and S^r. W^m. Woolfe Rector or Custos of Corsley, it was made a Parish Church of itself & the s^d. S^r W^m. & his successors were to pay yearly to y^e. s^d. D^r. Bennett and his Success^r. £1 6s. 8d., as by the s^d. Composition in writing remaining among

---

leat House. Transcribed by Canon Christopher Wordsworth by kind permission from the Marquis of Bath and translated by Miss S. E. Moffat.

[1] Sir Richard Colt Hoare, "History of Modern Wilts," Hund. of Warminster, p. 64. The original papal bull is among the papers belonging to Corsley Church.

the Writings in the Parish Church of Corsley at large doth appear." [1]

Besides the Chapel of St. James, which seems to have become the parish church of St. Margaret, there were, according to Sir Richard Colt Hoare, also many endowed chapels in Corsley. [2]

One of these, Kington Court Chapel, or Little Corsley Chapel, on the site of the house now known as Cley Hill Farm, remained till the Reformation. [3] This chapel is said to have belonged anciently to the Kingston family, and afterwards to St. John's Hospital, Wilton [4] The Commissioners in 7 Edward VI. found at this chapel 3 bells, a chalice or cup worth 7d., and some plate, which were to be safely kept to the King's use. [5]

An interesting seating order, comprising a plan of Corsley Church, dated 1635, and showing the name of the occupier of each seat, is among the parish records. The document runs as follows :—

"CORSLEY CHURCHE IN THE COUNTIE OF WILTES.

"The order and manner of placeing of the SEATES within the parish of Corsley by the Right worshipful MARMADUKE LYNN Doctor of the Civill lawe and Chancelor of the Diocese of Sarum in the Countie aforesaid the twenty sixe day of July Anno Dñi 1635 where the said Chancelor did order and appoint HENRY TEDBURY AND WILLIAM GODSELL CHURCH WARDENS And Stephen Holwey John Smith and Anthony Raxworthie their ASSISTANTS to settle and place every MAN and WOMAN in their several seates who were settled and placed accordinglie, as by the Churchbooke and also by this Mappe appeareth as ffolloweth vidzt

THE NORTH CORNER off the bodie
of the Church
SIR THOMAS THYNN Kᵗ.
FOR HIMSELF AND HIS LADY

---

[1] Corsley Perambulation, 1754, in Longleat Estate Office.
[2] Sir Richard Colt Hoare, "History of Modern Wilts," Hund. of Warminster, p. 64.
[3] *Ibid.* Also *Wilts Archæol. Mag.* x. p. 273.
[4] *Wilts Archæol. Mag.* x. p. 273.
[5] *Ibid.* xii. p. 265.

[The Nave of the Church]

	The piller		Sir Thomas Thynn	Sⁱ. Thomas Thynn
	John Stevens aᵗs Shepherd	Maurice Litlecot Henrye Tedbury	George Turner	Marie Lambe	Robert Rymell
	John Crosse	John Nevill	John Smith	Henry Feltham	Thomas Chace
John	Singer	Anthony · Rackesworthie	Robert Hopkins	William Raxworthie	Widdowe Dredge
John Barens	James Watts	William Holwey	Thomas Hill	Robert Knght	William Chace
William Smith aᵗs Singer	John Kennell	John Carr	Thomas Eyres	Thomas Holweye	John Watts
William Smith aᵗs Singer	William Smith aᵗs Singer	Richard Carpenter			
Stephen Crooch	William Downe	John Knight	Tobie Lambe	Robert Carpenter	John Withie
		Anthony Rackesworthe	Michael Ewestice	John Williams aᵗs Clarke	Hugh Holwey
The Fonte		Robert Hopkins	Thomas Mines	Edward Adlam	Henry George
			WOMENS SEATES		
Thomas Hill wives seate	Robert Rymell wives seate	John Stevens aᵗs Shepherd wives seate	Mathew Chandler wives seate	John Carrs wives seate	Robert Knight wives seate
George Turner		John Turner	Henry Feltham	Anthony Rackesworthy	Richard Carpenter
James Watts	John Kennell	Thomas Chace	John Watts	John Knight	John Holwey
John Withie	Christopher Hill	George Turner	Lewes Abraham	Widdowe Cloude	John Hopkins
Robert Watts		Wiliam Smith aᵗs Singer	William Smith aᵗs Singer	John Watts	Edward Daniell
			Thomas Mines		
John Rogers	John Laurence	Alexander Knight	John Beacham	Widdowe Paine	Stephen Crutch
				John Baylie	Robert Minete

The Vicars wives seate
for the Vicarage

The Farmers wife of Clyhill
for the Farme

MENS SEATES

Nichs Gibbins	Edward Couch	Humphrie Adlam
John Gratewood	Robert Hill	William Hooper
Peter Queile	John Turner	George Paine
Richard Dunnen	Christopher Dunnen	John Hunt
John Hooper	Anthony Coombes	Arthur Gaye
William Hancocks	Robert Watts	Henery Wates
HUNTENHULL	farme	CLYHILL
		Farme

WEOMENS SEATES

for Huntenhull Farme

John Carrs wives	Thomas Eyres wives seate	Thomas Allwood
Michael Ewestice wives seate	Robert Hopkins wives seate	Widdowe Dredge
Whiteborne Temple	Robert Hooper	John Nevill
Humphrie Adlam	Stephen Holweye	Roger Trolloppe
Nichs Dibbins	Anthony Coombs	John Rogers John Barens

| CHANCELL | | THE SOUTH CORNER |
| DOORE | Sᵣ. Thomas Thynn | of the bodie of the Church |

SIR THOMAS THYNN

| Thomas Carr | . Mathewe Chandler | . Fields Courte |
| Mᵣ. John Holweye | Mᵣ. John Holweye | Mᵣ. John Holweye |

THE VICARS SEATE   } Pull-
....   NICHO : FITZHUGH   } Pitt
    Clearck   And the.....................................

THE CLEARCKS SEATE	· Robert Hooper	
John Meare	John Hopkins	John Watts
Whiteborne Temple	Richard Carpenter	William Godsell
Lewes Abraham	George Turner	Stephen Holwcy
Edward Danyell	Roger Trolloppe	Michael Ewestice

WOMENS SEATES

William Godsells wives seates		M'. John	wives seates
		Holweyes	
Robert Hills	Arthur Gayes	William Raxworthies	Henry Tedbury
wife	wife	wife	wife
			The Porch

WEOMENS SEATES

John Williams	Richard	John Hoopers	Feilds Court
als Clarke	Carpenters wife	wife	seate for the
wives seate			woman
Elenor Meares	Mary Lambs	Maurice Litlecots	John Smithes
seate	seate	wives seate	wives seate
Wardes	William Holweys	Widdow Carpenters	Peter Queile
	wives	seate	wives seate
John Holweyes	John Bayly	Henry George	Thomas Holweys
wives seate	wives seate	his wives	
		seate	
William Claces	Robert Hopkins	Goodwife Francis	William Smith
wives seate			als Singer
John Kennell	William Watts	William Downe	John Singer
	Widdowe Greene."		

(B) LIST OF INCUMBENTS AND PATRONS AT CORSLEY 1250-1902.

Until 1485, when the predecessor of William Woolfe was appointed, the presentment is often noted as being either to the Chapel of Corsley, or to the Church (E.). Without further evidence it is not very clear whether there were usually two incumbents of Corsley up to this date, or whether the Chapel and Church alluded to are one and the same.

	Incumbent.	Patron.
A D		
1250	Thomas de Corsleya.	Prioress of Studley.
1306	William de Poiter.	,,
,,	Walter de Parco.	,,
1309	Nicholas de Hulprintune.	William de Lye.
1316	Richard Spakeman.	,,
,,	Walter de Stoville.	,,
1326	William de Petresfeld.	E. ,,
1333	John *dictus* de Bathon de Cirencester.	Capella Corslegh Will' Hasard de Malmsbury.
1338	John le Vake of Corsley.	{ Capella. John, son of William de Lye.
1348	William le Forester.	E. John de Lye.
1348	Joseph Southcote.	
1378	Henry Langham.	E. Robert Lye.
1394	John Guynterel.	E. Robert Leghe.
1396	John Bryd.	,,
1397	John Rome.	
1425	Thomas Wyddyngton.	E. Richard de Lye.
1430	Thomas Bonar.	,,
1433	John Butler.	,,
1439	John Fitz-Richard.	{ Capella. Nicholas Upton and other feoffees of Richard Lye.
1441	Nicholas Druell.	ditto.
1441	William Warmyll.	
1453	Richard Dyring.	{ Capella Thomas Tropenell and other feoffees of Robert Lye.
¹ 1454	Richard Gartham.	ditto.
1485	William Say.	E. Robert Ley de Corsley.
1505	William Wolf.	,,
1524	William Benet, jun.	Richard Powton, Gen.
1539	John Swynerton.	
1555	Thomas Scott.	John Gly . . . Yeoman.
1563	William Harrington.	John Thynne, Knight.
1576	Henry Schawe.	,,
1579	John Cutlett.	,,
1908	Nicholas Fitzhugh.	{ Joanna, widow of John Thynne of Longleat.

¹ Last presentation to the chapel.

A.D.	*Incumbent.*	*Patron.*
1625	Robert Nevill.	
1660	John Yarner.	
1667	Richard Jenkins.	James Thynne, Knight.
1668	Thomas Aylesbury.	
1725	Richard Moody.	{ Thomas, Viscount Weymouth.
1736	Lionel Seaman.	,,
1738	William Colville.	,,
1764	John Lacy.	,,
1768	Millington Massey.	,,
1774	William Slade.	,,
1783	Thomas Huntingford.	Lord Weymouth.
1787	Isaac Huntingford.	,,
1830	R. C. Griffith.	,,
1845	James H. Waugh.	,,
1886	Richard E. Coles.	,,
1902	John T. Kershaw.	,,

(C) PURCHASES OF SIR JOHN THYNNE IN CORSLEY PARISH, SIXTEENTH CENTURY.[1]

The following extracts from Hoare's "History of Modern Wilts" show how extensive were the purchases of Sir John Thynne in the parish of Corsley in the sixteenth century.

"Extracts from Inquisition Roll taken at the death of Sir John Thynne, the elder, of his manor lands with their yearly value. . . .

". . . Maner. de Hunthill, alias Huntenhull, cum pertinen⁵ in Com. Wiltes, ten. de quo vel de quibus ignoratur, et val. p. annᵐ £21. . . .

"Manerium de Corsley, cum pertinen ac domus mansionalis ejusd. Joh'is Thynne mil. una cum dominicis terris, et parcus de Corsley jacen. et existens in Warminster et Corsley, in praed Com. Wiltes. ten de D'na Reginâ in cap. per 20ᵃᵐ part 1 feod. mil. et val. darè p. annᵐ. £15. 12s.

"Dominium sive Manerium de Whitborne et Whitborne Temple cum suis pertinents in dicto Com. Wiltes, ten. de D'na Regina in cap. per 20ᵃᵐ part. 1 feod, mil. et valet darè p. annum £4. 18s.

* * * * *

[1] See Hoare, "History of Modern Wilts," Hundred of Heytesbury, pp. 74–78.

"Boscus vocat. Norridge Woods, jacen. et existen. in Warminster et Upton Scudmore, ten. de D'na Regina. 10ˢ. &c.

"Extracts Inquisition Roll, taken at the death of Sir John Thynne the elder (original at Longleat).

"Terræ, Maneria, et Possessiones Johannis Thynne, Wilts. Manor of Hunthill, alias Huntenhull, &c., £21.

* * * * *

"Manor of Corsley, with the *domus mansionalis* of John Thynne, together with the park at Corsley, &c., £15. 12s.

"Demesne or Manor of Whitborne and Whitborne Temple, &c., £4. 18s.

"Norridge Woods, in Warminster and Upton Scudmore, 10s.

* * * * *

"Lands, &c., &c., in Whitburne Temple &c., £2. 2s. 2d.

* * * * *

"Lands, &c., in Warminster, Bugley, &c , £5. 11s.

"Lands, &c., in Corsley, 4/1

* * * * *

"One tenement in Bugley, held of Lord Audley, £1. 6s. 8d."

Extract from MS. list at Longleat of purchases made by Sir John Thynne the elder.

The Manors of Whitborne and lands in Bugley and Corsley, Co. Wilts. Bought of Richard Andrews, de Hayles, Co. Gloucester, anno regni Henry VIII 36°, who had them by grant from the said king in the same year. They had been part of the possessions of the Monastery of Mayden Bradley, Co. Wilts."

Sir John Thynne died in 1580.

APPENDIX II

EXTRACTS FROM MS. CORSLEY OVERSEERS' ACCOUNTS

THE following is a summary of the expenditure on poor relief from May till October, 1729, and some full extracts from the list of "Extraordinaries" are also given.

During these months an average of thirty persons was in receipt of regular relief, the amount given varying from 1s. to 12s. per month, in different cases.

Expenditure on Poor, May 2 to Oct. 2, 1729.

Month.	Regular Relief	Extraordinaries.
	£ s. d	£ s. d.
May 2nd	6 1 6	8 18 10
May 29th	7 7 6	11 15 10
July 4th	7 2 6	5 18 3
July 31st	7 2 6	9 18 4
September 4th ...	6 18 0	6 19 9
October 2nd ...	6 15 6	6 19 6
Total, 6 months ...	41 7 6	50 10 6

Total expenditure on poor relief for six summer months: £91. 18s. 0d.

	1729, May 2nd.
Extraordinaries.	
	£ s. d.
The Wido Benet in yᵉ smalpox	1 0 6
Mosis Withy for Rent of a loome	0 7 0
John Napes wife for to by threed	0 1 0
Elisabeth West for keeping Grace Bartlets children	1 0 0
Mary Udil for qureing John Udiel's wife's	0 5 0
Washing John Bartlet (regular pauper)	0 1 0
Ester Tusdays expences	0 15 6
Suzan Coleses house rent (regular pauper) ...	0 10 0

Paeid for Briches for Will Langford (regular pauper) 0 3 8
Paeid for a shirt and making for Will Langford 0 2 10
John Saey for Moses Withey's loome 0 8 0
for careing Moses Withey Loome home 0 5 0
5 eles of doules for Wid Holawaey's children (regular pauper) 0 6 9
for making 5 shifts 0 1 4
John Haines's house rent (regular pauper) ... 1 15 0
Ann Pickford for Nap's family 0 4 0

Extorernieryes.

betay Clarke in ye smalpox 0 15 0
John Nap for a discharge & to by the children bread 0 12 0
Shift for Wid Brown 0 2 10
for feching Elisabeth withey home (regular pauper) 0 3 4
Sara Hunt for waishen John Bartlit (regular pauper) 0 2 0
Expenses for moving Mary Holoway 0 3 6
For feching a warint for Samuel Dunin 0 1 4
Ann pickford for house Rent for Naps 0 2 6

Extorernieryes.

too dozen of Read for Ales Gatood 0 11 0
For thatching of ales Gratood (regular pauper) house & Loft and naiels 0 16 0
Richard Whitaker for bilding ales Gratood's house 0 5 0
Wid. Turner for her family in ye smalpox ... 0 19 0
Mary Martin in ye smalpox 0 19 0
Issack Singer for building ales Gratoods house & for timber 1 16 0
Ann pickford for keeping John Napes children (two entries making) 1 16 0

<table>
<tr><td></td><td></td><td></td><td colspan="3">1729,</td></tr>
<tr><td>Extraordinaries.</td><td></td><td></td><td colspan="3">September 4th.</td></tr>
<tr><td></td><td></td><td></td><td>£</td><td>s</td><td>d</td></tr>
<tr><td>Mary Marten in the smalpox. ...   ...</td><td></td><td>...</td><td>1</td><td>3</td><td>0</td></tr>
<tr><td>(various items of clothing and shoes for paupers)</td><td></td><td></td><td></td><td></td><td></td></tr>
<tr><td>Mary Udiel for keeping Mary Martin's chield</td><td></td><td></td><td></td><td></td><td></td></tr>
<tr><td>   and tending them both...   ...   ...</td><td></td><td>...</td><td>1</td><td>5</td><td>0</td></tr>
</table>

		1729,
Extraordinaries.		October 2nd.

	£	s	d
Francis Mines his wages	0	12	6
George Biffen to send his Dafter to London ...	0	10	0
for careing of Mary Martin's goods	0	5	0
Ann Pickford for keeping John Naps children			
2 wickes	1	16	0
A paier of stockins for John Bartlet (regular			
pauper)	0	1	0

	1729
	[December 2nd].

	£	s	d
Booft of Timithey Bodman a pice of cloth 34			
yards att 1^s, 9^d. yard	2	13	10

APPENDIX III

EXTRACTS FROM CENSUS REPORTS RELATING TO CORSLEY

PARISH OF CORSLEY. AREA 2,580 ACRES.

Year	Inhabited Houses.	Uninhabited Houses.	Building.	Population.
1801	—	—	—	1,412
1811	—	—	—	1,352
1821	—	—	—	1,609
1831[1]	—	—	—	1,729
1841	351	28	2	1,621
1851[2]	334	17	—	1,473
1861[3]	303	24	—	1,235
1871	283	22	1	1,196
1881[4]	266	21	—	1,019

CIVIL PARISH OF CORSLEY. AREA 3,056 STATUTE ACRES

	Inhabited Houses	Uninhabited Houses	Building	Population
(1881[5]	268	21	—	1,023)
1891	236	26	8	926

		Uninhabited Houses		
	Inhabited	Occupied.	Unoccupied.	Population
1901	219	7	25	824

---

[1] 1831. About two hundred persons are stated to have emigrated within the last three years.

[2] 1851. In consequence of the discontinuance of a large cloth factory, several families have removed to other parishes in search of employment.

[3] 1861. "The decrease of population in the parish of Corsley is attributed to emigration. Many cottages have been pulled down" (Census Report, 1861, p. 667).

[4] Census Report, 1881, vol. ii. p. 253.

[5] Census Report, 1891, vol. ii. Transfers made from Corsley to Warminster of part of Bugley, and from Norton Bavant to Corsley. Census report says that a population of seventeen was transferred in both cases, so total population of Corsley not affected.

21

APPENDIX IV

EXTRACTS FROM MS. FARMING ACCOUNTS OF MR. JOHN BARTON

On October 18th, 1804, the farm stock was valued as follows :

	£	s.	d
Old wheat in two Ricks, 130 Sacks at 40ˢ/-	260	0	0
Do. in Barn 24 Doˢ at 40ˢ/-	52	0	0
New Wheat in two Ricks 90 Doˢ at 40/-	180	0	0
Old Barley in Rick 16 Qʳˢ at 40/-	32	0	0
New Dº in two Ricks 30 Dᵒˢ at 40/-	60	0	0
Old Oats in Rick 16 Qʳˢ at 30/-	24	0	0
New Dº in one Rick 30 Qʳˢ at 30/-	45	0	0
Old Beans in Granary 10 Sacks at 26/-	13	0	0
New Dº in Rick 15 Sacks at 26/-	19	10	0
Peas in Rick 20 Sacks at 25/-	25	0	0
Peas in Granary 8 Dº at 25/-	10	0	0
Clover seed, two sacks in Granary ...	20	0	0
Wool in Granary	31	0	0
Vetches in Granary—5 sacks	5	5	0
Six Cows at 15£	90	0	0
Two yearling Cows	12	0	0
Seven Cart Horses	125	0	0
Colt, two years old	23	0	0
Colt, sucking	7	0	0
Poultry	10	0	0
120 Ewes for Stock at 1 gā	126	0	0
40 Dº for Sale at 1£	40	0	0
Two Rams	4	0	0
50 chilver Lambs at 17/-	42	10	0
44 Wedder Dº at 16/-	35	4	0
Two fatting pigs	8	0	0
3 sows and 14 young pigs	16	0	0
Waggons, Harness, &c.	80	0	0

		£	s	d
Bills due for work with Cart Horses	...	8	0	0
Potatoes	...	10	0	0
Rent of potatoe ground ...	...	4	0	0
Grass Seeds sown 31 acres at 1£	...	31	0	0
Wheat bought for Seed and paid for	...	15	13	0
D° from Mr. Barter for wool	...	31	0	0
Due for Bills for poultry, Hay, &c. at Warm^r	...	10	17	4
D° at Corsley	...	42	16	10
To Hay there being 72 Ton, and which is supposed more than a usual quantity by 22 ton	...	80	0	0
		1,575	2	0

LIST OF REFERENCES TO CORSLEY

Hoare, Sir Richard Colt, History of Ancient Wilts, Hundred of Warminster. London, 1812-21.

Jones, William H., Domesday for Wilts. 1865.

Calendar Charter Rolls, Hen. III., vol. i., p. 283.

Rotuli Hundredorum (Record Commission), vol. ii., p. 276.

Calendar Patent Rolls, vols. 1334—38, p. 540.

MS. Extent of Manor of Whitbourne, 1364, in possession of Marquis of Bath.

Gairdner, Letters and Papers of Reign of Hen. VIII., vols. xii., xix.

MS. Wilts Quarter Sessions Records.

Hist. MS. Commission. Various Collections, i. 1901. Wilts Quarter Sessions Records.

Calendar State Papers, Domestic, Chas. I., vols. 1631—33.

Proceedings Court of Chancery, Haynes v. Carr. Chas. I. H. H. 69.

MS. Bayliffe's Account of Corsley Manor, 1634, at Longleat Estate Office.

MS. Certificates in Corsley Parish Chest.

MS. Indentures in Corsley Parish Chest.

MS. Examinations of Applicants for Relief in Corsley Parish Chest.

MS. Papers relating to bastardy cases in possession of C. N. Phipps, Esq.

MS. Corsley Overseers' Accounts, 1729—41, 1747—55, 1769—1836.

Enclosure Agreement of 1742, at Longleat Estate Office.

MS. Corsley Survey, 1745, at Longleat Estate Office.

MS. Corsley Perambulation in 1754, at Longleat Estate Office.

MS. Corsley Workhouse Accounts, 1774—1801.

Workhouse Insurance Policy, c. 1774, in Corsley Parish Chest.

MS. Corsley Churchwardens' Accounts, 1782, *et seq.*

MS. Corsley Vestry Minutes.

Warminster and Corsley Enclosure Award, with Maps, 1783, at Longleat Estate Office, and at Office of Clerk of the Peace, Devizes.

MS. Minutes of Manor Courts, Corsley, Huntenhull, &c., at Longleat Estate Office.

Davis, T , General View of the Agriculture of Wilts, 1794, and second edition, 1813.

Hoare, Sir Richard Colt, History of Modern Wilts, Hundred of Warminster and Hundred of Heytesbury. London, 1822-44.

Census Reports.

MS. Barton Farming Accounts, 1801—11, and 1828—36, at Corsley House.

Abstract Poor Returns, 1815.

MS. Account Book of Mr. Sparey, 1821.

Cobbett, William, Rural Rides, 1825.

MS. Terrier of Corsley, 1828, among parish records.

Scrope, Paulet, Extracts of Letters, from poor persons who emigrated last year to Canada and the United States. Printed for the information of the labouring poor in this country. London : Chippenham [printed], 1831.

Report Charity Commission, 1834, vol. xxviii.

Report Poor Law Commission, 1834, vol. xiii., Appendix B1, vol. xiv., Appendix B1, Part III., Appendix C.

Second Annual Report Poor Law Commission, 1836, vol. i.

Warminster and Westbury Journal, June 17, 1905.

Lea, J. Henry, The Lyes of Corsley. [To be published in America.]

Wiltshire Archæological Magazine, vols. x., xii., xv., xvi., xix., xxii , xxiii., xxvi.

Daniell, John, History of Warminster. Simpkin, Marshall & Co., London : Warminster [printed], 1879.

Doël, W., Twenty Golden Candlesticks. Trowbridge, 1890.

Tuck, Stephen, Wesleyan Methodism in Frome. Frome, 1837.

MS. Corsley Parish Registers.

Various documents and papers relating to the parish in the care of the Rector or of the Clerk to the Parish Council.

MS. Corsley Wesleyan Methodist Chapel Baptismal Register.

INDEX

313

The Gresham Press,
UNWIN BROTHERS, LIMITED.
WOKING AND LONDON

A

CLASSIFIED CATALOGUE

OF

T. FISHER UNWIN'S

PUBLICATIONS.

CONTENTS.

———

Book Buyers are requested to order any volumes they may require from their bookseller. On receipt of a post-card, Mr. Fisher Unwin will be pleased to furnish the address of the nearest local bookseller where the works detailed in this list may be inspected.

Should any difficulty arise, the Publisher will be happy to forward any book in the list to any country in the Postal Union, on receipt of the price marked and a sufficient sum to cover postage, together with full Postal Address. Any amount forwarded in excess will be returned to the sender.

Remittances may be made by Cheque, draft on London, Money Orders, or Stamps.

After reading this Catalogue, kindly pass it on to some book-buying friend, or send an address to which this or future editions may be sent.

INDEX of AUTHORS, some

ILLUSTRATORS, and EDITORS.

INDEX in order of Titles.

LITERARY HISTORY.

ABRAHAMS. A Short History of Jewish Literature, from the Fall of the Temple (70 C.E.) to the Era of Emancipation (1706 C.E.) By Israel Abrahams, M.A., Reader in Rabbinic Literature in the University of Cambridge Cr. 8vo, cloth. net 2/6

BAILEY. The Novels of George Meredith. By E. E. J. Bailey. Cr. 8vo, cloth net 5/-

BEERS. A Short History of American Literature. By Henry A. Beers. Large cr 8vo, cloth. net 3/6

BRERETON (Austin). The Literary History of the Adelphi and its Neighbourhood. See under " History."

BROWNE. A Literary History of Persia Vol. I From the Earliest Times until Firdawsi. By Edward G. Browne, M.A, M B., Fellow of Pembroke College With Photogravure Frontispiece. (Library of Literary History.) Demy 8vo, cloth. net 12/6

—— A Literary History of Persia Vol 2. From Firdawsi until Sa'di (A D 1000—1290). By Edward G. Browne. With Photogravure Frontispiece. (Library of Literary History.) Demy 8vo, cloth. net 12/6

BRÜCKNER. A Literary History of Russia. By Professor A Bruckner, of Berlin. Edited by Ellis H Minns, M A. Translated by H. Havelock, M A With Photogravure Frontispiece. (Library of Literary History) Demy 8vo, cloth. net 12/6

BRUNETIÈRE. Essays in French Literature. A Selection, translated by D. Nichol Smith, with a Preface by the Author specially written for this, the authorised English translation. Large cr 8vo, cloth. 7/6

—— Manual of the History of French Literature. By Ferdinand Brunetière. Demy 8vo., cloth. 12/-

CANNING. Shakespeare Studied in Eight Plays. By the Hon. Albert S. G. Canning. Demy 8vo, cloth net 16/-

—— Shakespeare Studied in Six Plays. By the Hon. Albert S. G Canning Demy 8vo, cloth. net 16/-

—— Shakespeare Studied in Three Plays. By the Hon. Albert S G Canning. Demy 8vo, cloth net 7/6

—— Literary Influence in British History. By the Hon Albert S. G. Canning. Demy 8vo, cloth. net 7/6

—— History in Scott's Novels. By the Hon. Albert S. G. Canning Demy 8vo, cloth. net 10/6

—— British Writers on Classic Lands By the Hon. Albert S G. Canning Demy 8vo, cloth net 7/6

DUFF. A Literary History of Rome. From the Origins to the Close of the Golden Age. By J Wight Duff, M A. With Photogravure Frontispiece. (Library of Literary History) Demy 8vo, cloth net 12/6

FAGUET. A Literary History of France By Emile Faguet, Member of the French Academy. With Photogravure Frontispiece (Library of Literary History) Demy 8vo, cloth. net 12/6

FRAZER. A Literary History of India. By R. W Frazer, LL B., I.C S Frontispiece (Library of Literary History.) Demy 8vo, cloth. net 12/6

HORRWITZ. A Short History of Indian Literature. By Ernest Horrwitz. With an Introduction by Professor T. W Rhys Davids. Cr. 8vo, cloth. net 2/6

HYDE. A Literary History of Ireland. By Douglas Hyde, LL.D. With Photogravure Frontispiece (Library of Literary History) Demy 8vo, cloth. net 12/6

—— **The Story of Early Gaelic Literature.** By Douglas Hyde, LL.D. (New Irish Library Vol. 6) Sm. cr. 8vo, paper covers, 1/-, cloth 2/-

JONES. Dafydd ap Gwilym A Welsh Poet of the Fourteenth Century. By W. Lewis Jones, M A., Professor of English Language and Literature, University College of North Wales. Large cr 8vo, cloth. [In Preparation.] net 7/6

JUSSERAND. The English Novel in the Time of Shakespeare. By J J Jusserand, Conseiller d'Ambassade Translated by Elizabeth Lee Second Edition Revised and enlarged by the Author. Illustrated. Large cr 8vo, cloth. 7/6

—— **A Literary History of the English People.** Vol 1 From the Origins to the Renaissance. By J J. Jusserand. With Photogravure Frontispiece Demy 8vo, cloth. net 12/6

—— **A Literary History of the English People.** Vol. 2. From the Renaissance to the Civil War. I By J J Jusserand. With Photogravure Frontispiece. Demy 8vo, cloth. net 12/6

—— **A Literary History of the English People.** Vol. 3 From the Renaissance to the Civil War II By J J Jusserand. With Photogravure Frontispiece Demy 8vo, cloth net 12/6

—— **Shakespeare in France** By J. J Jusserand. Illustrated. Demy 8vo, cloth. 21/-

LANGLAND'S (William) Vision of Piers Plowman. Edited by Kate Warren. Second Edition, revised Cloth. 3/6

LIBRARY OF LITERARY HISTORY, THE. Each with Photogravure Frontispiece. Demy 8vo, cloth each, net 12 6

[For full Titles see under Authors' names.]

Published :—

(1) **India.** By Professor R. W. Frazer

(2) **Ireland.** By Dr Douglas Hyde

(3) **America.** By Professor Barrett Wendell

(4) **Persia.** Vol 1. From the Earliest Times until Firdawsi By Professor E G. Browne.

(5) **Scotland** By J. H Millar.

(6) **Persia.** Vol 2 From Firdawsi until Sa'di By Professor E. G Browne

(7) **The Arabs** By R. A. Nicholson.

(8) **France** By Emile Faguet.

(9) **Russia.** By Professor A. Bruckner.

In Preparation —

Rome. By J. Wight Duff.

The Jews By Israel Abrahams, M.A.

MARBLE Heralds of American Literature By Annie Russell Marble Illustrated Cr. 8vo, cloth. net 6/6

MILLAR. A Literary History of Scotland By J H Millar, Balliol College, Oxford With Photogravure Frontispiece (Library of Literary History) Demy 8vo, cloth gilt net 12/6

Also a *Fine Edition*, limited to 25 copies, on hand-made paper. net 42/-

—— **A Short History of Scottish Literature.** By J H Millar Cr 8vo, cloth. [In Preparation] net 2/6

MILLS The Secret of Petrarch. By E. J Mills. With 13 Photogravure Plates, one in colour Demy 8vo. cloth net 12/-

MOTTRAM The True Story of George Eliot in relation to "Adam Bede." By William Mottram. Illustrated. Demy 8vo, cloth. net 7/6

NICHOLSON A Literary History of the Arabs. By R A Nicholson,
M.A., Lecturer in Persian in the University of Cambridge. With
Coloured Frontispiece. (Library of Literary History) Demy 8vo,
cloth.   net   12/6

REA. Schiller's Dramas and Poems in England. By Thomas Rea,
M.A, Lecturer in German and Teutonic Philology, University
College of North Wales   Cr. 8vo, cloth   net   3/6

SMITH. Shakespeare the Man : An Attempt to Find Traces of the
Dramatist's Personal Character in his Dramas. By Professor
Goldwin Smith. 8vo, cloth gilt   net   2/6

WENDELL. A Literary History of America By Barrett Wendell,
Professor of English at Harvard College With Frontispiece.
(Library of Literary History) Demy 8vo, cloth   net   12/6

[For reference see also under " Biography."]

POETRY and the DRAMA.

ADAMS The Lonely Way, and Other Poems By W. A. Adams,
M.A   Demy 12mo, cloth.   3/6

—— Rus Divinum. (Poems) By Auguste Smada. (W. A Adams.)
Demy 12mo, parchment binding.   3/6

Bards of the Gael and Gail. See under "Sigerson"

BLIND. The Complete Poems of Mathilde Blind. Edited by
Arthur Symons With an Introduction by Dr Garnett. Cr. 8vo,
cloth gilt.   7,6

—— A Selection from the Poems of Mathilde Blind. Edited by
Arthur Symons. Portrait Fcap 8vo, parchment gilt,   7/6
Edition de Luxe, in Japan paper, in vellum   net   10/6

BURNS. The Love Songs of Robert Burns Selected and Edited,
with Introduction, by Sir George Douglas, Bart With Frontispiece
Portrait (Cameo Series. Vol. 11.) Demy 12mo, half-bound, paper
boards.   3/6

CAMEO SERIES, THE. Demy 12mo, with Frontispiece, half-bound.
Paper boards, 3/6 each ; vols. 14-20, each, **net**   3/6
Also an Edition de Luxe, limited to 30 copies, printed on Japan paper.
Prices on Application
[For full Titles see under Authors' names]

(1) The Lady from the Sea. By Henrik Ibsen.

(2) Iphigenia in Delphi. By Richard Garnett.

(3) A London Plane Tree. By Amy Levy

(4) Wordsworth's Grave. By William Watson.

(5) Miréio. By Frederic Mistral.

(6) Lyrics. Selected from the Works of A. Mary F. Robinson.

(7) A Minor Poet By Amy Levy.

(8) Concerning Cats.

(9) A Chaplet from the Greek Anthology. By Richard Garnett.

(10) The Countess Kathleen. By W. B. Yeats

(11) The Love Songs of Robert Burns.

(12) Love Songs of Ireland. Collected by K. Tynan

(13) Retrospect. By A. Mary F. Robinson.

(14) Brand. By Henrik Ibsen.

(15) The Son of Don Juan. By Don José Echegaray.

(16) Mariana. By Don José Echegaray

(17) Flamma Vestalis. By Eugene Mason.

(18) The Soul's Departure. By E Willmore.

(19) The Unpublished and Uncollected Poems of William Cowper.

(20) Ultima Verba. By Alfred de Kantzow.

CAPES. Amaranthus. A Book of Little Songs. By Bernard Capes
Small cr. 8vo, cloth. net 3/6

CARDUCCI. Poems by Giosuè Carducci. Selected and Translated, and with an Introduction by Maud Holland. Cr. 8vo, half-parchment. net 5/-

Concerning Cats. A Book of Verses by many Authors Edited by Graham R Tomson. Illustrated. {Cameo Series. Vol. 8.) Demy 12mo, half-bound, paper boards 3/6

COWPER. The Unpublished and Uncollected Poems of William Cowper. Edited by Thomas Wright Frontispiece (Cameo Series. Vol. 19.) Demy 12mo, paper boards, half-bound net 3/6

CRUSO. Sir Walter Raleigh. A Drama in Five Acts By H. A A. Cruso Cr 8vo, cloth. net 5/-

DYER. The Poems of John Dyer. Edited by Edward Thomas. With Portrait of J. D (Welsh Library. Vol. 4) Fcap 8vo
Paper covers, 1/- ; cloth 2/-

ECHEGARAY. Mariana An Original Drama in 3 Acts and an Epilogue By Don José Echegaray Translated into English by James Graham. With a Photogravure of a recent Portrait of the Author (Cameo Series. Vol 16) Demy 12mo, half-bound, paper boards net 3/6

—— **The Son of Don Juan.** An Original Drama in 3 Acts. By Don José Echegaray. Translated into English, with Biographical Introduction by James Graham. With Etched Portrait of the Author by Don B Maura (Cameo Series. Vol. 15.) Demy 12mo, half-bound, paper boards. net 3/6

FIELD. Wild Honey from Various Thyme. By Michael Field Cr 8vo, cloth. net 5/-

GARNETT. A Chaplet from the Greek Anthology By Richard Garnett, LL.D. (Cameo Series. Vol. 9) Demy 12mo, half-bound, paper boards 3/6

—— **Iphigenia in Delphi.** A Dramatic Poem. With Homer's "Shield of Achilles" and other Translations from the Greek. By Richard Garnett, LL D Frontispiece. (Cameo Series Vol 2.) Demy 12mo, half-bound, paper boards. 3/6

GOETHE'S Werke Mit Goethe's Leben Bildnis and Faksimile, Einleitungen und Anmerkungen Unter Mitwirkung mehrerer Fachgelehrter herausgegeben von Professor Dr K. Heinemann. 15 vols., large cr. 8vo cloth net 30/-

GRAVES. The Irish Poems of Alfred Perceval Graves. In two volumes Cloth, each, net 2/- , leather, each, net 3/-

HALL. God's Scourge A Drama in Four Acts. By Moreton Hall Cr. 8vo, cloth. net 3/6

HEINRICH HEINE'S Samtliche Werke. Herausgegeben von Professor Dr Ernst Elster. Kritisch durchgesehene und erlauterte Ausgabe. With Frontispiece and Facsimile. 7 vols., large cr. 8vo, cloth, net 16/-

HERBERT. The Temple By George Herbert. Sacred Poems. Facsimile Reprint of the First Edition, 1633 With an Introduction by J. H. Shorthouse Sixth Edition. Fcap 8vo, cloth net 3/6

HILL. Alfred the Great. A Play in Three Acts, wrought in Blank Verse. By Edmund L, Hill Demy 12mo, cloth net 2/6

HOBBES. The Ambassador : A Comedy in 4 Acts. By John Oliver Hobbes With Frontispiece. Cr 8vo, paper, net 2/- , cloth, net 3/6

—— **The Wisdom of the Wise** A Comedy in 3 Acts. By John Oliver Hobbes Cr 8vo. Paper covers, net 2/- , cloth, net 3/6

HYDE. The Religious Songs of Connacht   By Douglas Hyde, LL.D., M R.I A   Author of "A Literary History of Ireland," "Love Songs of Connacht," &c.   2 vols , cloth   **net**   10/-

IBSEN. Brand. A Dramatic Poem. By Henrik Isben. Translated by F. Edmund Garrett. With Frontispiece. (Cameo Series. Vol. 14.) Demy 12mo, half-bound, paper boards   **net**   3/6

—— The Lady from the Sea   By Henrik Ibsen. Translated by Eleanor Marx-Aveling. With Critical Introduction by Edmund Gosse   Third Edition   Portrait   (Cameo Series. Vol 1.) Demy 12mo, half-bound, paper boards.   3/6

LAW Songs of the Uplands   By Alice Law.   Cr 8vo, cloth, net   3/6

LEVY. A London Plane Tree. By Amy Levy   Illustrated by Bernard Partridge. (Cameo Series. Vol. 3) Demy 12mo, half-bound, paper boards.   3/6

—— A Minor Poet. By Amy Levy   With Frontispiece   Second Edition. (Cameo Series. Vol 7) Demy 12mo, half-bound, paper boards   3/6

LYTTELTON   Warp and Woof   A Play. By Edith Lyttelton. Cr 8vo, cloth   **net**   3/6

MACDONALD. A Wanderer, and Other Poems. By Leila Macdonald   Cr 8vo, white cloth, gilt   **net**   3/6

MASON. Flamma Vestalis, and Other Poems. By Eugene Mason Frontispiece after Sir Edward Burne-Jones   (Cameo Series Vol 17) Demy 12mo, half-bound, paper boards.   **net**   3/6

MERMAID SERIES (THE)   The Best Plays of the Old Dramatists Literal Reproductions of the Old Text. With Photogravure Frontispieces. The volumes may now be obtained bound in the following styles :

1. Cr. 8vo, uncut   Brown paper boards, with label   3/6
2. Cr. 8vo, uncut.   Green cloth, with gilt lettering on ink panel.   3/6
3. Cr 8vo, uncut top.   Brown cloth, with gilt lettering and decorative design in brown.   3/6
4. Cr. 8vo   Full vellum, with gilt lettering and gilt top   **net**   6/-

The Thin Paper Edition is also obtainable in cloth at 2/6 **net** , and in leather, at   **net**   3/6

	No
Beaumont. The Best Plays of Beaumont and Fletcher. Introduction and Notes by J St. Loe Strachey 2 vols	9, 10
Chapman. The Best Plays of George Chapman. Edited by William Lyon Phelps, Instructor in English Literature at Yale College.	
Congreve. The Complete Plays of William Congreve. Edited by Alex. C. Ewald.	21
Dekker. The Best Plays of Thomas Dekker. Notes by Ernest Rhys.	11
Dryden. The Best Plays of John Dryden. Edited by George Saintsbury 2 vols.	16
Farquhar. The Best Plays of George Farquhar. Edited, and with an Introduction, by William Archer.	24, 25
Fletcher. See Beaumont.	26
Ford The Best Plays of John Ford. Edited by Havelock Ellis	
Greene. The Complete Plays of Robert Greene. Edited with Introduction and Notes by Thomas H. Dickinson	3 / 27
Heywood. The Best Plays of Thomas Heywood. Edited by A W. Verity. With Introduction by J. A. Symonds.	6

MERMAID SERIES, THE—*continued*   No .

Jonson. **The Best Plays of Ben Jonson.** Edited, with Introduction and Notes, by Brinsley Nicholson and C. H. Herford 3 vols.   17, 19, 20

Marlowe. **The Best Plays of Christopher Marlowe.** Edited, with Critical Memoir and Notes, by Havelock Ellis ; and containing a General Introduction to the Series by John Addington Symonds   1

Massinger. **The Best Plays of Philip Massinger.** With Critical and Biographical Essay and Notes by Arthur Symons 2 vols   4, 5

Middleton. **The Best Plays of Thomas Middleton.** With an Introduction by Algernon Charles Swinburne. 2 vols   13, 14

Nero, and Other Plays. Edited by H. P Horne, Arthur Symons, A W. Verity, and H. Ellis   8

Otway **The Best Plays of Thomas Otway.** Introduction and Notes by the Hon. Roden Noel   2

Shadwell. **The Best Plays of Thomas Shadwell** Edited by George Saintsbury.   23

Shirley. **The Best Plays of James Shirley.** With Introduction by Edmund Gosse   15

Steele. **The Complete Plays of Richard Steele.** Edited, with Introduction and Notes, by G A Aitken   18

Tourneur. See Webster.

Vanbrugh. **The Select Plays of Sir John Vanbrugh** Edited, with an Introduction and Notes, by A. E. H. Swain.   22

Webster. **The Best Plays of Webster and Tourneur.** With an Introduction and Notes by John Addington Symonds.   12

Wycherley. **The Complete Plays of William Wycherley.** Edited, with Introduction and Notes, by W C Ward   7

MILLER The Tragedies of Seneca. By Frank Justus Miller Large cr. 8vo, cloth.   net 12/6

MISTRAL Mirèio A Provençal Poem By Frederic Mistral. Translated by H W. Preston. Frontispiece by Joseph Pennell. (Cameo Series Vol 5) Demy 12mo, half-bound, paper boards.   3/6

MOORE The Bending of the Bough. (Drama) By George Moore Cr 8vo, cloth   net 3/6

MYRON Of Una, and other African Memories. (Poems) By A. Kiel Myron. Cr 8vo, cloth   2/6

NICHOLSON (F. C.). Old German Love Songs Translated from the Minnesingers of the 12th—14th centuries. By F. C Nicholson, M.A. Large cr 8vo, cloth.   6/-

—— (L.) Vagrant Songs. By L Nicholson. Crown 8vo, cloth net 3/6

PRESLAND The Marionettes A Puppet Show in Two Acts. With other Poems By John Presland. Cr 8vo, half-parchment   net 5/-

RICHARDSON. Artist Songs. By E Richardson, LL.A., Author of "Sun, Moon, and Stars," and "Songs of Near and Far Away" Illustrated. Fcap 8vo, cloth   net 3/6

ROBINSON. The Collected Poems of Mary F. Robinson. Cr. 8vo, cloth.   7/6

—— Lyrics. Selected from the Works of A Mary F. Robinson (Cameo Series. Vol 6)   3/6

—— The New Arcadia. (Poems.) By A Mary F. Robinson (Mme. James Darmesteter) Cr. 8vo, paper covers.   3/6

—— Retrospect, and Other Poems By A. Mary F. Robinson (Cameo Series. Vol 13) Demy 12mo, half-bound, paper boards   3/6

AUTONYM LIBRARY, THE. Uniform in style and price with "The Pseudonym Library."   Paper covers, each, 1/6 , cloth, each   **2/-**

(1) **The Upper Berth.** By F. Marion Crawford

(2) **Mad Sir Uchtred of the Hills.** By S. R. Crockett.

(3) **By Reef and Palm** By Louis Becke.

(4) **The Play-Actress.** By S. R. Crockett.

(5) **A Bachelor Maid.** By Mrs Burton Harrison.

(6) **Miserrima.** By G. W. T. Omond.

(7) **The Two Strangers.** By Mrs Oliphant

(8) **Another Wicked Woman.** By S. De Pentheny

(9) **The Spectre of Strathannan.** By W. E. Norris.

(10) **Kafir Stories.** By W. C. Scully

(11) **Molly Darling.** By Mrs Hungerford

(12) **A Game of Consequences** By Albert Kinross.

(13) **Sleeping Fires.** By George Gissing.

(14) **The Red Star.** By L. McManus.

(15) **A Marriage by Capture.** By Robert Buchanan

(16) **Leaves from the Life of an Eminent Fossil.** By W. Dutton Burrard

(17) **An Impossible Person.** By Constance Cotterell.

(18) **Which is Absurd.** By Cosmo Hamilton

BACHELLER. Eben Holden. By Irving Bacheller Cr. 8vo, cloth, net   **2/6**
Also paper covers.   **6d.**

—— **Silas Strong** By Irving Bacheller. Cr. 8vo, cloth. (Unwin's Green Cloth Library.)   **6/-**

BAILLIE-SAUNDERS. London Lovers. By Margaret Baillie-Saunders, Author of the Prize Novel, "Saints in Society" Cr 8vo, cloth   Decorative binding.   **6/-**

—— **Saints in Society.** By Margaret Baillie-Saunders. £100 prize novel. Cr. 8vo, cloth. (First Novel Library.)   **6/-**
Also paper covers.   **6d.**

BAKER (H. B). Margaret Grey. See under "Little Novels" No. 4

BAKER (J.). A Double Choice. By James Baker. (Unwin's Green Cloth Library) Cr 8vo, cloth   **6/-**

BARLOW. By Beach and Bogland. By Jane Barlow, Author of "Irish Idylls," &c. With Frontispiece. Cr. 8vo cloth. (Unwin's Green Cloth Library.)   **6/-**

BARR (A. E.). The Black Shilling. By Amelia E. Barr. (Unwin's Red Cloth Library) Cr. 8vo, cloth   **6/-**

—— **Cecilia's Lover.** By Amelia E Barr. Cr. 8vo, cloth (Unwin's Red Cloth Library.)   **6/-**

—— **I, Thou, and the Other One.** By Amelia E. Barr. (Unwin's Green Cloth Library.) Cr 8vo, cloth.   **6/-**
Also (Popular Copyright Novels), cloth   **2/6**

—— **The Lion's Whelp.** By Amelia E. Barr. (Unwin's Green Cloth Library) Cr 8vo, cloth   **6/-**

—— **The Maid of Maiden Lane.** By Amelia E. Barr. Fully Illustrated. (Unwin's Green Cloth Library.) Cr 8vo, cloth.   **6/-**

—— **Prisoners of Conscience.** By Amelia E. Barr. Cr. 8vo, cloth   **6/-**
Popular Series for Boys and Girls Illustrated, cloth.   **3/6**
Also (Popular Copyright Novels), cloth.   **2/6**

—— **A Song of a Single Note.** By Amelia E Barr (Unwin's Red Cloth Library) Cr 8vo, cloth.   **6/-**

—— **Souls of Passage.** By Amelia E Barr (Unwin's Green Cloth Library) Cr. 8vo, cloth.   **6/-**

BARR (A. E) **Thyra Varrick.** By Amelia E Barr. (Unwin's Red Cloth Library) Cr 8vo, cloth.   6/-

—- **Trinity Bells.** A Tale of Old New York By Amelia E Barr Fully Illustrated in handsome decorated cover. Cr 8vo, cloth gilt.   6/-

—— **Was it Right to Forgive?** A Domestic Romance By Amelia E. Barr (Unwin's Green Cloth Library) Cr 8vo, cloth   6/-
Also (Popular Copyright Novels), cloth   2/6

BARR (W). **Shacklett** The Evolution of a Statesman. By Walter Barr Large cr. 8vo, cloth   6/-

BARRY. **Arden Massiter.** By William Barry. (Unwin's Green Cloth Library) Cr 8vo, cloth.   6/-

—— **The Dayspring—A Romance.** By William Barry, D D (Unwin's Red Cloth Library.) Cr. 8vo   6/-

—— **The Two Standards.** By William Barry, D.D. (Unwin's Green Cloth Library) Cr. 8vo, cloth.   6/-

—— **The Wizard's Knot.** By William Barry. (Unwin's Green Cloth Library) Cr. 8vo, cloth   6/-

BARTRAM. **People of Clopton.** By George Bartram. (Unwin's Green Cloth Library) Cr. 8vo, cloth.   6/-

—— **The White-headed Boy.** By George Bartram (Unwin's Green Cloth Library) Cr 8vo, cloth   6/-

BEALBY **A Daughter of the Fen** By J T Bealby (Unwin's Green Cloth Library) Cr. 8vo, cloth   6/-

BECKE. **The Adventures of a Supercargo.** By Louis Becke. (Unwin's Red Cloth Library) Cr. 8vo, cloth   6/-

—— **Breachley · Black Sheep.** By Louis Becke. (Unwin's Red Cloth Library) Cr 8vo, cloth.   6/-

—— **By Reef and Palm,** See Autonym Library. Vol 3

—— **By Reef and Palm, and Other Stories.** By Louis Becke. (Popular Copyright Novels) Cr 8vo, cloth   2/6

—— **By Rock and Pool.** By Louis Becke (Unwin's Green Cloth Library.) Cr. 8vo, cloth   6/-

—— **Chinkie's Flat, and Other Stories.** By Louis Becke (Unwin's Red Cloth Library) Cr 8vo, cloth   6/-

—— **The Ebbing of the Tide** By Louis Becke (Unwin's Green Cloth Library) Cr 8vo, cloth.   6/-

—— **Edward Barry · South Sea Pearler.** By Louis Becke. (Unwin's Green Cloth Library) Cr 8vo. cloth.   6/-

—— **Helen Adair.** By Louis Becke. (Unwin's Red Cloth Library) Cr 8vo, cloth   6/-

—— **His Native Wife.** By Louis Becke. (Century Library No. 4) Paper covers, 1/6 , cloth   2/-
Also paper covers.   6d.

—— **Old Convict Days.** Edited by Louis Becke. Cr. 8vo, cloth.   6/-

—— **Pacific Tales.** By Louis Becke Frontispiece Portrait of the Author (Unwin's Green Cloth Library) Cr 8vo, cloth.   6/-

—— **Ridan the Devil, and Other Stories.** By Louis Becke. (Unwin's Green Cloth Library) Large cr. 8vo, cloth.   6/-

—— **Rodman the Boatsteerer.** By Louis Becke. (Unwin's Green Cloth Library) Cr. 8vo, cloth.   6/-

—— **The Strange Adventure of James Shervington, and Other Stories** By Louis Becke (Unwin's Red Cloth Library) Cr 8vo, cloth   6/-
Also (Popular Copyright Novels), cloth.   2/6

CLIFFORD. Mrs Keith's Crime By Mrs. W K Clifford (Unwin's Green Cloth Library.) Cr. 8vo, cloth   6/-

CLYDE. A Pagan's Love. By Constance Clyde. (Unwin's First Novel Library.) Cr. 8vo, cloth.   6/-

COBBLEIGH (Tom) Gentleman Upcott's Daughter. See Pseudonym Library No. 19.

—— **Young Sam** See Pseudonym Library No. 40.

CONRAD. Almayer's Folly : A Romance of an Eastern River By Joseph Conrad. (Unwin's Green Cloth Library) Cr 8vo, cloth.   6/-

—— **An Outcast of the Islands.** By Joseph Conrad (Unwin's Green Cloth Library) Cr. 8vo, cloth.   6/-

—— **Tales of Unrest.** By Joseph Conrad. (Unwin's Green Cloth Library) Cr. 8vo, cloth   6/-
Also (The Adelphi Library). Cloth.   3/6

CORKRAN Lucie and I. By Henriette Corkran. Cr. 8vo, cloth   6/-

COSTELLOE. The World at Eighteen. By Ray Costelloe. Cr. 8vo, cloth   3/6

COTTERELL. An Impossible Person. By Constance Cotterell. (The Autonym Library.)   Paper covers, 1/6 , cloth   2/-

—— **Love is Not so Light.** By Constance Cotterell. (Unwin's Green Cloth Library.) Cr. 8vo, cloth   6/-

COURLANDER. Eve's Apple. By Alphonse Courlander. With Frontispiece Cr. 8vo, cloth   6/-

—— **The Sacrifice.** By Alphonse Courlander. With a coloured Frontispiece. (Green Cloth Library.) Cr. 8vo.   6/-

CRAMPTON. The Story of an Estancia. By George Crampton. Cr 8vo, cloth.   3/6

CRAWFORD (F. Marion.) The Upper Berth. See Autonym Library. Vol. I.

CRESPIGNY. From Behind the Arras. By Mrs. Philip Champion de Crespigny. (First Novel Library) Cr. 8vo, cloth   6/-

—— **The Mischief of a Glove.** By Mrs Philip Champion de Crespigny. (Unwin's Red Cloth Library.) Cr. 8vo, cloth.   6/-
Also paper covers   6d

Cricket on the Brain. By M. C C.   Illustrated by "Gil" Fcap. 4to, paper covers.   net 11d.

CROCKETT. Cinderella. By S. R. Crockett. (Unwin's Green Cloth Library) With 8 Illustrations. Cr. 8vo, cloth.   6/-

—— **The Grey Man.** By S R Crockett. (Unwin's Green Cloth Library) Cr. 8vo, cloth, gilt tops.   6/-
Also an Edition de Luxe, cr 4to, cloth gilt.   net 21/-

—— **Kit Kennedy : Country Boy** By S. R. Crockett. (Unwin's Green Cloth Library. Cr. 8vo, cloth gilt   6/-

—— **The Lilac Sunbonnet.** By S R Crockett. (Unwin's Green Cloth Library) Cr. 8vo, cloth, gilt tops.   6/-

—— **Mad Sir Uchtred of the Hills.** See Autonym Library. Vol. 2.

—— **Me and Myn.** By S R Crockett. (Unwin's Green Cloth Library) Cr 8vo.   6/-

—— **The Play Actress.** See Autonym Library Vol. 4.

—— **The Play Actress and Mad Sir Uchtred.** By S R Crockett With a new Preface. (Popular Copyright Novels) Cr. 8vo, cloth. 2/6

—— **The Raiders** By S. R. Crockett. (Unwin's Green Cloth Library) Cr. 8vo, cloth, gilt tops   6/-

CROCKETT. The Stickit Minister. By S. R Crockett. (Unwin's
Green Cloth Library.) Crown 8vo, cloth, gilt tops 6/-
   Cheap Edition. (Popular Copyright Novels) Cloth 2/6
   Also cr. 8vo, cloth. 1/- net   Paper covers 6d.

CROTTIE. The Lost Land. By Julia M Crottie. (Unwin's Green
Cloth Library) Cr 8vo, cloth. 6/-
—— Neighbours Being Annals of a Dull Town By Julia M. Crottie.
Cr 8vo, cloth. 6/-

DALIN (Talmage). European Relations See Pseudonym Library.
No. 9.

DALTON. Olive in Italy. By Moray Dalton. Cr 8vo, cloth. 6/-

DALZIEL. In the First Watch, and Other Engine-Room Stories.
By James Dalziel. Cr 8vo, cloth 6/-
—— High Life in the Far East. By James Dalziel. Cr. 8vo, cloth.

DAVIDSON. The Confessions of a Match-making Mother. By
Lillias Campbell Davidson. (Idle Hour Series No 6)
               Paper covers, 1/- ; cloth 2/-

DEAN (Mrs. Andrew). Splendid Cousin. See Pseudonym Library.
No 20.
—— Lesser's Daughter. See Pseudonym Library No. 43.

von DEGEN. Mystery of the Campagna. See Pseudonym Library.
No 3

DEW-SMITH. Diary of a Dreamer. By Mrs. Dew-Smith Cr. 8vo,
cloth gilt. 6/-

DICKESON. Tychiades. A Tale of the Ptolemies. Written in the
Third Century, B.C , by Ornithovius, and now faithfully translated
out of the Original by Alfred Dickeson Cr. 8vo, cloth 6/-

DRACHMANN (Holger). Cruise of the "Wild Duck." See
Pseudonym Library. No. 24

DROSINES (Georgios). Amaryllis. See Pseudonym Library. No 5.
—— Herb of Love. See Pseudonym Library No 16

DUMILLO (Alice). On the Gogmagogs. See "Little Novels" No. 10.

DUNDAS. The Journeys of Antonia By Christian Dundas
(Unwin's Red Cloth Library.) Cr. 8vo. 6/-

DUTT. The Lake of Palms. By Romesh Dutt, C I.E With Frontispiece. Cr. 8vo, cloth. 6/-

DYKE. As Others See Us. By Watson Dyke. (Unwin's Green Cloth
Library) Cr 8vo 6/-

von EBNER-ESCHENBACH (Marie). Two Countesses. See
Pseudonym Library. No. 27

van EEDEN. The Deeps of Deliverance. By F. Van Eeden.
(Unwin's Red Cloth Library) Cr 8vo, cloth 6/-

FALCONER (Lanoe) Mademoiselle Ixe See Pseudonym Library.
No 1
—— Hotel d'Angleterre. See Pseudonym Library No 6
—— Mademoiselle Ixe, The Hotel d'Angleterre, and Other
Stories. By Lanoe Falconer Popular Ed Cr 8vo, cloth. net 1/-

FARRER. The Great Noodleshire Election A Comedy of Political
Life By J. A Farrer. Cr 8vo, cloth. 3/6

FERGUSON. Lays of the Red Branch. By Sir Samuel Ferguson.
(New Irish Library) Small cr. 8vo.   Paper covers, 1/- ; cloth 2/-

FIRST NOVEL LIBRARY, THE. First Novels of New Authors.
Cr 8vo, cloth   each   6/-

(1) **Wistons.** By Miles Amber
(2) **The Searchers.** By Margaretta Byrde
(3) **A Lady's Honour.** By Bass Blake.
(4) **From Behind the Arras.** By Mrs. Philip Champion de Crespigny.
(5) **The Flame and the Flood.** By Rosamond Langbridge
(6) **A Drama of Sunshine.** By Mrs Aubrey Richardson
(7) **Rosemonde.** By Beatrice Stott.
(8) **The Cardinal's Pawn.** By K L. Montgomery.
(9) **Tussock Land.** By Arthur H. Adams
(10) **The Kingdom of Twilight.** By Forrest Reid
(11) **A Pagan's Love** By Constance Clyde
(12) **Saints in Society.** By Margaret Baillie-Saunders.
(13) **At the Sign of the Peacock** By K. C. Ryves.
(14) **From One Man's Hand to Another.** By G. H. Breda
(15) **Woman and the Sword.** By Rupert Lorraine.

FITZGERALD. Josephine's Troubles. A Story of the Franco-German War. By Percy Fitzgerald. Illustrated. Cr 8vo, cloth.   5/-

FLETCHER. Grand Relations. By J. S. Fletcher. Author of " The Arcadians " (Unwin's Red Cloth Library.) Cr. 8vo, cloth.   6/-
Also paper covers.   6d

—— **Paradise Court.** By J. S. Fletcher   Cr. 8vo, cloth   6/-

—— **The Queen of a Day.** By J. S Fletcher (Unwin's Red Cloth Library) Cr 8vo.   6/-

—— **The Threshing Floor** By J S. Fletcher. Cr. 8vo, cloth   6/-

FLOWERDEW. The Ways of Men. By Herbert Flowerdew. Cr. 8vo, cloth.   6/-

FOGAZZARO The Woman (Malombra) By Antonio Fogazzaro Translated by F Thorold Dickson. Cr. 8vo, cloth   6/-

FORREST The Bond of Blood See under " Little Novels " No. 6.

FRAPAN (Ilse). Heavy Laden. See Pseudonym Library No 13.
—— **Goo's Will.** See Pseudonym Library. No. 31

FRASER Death, the Showman. By John Fraser (Unwin's Green Cloth Library) Cr 8vo   6/-

FREDERIC. Marsena. By Harold Frederic. (Yellow Library. Vol. 2)   Paper covers, 1/- ; cloth   2/-

FRENCH. Desmonde, M.D. By Henry Willard French (Popular Copyright Novels.) Cr. 8vo, cloth.   2/6

FURNESS. The Melpomene Papers. By Annette Furness. Cr. 8vo, cloth.   3/6

GISSING (George). Sleeping Fires. See Autonym Library. Vol. 13.

GORKY Foma Gordyeeff. By Maxim Gorky Illustrated and unabridged. (Unwin's Green Cloth Library) Cr 8vo, cloth.   6/-

—— **The Man who was Afraid (Foma Gordyeeff).** By Maxim Gorky. Popular Edition. Cr. 8vo, cloth   net   1/-

—— **The Outcasts, and Other Stories.** By Maxim Gorky Cr. 8vo, cloth   3/6
Contents —The Outcasts, and Waiting for the Ferry Translated by Dora B. Montefiore. The Affair of the Clasps. Translated by Vera Volkhovsky.
New Popular Edition Cr. 8vo, cloth.   net   1/-

—— **Three of Them** By Maxim Gorky. Cr. 8vo, cloth.   2/6
New Popular Edition. Cr. 8vo, cloth   net   1/-

Grandmother's Advice to Elizabeth. See under "Trowbridge."

GREEN. The Filigree Ball. By Anna Katherine Green, Author of "The Leavenworth Case" (Unwin's Red Cloth Library) Cr 8vo, cloth. 6/-
Also paper covers. 6d.

GREEN CLOTH LIBRARY. See Unwin's Green Cloth Library.

GRIFFITHS (Arthur). A Royal Rascal. By Major Arthur Griffiths Cr. 8vo (Unwin's Red Cloth Library). 6/-
Also paper covers. 6d.

GRIFFITHS (D.R.) Elgiva, Daughter of the Thegn. By D R. Griffiths. Cr 8vo, cloth gilt 6/-

GUEST (Lady Charlotte). See under "Mabinogion"

GYP. Ginette's Happiness. By Gyp Translated by Ralph Derechef. (Popular Copyright Novels) Cr.8vo, cloth 2/6

HALES. A Lindsay o' the Dale. By A G Hales. With a Frontispiece by Stanley L. Wood. Crown 8vo, cloth. 6/-

—— Marozia. By A. G Hales. Cr. 8vo, cloth 6/-

—— The Watcher on the Tower. By A G. Hales (Unwin's Red Cloth Library) Cr. 8vo, cloth. 6/-
Also paper covers. 6d.

HAMILTON (Cosmo). Which is Absurd. See Autonym Library: Vol. 18.

HAMILTON (E.). The Mawkin of the Flow. By Lord Ernest Hamilton. (Unwin's Green Cloth Library.) Cr 8vo, cloth 6/-

—— Outlaws of the Marches. By Lord Ernest Hamilton. (Unwin's Green Cloth Library) Cr. 8vo, cloth. 6/-

—— The Perils of Josephine. By Lord Ernest Hamilton. (Unwin's Green Cloth Library) Cr 8vo, cloth. 6/-

HARDING. The Woman Who Vowed (The Demetrian) By Ellison Harding. Cr. 8vo, cloth. 6/-

HARDY. Pen Portraits of the British Soldier. By the Rev E. J. Hardy Illustrated. Demy 12mo, cloth, decorated cover. 1/-

—— Mr. Thomas Atkins. A study in Red, Blue, Green and Khaki. By the Rev. E J Hardy, M.A. 6/-
Also decorative paper covers. net 1/-

HARRISON (B.). Latter-day Sweethearts. By Mrs. Burton Harrison, Cr 8vo, cloth. 6/-

—— Transplanted Daughters. By Mrs. Burton Harrison, Cr. 8vo, cloth 6'-

—— A Triple Entanglement. By Burton Harrison. Cr. 8vo, cloth. 6/-

—— A Bachelor Maid. See Autonym Library. Vol. 5.

HARRISON (D.). Master Passions. By Mrs Darent Harrison Cr. 8vo, cloth. 6/-

HAY. Herridge of Reality Swamp By William Hay Cr 8vo, cloth. 6/-

HENSHAW. Why Not, Sweetheart? By Julia W. Henshaw. Cr. 8vo, cloth. 6/-

HENTY. The Lost Heir. By G. A. Henty. Cr. 8vo, cloth. 6/-
Also Popular Series for Boys and Girls Illustrated, cloth 3/6

HERTZ-GARTEN (Theodor). Red-Litten Windows. See Pseudonym Library. No. 11.

HINKSON   Father Alphonsus   By H A. Hinkson. Cr. 8vo, cloth   6/-

HOBBES   A Bundle of Life   See Pseudonym Library, No. 34.

—— The Dream and the Business. By John Oliver Hobbes
With a cover design by Aubrey Beardsley   Cr. 8vo, cloth.   6/-

—— The Flute of Pan.   By John Oliver Hobbes.   (Unwin's
Red Cloth Library.) Cr 8vo, cloth   6/-

—— The Gods, Some Mortals, and Lord Wickenham. By John
Oliver Hobbes (Unwin's Green Cloth Library) Cr. 8vo, cloth   6/-
Also (Idle Hour Series. No 3).   Paper covers, 1/- , cloth   2/-
Also paper covers.   6d·

—— The Herb-Moon   By John Oliver Hobbes (Unwin's Green Cloth
Library) Large cr. 8vo, cloth   6/-
Also (Popular Copyright Novels).   2/6

—— Love and the Soul Hunters By John Oliver Hobbes. (Unwin's
Red Cloth Library) Cr. 8vo, cloth.   6/-
Popular Edition   Cr. 8vo.   Paper covers, net, 6d ; cloth, net   1/-

—— Robert Orange : A Sequel to "The School for Saints." (Unwin's
Green Cloth Library.) Cr. 8vo, cloth   6/-
Also paper covers.   6d.

—— The School for Saints. By John Oliver Hobbes. (Unwin's Green
Cloth Library) Large cr 8vo, cloth   6/-
Also paper covers.   6d.

—— The Sinner's Comedy. See Pseudonym Library, No 28

—— Some Emotions and a Moral, and The Sinner's Comedy
By John Oliver Hobbes   Cr. 8vo, cloth.   net   1/-

—— Some Emotions and a Moral   See Pseudonym Library, No. 8.
Also paper covers.   6d.

—— A Study in Temptations, and A Bundle of Life By John Oliver
Hobbes. Cr. 8vo.   Paper covers, net, 6d. ; cloth, net   1/-

—— A Study in Temptations. See Pseudonym Library, No. 23.

—— Tales about Temperaments. By John Oliver Hobbes. Cr. 8vo,
cloth gilt,   net   2/6

—— The Tales of John Oliver Hobbes.   Portrait of the Author.
(Unwin's Green Cloth Library) Large cr. 8vo, cloth
Contents :—Some Emotions and a Moral   A Bundle of Life.   6/-
A Study in Temptations.   The Sinner's Comedy.
Also (The Adelphi Library), cloth.   3/6

—— The Vineyard. By John Oliver Hobbes. (Unwin's Red Cloth
Library.) With Six Illustrations. Cr. 8vo, cloth,   6/-
Also paper covers.   6d.

—— Life and To-morrow. Selections from the Writings of John
Oliver Hobbes. Edited by Zoe Procter. Cr. 8vo, cloth.   6/-

HOCKING. Meadowsweet and Rue. By Silas K. Hocking (Unwin's
Red Cloth Library) Cr. 8vo, cloth.   6/-

HOLDSWORTH.   The Iron Gates.   By Annie E. Holdsworth.
(Unwin's Green Cloth Library) Cr. 8vo, cloth.   6/-

HORNIMAN. That Fast Miss Blount. A Novel. By Roy Horniman. (Unwin's Red Cloth Library.) Cr. 8vo, cloth. 　　6/-
Also paper covers. 　　6d.

—— **The Living Buddha.** By Roy Horniman. (Unwin's Red Cloth Library.) Cr. 8vo, cloth. 　　6/-

HUDSON A Crystal Age. By W. H. Hudson. Cr. 8vo, cloth, decorative binding. 　　6/-

HUMPHREY (Frank Pope). New England Cactus. See Pseudonym Library, No. 15.

HUMPHREY (Mrs.) Beauty Adorned. By Mrs. Humphrey. Long 8vo, cloth, decorated cover 　　1/-

HUNGERFORD (Mrs.) Molly Darling. See Autonym Library. Vol. 11.

IDLE HOUR SERIES, THE. Cr. 8vo. 　　Paper covers, 1/-; cloth 　　2/-

(1) **Another Englishwoman's Love Letters.** By Barry Pain
(2) **The Letters of Her Mother to Elizabeth.** By W. R. H. Trowbridge
(3) **The Gods, Some Mortals, and Lord Wickenham.** By John Oliver Hobbes (Mrs. Craigie).
(4) **De Omnibus.** By the Conductor (Barry Pain).
(5) **Certain Personal Matters.** By H. G. Wells
(6) **The Confessions of a Match-making Mother.** By Lillias C. Davidson.
(7) **The Grandmother's Advice to Elizabeth.** By W. R H. Trowbridge.
(8) **Hookey.** By A. Neil Lyons
(9) **The Adventures of Prince Aga Mirza.** By Aquila Kempster.

IRVING. Six Girls. By Fanny Belle Irving Illustrated. (Unwin's Popular Series for Boys and Girls) Cloth 　　3/6

IRWIN. With Sword and Pen. A Story of India in the Fifties. By H. C. Irwin. (Unwin's Red Cloth Library) Cr. 8vo, cloth. 　　6/-

JEFFERY (Walter). See "Becke (Louis)."

JENNINGS Under the Pompadour. A Romance. By Edward W. Jennings. Cr. 8vo, cloth. 　　6/-

JEPSON. The Lady Noggs, Peeress. By Edgar Jepson. With 8 Illustrations. Cr. 8vo, cloth. 　　6/-
Also decorative paper covers 1/- net. 　　Also paper covers. 　　6d.

—— **The Four Philanthropists.** By Edgar Jepson. Crown 8vo, cloth. 　　6/-

JERNINGHAM. Monsieur Paulot. By Sir Hubert Jerningham. (Century Library. No 3.) 　　Paper covers, 1/6; cloth 　　2/-

JESSOPP. Frivola, and Simon Ryan the Peterite. By Augustus Jessopp, D D. New Edition. Revised and Expanded. With portrait. Cr. 8vo, limp cloth, silk sewn. 　　3/6

—— **Simon Ryan the Peterite.** By Augustus Jessopp, D.D (Yellow Library. Vol 1.) 　　Paper covers, 1/-; cloth 　　2/-

KEARY. High Policy. By C. F. Keary. (Unwin's Red Cloth Library) Cr. 8vo, cloth 　　6/-

—— **A Mariage de Convenance.** By C. F. Keary. (Unwin's Green Cloth Library) Cr. 8vo, cloth. 　　6/-

KELLER (Gottfried) A Selection of his Tales. Translated, with a Memoir, by Kate Freiligrath Kroeker. With Portrait Cr. 8vo, cloth. 　　6/-

KEMPSTER. The Adventures of Prince Aga Mirza. By Aquila Kempster. (Idle Hour Series. No. 9). 　　Paper covers, 1/-; cloth 　　2/-

MANN. Among the Syringas. By Mary E Mann. (Unwin's Green
Cloth Library.) Cr. 8vo.   6/-
—— **In Summer Shade.** By Mary E. Mann. Cr. 8vo, cloth.   6/-
Also in decorative paper covers.   net   1/-
—— **The Mating of a Dove.** By Mary E. Mann. (Unwin's Green Cloth
Library.) Cr. 8vo, cloth.   6/-
—— **Moonlight.** By Mary E. Mann. (Unwin s Green Cloth Library.)
Cr 8vo.   6/-
—— **The Patten Experiment.** By Mary E. Mann. (Unwin's Green
Cloth Library.) Cr. 8vo, cloth.   6/-
—— **Susannah.** By Mary E. Mann. (Unwin's Green Cloth Library)
Cr. 8vo, cloth.   6/-

MARQUIS. Marguerite de Roberval. By T. G. Marquis. Cr. 8vo,
cloth.   6/-

MARSH. The Beetle A Mystery By Richard Marsh.   With Illustrations by John Williamson   Cr. 8vo, cloth   6/-
Also (The Adelphi Library), cloth.   3/6

MARTYN. The Tale of a Town and an Enchanted Sea. By Edward
Martyn   Cr. 8vo, cloth.   5/-

MAUGHAM. 'Liza of Lambeth. By W. Somerset Maugham. Cr. 8vo.
cloth.   3/6
Also paper covers.   6d.
—— **The Making of a Saint.** By W. Somerset Maugham. (Unwin's
Green Cloth Library.) Cr 8vo, cloth.   6/-
—— **Orientations, and Other Stories.** By W. Somerset Maugham.
Cr. 8vo, cloth   6/-

MAYNE. The Clearer Vision. By Ethel Colburn Mayne. Cr. 8vo,
cloth gilt.   5/-

MEADE. Love Triumphant. By Mrs. L. T. Meade. (Unwin's Red
Cloth Library.) Cr 8vo, cloth.   6/-
Also Popular Series for Boys and Girls.   Illustrated, cloth.   3/6

MEIRION (Ellinor). Cause and Effect. See Pseudonym Library.
No. 49.

MIKOULITCH (V.). Mimi's Marriage. See Pseudonym Library.
No 35

MILNE. The Epistles of Atkins. By James Milne. With 12 Illustrations from War Sketches. Cr. 8vo, cloth.   6/-

MITCHELL. Hugh Wynne. By S. Weir Mitchell. (Unwin's Green
Cloth Library) Cr 8vo.   6/-
—— **Far in the Forest.** By S. Weir Mitchell. Cr. 8vo, cloth.   6/-

MONTAGU. Naomi's Exodus. By Lily H. Montagu Cr. 8vo, cloth. 3/6

MONTGOMERY. The Cardinal's Pawn. By K L Montgomery.
(First Novel Library. No. 8) Cr. 8vo, cloth.   6/-
Also paper covers.   6d.
—— **Love in the Lists.** By K. L. Montgomery. Cr. 8vo, cloth.   6/-
—— **Major Weir.** By K. L. Montgomery. With 8 Illustrations.
(Unwin's Red Cloth Library.) Cr. 8vo, cloth.   6/-

MOORE. Evelyn Innes. By George Moore. (Unwin's Green Cloth
Library) Cr. 8vo, cloth.   6/-
Also (The Adelphi Library), cloth.   3/6
Also paper covers.   6d.

MOORE. **Sister Teresa.** A Novel. By George Moore. (Unwin's Green Cloth Library.) Cr. 8vo, cloth. — 6/-
Also (The Adelphi Library). Cloth. — 3/6
Paper covers. — 6d.

—— **The Untilled Field.** By George Moore. (Unwin's Red Cloth Library) Cr 8vo, cloth. — 6/-

MUIR. **The Mystery of Muncraig.** By Robert James Muir. Cr. 8vo, cloth gilt. — 6/-

MURRAY. **He that had Received the Five Talents.** By J. Clark Murray. (Unwin's Red Cloth Library) Cr. 8vo, cloth. — 6/-

NELSON (Jane). **The Rousing of Mrs. Potter.** See Pseudonym Library. No 36.

NESBIT. **Man and Maid** By E. Nesbit Cr. 8vo, cloth. — 6/-

NESBIT'S Children's Stories. See under "Books for Children."

NORMYX. **Unprofessional Tales.** By Normyx. Cr. 8vo, cloth. — 6/-

NORRIS (W. E). **The Spectre of Strathannan.** See Autonym Library. Vol 9.

O'GRADY. **The Bog of Stars, and Other Stories of Elizabethan Ireland.** By Standish O'Grady. (New Irish Library. No 2) Small cr. 8vo. Paper covers, 1/- ; cloth — 2/-

OLIPHANT (Mrs.). **The Two Strangers.** See Autonym Library. Vol. 7.

OMOND (G. W. T.). **Miserrima.** See Autonym Library. Vol. 6.

ORCZY. **The Case of Miss Elliott.** By the Baroness Orczy, Author of "The Scarlet Pimpernel," &c. With 16 Illustrations Cr. 8vo, cloth. — 6/-

OUIDA. **A Rainy June and Don Gesualdo.** By Ouida. (Popular Copyright Novels) Cr 8vo, cloth. — 2/6

—— **The Silver Christ, and Other Stories.** By Ouida. (Unwin's Green Cloth Library) Cr 8vo, cloth. — 6/-
See also Pseudonym Library. No. 41.

—— **Toxin.** See Century Library. No. 1.

OWEN. **Captain Sheen.** By Charles Owen. Cr 8vo, cloth. — 6/-

PAIN. **Another Englishwoman's Love Letters.** By Barry Pain. (Idle Hour Series. No. 1) Paper covers, 1/- ; cloth — 2/-

—— **Curiosities.** By Barry Pain. Paper covers. — 1/-

—— **De Omnibus.** By The Conductor (Barry Pain). Paper covers, 1/- Cloth. — 2/-

—— **De Omnibus and Another Englishwoman's Love Letters.** By Barry Pain. Paper covers — 6d.

—— **Little Entertainments.** By Barry Pain. Cr. 8vo. Paper covers, 1/- Cloth. — 2/-

—— **The Memoirs of Constantine Dix.** By Barry Pain. Cr. 8vo, cloth — 3/6
Also in decorative paper covers. 1/- net. Also paper covers 6d.

de PENTHENY (S.) **Another Wicked Woman.** See Autonym Library. Vol. 8.

PIDGIN. **Quincy Adams Sawyer.** By Charles F. Pidgin. Cr. 8vo, cloth. — 6/-

PINSENT. **No Place for Repentance.** See under Little Novels. No. 2.

PLAYNE. **The Romance of a Lonely Woman.** By C. E. Playne. Cr 8vo, cloth. — 6/-

MANN. Among the Syringas. By Mary E Mann. (Unwin's Green
Cloth Library.) Cr. 8vo.   6/-

—— **In Summer Shade.** By Mary E Mann. Cr. 8vo, cloth.   6/-
Also in decorative paper covers.   **net** 1/-

—— **The Mating of a Dove.** By Mary E. Mann. (Unwin's Green Cloth
Library) Cr. 8vo, cloth.   6/-

—— **Moonlight.** By Mary E. Mann. (Unwin s Green Cloth Library.)
Cr 8vo.   6/-

—— **The Patten Experiment.** By Mary E. Mann. (Unwin's Green
Cloth Library.) Cr 8vo, cloth.   6/-

—— **Susannah.** By Mary E. Mann. (Unwin's Green Cloth Library.)
Cr 8vo, cloth.   6/-

MARQUIS. Marguerite de Roberval. By T. G. Marquis. Cr. 8vo,
cloth.   6/-

MARSH The Beetle A Mystery. By Richard Marsh. With.Illustra-
tions by John Williamson Cr. 8vo, cloth.   6/-
Also (The Adelphi Library), cloth.   3/6

MARTYN. The Tale of a Town and an Enchanted Sea. By Edward
Martyn. Cr. 8vo, cloth.   5/-

MAUGHAM. 'Liza of Lambeth. By W. Somerset Maugham. Cr. 8vo.
cloth   3/6
Also paper covers.   6d.

—— **The Making of a Saint.** By W. Somerset Maugham. (Unwin's
Green Cloth Library) Cr. 8vo, cloth.   6/-

—— **Orientations, and Other Stories.** By W. Somerset Maugham.
Cr. 8vo, cloth.   6/-

MAYNE. The Clearer Vision. By Ethel Colburn Mayne. Cr 8vo,
cloth gilt.   5/-

MEADE. Love Triumphant. By Mrs. L. T. Meade. (Unwin's Red
Cloth Library) Cr. 8vo, cloth.   6/-
Also Popular Series for Boys and Girls. Illustrated, cloth.   3/6

MEIRION (Ellinor). Cause and Effect. See Pseudonym Library.
No. 49.

MIKOULITCH (V.). Mimi's Marriage. See Pseudonym Library.
No 35.

MILNE. The Epistles of Atkins. By James Milne. With 12 Illustrations from War Sketches. Cr. 8vo, cloth.   6/-

MITCHELL. Hugh Wynne. By S. Weir Mitchell. (Unwin's Green
Cloth Library) Cr. 8vo.   6/-

—— **Far in the Forest.** By S. Weir Mitchell. Cr. 8vo, cloth.   6/-

MONTAGU. Naomi's Exodus. By Lily H. Montagu. Cr. 8vo, cloth. 3/6

MONTGOMERY. The Cardinal's Pawn. By K. L. Montgomery.
(First Novel Library. No. 8) Cr. 8vo, cloth.   6/-
Also paper covers.   6d.

—— **Love in the Lists.** By K. L. Montgomery. Cr. 8vo, cloth.   6/-

—— **Major Weir.** By K. L. Montgomery. With 8 Illustrations.
(Unwin's Red Cloth Library.) Cr. 8vo, cloth.   6/-

MOORE. Evelyn Innes. By George Moore. (Unwin's Green Cloth
Library) Cr 8vo, cloth.   6/-
Also (The Adelphi Library), cloth.   3/6
Also paper covers.   6d.

MOORE. Sister Teresa. A Novel. By George Moore. (Unwin's Green Cloth Library) Cr. 8vo, cloth.   6/-
Also (The Adelphi Library). Cloth.   3/6
Paper covers.   6d.

—— **The Untilled Field.** By George Moore. (Unwin's Red Cloth Library.) Cr. 8vo, cloth.   6/-

MUIR. The Mystery of Muncraig. By Robert James Muir. Cr. 8vo, cloth gilt.   6/-

MURRAY. He that had Received the Five Talents. By J. Clark Murray. (Unwin's Red Cloth Library) Cr. 8vo, cloth.   6/-

NELSON (Jane). The Rousing of Mrs. Potter. See Pseudonym Library. No. 36

NESBIT. Man and Maid By E. Nesbit. Cr. 8vo, cloth.   6/-

NESBIT'S Children's Stories. See under "Books for Children."

NORMYX. Unprofessional Tales. By Normyx. Cr. 8vo, cloth.   6/-

NORRIS (W. E). The Spectre of Strathannan. See Autonym Library. Vol 9.

O'GRADY. The Bog of Stars, and Other Stories of Elizabethan Ireland By Standish O'Grady. (New Irish Library. No. 2) Small cr. 8vo.   Paper covers, 1/- ; cloth   2/-

OLIPHANT (Mrs.). The Two Strangers. See Autonym Library. Vol. 7.

OMOND (G. W. T.). Miserrima. See Autonym Library Vol. 6.

ORCZY. The Case of Miss Elliott. By the Baroness Orczy, Author of "The Scarlet Pimpernel," &c. With 16 Illustrations. Cr. 8vo, cloth.   6/-

OUIDA. A Rainy June and Don Gesualdo. By Ouida. (Popular Copyright Novels) Cr. 8vo, cloth.   2/6

—— **The Silver Christ, and Other Stories.** By Ouida. (Unwin's Green Cloth Library.) Cr 8vo, cloth.   6/-
See also Pseudonym Library. No 41.

—— **Toxin.** See Century Library. No 1.

OWEN. Captain Sheen. By Charles Owen. Cr. 8vo, cloth.   6/-

PAIN. Another Englishwoman's Love Letters. By Barry Pain. (Idle Hour Series No 1)   Paper covers, 1/- ; cloth   2/-

—— Curiosities. By Barry Pain. Paper covers.   1/-

—— De Omnibus. By The Conductor (Barry Pain). Paper covers, 1/- Cloth.   2/-

—— De Omnibus and Another Englishwoman's Love Letters. By Barry Pain Paper covers   6d.

—— Little Entertainments By Barry Pain. Cr. 8vo. Paper covers, 1/- Cloth.   2/-

—— The Memoirs of Constantine Dix. By Barry Pain. Cr. 8vo, cloth   3/6
Also in decorative paper covers. 1/- net.   Also paper covers   6d.

de PENTHENY (S.) Another Wicked Woman. See Autonym Library Vol. 8.

PIDGIN. Quincy Adams Sawyer. By Charles F. Pidgin. Cr 8vo, cloth.   6/-

PINSENT. No Place for Repentance. See under Little Novels. No. 2.

PLAYNE. The Romance of a Lonely Woman. By C. E. Playne. Cr. 8vo, cloth   6/-

de POLEN. Clairice · The Story of a Crystal Heart. By Narcisse
      Lucien de Polen   Cr 8vo, cloth   3/6

POPULAR COPYRIGHT NOVELS. Cheap re-issue. In cr. 8vo,
      cloth gilt.   each   2/6

ALEXANDER (MRS).
    Brown, V.C.
    Stronger than Love.
    Through Fire to Fortune.
    A Winning Hazard.
BARR (AMELIA E)
    I, Thou, & the Other One.
    Prisoners of Conscience,
    Was it Right to Forgive?
BECKE (LOUIS).
    By Reef & Palm,
    The Strange Adventures
        of James Shervington.
    Tessa and The Trader's
        Wife.
BUCHANAN (ROBERT).
    Effie Hetherington.
CROCKETT (S R).
    The Play Actress and
        Mad Sir Uchtred.
    The Stickit Minister.
CROMMELIN (MAY)
    Half Round the World for
        a Husband.

FRENCH (H. W.).
    Desmonde, M D.
GYP
    Ginette's Happiness.
HOBBES (JOHN OLIVER).
    The Herb-Moon.
McMANUS (L)
    Lally of the Brigade.
OUIDA.
    A Rainy June.
RITA.
    The Ending of My Day.
    Vanity! The Confessions
        of a Court Modiste.
RUSSELL (W CLARK).
    The Romance of a Mid-
        shipman.
SALÀ (GEORGE AUGUS-
    TUS).
    Margaret Forster.
SCHREINER (OLIVE).
    Trooper Peter Halket.

POTAPENKO (J)   Russian Priest. See Pseudonym Library. No 7.

——— **General's Daughter.** See Pseudonym Library. No. 17.

——— **Father of Six.** See Pseudonym Library. No 26.

PRAED. The Insane Root. By Mrs. Campbell Praed. (Unwin's Green
      Cloth Library) Cr 8vo, cloth   6/-

——— **Nyria.** By Mrs. Campbell Praed. (Unwin's Red Cloth Library.)
      Cr. 8vo, cloth.   6/-

PRICHARD. The New Chronicles of Don Q. By K and Hesketh
      Prichard Illustrated   Cr. 8vo, cloth   6/-

PRYCE. John Jones, Curate. By G. Pryce. (Unwin's Green Cloth
      Library) Cr. 8vo, cloth.   6/-

——— **A Son of Arvon.** A Welsh Novel By Gwendolen Pryce.
      (Unwin's Green Cloth Library) Cr. 8vo.   6/-

PSEUDONYM LIBRARY, THE. 24mo. Paper covers, 1/6 ; cloth, each   2/-

(1) Mademoiselle Ixe. By
    Lanoe Falconer.
(2) The Story of Eleanor
    Lambert. By Magdalene
    Brooke
(3) A Mystery of the Cam-
    pagna. By von Degen.
(4) The School of Art. By
    Isabel Snow.
(5) Amaryllis. By Georgios
    Drosines.

(6) The Hotel d' Angleterre.
    By Lanoe Falconer.
(7) A Russian Priest. By
    J. Potapenko. Translated
    by W. Gaussen.
(8) Some Emotions and a
    Moral. By John Oliver
    Hobbes
(9) European Relations. A
    Tirolese Sketch. By Tal-
    mage Dalin

PSEUDONYM LIBRARY, THE.—*continued.*

(10) **John Sherman, & Dhoya.** By Ganconagh (W B. Yeats).

(11) **Through the Red-Litten Windows.** By Theodor Hertz-Garten.

(12) **Green Tea.** A Love Story. By V. Schallenberger

(13) **Heavy Laden, and Old Fashioned Folk.** By Ilse Frapan. Translated by Helen A. Macdonell.

(14) **Makar's Dream, and Other Russian Stories.** By V Korolenko, and Others

(15) **A New England Cactus.** By Frank Pope Humphrey

(16) **The Herb of Love.** By Georgios Drosines. Translated by Eliz. M Edmonds.

(17) **The General's Daughter.** By J Potapenko Translated by W. Gaussen

(18) **The Saghalien Convict, and Other Russian Stories** By V. Korolenko, and Others

(19) **Gentleman Upcott's Daughter.** By Tom Cobbleigh

(20) **A Splendid Cousin.** By Mrs Andrew Dean

(21) **Colette.** By Philippe St. Hilaire.

(22) **Ottilie.** By Vernon Lee

(23) **A Study in Temptations.** By John Oliver Hobbes.

(24) **The Cruise of the "Wild Duck."** By Holger Drachmann.

(25) **Squire Heilman, and Other Finnish Stories.** By Juhani Aho. Translated by R Nisbert Bain.

(26) **A Father of Six, and An Occasional Holiday.** By J. Potapenko Translated by W Gaussen.

(27) **The Two Countesses.** By Marie von Ebner-Eschenbach. Translated by Mrs Waugh.

(28) **The Sinner's Comedy.** By John Oliver Hobbes.

(29) **Cavalleria Rusticana, and Other Tales of Sicilian Peasant Life.** By Giovanni Verga Translated by Alma Strettell.

(30) **The Passing of a Mood, and Other Stories.** By V. O. C S.

(31) **God's Will, and Other Stories.** By Ilse Frapan Translated by Helen A. Macdonell.

(32) **Dream Life and Real Life.** By Ralph Iron (Olive Schreiner).

(33) **The Home of the Dragon.** A Tonquinese Idyll. By Anna Catharina

(34) **A Bundle of Life.** By John Oliver Hobbes

(35) **Mimi's Marriage.** By V. Mikoulitch.

(36) **The Rousing of Mrs. Potter, and Other Stories.** By Jane Nelson.

(37) **A Study in Colour** By Alice Spinner.

(38) **The Hon Stanbury.** By Two.

(39) **The Shen's Pigtail, and Other Stories of Anglo-China Life.** By Mr. M—

(40) **Young Sam and Sabina.** By Tom Cobbleigh

(41) **The Silver Christ, and a Lemon Tree.** By Ouida

(42) **A Husband of No Importance.** By Rita

(43) **Lesser's Daughter.** By Mrs. Andrew Dean.

(44) **Helen.** By Oswald Valentine.

(45) **Cliff Days.** By Brian Rosegarth.

(46) **Old Brown's Cottages** By John Smith.

(47) **Under the Chilterns.** By Rosemary

(48) **Every Day's News.** By R. E. Francis

(49) **Cause and Effect** By Ellinor Merrion

(50) **A White Umbrella, and Other Stories.** By Sarnia.

(51) **When Wheat is Green.** By Jos. Wilton.

(52) **Anthony Jasper.** By Ben Bolt

(53) **As a Tree Falls.** By L. Parry Truscott.

(54) **A Ne'er-Do-Weel.** By Valentine Caryl.

(55) **Penelope Brandling.** By Vernon Lee

RED CLOTH LIBRARY. See Unwin's Red Cloth Library.

REETH. Legions of the Dawn. By Allan Reeth. Cr. 8vo, cloth. 6/-

REID. The Kingdom of Twilight. By Forrest Reid. (First Novel Library) Cr. 8vo, cloth. 6/-

RICHARDSON. A Drama of Sunshine—Played in Homburg. By Mrs Aubrey Richardson. (First Novel Library.) Cr. 8vo, cloth. 6/-

—— They Twain. By Mrs. Aubrey Richardson. (Unwin's Red Cloth Library) Cr. 8vo, cloth. 6/-

RICHINGS. In Chaucer's Maytime. By Emily Richings. (Unwin's Red Cloth Library) Cr. 8vo, cloth gilt. 6/-

RITA. The Ending of My Day. By Rita. (Popular Copyright Novels.) Cr. 8vo, cloth gilt. 2/6

—— A Husband of No Importance. See Pseudonym Library. No. 42.

—— A Jilt's Journal. (Unwin's Green Cloth Library.) Cr 8vo, cloth. 6/-

—— Vanity: The Confessions of a Court Modiste. By Rita. Cr. 8vo, cloth. 6/-
  Also (Popular Copyright Novels), cloth. 2/6

ROOSEVELT. The Siren's Net. By Florence Roosevelt. (Unwin's Red Cloth Library) Cr. 8vo, cloth 6/-

ROSEGARTH (Brian). Cliff Days. See Pseudonym Library. No. 45.

ROSEGGER. The Light Eternal. By Peter Rosegger. Cr. 8vo, cloth. 6/-

ROWBOTHAM. Tales from Plutarch. By F Jameson Rowbotham. Fully illustrated. Cr 8vo, cloth. 5/-

ROWLANDS. The Passion of Mahael. See under "Bowen-Rowlands."

RUSSELL. The Honour of the Flag. By W. Clark Russell. Demy 12mo, cloth 2/6

—— A Noble Haul. See under "Little Novels" No 11.

—— The Romance of a Midshipman. By W. Clark Russell. (Popular Copyright Novels) Cr 8vo, cloth. 2/6

—— The Yarn of Old Harbour Town. A Sea Romance. By W. Clark Russell (Unwin's Red Cloth Library) Cr. 8vo, cloth. 6/-

RUTHERFORD. The Autobiography of Mark Rutherford. Edited by Reuben Shapcott. Cr. 8vo, cloth. 3/6

—— Catherine Furze: A Novel by Mark Rutherford. Cr. 8vo, cloth. 3/6

—— Clara Hopgood. By Mark Rutherford Cr 8vo, cloth. 3/6

—— Mark Rutherford's Deliverance. Cr 8vo, cloth. 3/6

—— Miriam's Schooling, and Other Papers. By Mark Rutherford. With Frontispiece by Walter Crane. Cr. 8vo, cloth. 3/6

—— The Revolution in Tanner's Lane. Cr. 8vo, cloth. 3/6

—— Pages from a Journal. By Mark Rutherford. Cr. 8vo, cloth. 6/-

—— A New Popular Edition. Each vol cr. 8vo, cloth gilt, each, net 1/-

LIST OF VOLUMES.

(1) The Autobiography of Mark Rutherford.

(2) Mark Rutherford's Deliverance.

(3) The Revolution in Tanner's Lane.

(4) Miriam's Schooling.

(5) Catherine Furze.

(6) Clara Hopgood.

RYVES. At the Sign of the Peacock. By K C. Ryves (First Novel Library.) Cr 8vo, cloth.   6/-

ST. HILAIRE (Philippe). Colette. See Pseudonym Library. No. 21.

SALA. Margaret Forster: A Novel By George Augustus Sala (Popular Copyright Novels) Cr. 8vo, cloth gilt.   2/6

SANDERS. A Comedy of Three. See under "Little Novels." No. 8.

SARNIA. White Umbrella. See Pseudonym Library. No. 50.

SCHALLENBERGER (V.). Green Tea. See Pseudonym Library. No. 12.

von SCHLICHT. Life in a Crack Regiment (Erstklassige Menschen). A Novel of German Military Manners and Morals By Baron von Schlicht. Translated by F. B. Low. Cr. 8vo, cloth.   6/-
Also paper covers.   6d

SCHREINER. Dream Life and Real Life. By Olive Schreiner. Cloth.   2/-

—— (RALPH IRON) Dream Life and Real Life. See Pseudonym Library. No. 32.

—— Dreams. By Olive Schreiner. Demy 12mo, cloth.   2/6

—— Trooper Peter Halket of Mashonaland. By Olive Schreiner. Frontispiece. (Popular Copyright Novels.) Cr. 8vo, cloth gilt.   2/6
Cheap Edition, cr. 8vo, cloth.   net   1/-

SCOTT (Sir Walter). The "Century" Scott. In 25 vols. Fcap. 8vo (6 by 4) Each with Collotype Frontispiece, and with book plate, title-pages, binding, and devices in two colours by James Allen Duncan.   Decorative cloth, 1/- ; green leather   2/6

LIST OF VOLUMES.

Ivanhoe.	The Bride of Lammermoor.
Waverley.	The Fortunes of Nigel.
Guy Mannering.	Quentin Durward.
Old Mortality.	St Ronan's Well.
Rob Roy.	Redgauntlet.
The Antiquary.	The Betrothed and Highland
The Heart of Midlothian.	Widow, &c.
The Monastery.	The Talisman.
The Abbot.	Woodstock.
Kenilworth.	The Fair Maid of Perth.
The Pirate.	Anne of Geierstein.
Peveril of the Peak.	The Surgeon's Daughter and
The Legend of Montrose and	Castle Dangerous.
Black Dwarf.	Count Robert of Paris.

SCULLY (W. C.). Kafir Stories. See Autonym Library. Vol. 10

—— By Veldt and Kopje. By W. C. Scully. Cr. 8vo, cloth.   6/-

SHEEHAN. A Spoiled Priest, and Other Stories By the very Rev. P A. Sheehan, D.D. Illustrated. Cr. 8vo, cloth.   5/-

SHENSTONE. A Painter's Honeymoon. See under "Little Novels."

SHERWOOD. Tongues of Gossip. By A. Curtis Sherwood. Cr. 8vo   6/-

SHOLL. The Greater Love. By Anna McClure Sholl. Cr. 8vo, cloth   6/-

SMITH (F. C.) A Daughter of Patricians. By F. Clifford Smith. Illustrated. Cr. 8vo, cloth   6/-

SMITH (I.). The Minister's Guest. By Isabella Smith. (Unwin's Green Cloth Library.) Cr. 8vo, cloth.   6/-

SMITH (John). Old Brown's Cottages. See Pseudonym Library, 46.

SNOW (Isabel). School of Art. See Pseudonym Library. No 4.

SPINNER (Alice). Study in Colour. See Pseudonym Library, 37.

STACPOOLE. The Bourgeois. By H. de Vere Stacpoole. (Unwin's Green Cloth Library.) Cr 8vo, cloth.   6/-

—— **The Blue Lagoon** A Romance. By H de Vere Stacpoole Cr. 8vo, cloth.   6/-
Also in decorative paper covers.   **net**   1/-

—— **The Crimson Azaleas.** By H. de Vere Stacpoole. Cr 8vo, cloth.   6/-
Also paper covers.   6d.

—— **The Doctor.** By H. de Vere Stacpoole. (Unwin's Green Cloth Library.) Cr. 8vo, cloth gilt.   6/-

—— **Fanny Lambert.** By H. de Vere Stacpoole. (Unwin's Red Cloth Library) Cr 8vo, cloth.   6/-
Also Paper covers.   6d.

—— **The Lady Killer.** By H de Vere Stacpoole. (Unwin's Red Cloth Library.) Cr. 8vo   6/-

—— **Patsy.** By H. de Vere Stacpoole. With Frontispiece. Cr. 8vo, cloth   6/-

—— **The Vulture's Prey.** By H. de Vere Stacpoole. Cr. 8vo, cloth   6/-

STEVENS. The Perils of Sympathy. By Nina Stevens. (Unwin's Red Cloth Library) Cr 8vo, cloth.   6/-

STOTT. Rosemonde. By Beatrice Stott. (First Novel Library) Cr. 8vo, cloth   6/-

STRAIN. Laura's Legacy. By E. H. Strain (Unwin's Red Cloth Library.) Cr. 8vo, cloth.   6/-

SUMMERS. Renunciation. By Dorothy Summers. Cr. 8vo, cloth   6/-

—— **A Man's Love.** By Dorothy Summers. Cr 8vo, cloth   6/-

SUTCLIFFE. A Bachelor in Arcady. By Halliwell Sutcliffe. With Frontispiece. (Unwin's Green Cloth Library) Cr. 8vo, cloth.   6/-
Also a Presentation Edition   **net**   6/-

—— **By Moor and Fell :** Landscape and Lang-Settle Talk in West Yorkshire. By Halliwell Sutcliffe Cr. 8vo, cloth.   6/-

—— **Mistress Barbara Cunliffe.** By Halliwell Sutcliffe. (Unwin's Green Cloth Library) Cr. 8vo, cloth.   6/-

—— **Ricroft of Withens.** By Halliwell Sutcliffe. (Unwin's Green Cloth Library.) Cr. 8vo, cloth.   6/-
Paper covers.   6d.

—— **Shameless Wayne.** By Halliwell Sutcliffe. (Unwin's Green Cloth Library) Cr. 8vo.   6/-

—— **Through Sorrow's Gates.** A Tale of the Wintry Heath. By Halliwell Sutcliffe (Unwin's Green Cloth Library) Cr. 8vo, cloth   6/-
Also (The Adelphi Library), cloth.   3/6

—— **Willowdene Will** By Halliwell Sutcliffe. (Adelphi Library) Cloth   3/6

SWIFT. The Destroyer. By Benjamin Swift. (Unwin's Green Cloth Library) Cr. 8vo, cloth   6/-

—— **Nancy Noon.** By Benjamin Swift. (Unwin's Green Cloth Library.) Cr 8vo, cloth   6/-

—— **The Tormentor.** By Benjamin Swift (Unwin's Green Cloth Library) Cr. 8vo, cloth   6/-

SYNGE. The Coming of Sonia. By Mrs. Hamilton Synge Cr. 8vo, cloth   6/-

—— **A Supreme Moment.** By Mrs. Hamilton Synge. (Unwin's Green Cloth Library.) Cr 8vo, cloth.   6/-

TAYLER. The Long Vigil. By F. Jenner Tayler. (Unwin's Red
Cloth Library.) Cr. 8vo, cloth.   6/-

TAYLOR. A Thousand Pities By Ellen Taylor. Cr. 8vo, cloth.   2/6

THYNNE. Facing the Future; or, the Parting of the Ways. By
R. Thynne. Cr. 8vo, cloth   6/-

TREHERNE. A Love Cure. By Philip Treherne. Cr. 8vo, cloth.   3/6

TROUBRIDGE The Millionaire By Lady Troubridge. Cr 8vo, cloth.   6/-
—— The Woman Thou Gavest. By Lady Troubridge. Cr. 8vo, cloth.   6/-
  Also paper covers.   6d.

TROWBRIDGE. A Girl of the Multitude   By W R. H. Trowbridge.
Cr 8vo, cloth   6/-

—— A Dazzling Reprobate. By W. R. H. Trowbridge. (Unwin's
Red Cloth Library.) Cr. 8vo   6/-

—— The Grandmother's Advice to Elizabeth. A companion
volume to "The Letters of Her Mother to Elizabeth." (Idle Hour
Series No. 7)   Paper covers, 1/- ; cloth   2/-

—— The Letters of Her Mother to Elizabeth. A Series of Smart
Letters for Admirers of "The Visits of Elizabeth " (Idle Hour
Series No 2)   Paper covers, 1/- ; cloth   2/-
  Also an Edition in paper covers.   6d.

—— The Situations of Lady Patricia A Satire for Idle People. By
W. R. H. Trowbridge. (Unwin's Red Cloth Library.) Cr 8vo,
cloth   6/-

TRUSCOTT. As a Tree Falls. See Pseudonym Library. No 53
—— The Mother of Pauline By L Parry Truscott Paper covers.   6d
—— Motherhood. By L. Parry Truscott (Unwin's Red Cloth Library.)
Cr 8vo, cloth.   6/-
—— The Poet and Penelope. By L. Parry Truscott. Cr 8vo, cloth.   6/-
—— Stars of Destiny. By L. Parry Truscott. (Unwin's Red Cloth
Library.) Cr 8vo, cloth.   6/-

TURNER That Girl. By Ethel Turner (Mrs. Curlewis). With 25
Illustrations by Frances Ewan. Large cr 8vo, cloth.   6/-

TWEEDDALE. Moff. By John Tweeddale. (Century Library. No 2)
          Paper covers, 1/6 , cloth   2/-

UNWIN'S GREEN CLOTH LIBRARY. In uniform green cloth, gilt
tops   each   6/-

ALEXANDER (Mrs). ￼
    The Yellow Fiend.
￼   Through Fire to Fortune.
"ALIEN"
    The Devil's Half-Acre.
ASKEW (ALICE and MAUDE).
    The Shulamite
BACHELLER (IRVING).
    Silas Strong.
BAKER (JAMES)
    A Double Choice.
BARLOW (JANE).
    By Beach and Bogland.

BARR (AMELIA E).
    Was it Right to Forgive?
    I, Thou, and the Other
        One.
    Souls of Passage.
    The Maid of Maiden Lane
    The Lion's Whelp. ￼
BARRY (WILLIAM).
    Arden Massiter.
    The Two Standards.
    The Wizard's Knot
BARTRAM (GEORGE)
    The People of Clopton.
    The White-Headed Boy

UNWIN'S GREEN CLOTH LIBRARY—*continued.*

BEALBY (J T).
A Daughter of the Fen.

BECKE (LOUIS)
By Rock and Pool.
Edward Barry.
Rodman, the Boat-
steerer.
Yorke the Adventurer.
Ridan the Devil.
The Ebbing of the Tide.
Pacific Tales.

BECKE (L.) and WALTER
JEFFREY.
A First Fleet Family.
The Mutineer.

CHOMLEY (C H).
The Wisdom of Esau.

CLEEVE (LUCAS).
Blue Lilies.

CLIFFORD (Mrs W K).
Mrs. Keith's Crime

CONRAD (JOSEPH).
An Outcast of the Islands.
Almayer's Folly.
Tales of Unrest.

COTTERELL (CONSTANCE).
Love is not so Light

COURLANDER (ALPHONSE).
The Sacrifice

CROCKETT (S. R).
Kit Kennedy.
The Stickit Minister.
The Lilac Sunbonnet.
Cinderella.
The Raiders.
The Grey Man.
Me and Myn.

CROTTIE (JULIA M).
The Lost Land.

DYKE (WATSON)
As Others See Us.

FRASER (JOHN)
Death the Showman.

GORKY (MAXIM).
Foma Gordyeeff.

HAMILTON (ERNEST).
Outlaws of the Marches.
The Perils of Josephine.
The Mawkin of the Flow.

HOBBES (JOHN OLIVER).
The Herb-Moon.
The Gods, Some Mortals,
and Lord Wickenham.
The School for Saints.
Robert Orange.
The Tales of John
Oliver Hobbes.

HOLDSWORTH (ANNIE E)
The Iron Gates.

KEARY (C. F.).
Marriage de Convenance

McAULAY (ALLAN).
Black Mary.
The Rhymer.

MANN (MARY E),
Moonlight.
Susannah.
The Patten Experiment.
Among the Syringas.
The Mating of a Dove.

MAUGHAM (W. SOMERSET).
The Making of a Saint.
Orientations.

MITCHELL (S. WEIR).
Hugh Wynne.

MOORE (GEORGE).
Evelyn Innes.
Sister Teresa.

NESBIT (E)
The Treasure Seekers.

OUIDA
The Silver Christ.

PRAED (Mrs CAMPBELL).
The Insane Root.

PRYCE (GWENDOLEN).
A Son of Arvon.
John Jones, Curate.

RITA.
A Jilt's Journal.

SMITH (ISABELLA)
The Minister's Guest.

STACPOOLE (H DE VERE).
The Doctor.
The Bourgeois.

SUTCLIFFE (HALLIWELL).
Ricroft of Withens.
Shameless Wayne.
Mistress Barbara Cun-
liffe.
Through Sorrow's Gates
A Bachelor in Arcady.

SWIFT (BENJAMIN).
Nancy Noon.
The Tormentor.
The Destroyer.

SYNGE (Mrs. HAMILTON).
A Supreme Moment.

WATSON (J. R)
In a Man's Mind.

WATSON (MARGARET).
Driven.

UNWIN'S RED CLOTH LIBRARY. Cr. 8vo, cloth.   each 6/-

ALEXANDER (Mrs).
  Kitty Costello.
  Stronger than Love.
ARCHER (L. M. PALMER).
  A Bush Honeymoon.
BARR (AMELIA E).
  The Black Shilling.
  A Song of a Single
    Note.
  Thyra Varrick.
  Cecilia's Lovers.
BARRY (WILLIAM).
  The Dayspring.
BECKE (LOUIS)
  Breachley, Black Sheep.
  Chinkie's Flat.
  Adventures of a Super-
    cargo.
  Helen Adair.
  The Strange Adventure
    of James Shervington.
  Tom Gerrard.
  Under Tropic Skies.
BOURGET (PAUL).
  Divorce
CLARE (AUSTIN).
  Court Cards.
CLEEVE (LUCAS).
  Anglo-Americans.
  Children of Endurance.
  Counsels of the Night.
  Progress of Priscilla.
  Stolen Waters.
  The Fool-killer.
  The Man in the Street.
  A Double Marriage.
  Seven Nights in a Gondola
DE CRESPIGNY (Mrs. P.
  CHAMPION).
  The Mischief of a Glove.
DUNDAS (CHRISTIAN).
  Journeys of Antonia.
Van EEDEN (F.)
  The Deeps of Deliverance.
FLETCHER (J. S)
  Grand Relations.
  The Queen of a Day
GREEN (A. KATHERINE).
  The Filigree Ball
GRIFFITHS (MAJ. ARTHUR.)
  A Royal Rascal.
HALES (A. G).
  The Watcher on the
    Tower.
HOBBES (JOHN OLIVER).
  The Flute of Pan.
  Love and the Soul
    Hunters.
  The Princess of Bene-
  The Vineyard.   [vento.

HOCKING (SILAS K.).
  Meadow-sweet and Rue.
HORNIMAN (ROY)
  That Fast Miss Blount.
  The Living Buddha.
IRWIN (H. C.).
  With Sword and Pen.
KEARY (C. F)
  High Policy.
LANGBRIDGE (ROSAMOND).
  The Third Experiment.
LITTLE (Mrs. ARCHIBALD).
  A Millionaire's Courtship.
MACK (LOUISE).
  An Australian Girl in
    London.
MEADE (L. T.).
  Love Triumphant.
MONTGOMERY (K L).
  Major Weir.
MOORE (GEORGE).
  The Untilled Field.
MURRAY (J. CLARK).
  Five Talents.
PRAED (Mrs. CAMPBELL).
  Nyria.
RICHARDSON (Mrs.
  AUBREY).
  They Twain.
RICHINGS (EMILY).
  In Chaucer's Maytime.
ROOSEVELT (FLORENCE).
  The Siren's Net
RUSSELL (W. CLARK).
  Yarn of Old Harbour
    Town.
STACPOOLE (H. DE VERE).
  Fanny Lambert.
  The Lady Killer.
STEVENS (NINA).
  The Perils of Sympathy.
STRAIN (E H).
  Laura's Legacy.
TAYLER (F. JENNER).
  The Long Vigil.
TROWBRIDGE (W. R. H.).
  A Dazzling Reprobate.
  The Situations of Lady
    Patricia.
TRUSCOTT (L. PARRY).
  Motherhood.
  Stars of Destiny.
VIELE (HERMAN K.).
  Myra of the Pines.
WHITECHURCH.
  The Canon in Residence.
YEIGH (KATE WESTLAKE).
  A Specimen Spinster.
YSTRIDDE (G).
  Three Dukes.

UNWIN'S SHILLING REPRINTS OF STANDARD NOVELS.

Cr 8vo, cloth.   each, net   1/-

CROCKETT (S. R.).
  The Stickit Minister.
FALCONER (LANOE).
  Mademoiselle Ixe, and
  the Hotel d'Angleterre.
GORKY (MAXIM).
  Three of Them.
  The Outcasts, and other
  Stories.
  The Man who was afraid
  (Foma Gordyeeff).
HOBBES (JOHN OLIVER).
  Love and the Soul
  Hunters.
  Some Emotions and a
  Moral, and The Sin-
  ner's Comedy.

HOBBES (JOHN OLIVER).
  A Study in Temptations, and
  A Bundle of Life.
RUTHERFORD (MARK).
  The Autobiography of Mark
  Rutherford.
  Mark Rutherford's Deliverance.
  The Revolution in Tanner's
  Lane.
  Miriam's Schooling.
  Catherine Furze.
  Clara Hopgood.
SCHREINER (OLIVE).
  Trooper Peter Halket of
  Mashonaland.

UNWIN'S SIXPENNY EDITIONS.

In paper covers.   each   6d.

Canon in Residence, The. By
  Victor L Whitechurch.
Cardinal's Pawn, The. By K.
  L. Montgomery
Crimson Azaleas, The   By
  H. de Vere Stacpoole.
De Omnibus and Another
  Englishwoman's Love Let-
  ters. By Barry Pain
Eben Holden. By Irving
  Bacheller. 393rd Thousand
Evelyn Innes. By Geo. Moore.
Fanny Lambert. By H de
  Vere Stacpoole
Filigree Ball, The. By Anna
  Katherine Green.
Gods, Some Mortals, and
  Lord Wickenham, The. By
  John Oliver Hobbes (Mrs
  Craigie)
Grand Relations. By J. S.
  Fletcher.
His Native Wife   By Louis
  Becke.
House by the River, The. By
  Florence Warden.
How to be Happy though
  Married. By E J Hardy
Lady Mary of the Dark House.
  By Mrs. C N. Williamson
Lady Noggs, The   By Edgar
  Jepson.
Letters of Her Mother to
  Elizabeth. 63rd Thousand.
Life in a Crack Regiment.
  By Baron Von Schlicht.

Liza of Lambeth. By W.
  Somerset Maugham   Revised
  Edition
Memoirs of Constantine Dix,
  The. By Barry Pain
Mischief of a Glove, The By
  Mrs Philip Champion de
  Crespigny.
Mother of Pauline, The   By
  L. Parry Truscott
Motor Cracksman, The. By
  Charles Carey.
Ricroft of Withens. By Halli-
  well Sutcliffe.
Robert Orange.   By John
  Oliver Hobbes.
Royal Rascal, A.   By Major
  Arthur Griffiths.
Saints in Society. By Margaret
  Baillie-Saunders
School for Saints, The. By
  John Oliver Hobbes
Sister Teresa   By George
  Moore. Revised Edition.
Some Emotions and a Moral.
  By John Oliver Hobbes.
Stickit Minister, The. By
  S. R. Crockett.
Stolen Waters. By Lucas
  Cleeve
That Fast Miss Blount   By
  Roy Horniman
Vineyard, The. By John Oliver
  Hobbes
Watcher on the Tower, The.
  By A G'Hales.
Woman Thou Gavest, The.
  By Lady Troubridge.

UNWIN'S SHILLING NOVELS. A new series of high-class Novels by popular writers In paper covers (see page 87)   Each net   1/-

VALENTINE The Red Sphinx   By E. U. Valentine and S. Eccleston Harper   Cr. 8vo, cloth.   6/-

VERGA (Giovanni). Cavalleria Rusticana. See Pseudonym Library No 29

VIELE. Myra of the Pines. By Herman K. Viele. (Unwin's Red Cloth Library.) Cr 8vo, cloth.   6/-

WARDEN The Dazzling Miss Davison. By Florence Warden. Cr. 8vo, cloth.   6/-

—— The House by the River. By Florence Warden. Cr. 8vo, cloth.   6/-
Also paper covers.   6d.

—— The Mis-Rule of Three. By Florence Warden. Cr 8vo, cloth.   6/

WARRY. The Sentinel of Wessex. By C. King Warry. Cr. 8vo, cloth   6/-

WATSON (M). Driven l By Margaret Watson. (Unwin's Green Cloth Library) Cr 8vo.   6/-

WATSON (J. R.). In a Man's Mind. By John Reay Watson. (Unwin's Green Cloth Library.) Cr 8vo, cloth.   6/-

WELLS. Certain Personal Matters. By H. G. Wells. (Idle Hour Series. No. 5.)   Paper covers, 1/- , cloth   2/-

WHITE. Uncle Jem. By Hester White   Cr 8vo, cloth.   6/-

WHITECHURCH. The Canon in Residence. By Victor L Whitechurch (Unwin's Red Cloth Library.) Cr. 8vo, cloth..   6/-
Also (The Adelphi Library), cloth.   3/6
Also decorative paper covers. 1/- net   Also paper covers   6d.

—— Concerning Himself By Victor L. Whitechurch   Cr. 8vo, cloth   6/-
—— The Locum Tenens By Victor L. Whitechurch. Cr. 8vo, cloth   6/-

WILKINS. Doctor Gordon. By Mary E. Wilkins. Cr. 8vo, cloth.   6/-

WILLIAMSON. Lady Mary of the Dark House. By Mrs. C. N. Williamson   Cr. 8vo, cloth   6/-
Also decorative paper covers. 1/- net.   Also paper covers   6d.

WILLIAMSON (W H.). The Traitor's Wife. By W. H. Williamson. Cr 8vo, cloth.   6/-

—— The Prince's Marriage. By W H. Williamson   Cr. 8vo, cloth.   6/-

WILTON (Jos.). When Wheat is Green. See Pseudonym Library 51.

WITT. Innocent of a Crime. By Captain Paul Witt. Cr. 8vo, cloth gilt.   6/-

WYLWYNNE. The Dream Woman. By Kythe Wylwynne. Cr. 8vo, cloth.   6/-

YEATS, (W. B.). John Sherman and Dhoya. See Pseudonym Library, No. 10.

YEIGH. A Specimen Spinster. By Kate Westlake Yeigh. (Unwin's Red Cloth Library,) Cr. 8vo, cloth,   6/-

YELLOW LIBRARY. A bijou series printed on yellow paper (6½ by 3¾ inches)   Paper covers, 1/- ; cloth   2/-

(1) **Simon Ryan the Peterite.** (3) **The Mystery of the Laughlin Islands.** By Louis Becke and Walter Jeffery.
-By Canon Augustus Jessopp, D.D.

(2) **Marsena.** By Harold Frederic

YSTRIDDE. Three Dukes. By G. Ystridde. (Unwin's Red Cloth Library) Cr. 8vo, cloth.

a   2/-

<table>
ESSAYS, CRITICISM,
PHILOSOPHY, &c.
</table>

BIGELOW. The Mystery of Sleep. By John Bigelow, LL.D. Cr. 8vo, cloth.   net   6/-

BOUTMY. The English People : A Study of their Political Psychology. By Emile Boutmy, Membre de l'Institut. Translated by E. English. With an Introduction by J E. C. Bodley. Demy 8vo, cloth gilt.   16/-

BROOKE The Need and Use of getting Irish Literature into the English Tongue. By the Rev Stopford A. Brooke.   1/- ; cloth   2/-

CHRISTY. Proverbs, Maxims, and Phrases of all Ages. Classified subjectively and arranged alphabetically. By Robert Christy. One vol. Cr. 8vo, cloth   7/6

CRIMINOLOGY SERIES, THE. Large cr. 8vo, cloth.   each   6/-
   (1) **The Female Offender.** By   (3) **Juvenile Offenders.** By
      Professor Lombroso.   W. Douglas Morrison.
   (2) **Criminal Sociology.** By   (4) **Political Crime.** By Louis
      Professor Enrico Ferri   Proal
                     [For full Titles see under Authors' names.]

DETHRIDGE. The "Lucas Malet" Birthday Book. By G. Olivia Dethridge. Large cr. 12mo, cloth.   net   4/-

DUFFY. The Revival of Irish Literature. A Series of Addresses by Sir Chas Gavan Duffy, and others.   Paper covers, 1/- ; cloth   2/-

FERRI. Criminal Sociology. By Professor Enrico Ferri. With Preface by W. Douglas Morrison. M.A. (Criminology Series. Vol. 2) Large cr. 8vo, cloth.   6/-

Good Reading About Many Books. Nos. 1, 2, and 3   By their Authors. With Portraits and Facsimile Autographs. Demy 12mo.
                     Paper covers, 1/- each net , cloth, each net   2/-

GORDON. The Social Ideals of Alfred Tennyson. By William Clark Gordon. Large cr. 8vo, cloth.   net   6/6

HORNBY. Great Minds at One. A Year's Parallels in Prose and Verse. Compiled by F. M. Hornby. Fcap 8vo, cloth.   net   3/6

JESSOPP. Frivola. By Augustus Jessopp, D.D. See also " The Yellow Library." Cr. 8vo, cloth.   3/6

—— Frivola, Simon Ryan, and other Papers. By Augustus Jessopp, D.D. Cr. 8vo, limp cloth.   3/6

JUSSERAND. English Essays from a French Pen. By J. J. Jusserand. Photogravure Frontispiece and 4 other full-page Illustrations. Large cr 8vo, cloth.   7/6

LE BON. The Crowd : A Study of the Popular Mind. By Gustave Le Bon. Cr. 8vo, cloth.   6/-
Also in "Reformer's Bookshelf." Large cr 8vo, cloth.   3/6

LEE. Baldwin : Being Dialogues on Views and Aspirations. By Vernon Lee. Demy 8vo, cloth.   12/-

—— Belcaro : Being Essays on Sundry Æsthetical Questions. By Vernon Lee. Cr. 8vo, cloth.   5/-

—— Euphorion : Studies of the Antique and the Mediæval in the Renaissance. By Vernon Lee. Fourth Impression, Cheap Edition. Demy 8vo, cloth.   7/6

—— Gospels of Anarchy, and other Contemporary Studies. By Vernon Lee. Demy 8vo, cloth.   net   10/6

—— Juvenilia. Essays on Sundry Æsthetical Questions. By Vernon Lee. Two vols., leather.   14/-

LOMBROSO. The Female Offender. By Professor Lombroso. Edited, with Introduction, by W. Douglas Morrison, M.A. Illustrated (Criminology Series Vol. 1) Large cr. 8vo, cloth   6/-

MALET. The "Lucas Malet" Birthday Book. Compiled by G. Olivia Dethridge. Cloth, large cr 12mo.   net   4/-

MALLIK The Problem of Existence: Its Mystery, Struggle, and Comfort in the Light of Aryan Wisdom. By Manmath C. Mallik Demy 8vo, cloth   10/6

MARSHALL. Aristotle's Theory of Conduct. By Thomas Marshall. Medium 8vo, cloth   net   21/-

MARTINENGO-CESARESCO. The Place of Animals in Human Thought. By Countess Martinengo-Cesaresco Illustrated. Demy 8vo, cloth.   net   10/6

MASTERMAN. In Peril of Change Essays written in Time of Tranquillity By C. F G. Masterman Large cr. 8vo, cloth.   6/-

MENCKEN. The Philosophy of Friedrich Nietzsche. By Henry L. Mencken. Demy 8vo, cloth.   net   7/6

MORRISON. Juvenile Offenders By W Douglas Morrison, M.A. (Criminology Series. Vol 3) Large cr. 8vo, cloth.   6/-

MÜGGE. Nietzsche: His Life and Work. By M. A Mugge, Ph.D. Demy 8vo, cloth.   net   10/6

MUIR. Plato's Dream of Wheels: Socrates, Protagoras, and the Hegeleatic Stranger. With an Appendix by certain Cyclic Poets By R. J. Muir, Magd. Coll , Oxon. Cr. 8vo, cloth   net   2/-

New Spirit of the Nation, The. Edited by Martin MacDermott (New Irish Library) Small cr. 8vo   Paper covers, 1/- , cloth   2/-

NIETZSCHE. The Works of Friedrich Nietzsche. Uniform demy 8vo, cloth gilt.   each net   8/6

(1) **A Genealogy of Morals and Poems.**

(2) **Thus Spake Zarathustra.** A Book for All and None.

(3) **The Case of Wagner.** Nietzsche contra Wagner. The Twilight of the Idols. The Anti-Christ.

(4) **The Dawn of Day.**

PROAL. Political Crime. By Louis Proal. (Criminology Series. Vol 4) Large cr 8vo, cloth.   6/-

RUSSELL (E). An Editor's Sermons. By Sir Edward Russell With an Introduction by the Lord Bishop of Hereford Large cr 8vo, cloth.   net   6/-

RUSSELL (G. W. E.). "For Better? For Worse?": Notes on Social Changes. By George W. E. Russell. Cr. 8vo, cloth gilt.   3/6

RUSSELL (T Baron). A Hundred Years Hence. The Expectations of an Optimist. By T. Baron Russell. Large cr. 8vo, cloth.   7/6

SAMHAIN: An Occasional Review. Edited by W B. Yeats. Contributors · J M Synge, Lady Gregory, Douglas Hyde, George Moore, Edward Martyn, and others First Number (October, 1901) Second Number (October, 1902) Third Number (September, 1903) Paper covers   net   6d. Fourth Number (December, 1904). Fifth Number (December, 1905)   1/-

SCHMIDT. Happy-Go-Lucky Land. England Through German Glasses. By Max Schmidt.   Paper covers, 1/- , cloth   2/-

Society in the New Reign. By A Foreign Resident. With Photogravure Frontispiece. Demy 8vo, cloth.   16/-

THOMAS Sex and Society. Studies in the Social Psychology of Sex. By William J. Thomas. Large cr. 8vo, cloth.   net

THRING. Addresses. By Edward Thring, M.A With Portrait. Second Edition. Small cr. 8vo, cloth.

WELLS. The Discovery of the Future. A Discourse delivered at the Royal Institution by H. G. Wells. Paper covers

ART and MUSIC.

BLACKER. Chats on Oriental China. By J F Blacker. With a Coloured Frontispiece and about 70 other Illustrations. (Unwin's "Chats" Series. Large cr. 8vo, cloth.   **net**   5/-

BLOOM Shakespeare's Church, Otherwise the Collegiate Church of the Holy Trinity of Stratford-on-Avon An Architectural and Ecclesiastical History of the Fabric and its Ornaments By J Harvey Bloom, M A Illustrated from photographs by L. C. Keighley-Peachr Large cr. 8vo, cloth.   **net**   7/6

CARROLL. The Lewis Carroll Picture Book Edited by Stuart Dodgson Collingwood. Profusely illustrated. Large cr. 8vo, cloth.   6/-

THE "CHATS" SERIES. Practical Guides for Collectors. Each volume fully Illustrated. Large cr. 8vo, cloth.   **net**   5/-

(1) Chats on English China By Arthur Hayden.

(2) Chats on Old Furniture. By Arthur Hayden.

(3) Chats on Old Prints By Arthur Hayden

(4) Chats on Costume A Practical Guide to Historic Dress By G. Woolliscroft Rhead.

(5) Chats on Old Miniatures. By J. J. Foster, F.S.A.

(6) Chats on Old Lace and Needlework. By Mrs. Lowes.

(7) Chats on Oriental China. By J. F Blacker.

In Preparation :—

Chats on Book-Plates. By H K. Wright.

Chats on Earthenware. By Arthur Hayden

DITTRICH The Horse A Guide to its Anatomy for Artists 110 Drawings (reproduced by Photo Lithography) by Hermann Dittrich, with Explanatory Notes by Prof Ellenberger and Prof. Baum In portfolio, quarto.   **net**   30/-

van DYKE. Modern French Masters. A series of Biographical and Critical Reviews By American Artists With 37 Wood Engravings by Timothy Cole and others, and 28 Half-Tone Illustrations. Edited by John C van Dyke. Royal 8vo, elegantly bound in cloth gilt.   42/-

—— Old Dutch and Flemish Masters. The Text by John C van Dyke, and the Notes on the Pictures by Timothy Cole. Imp. 8vo, cloth elegant   42/-

ERSKINE. Lady Diana Beauclerk: Her Life and Work. By Mrs. Steuart Erskine. Illustrated with Coloured Plates, and many reproductions in half tone. Royal 4to.   **net** 42/-
Also a *Fine Edition.*   net126/-

FISHER The Harrison Fisher Book A Collection of Drawings in Colours and Black and White. With an Introduction by James B. Carrington Quarto   **net** 10/6

FITZGERALD. Robert Adam, Artist and Architect. His Works and his System By Percy Fitzgerald, M A., F.S A. With collotype plates, and many other illustrations. Cr 4to, cloth.   **net** 10/6

STER. Chats on Old Miniatures By J. J Foster, F.S A. Copiously illustrated with examples from celebrated collections. —— Goodwin's "Chats" Series.) Large cr. 8vo, cloth.   **net**   5/-
Lee. Large Paper Edition Medium 8vo With 8 Illustrations in venilia. Collotype and about 100 reproductions in Black and two   **net** 10/6

FURNISS. **Harry Furniss at Home.** By Himself. With over 120 Illustrations. Medium 8vo, cloth gilt. net 16/-

——. **The Confessions of a Caricaturist.** Being the Reminiscences of Harry Furniss. Illustrated with over 300 Illustrations, many made specially for the volume. In 2 vols. Super royal 8vo. 32/-
New and Cheap Edition in 1 vol., medium 8vo, cloth. net 10/6

GRAVES. **The Irish Song Book,** with Original Irish Airs. Edited by Alfred Perceval Graves. Eighth Impression (New Irish Library.) Paper covers, 1/- ; cloth 2/-

GWYNN. **Memorials of an Eighteenth Century Painter (James Northcote).** By Stephen Gwynn Fully Illustrated with Photogravures, &c. Demy 8vo, cloth gilt. 12/-

HARRISON. **Introductory Studies in Greek Art.** By Jane E. Harrison. Fourth Edition. Map and 10 Illustrations. Large cr. 8vo, cloth. 7/6

HAYDEN. **Chats on English China.** By Arthur Hayden. Illustrated with over 100 Specimens of Old China, and with over 150 China Marks. Three-colour Frontispiece. (Unwin's " Chats " Series.) Large cr. 8vo, cloth gilt net 5/-

—— **Chats on Old Furniture** By Arthur Hayden With 106 illustrations. (Unwin's " Chats " Series.) Large cr. 8vo, cloth. net 5/-

—— **Chats on Earthenware** [In Preparation]

—— **Chats on Old Prints** By Arthur Hayden. With a Coloured Frontispiece and 70 full-page Plates. (Unwin's " Chats " Series.) Large cr. 8vo, cloth. net 5/-

LA FARGE. **An Artist's Letters from Japan.** See under "Geography."

LAWTON. **The Life and Work of Auguste Rodin** By Frederick Lawton. With many Illustrations. Demy 8vo, cloth. net 15/-

LEGGE. **Some Ancient Greek Sculptors.** By H Edith Legge. With a Preface by Professor Percy Gardner, and illustrated by about 40 Plates. Cr. 8vo, cloth. 6/-

LOWES **Chats on Old Lace and Needlework.** By Mrs Lowes. With a Coloured Frontispiece and about 70 other Illustrations. (Unwin's " Chats " Series) Large cr 8vo, cloth. net 5/-

MOSCHELES. **In Bohemia with Du Maurier.** By Felix Moscheles Illustrated with 63 Original Drawings by G. Du Maurier. Third Edition. Demy 8vo, cloth. 10/6

MOSSO **The Palaces of Crete and their Builders** By Angelo Mosso, Author of " The Life of Man on the High Alps." With 187 Illustrations and 2 Plans. Royal 8vo, cloth. 21/-

NORDAU. **On Art and Artists.** By Max Nordau. With a Portrait Frontispiece Large cr 8vo, cloth. net 7/6

PENNELL. **The Illustration of Books:** A Manual for the use of Students By Joseph Pennell, Lecturer on Illustration at the Slade School, University College. With Diagrams. Cr. 8vo, cloth. 2/-

—— **Lithography and Lithographers·** Some Chapters on the History of the Art With Technical Remarks and Suggestions Joseph and Elizabeth Robins Pennell Lithographic Frontis Portrait of Mr Pennell by J McNeill Whistler, and numerous trations and Plates Large royal 4to.

Also a *Fine Edition,* on Japan paper.

PENNELL. The Work of Charles Keene. Introduction and Notes by Joseph Pennell, many pictures illustrative of the artist's method and vein of humour, and Bibliographical Notes by W. H. Chesson Large royal 4to.   net 73/6

Fine Edition.   net 315/-

de QUEVEDO. Pablo de Segovia. By Francisco de Quevedo Illustrated by Daniel Vierge. Introduction by Joseph Pennell. Super royal 4to, cloth.   net 73/6

van RENSSELAER. English Cathedrals. Described by Mrs. van Rensselaer, and Illustrated by Charles Pennell. Royal 8vo, cloth elegant.   25/-

—— **Hand-Book of English Cathedrals.** By Mrs. van Rensselaer. Fully Illustrated. Cr. 8vo, cloth.   10/6

RHEAD. Chats on Costume · A Practical Guide to Historic Dress. By G. Woolliscroft Rhead, R E., A R C A , Lond. With a Coloured Frontispiece and many Illustrations. (Unwin's "Chats" Series) Large cr 8vo, cloth.   net 5/-

SCOTSON-CLARK. The "Halls." A Collection of Portraits of eminent Music Hall Performers, Drawn in 3 Colours by Scotson-Clark Introduction by George Gamble. Imperial 8vo, decorated title, &c., buckram, gilt.   net 6/-

SEYMOUR. Siena and Her Artists. By Frederick H A. Seymour, Author of "Saunterings in Spain" With 16 Illustrations. Large cr. 8vo, cloth.   6/-

STILLMAN. Old Italian Masters. By W J Stillman. Engravings and Notes by T. Cole. Royal 8vo, cloth elegant.   42/-

STUART and PARKE. The Variety Stage. By C. Douglas Stuart and A T. Parke. Cr. 8vo, cloth.   3/6

STURGIS. The Arts of Design. By Russell Sturgis, M.A., Ph.D , Fellow of the National Sculpture Society, &c. With 107 Illustrations. Royal 8vo, cloth.   net 7/6

VELDHEER. Old Dutch Towns and Villages of the Zuiderzee. By J G. Veldheer With Illustrations by J G Veldheer, W. J Tuin, and W. O. J. Nieuwenkamp, and with Decorative Initials. Imperial cloth.   21/-

VIERGE Don Quixote. By Miguel de Cervantes. With 260 Drawings by Daniel Vierge. 4 vols. Super royal 8vo. Edition limited to 155 copies.   net £15

Fine Edition (limited to 10 copies) on Imperial Japan paper, with extra set of full-page Plates   net £30

—— **The Nun-Ensign.** Translated from the Original Spanish with an Introduction and Notes by James Fitzmaurice-Kelly, Fellow of the British Academy Also La Monja Alferez, a Play in the Original Spanish by D. Juan Perez de Montalban. With Illustrations by Daniel Vierge, Illustrator of "Pablo de Segovia" and "Don Quixote." Large cr. 8vo, cloth.   net 7/6

—— ?ARI. Giovanni Segantini His Life and Work. Edited by Luigi 'llari. With upwards of 80 Illustrations reproduced direct from Gooriginal paintings. In one volume. With Photogravure Frontispiece. Imperial 8vo, with specially designed cover, and boxed, net 21/-

venilia. Cathedral. A Free Criticism By an Architectural two 9 Plates. Quarto, cloth.   net 6/-

BIOGRAPHY, MEMOIRS, CORRESPONDENCE, &c.

ADAM. My Literary Life. By Madame Edmond Adam. (Juliette Lamber). 8vo, cloth, gilt top, with Portraits.   net   8/6

—— Robert Adam, Artist and Architect. By Percy Fitzgerald. See under "Art"

ADVENTURE SERIES, The. See at the end of this Section.

AUSTIN (Mrs. Sarah). See Ross, "Three Generations."

BAMFORD'S Passages in the Life of a Radical.   See under "Politics."

BEACONSFIELD. Lord Beaconsfield. By T. P. O'Connor. Popular Edition. With Frontispiece. Large cr. 8vo, cloth.   net   2/6

BEARNE (Mrs.) Works. See under "History."

BEAUCLERK (Lady Diana). By Mrs Steuart Erskine See under "Art"

BELGIOJOSO. A Revolutionary Princess: Christina Belgiojoso-Trivulzio. Her Life and Times (1808-1871) By H. Remsen Whitehouse. With Photogravure Frontispiece and many other Illustrations. Demy 8vo, cloth.   net   10/6

BERNARD. Claude Bernard. By Sir Michael Foster. With Photogravure Frontispiece (Masters of Medicine. Vol. 6.) Large cr. 8vo, cloth.   3/6

BESANT. Annie Besant: An Autobiography. New Edition, with a new Preface Illustrated. Large cr 8vo, cloth.   net   5/-

BRADLAUGH. Charles Bradlaugh: A Record of His Life and Work. By His Daughter, Hypatia Bradlaugh Bonner. 2 vols. (Reformer's Bookshelf) Large cr. 8vo, cloth.   7/-

Also in Unwin's Half-Crown Standard Library. 1 vol. Cloth.   net   2/6

BRIGHTWEN. The Life and Thoughts of a Naturalist. Mrs. Brightwen. Edited by W. H. Chesson. With Portrait and Illustrations, and an Introduction by Edmund Gosse. Large cr. 8vo, cloth.   net   5/-

BRODIE. Sir Benjamin Brodie. By Timothy Holmes. With Photogravure Frontispiece. (Masters of Medicine Vol. 5) Large cr. 8vo, cloth.   3/6

BROOKE. Rajah Brooke: The Englishman as Ruler of an Eastern State By Sir Spencer St. John, G C.M G. With Frontispiece and Maps. (Builders of Greater Britain Vol. 7.) Large cr 8vo, cloth.   5/-

BROWN. Captain John Brown of Harper's Ferry. By John Newton. Fully Illustrated. Cr. 8vo, cloth.   6/-
"John Brown's body lies a 'mould'ring in the grave
But his soul's marching on"

Also (Lives Worth Living Series).   3/6

BUCHANAN. Robert Buchanan: Some Account of His Life, His Life's Work, and His Literary Friendships. By Harriett Jay. Illustrated with Portraits and from other sources   Demy 8vo, cloth. net   10/6

BUILDERS OF GREATER BRITAIN. Edited by H. F. Wilson A Set of 8 volumes, with Photogravure Frontispiece and Maps to each. Large cr. 8vo, cloth.   each

[For full titles see under:]

(1) Sir Walter Ralegh.	(5) Lord Clive.
(2) Sir Thomas Maitland.	(6) Admiral Phillip..es.
(3) John and Sebastian Cabot.	(7) Rajah Brooke
(4) Edward Gibbon Wakefield.	(8) Sir Stamf○NS.

BURTON. The Real Sir Richard Burton   By Walter Phelps Dodge
With a Frontispiece.   Large cloth   net   6/-

CABOT   John and Sebastian Cabot; the Discovery of North America.
By C Raymond Beazley, M A   With Frontispiece and Maps.
(Builders of Greater Britain.   Vol 3)   Large cr. 8vo, cloth.   5/-

CARLYLE   The Story of Thomas Carlyle   By A. S Arnold.   With
6 Illustrations   (Lives Worth Living Series.   Vol. II.)   Cr. 8vo,
cloth.   3/6

CARROLL   The Life and Letters of Lewis Carroll (G L. Dodgson).
By S. D Collingwood.   With about 100 Illustrations.   Large cr
8vo, cloth.   3/6

CESARESCO.   Italian Characters in the Epoch of Unification.
By Countess Martinengo Cesaresco   Cheap Edition.   Demy 8vo,
cloth   7/6

CHEVALIER.   Before I Forget.   Being the Autobiography of a
Chevalier d'Industrie   Written by Albert Chevalier   Very fully
Illustrated   Demy 8vo.   net   16/-

CLIVE.   Lord Clive: The Foundation of British Rule in India.   By Sir
A. J Arbuthnot, K.C S I, C I E.   With Frontispiece and Maps.
(Builders of Greater Britain   Vol. 5)   Large cr. 8vo, cloth.   5/-

COBDEN.   The Life of Richard Cobden.   By the Right Hon John
Morley, M.A. (Oxford), Hon. LL.D.   With Photogravure Portrait
from the Original Drawing by Lowes Dickinson   Jubilee Edition.
(Reformer's Bookshelf)   2 vols.   Large cr 8vo, cloth   7/-
   New Binding   Demy 8vo, cloth   3/6
   New Popular Unabridged Edition in 1 vol.   Large cr. 8vo, cloth   net   2/6
   The "Free Trade" Edition.   Popular Re-issue, abridged.   Demy 4to
Paper covers   6d.
   Special Edition, in 5 Parts.   Demy 8vo, paper covers   Each, net   6d
—— Cobden as a Citizen.   A Chapter in Manchester History.   Con-
taining a facsimile of Cobden's pamphlet, "Incorporate Your
Borough!" with an Introduction and a complete Cobden Biblio-
graphy, by William E. A. Axon.   With 7 Photogravure Plates and
3 other Illustrations   Demy 8vo, full vellum or buckram.   net   21/-
—— Richard Cobden and the Jubilee of Free Trade. See under
"Politics."
—— Cobden's Work and Opinions.   By Welby and Mallet.   See
under "Politics."
—— The Political Writings of Richard Cobden.   See under
"Politics."

COILLARD.   Coillard of the Zambesi.   The Lives of François and
Christina Coillard, of the Paris Missionary Society (1834-1904).   By
C W. Mackintosh   With a Photogravure Frontispiece, a Map, and
64 other Illustrations   Demy 8vo, cloth   net   15/-

COLERIDGE   The Story of a Devonshire House.   By Lord Coleridge,
K.C.   Illustrated.   Demy 8vo, cloth.   net   15/-

CREMER.   Life of W. Randal.   See page 42.

CROMWELL   Oliver Cromwell and His Times.   By G. Holden
Pike   Cr 8vo, cloth.   Illustrated   6/-
   Also "Lives Worth Living" Series.   3/6

DAVIDSON.   Memorials of Thomas Davidson the Wandering
Scholar   Collected and Edited by William Knight, LL.D.,
formerly Professor of Moral Philosophy in the University of St.
Andrews.   With a Portrait.   net   7/6

DAVIS A   Short Life of Thomas Davis.   By Sir Charles Gavan
Duffy.   (New Irish Library.   Vol. 10.)   Small cr 8vo
Paper covers. 1/-   cloth   2/-

DAVITT. Michael Davitt: Revolutionary, Agitator, and Labour Leader. See "Sheehy-Skeffington."

DE LA REY. A Woman's Wanderings and Trials During the Anglo-Boer War. By Mrs (General) De La Rey Illustrated. 2nd Edition. Cr. 8vo, cloth. 2/6

DOYLE. Bishop Doyle. By Michael MacDonagh (New Irish Library. Vol 11.) Small cr. 8vo Paper covers, 1/-, cloth 2/-

DUFFY. My Life in Two Hemispheres. By Sir Charles Gavan Duffy, K C M G Two vols. demy 8vo, cloth. 32/-
Cheap Edition. 2 vols (Reformer's Bookshelf) Large cr. 8vo, cloth. 7/-

DU MAURIER. By Felix Moscheles See under "Art."

ELIZABETH. The Correspondence of Princess Elizabeth of England, Landgravine of Hesse-Homburg, for the most part with Miss Louisa Swinburne. With Portraits, and Edited with Preface by Philip C. Yorke, M A, Oxon. With a Photogravure and other Illustrations. Demy 8vo, cloth. 12/-

EVANS. The Memoirs of Dr. Thomas W Evans. Recollections of the Second French Empire. Edited by Edward A. Crane, M.D Illustrated. 2 vols Demy 8vo, cloth. net 21/-

FITCH. Ralph Fitch: England's Pioneer to India and Burma His Companions and Contemporaries. By J. Horton Ryley, Member of the Hakluyt Society. With 16 full-page and 3 smaller Illustrations Large cr. 8vo, cloth. net 10/6

FITZMAURICE-KELLY The Nun-Ensign. Translated from the Original Spanish with an Introduction and Notes by James Fitzmaurice-Kelly, Fellow of the British Academy Also La Monja Alferez, a Play in the Original Spanish by D. Juan Perez de Montalban With Illustrations by Daniel Vierge, Illustrator of "Pablo de Segovia" and "Don Quixote." Large cr 8vo, cloth net 7/6

FULLER. The Love-Letters of Margaret Fuller (1845-1846). With an Introduction by Julia Ward Howe To which are added the Reminiscences of Ralph Waldo Emerson, Horace Greeley, and Charles T Congdon With Portrait. 12mo, cloth, gilt top. net 5/-

FURNISS (Harry). Confessions of a Caricaturist. See under "Art"

—— At Home. See under "Art"

GAMBIER. Links in My Life on Land and Sea. By Commander J W. Gambier, R.N. With Frontispiece and 7 other Illustrations. Demy 8vo, cloth. net 15/-
Cheap Edition, with Frontispiece. (Modern Travel Series.) Large cr. 8vo, cloth. 5/-

GLADSTONE My Memory of Gladstone. By Goldwin Smith. With Portrait Cr 8vo, cloth net 2/6

GORDON. The Life of General Gordon. By Demetrius C Boulger. Illustrated New and Cheaper Edition Demy 8vo, cloth 6/-

—— (Lady Duff). See Ross, "Three Generations."

GOETHE. Life of Goethe. By Heinrich Düntzer. Translated by Thomas W. Lyster, Assistant Librarian, National Library of Ireland. With Authentic Illustrations and Facsimiles. (Unwin's Half-Crown Standard Library.) Large cr. 8vo, cloth. net 2/

GOULD. Concerning Lafcadio Hearn. By G. M. Gould, M.D. With 5 Illustrations Demy 8vo, cloth

GRATTAN. Henry Grattan. (The Gladstone Prize Essay in the University of Oxford, 1902) By Percy M. Roxby, Scholar of Christ With Frontispiece Cr 8vo, cloth. 3/6

GRAY. Wise Words and Loving Deeds. See under " Living."

HAECKEL. Haeckel: His Life and Work. By Wilhelm Bölsche. Translated and with an Introduction and Supplementary Chapter by Joseph McCabe. With four Coloured Frontispieces and many other Illustrations. Demy 8vo, cloth. **net** 15/-

HARDY. The Love Affairs of Some Famous Men. By the Rev. E. J Hardy, M A. Imp. 16mo, cloth. 6/-
Cheaper Edition, cr 8vo, cloth. 3/6

HARVEY. William Harvey. By D'Arcy Power. With Photogravure Frontispiece. (Masters of Medicine. Vol. 2) Large cr. 8vo, cloth 3/6

HELMHOLTZ. Hermann von Helmholtz. By Prof. John G. McKendrick. With Photogravure Frontispiece. (Masters of Medicine. Vol. 7) Large cr. 8vo, cloth. 3/6

HILL. Sir Rowland Hill The Story of a Great Reform. Told by his Daughter, Eleanor C. Smyth With a Photogravure Frontispiece and 16 other Illustrations. Large cr. 8vo, cloth. **net** 5/-

HOLYOAKE. Bygones Worth Remembering. A Sequel to "Sixty Years of an Agitator's Life." By George Jacob Holyoake. With a Photogravure Frontispiece, and 18 other Portraits. 2 vols. Demy 8vo, cloth. 21/-

Also Reformer's Bookshelf, 2 vols Large cr. 8vo, cloth. 7/-
—— Sixty Years of an Agitator's Life. George Jacob Holyoake's Autobiography 2 vols. (Reformer's Bookshelf.) Large cr 8vo, cloth. 7/-
Also in Unwin's Half-Crown Standard Library. 1 vol. cloth **net** 2/6

HORRIDGE. Lives of Great Italians. By Frank Horridge Illustrated. Large cr. 8vo, cloth. 7/6
Prize Edition. 3/6

HUNTER. John Hunter. By Stephen Paget With Photogravure Frontispiece. (Masters of Medicine Vol. 1.) Large cr. 8vo, cloth. 3/6

IRVING Sir Henry Irving. A Biography. By Percy Fitzgerald. With a Photogravure Frontispiece and 35 other Illustrations. Demy 8vo, cloth. **net** 10/6

JAPP. Master Missionaries. See under "Lives Worth Living."
—— Labour and Victory. See under "Lives Worth Living"
—— Good Men and True. See under "Lives Worth Living."

JULIAN The Apostate A Historical Study. By Gaetano Negri. Translated by the Duchess Lita-Visconti-Arese. With an Introduction by Professor Pasquale Villari. Illustrated. 2 vols. Demy 8vo, cloth. **net** 21/-

KEENE (Charles). By Joseph Pennell and W. H. Chesson. See under "Art"

KERR. Commissioner Kerr—An Individuality. By G. Pitt-Lewis, K.C. With Photogravure and half-tone Portraits. Demy 8vo, cloth. **net** 10/6

KRUGER. The Memoirs of Paul Kruger. Four Times President of the South African Republic. Told by Himself. Translated by A. Teixeira de Mattos. With Portraits and Map 2 vols. Demy 8vo, cloth gilt 32/-
Also a *Fine Edition* on Japan paper Price on application.

LAURENSON. Memoirs of Arthur Laurenson. Edited by Catherine Spence. With Portrait Cr. 8vo, cloth. 7/6

LEAR. The Letters of Edward Lear (Author of "The Book of Nonsense") to Chichester Fortescue, Lord Carlingford, and Frances, Countess Waldegrave (1848 to 1864). Edited by Lady Strachey, of Sutton Court). With a Photogravure Frontispiece, 3 Coloured Plates, and many other Illustrations. Demy 8vo, cloth: **net** 15/-

LINCOLN. Abraham Lincoln A History. By John G. Nicolay and Colonel John Hay With many full-page Illustrations, Portraits and Maps. 10 vols. Royal 8vo, cloth. 120/-

"LIVES WORTH LIVING," THE, Series of Popular Biographies. Illustrated. Cr 8vo, cloth extra, gilt edges. per vol. 3/6

(1) **Leaders of Men.** By H. A Page.

(2) **Wise Words and Loving Deeds.** By E. Conder Gray

(3) **Master Missionaries.** Studies in Heroic Pioneer Work. By A H Japp.

(4) **Labour and Victory.** By A. H. Japp, LL.D.

(5) **Heroic Adventure.** Chapters in Recent Explorations and Discovery. Illustrated

(6) **Great Minds in Art.** By William Tirebuck.

(7) **Good Men and True.** By Alex H. Japp, LL D.

(8) **Famous Musical Composers.** By Lydia Morris.

(9) **Oliver Cromwell and His Times.** By G Holden Pike.

(10) **Captain John Brown.** By John Newton.

(11) **Story of Thomas Carlyle.** By A S. Arnold.

(12) **Wesley and His Preachers.** By G. Holden Pike

(13) **Dr Parker & His Friends.** By G. Holden Pike.

McCARTHY. British Political Leaders By Justin McCarthy. Illustrated from Photographs. Large cr. 8vo, cloth, gilt top. net 7/6
Popular Edition. net 3/6

—— Portraits of the Sixties. By Justin McCarthy. M.P., Author of "A History of our Own Times," &c. Illustrated. Demy 8vo, cloth. net 15/-

MACHIAVELLI. Life and Times of Niccolo Machiavelli. By Professor Pasquale Villari Revised Edition. Translated by Linda Villari. Illustrated. Demy 8vo, cloth. 7/6
Also in Unwin's Half-Crown Standard Library. 1 vol., cloth. net 2/6

MADDISON. The Life of W. Randal Cremer, M.P. By Fred Maddison, M.P, and Howard Evans. net 5/-

MAITLAND. Sir Thomas Maitland: The Mastery of the Mediterranean. By Walter Frewen Lord. With Frontispiece and Maps. (Builders of Greater Britain. Vol. 2.) Large cr. 8vo, cloth. 5/-

MASTERS OF MEDICINE. Edited by C. Louis Taylor. Cr. 8vo, cloth. each 3/6

For full Titles see under :

(1) **John Hunter.**
(2) **William Harvey.**
(3) **Sir James Y. Simpson.**
(4) **William Stokes.**
(5) **Sir Benjamin Brodie.**
(6) **Hermann von Helmholtz.**
(7) **Claude Bernard.**
(8) **Thomas Sydenham.**

MAUDE. Oriental Campaigns and European Furloughs. The Autobiography of an Indian Mutiny Veteran. By Colonel Edwin Maude, late H.M. 2nd (Leinster) Regiment. With a Photogravure Frontispiece. Demy 8vo, cloth. net 7/6

MOFFAT. The Lives of Robert and Mary Moffat. By their Son, John Smith Moffat Illustrated Cr. 8vo, cloth. 6/-
Also in Unwin's Half-Crown Standard Library. 1 vol., cloth. net 2/6

MORRIS. Famous Musical Composers. See under "Lives Worth Living"

NAPOLEON. Napoleon's Last Voyages. Being the Diaries of Admiral Sir Thomas Usher, R.N., K.C.B. (on board the "Undaunted") and John R Glover, Secretary to Rear-Admiral of Cockburn (on board the "Northumberland"). New Ed with Introduction and Notes by J Holland Rose, Litt.D, Art." "Life of Napoleon I.," &c. Illustrated. Demy 8vo, net 10/6

NORTHCOTE (James). By Stephen Gwynn. See

O'NEILL. Owen Roe O'Neill. By J. F. Taylor, K C. (New Irish Library. Vol. 8) Small cr. 8vo   Paper covers, 1/- ; cloth   2/-

PAGE. Leaders of Men. See under "Lives Worth Living."

PARKER. Dr. Parker and his Friends. By G. Holden Pike. With Portraits. Cr. 8vo, cloth.   net   5/-
Also "Lives Worth Living" Series, cr 8vo, cloth.   3/6

PHILLIP. Admiral Phillip ; the Founding of New South Wales. By Louis Becke and Walter Jeffery. With Frontispiece and Maps (Builders of Greater Britain Vol 6) Large cr 8vo, cloth.   5/-

PLOWDEN. Grain or Chaff ? The Autobiography of a Police Magistrate. By A C. Plowden. With Photogravure Frontispiece. Demy 8vo, cloth gilt.   net 16/-
Popular Edition, cloth.   6/-

PORTER   Life and Letters of Mr. Endymion Porter. By Dorothea Townshend. Illustrated   Demy 8vo, cloth   12/-

PRAED. My Australian Girlhood. By Mrs. Campbell Praed. With many Illustrations   Demy 8vo, cloth.   16/-
Popular Edition, cloth.   net   6/-

RAFFLES. Sir Stamford Raffles ; England in the Far East. By Hugh E. Egerton. With Frontispiece and Maps, (Builders of Greater Britain Vol 8.) Large cr 8vo, cloth.   5/-

RALEGH. Sir Walter Ralegh ; the British Dominion of the West By Martin A. S. Hume. With Frontispiece and Maps (Builders of Greater Britain. Vol 1) Large cr. 8vo, cloth.   5/-
Also in Unwin's Half-Crown Standard Library. 1 vol., cloth.   net   2/6

RODIN. The Life of Auguste Rodin. By Frederick Lawton. With many Illustrations   Demy 8vo, cloth   net 15/-

ROSS   Three Generations of Englishwomen : Memoirs and Correspondence of Mrs. John Taylor, Mrs Sarah Austin, and Lady Duff Gordon. By Janet Ross.   New Edition, Revised and Augmented. With Portraits. Large cr 8vo, cloth.   7/6

ROSSETTI. Letters of Dante Gabriel Rossetti to William Allingham (1854-70). Edited by George Birkbeck Hill, D.C L, LL D. Illustrated   Demy 8vo, cloth.   12/-

SARSFIELD. Life of Patrick Sarsfield. By Dr. John Todhunter. (New Irish Library. Vol 7)   Paper covers, 1/- , cloth   2/-

SAVONAROLA. The Life and Times of Girolamo Savonarola. By Prof. Pasquale Villari. Translated by Linda Villari. Fully Illustrated. Large cr. 8vo, cloth.   7/6
Also in Unwin's Half-Crown Standard Library. 1 vol., cloth.   net   2/6

SECCOMBE. Lives of Twelve Bad Men. Edited by Thomas Seccombe, M A   Second Edition   Cr 8vo, cloth.   6/-

SEGANTINI (Giovanni). By Luigi Villari. See under "Art"

de SEGOVIA (Pablo). By F. de Quevedo. Illustrated by Daniel Vierge. See under "Art."

SEYMOUR. The "Pope" of Holland House. By Lady Seymour. Biographical Introduction and Supplementary Chapter by W. P. Courtney. With a Photogravure Frontispiece and 8 other Illustrations   Demy 8vo, cloth   net 10/6

SKEFFINGTON. Michael Davitt : Revolutionary, Agitator, and Labour Leader. By F. Sheehy-Skeffington   With Introduction by Justin McCarthy and a Portrait. Demy 8vo, cloth   net   7/6

T. FISHER

SHERVINTON. The Shervintons—Soldiers of Fortune. By Kathleen Shervinton Illustrated. Small demy 8vo.   net 10/6

SIMPSON. Sir James Y. Simpson. By H. Laing Gordon. With Photogravure Frontispiece (Masters of Medicine. Vol. 3) Large cr 8vo, cloth.   3/6

SIMPSON. The Autobiography of William Simpson, R.I. (Crimean Simpson). Edited by George Eyre-Todd. Illustrated with many Reproductions of his Pictures Royal 8vo, cloth   net 21/-
Also a *Fine Edition*, limited to 100 copies, printed on Arnold's unbleached, hand-made paper, with Plates on Japan paper.   net 42/-

SKIPSEY (Joseph). A Memoir See "Watson."

SMITH. Forty Years of Washington Society. From the Letters and Journals of Mrs. Samuel Harrison Smith (Margaret Bayard). Edited by Gaillard Hunt. With numerous Illustrations and Portraits Demy 8vo, cloth.   net 10/6

STANSFELD. James Stansfeld. By Jessie White Mario. Demy 8vo, cloth.   21/-

STOKES. William Stokes. By Sir William Stokes. With Photogravure Frontispiece. (Masters of Medicine Vol. 4) Large cr. 8vo, cloth   3/6

SULLIVAN. Barry Sullivan and his Contemporaries. By Robert M Sillard. 2 vols. Illustrated. Demy 8vo   net 21/-

SWANWICK. Anna Swanwick. A Memoir and Recollections. By Mary L. Bruce. Illustrated with a Photogravure Portrait, and five others in half-tone Cr 8vo, cloth   net 6/-

SWIFT. Unpublished Letters of Dean Swift. Edited by George Birkbeck Hill, D.C.L., LL D. Illustrated Demy 8vo, cloth   12/-

—— Swift in Ireland. By Richard Ashe King, M.A (New Irish Library) Small cr. 8vo   Paper covers, 1/-, cloth   2/-

SYDENHAM Thomas Sydenham. By J, F Payne With Photogravure Frontispiece (Masters of Medicine. Vol. 8) Large cr. 8vo, cloth   3/6

TAYLOR (Mrs. John). See Ross, "Three Generations."

TETLEY. Old Times and New. By J. George Tetley, D.D, Canon Residentiary of Bristol With Frontispiece. Demy 8vo, cloth, net   7/6

TIREBUCK. Great Minds in Art. See under "Lives Worth Living."

TOURGUENEFF. Tourgueneff and his French Circle. Edited by H. Halpérine-Kaminsky Translated by Ethel M Arnold Cr 8vo, cloth   7/6

TREHERNE, Spencer Perceval A Biography. By Philip Treherne With portraits Cr. 8vo, cloth   net 5/-

TROWBRIDGE (W R. H). Works. See under "History'

TROWBRIDGE. Mirabeau the Demi-God. Being the True and Romantic Story of his Life and Adventures By W. R H Trowbridge. With a Photogravure Frontispiece and 32 other Illustrations Demy 8vo, cloth.   net 15/-

VAMBERY. The Story of My Struggles. The Memoirs of Arminius Vambéry, C.V.O. With Photogravure and other Illustrations 2 vols Demy 8vo, cloth   net
Popular Edition in 1 vol. Demy 8vo, cloth.   th

—— Arminius Vambery:, His Life and Adventures. By Br of Imperial 16mo, cloth.   net 10/6
Boys' Edition, cr 8vo, cloth gilt, gilt edges.   Art."

VERNON. Admiral Vernon and the Navy. A Mem tion, with Sundry Sidelights. By Douglas Demy 8vo, cloth.   TIONS.

VINCENT. Twelve Bad Women : A Companion Volume to "Twelve Bad Men." Edited by Arthur Vincent. Illustrated. Large cr. 8vo, cloth   6/-

WAKEFIELD. Edward Gibbon Wakefield ; the Colonisation of South Australia and New Zealand. By R. Garnett, C.B., LL.D With Frontispiece and Maps. (Builders of Greater Britain. Vol 4.) Large cr 8vo, cloth   5/-

WALPOLE. Essays Political and Biographical. By Sir Spencer Walpole, K.C B. Edited by Francis Holland. With a Memoir by his Daughter, and a Photogravure Frontispiece. Demy 8vo, cloth. **net** 10/6

—— Studies in Biography. By Sir Spencer Walpole, K.C.B. With Photogravure Frontispiece. Demy 8vo, cloth.   **net** 15/-

WASHINGTON. From Slave to College President Being the Life Story of Booker T Washington. By G. Holden Pike. With Frontispiece Cr 8vo, half-bound cloth.   1/6

—— The Youth of George Washington. Told in the form of an Autobiography. By S. Weir Mitchell. Large cr. 8vo, cloth   6/-

WATSON The Savage Club. A Medley of History, Anecdote and Reminiscence. By Aaron Watson. With a chapter by Mark Twain, and a Photogravure Frontispiece, 4 Coloured Plates, and 64 other Illustrations Medium 8vo, cloth.   **net** 21/-

WATSON. Joseph Skipsey, a Memoir. By the Rt. Hon. Robert Spence Watson With 3 Portraits. Crown 8vo, cloth   **net** 2/6

WESLEY and his Preachers : Their Conquest of Britain. By G. Holden Pike Fully Illustrated. Cr 8vo, cloth.   7/6

Also "Lives Worth Living" Series.   3/6

WILBERFORCE. The Private Papers of William Wilberforce. Collected and Edited by A M. Wilberforce. Illustrated. Demy 8vo, cloth.   12/-

WILKINSON. The Personal Story of the Upper House. By Kosmo Wilkinson Demy 8vo, cloth.   16/-

---

UNWIN'S HALF-CROWN STANDARD LIBRARY OF HISTORY AND BIOGRAPHY. Illustrated. Large cr. 8vo, cloth, each, net   2/6

(1) The Life of Richard Cobden. By the Right Hon. John Morley.

(2) The Life of Girolamo Savonarola. By Professor Pasquale Villari.

(3) The Life of Niccolò Machiavelli. By Professor Pasquale Villari.

(4) The Lives of Robert and Mary Moffat. By John Smith Moffat.

(5) The History of Florence (for the first two centuries). By Prof. Pasquale Villari

(6) English Wayfaring Life in the Middle Ages (XIVth Century). By J. J. Jusserand.

(7) Lord Beaconsfield. By T. P. O'Connor

(8) Rome and Pompeii : Archæological Rambles. By Gaston Boissier.

(9) Holyoake : Sixty Years of an Agitator's Life. By George Jacob Holyoake.

(10) Sir Walter Ralegh. By Martin A. S Hume.

(11) The Dawn of the Nineteenth Century in England. By John Ashton

(12) Life of Goethe. By Heinrich Duntzer

(13) Charles Bradlaugh. By Hypathia Bradlaugh Bonner

(14) Augustus. The Life and Times of the Founder of the Roman Empire. By E. S. Shuckburgh.

ADVENTURE SERIES, THE. Popular Re-issue. Large cr. 8vo, fully Illustrated, cloth. Per vol. 3/6

(1) **Adventures of a Younger Son.** By Edward J. Trelawny. Introduction by Edward Garnett

(2) **Madagascar ;** or, Robert Drury's Journal during his Captivity on that Island. Preface and Notes by Captain S P. Oliver, R.A.

(3) **Memoirs of the Extraordinary Military Career of John Shipp.** Written by Himself Introduction by H Manners Chichester.

(4) **The Buccaneers and Marooners of America.** Edited and Illustrated by Howard Pyle.

(5) **The Log of a Jack Tar.** Being the Life of James Choyce, Master Mariner. Edited by Commander V. Lovett Cameron

(6) **Ferdinand Mendez Pinto, the Portuguese Adventurer.** New Edition. Annotated by Prof. Arminius Vambéry.

(7) **Adventures of a Blockade Runner.** By William Watson Illustrated by Arthur Byng, R N.

(8) **The Memoirs and Travels of Count de Benyowsky** in Siberia, Kamtschatka, Japan, the Liukiu Islands, and Formosa. Edited by Captain S. P Oliver, R A

(9) **The Life and Adventures of James P. Beckwourth.** New Edition. Edited and with Preface by C. G. Leland ("Hans Breitmann")

(10) **A Particular Account of the European Military Adventurers of Hindustan (1784-1803).** Compiled by Henry Compton. New and Cheaper Edition Maps and Illustrations.

(11) **A Master Mariner.** The Life of Captain Robert W. Eastwick. Edited by Herbert Compton.

(12) **Kolokotrones· Klepht and Warrior.** Translated from the Greek by Mrs. Edmonds. Introduction by M Gennadius.

(13) **Missing Friends.** The Adventures of an Emigrant in Queensland.

The following Volumes are done at 5/- only. 5/-

The Escapes of Latude and Casanova from Prison. Edited, with Introduction, by P. Villars.

The Story of the Filibusters By James Jeffrey Roche. And, The Life of Colonel David Crockett.

The following Volumes are done at 7/6 each. 7/6

The Women Adventurers. Edited by Menie Muriel Dowie.

The Life and Adventures of James Beckwourth. Mountaineer, Scout, Pioneer, and Chief of the Crow Nation of Indians Edited by Charles G. Leland (" Hans Breitmann")

A Particular Account of the European Military Adventurers of Hindustan (1784-1803). Compiled by Henry Compton. New and Cheaper Edition. Maps and Illustrations.

Famous Prison Escapes of the Civil War. Edited by G. W Cable.

HISTORY and HISTORICAL LITERATURE.

ARCHER and KINGSFORD The Crusades : The Story of the Latin
Kingdom of Jerusalem   By T. A. Archer and Charles Lethbridge
Kingsford   Third Impression.   With 58 Illustrations and 3 Maps.
(Story of the Nations. Vol. 40.)   Large cr. 8vo, cloth.   5/-

ASHTON. The Dawn of the Nineteenth Century in England : A
Social Sketch of the Times.   By John Ashton.   Third Edition.
Illustrated   Large cr 8vo, cloth.   7/6

Cheap Edition, "England 100 Years Ago."   3/6

Also in Unwin's Half-Crown Standard Library. 1 vol., cloth,   net   2/6

BARING-GOULD. Germany. By S Baring-Gould, M.A. Seventh
Impression.   With 108 Illustrations and Maps,   (Story of the
Nations. Vol. 3.) Large cr. 8vo, cloth.   5/-

BARRY. The Papal Monarchy · From Gregory the Great to Boniface
VIII. (590-1303). By William Barry, D.D. With 61 Illustrations and
Maps (Story of the Nations. Vol. 58) Large cr. 8vo, cloth.   5/-

BATESON. Mediæval England (1066-1350). By Mary Bateson,
Associate and Lecturer of Newnham College, Cambridge.   With 93
Illustrations   (Story of the Nations. Vol. 62.) Large cr 8vo, cloth   5/-

BEARNE. Heroines of French Society in the Court, the Revolution,
the Empire, and the Restoration. By Mrs. Bearne. With many
Illustrations. Large cr. 8vo, cloth   net   10/6

—— A Leader of Society at Napoleon's Court (Laura Permon). By
Mrs. Bearne. Fully Illustrated. Large cr 8vo, cloth   10/6

—— Lives and Times of the Early Valois Queens. By Mrs. Bearne.
Illustrated by E. H. Bearne. Small demy, cloth   10/6

—— Pictures of the Old French Court. By Mrs Bearne   Second
Edition, Revised. Illustrated. Small demy 8vo, cloth.   10/6

—— A Royal Quartette. By Mrs. Bearne. Fully Illustrated. Large cr.
8vo, cloth   net   10/6

—— A Sister of Marie Antoinette   The Life Story of Maria Carolina,
Queen of Naples. By Mrs. Bearne. Fully Illustrated. Large cr.
8vo, cloth.   net 10/6

—— A Queen of Napoleon's Court · The Life Story of Désirée
Bernadotte. By Mrs. Bearne. Fully Illustrated. Large cr 8vo,
cloth.   10/6

BENJAMIN. Persia. By S. G. W. Benjamin, late U S Minister to Persia.
Fourth Edition.   With 56 Illustrations and Maps.   (Story of the
Nations. Vol. 17) Large cr 8vo, cloth.   5/-

BIRCH. History of Scottish Seals, from the Eleventh to the
Seventeenth Century. By Walter de Gray Birch, LL D , F S A ,
of the British Museum. With many Illustrations derived from the
finest and most interesting examples extant. Vol. 1, The Royal Seals
of Scotland. Crown 4to, buckram, gilt top.   net 12/6

Also a *Fine Edition* on large paper.   net 21/-

BLISS. Turkey and the Armenian Atrocities. By Edwin M. Bliss.
Introduction by Frances E Willard. Cloth gilt.   10/6

BLUNT. **Secret History of the English Occupation of Egypt.** Being a Personal Narrative of Events. By Wilfrid Scawen Blunt Second Edition, Revised, with an Introduction by Sir William F. Butler, K.C.B. With a Photogravure Frontispiece. Demy 8vo, cloth. net 15/-

BOISSIER (Gaston). **The Country of Horace and Virgil.** See under "Geography"

—— **Rome and Pompeii.** See under "Geography"

BOURINOT. **Canada.** By Sir John Bourinot, K.C M G. With 63 Illustrations and Maps. New Edition, with a new Map, and revisions and a supplementary chapter by Edward Porritt. (Story of the Nations. Vol. 45) Large cr 8vo, cloth - - 5/-

BOXALL. **The Anglo-Saxon :** A Study in Evolution. By George E. Boxall Crown 8vo, cloth. 5/-

—— **The History of the Australian Bushrangers** By G. E Boxall Large cr 8vo, cloth. net 5/-

BOYESEN. **A History of Norway.** From the Earliest Times. By Professor Hjalmar H Boyesen With a Chapter by C F Keary With 77 Illustrations and Maps. (Story of the Nations. Vol 55) Large cr. 8vo, cloth 5/-

BRADLEY. **The Goths.** From the Earliest Times to the End of the Gothic Dominion in Spain. By Henry Bradley Fifth Edition. With 35 Illustrations and Maps. (Story of the Nations Vol. 12) Large cr. 8vo, cloth 5/-

BRERETON. **The Literary History of the Adelphi and its Neighbourhood.** By Austin Brereton. With a new Introduction, a Photogravure Frontispiece, and 26 other full-page Illustrations. Demy 8vo, cloth. net 10/6

BROOKS. **Dames and Daughters of the French Court.** By Geraldine Brooks. With a Photogravure Frontispiece and 10 other Illustrations. Large cr 8vo, cloth net 8/6

BROWNE **Bonaparte in Egypt and the Egyptians of To-day** By Haji A Browne. With Frontispiece. Demy 8vo, cloth. net 10/6

BUEL (Clarence C.). See "Johnson"

BUTLER. **The Lombard Communes** A History of the Republics of North Italy. By W. F. Butler. With Maps and Illustrations. Demy 8vo, cloth net 15/-

BUTLER **Wellington's Operations in the Peninsula (1808-1814)** By Captain Lewis Butler. With Maps. 2 vols. Demy 8vo, cloth. net 32/- Also in Six paper Parts. each, net 5/-

CARSE **All the Monarchs of Merry England** William I. to Edward VII By Roland Carse. With 40 full-page Coloured Illustrations by W Heath Robinson. 252 pages, bound in full leather and gold-blocked. 15/-

—— **The Monarchs of Merry England.** William I to Richard III By Roland Carse. With 20 full-page Coloured Illustrations by W. Heath Robinson. 124 pages, bound in full cloth. 6/- Also bound in art picture boards cloth back 5/-

—— **More Monarchs of Merry England** Henry VII to Edward VII By Roland Carse. With 20 full-page Coloured Pictures by W. Heath Robinson 128 pages, bound in full cloth. 6/- Also bound in picture boards, cloth back. 5/-

—— **The Monarchs of Merry England.** In Four Parts, each containing 10 full-page Coloured Illustrations by W Heath Robinson. 60 pages, bound in art picture boards, cloth back.

Part 1. William I. to Henry III		2/6
„ 2. Edward I. to Richard III.		2/6
„ 3 Henry VII to Elizabeth.		2/6
„ 4 James I. to Edward VII.		2/6

CESARESCO. Lombard Studies. By Countess Evelyn Martinengo
Cesaresco. Photogravure Frontispiece, and many other Illustra-
tions. Demy 8vo, cloth.   16/-

CHURCH. Carthage; or, the Empire of Africa. By Professor Alfred
J. Church, M A. Eighth Edition. With the Collaboration of Arthur
Gilman, M.A. With 43 Illustrations and Maps (Story of the
Nations. Vol. 4.) Large cr. 8vo, cloth.   5/-

—— **Early Britain.** By Professor Alfred J. Church, M A., Author of
"Carthage," &c   Sixth Impression. With 57 Illustrations and
Maps. (Story of the Nations. Vol. 21.) Large cr 8vo, cloth.   5/-

CLAYDEN. England Under the Coalition: The Political History of
England and Ireland from 1885 to 1892. By P. W. Clayden. Small
demy 8vo, cloth.   12/-

CLERIGH History of Ireland to the Coming of Henry II. By Arthur
Ua Clerigh, M.A , K.C. Demy 8vo, cloth.   net 10/6

COLERIDGE. The Story of a Devonshire House. By Lord Coleridge, K.C. Illustrated. Demy 8vo, cloth.   net 15/-

COPINGER. The Manors of Suffolk. Notes on their History and
Devolution and their Several Lords. The Hundreds of Babergh
and Blackbourn By W. A. Copinger, LL.D , F.S A., F.R S A.
Illustrated. Folio, cloth.   net 21/-

**CRICHFIELD. The Rise and Progress of the South American
Republics.** By George W. Crichfield. Illustrated. 2 vols Royal
8vo, cloth.   net 25/-

DAVIDS Buddhist India By T. W. Rhys Davids, LL.D., Ph D.
With 57 Illustrations and Maps. (Story of the Nations. Vol. 61)
Large cr 8vo, cloth.   5/-

**DAVIS. The Patriot Parliament of 1689, with its Statutes, Votes
and Proceedings.** By Thomas Davis. Edited by Ch. G Duffy.
Third Edition. (New Irish Library. Vol. 1.) Small cr. 8vo .
                                                    Paper covers, 1/- ; cloth   2/-

DIEULAFOY. David the King: An Historical Inquiry. By Marcel
Auguste Dieulafoy. (Membre de l'Institut.) Translated by Lucy
Hotz. Small demy 8vo, cloth   net 7/6

DODGE. From Squire to Prince: Being the Rise of the House of
Alksena. By Walter Phelps Dodge. Illustrated. Demy 8vo, cloth 10/6

DOUGLAS China. By Prof. Robert K Douglas. Third Edition.
With a new preface and a chapter on recent events. With 51 Illustrations and a Map. (Story of the Nations. Vol 51) Large cr. 8vo,
cloth   5/-

**DUFFY (B.). The Tuscan Republics (Florence, Siena, Pisa, and
Lucca) with Genoa.** By Bella Duffy. With 40 Illustrations and
Maps. (Story of the Nations. Vol. 32) Large cr. 8vo, cloth.   5/-
Also Tourist Edition in Baedeker Binding.   5/-

DUFFY (Ch. G.) Young Ireland: A Fragment of Irish History. By
the Hon. Sir Charles Gavan Duffy. Illustrated. Two Parts, in stiff
wrapper.   each   2/-
In one Volume, demy 8vo, cloth.   5/-

EDWARDS. A Short History of Wales. By Owen M. Edwards,
Lecturer on Modern History at Lincoln College, Oxford. With
Maps. Cr. 8vo, cloth.   net   2/-

—— **Wales.** By Owen M Edwards With 47 Illustrations and 7 Maps.
(Story of the Nations Vol. 56) Large cr. 8vo, cloth.   5/-

ESCOTT. Society in the Country House. Anecdotal Records of Six
Centuries By T. H. S Escott, Author of "King Edward and His
Court," &c. With Photogravure Frontispiece. Demy 8vo, cloth. 16/-

FITZGERALD. Lady Jean : The Romance of the Great Douglas Cause. By Percy Fitzgerald, F.S.A. With Photogravure Frontispiece and other Illustrations. Demy 8vo, cloth. net 12/-

FORREST. The Development of Western Civilization. By J. Dorsey Forrest. Large cr. 8vo, cloth. net 9/-

FOSTER The Stuarts. Being Outlines of the Personal History of the Family from James V to Prince Charles Edward. By J. J. Foster, F S A. Illustrated with 30 full-page Photogravure Plates Cloth net 25/-

FRAZER. British India. By R. W. Frazer, LL.D. Third Edition With 30 Illustrations and Maps. (Story of the Nations. Vol. 46.) Large cr. 8vo, cloth 5/-

FREEMAN. Sicily : Phœnician, Greek, and Roman. By Prof Edward A Freeman, M A, Hon. D.C.L, LL D., Oxford. Third Edition With 45 Illustrations. (Story of the Nations. Vol 31.). Large cr. 8vo, cloth. 5/-
Also Tourist Edition in Baedeker Binding. 5/-

GANNON. A Review of Irish History in Relation to the Social Development of Ireland. By John P. Gannon. 288 pp , cr. 8vo, green buckram. 6/-

GARDNER. A History of Jamaica. From its discovery by Christopher Columbus to the year 1872. By W J. Gardner. Large cr. 8vo. net 7/6

GILMAN. Rome : From the Earliest Times to the End of the Republic By Arthur Gilman, M A. Third Edition With 43 Illustrations and Maps. (Story of the Nations Vol 1) Large cr 8vo, cloth. 5/-

—— The Saracens : From the Earliest Times to the Fall of Bagdad. By Arthur Gilman, M.A. Fourth Edition. With 57 Illustrations and Maps (Story of the Nations. Vol. 9) Large cr 8vo, cloth. 5/-

GOMME. The Governance of London. Studies of the place of London in English Institutions. By G Lawrence Gomme, F S A With Maps. Demy 8vo, cloth. net 15/-

GORDON. The Old Bailey and Newgate. By Charles Gordon With about 100 Illustrations and a Frontispiece in tint Med. 8vo, cloth net 21/-

—— Old Time Aldwych, Kingsway, and Neighbourhood. By Charles Gordon Fully Illustrated and with Map. Medium 8vo, cloth, net 21/-
Popular Edition. Fully illustrated and with Map. Medium 8vo, cloth. net 7/6

GRAY. The Buried City of Kenfig. By Thomas Gray. With a Map and Illustrations. Demy 8vo, cloth. net 10/6

GRIFFITHS. Famous British Regiments. By Major Arthur Griffiths. Fully Illustrated. Cr. 8vo, cloth gilt 2/6

HALE. Mexico. By Susan Hale Third Impression With 47 Illustrations and Maps. (Story of the Nations. Vol 27) Large cr 8vo, cloth 5/-

HANNAH. A Brief History of Eastern Asia. By I. C. Hannah, M.A. Cr. 8vo, cloth 7/6

HASEN. Contemporary American Opinion of the French Revolution. By Charles Downer Hasen. Demy 8vo, cloth. net 8/6

HERTZ. English Public Opinion after the Restoration. By Gerald Berkeley Hertz Cr. 8vo, cloth net 3/6

HOLYOAKE (G.T). History of Co-operation. See under " Politics "

HOSMER. The Jews : In Ancient, Mediæval, and Modern Times By Prof James K Hosmer. Seventh Edition With 37 Illustrations and Maps. (Story of the Nations Vol. 2) Large cr 8vo, cloth 5/-

HOUGHTON. Hebrew Life and Thought Being Interpretative Studies in the Literature of Israel. By Louis Seymour Houghton. Large cr. 8vo, cloth. net 6/6

HOWARD. A History of Matrimonial Institutions. By George Elliott Howard, Ph.D , University of Chicago. 3 vols. Super royal 8vo.   net 42/-

HUG and STEAD. Switzerland. By Lina Hug and Richard Stead, B A. Third Impression. With over 54 Illustrations, Maps, &c. (Story of the Nations. Vol 26) Large cr 8vo, cloth   5/-
Also Tourist Edition in Baedeker Binding.   5/-

HUME. Modern Spain (1878-1898). By Martin A. S. Hume, F.R.H.S., Second Impression. With 37 Illustrations and a Map. (Story of the Nations. Vol 53) Large cr 8vo, cloth.   5/-

HUNGARY Its People, Places and Politics. The Journey of the Eighty Club in 1906 With 60 Illustrations. Demy 8vo, cloth.   10/6

JAMAICA (A History of). See " Gardner "

JAMES. The Siege of Port Arthur. Records of an Eye-Witness. By David H. James, Special War Correspondent for the London *Daily Telegraph* with the Third Japanese Army. With 4 Maps and Plans and 16 Illustrations Demy 8vo, cloth.   net 10/6

JANE. The Coming of Parliament. (England from 1350 to 1660.) By L. Cecil Jane With 51 Illustrations and 1 Map. (Story of the Nations. Vol. 63) Large cr. 8vo, cloth.   5/-

JENKS. Parliamentary England. The Evolution of the Cabinet System. By Edward Jenks, M A. With 47 Illustrations. (Story of the Nations Vol. 60) Large cr. 8vo, cloth.   5/-

JESSOPP. Arcady : for Better, for Worse. By Augustus Jessopp, D.D. Seventh Edition. Cr. 8vo, limp cloth, silk sewn.   3/6

—— **Before the Great Pillage,** with other Miscellanies. By Augustus Jessopp, D D., Cr. 8vo, cloth   7/6
New Cheap Edition, cr 8vo, cloth.   3/6

—— **The Coming of the Friars,** and other Mediæval Sketches. By Augustus Jessopp, D.D. Cr 8vo, limp cloth, silk sewn.   3/6

—— **Frivola, Simon Ryan and other Papers.** By Augustus Jessopp, D.D Cr. 8vo, limp cloth.   3/6

—— **One Generation of a Norfolk House.** A contribution to Elizabethan History. By Augustus Jessopp, D.D Large cr. 8vo, cloth.   7/6

—— **Random Roaming, and other Papers.** With Portrait. By Augustus Jessopp, D D. Cr. 8vo, limp cloth, silk sewn.   3/6

—— **Studies by a Recluse : In Cloister, Town, and Country.** By Augustus Jessopp, D.D. Cr. 8vo, limp cloth, silk sewn.   3/6

—— **The Trials of a Country Parson : Some Fugitive Papers.** By Augustus Jessopp, D.D. Cr 8vo, limp cloth, silk sewn.   3/6

JEWETT. The Story of the Normans. Told Chiefly in Relation to their Conquest of England. By Sarah Orne Jewett. Third Impression With 35 Illustrations and Maps. (Story of the Nations. Vol. 29.) Large cr. 8vo, cloth.   5/-

JOHNSON and BUEL. Battles and Leaders of the American Civil War. By Robert U Johnson and Clarence C. Buel. An Authoritative History written by Distinguished Participants on both sides, and Edited by the above. Four volumes, royal 8vo, elegantly bound. Fully Illustrated.   105/-

JONES (David Brynmor). See " Welsh People "

JONES (H. S) The Roman Empire, B.C. 29—A.D. 476. By H. Stuart Jones, M A. With a Map and many Illustrations. (Story of the Nations Vol. 65) Large cr. 8vo, cloth.   5/-

JUSSERAND. English Wayfaring Life in the Middle Ages (XIVth Century). By J. J. Jusserand, Conseiller d'Ambassade Translated from the French by Lucy A Toulmin Smith. With over 60 Illustrations. Large cr. 8vo, cloth. **7/6**
Also in Unwin's Half-crown Standard Library. 1 vol. Cloth. net **2/6**

—— A French Ambassador at the Court of Charles II., Le Comte de Cominges. From his unpublished Correspondence. By J. J. Jusserand, Conseiller d'Ambassade. Second Edition. Large cr. 8vo, cloth. **7/6**

—— The Romance of a King's Life. By J. J. Jusserand. With Illustrations Fcap. 8vo, cloth. **6/-**

LANE-POOLE. The Barbary Corsairs. By Stanley Lane-Poole With Additions by J. D. J. Kelly. Fourth Edition. With 39 Illustrations and Maps. (Story of the Nations. Vol. 22) Large cr. 8vo, cloth. **5/-**

—— Mediæval India under Mohammedan Rule (A D. 712-1764). By Stanley Lane-Poole. With 59 Illustrations. (Story of the Nations. Vol. 59.) Large cr. 8vo, cloth. **5/-**

—— The Moors in Spain. By Stanley Lane-Poole. With Collaboration of Arthur Gilman, M A. Eighth Edition. With 29 Illustrations and Maps. (Story of the Nations. Vol. 6) Large cr. 8vo, cloth **5/-**

—— Turkey. By Stanley Lane-Poole. Assisted by E. J W Gibb and Arthur Gilman New Edition. With a new chapter on recent events. (1908) With 43 Illustrations, Maps, &c. (Story of the Nations. Vol. 14) Large cr. 8vo, cloth. **5/-**

LATANE. The Diplomatic Relations of the United States and Spanish America. By John H. Latane, Large cr 8vo, cloth. net **6/6**

LAWLESS Ireland. By the Hon Emily Lawless Seventh Impression With some Addition by Mrs. Arthur Bronson. With 58 Illustrations and Maps. (Story of the Nations. Vol. 10.) Large cr 8vo, cloth **5/-**

LEBON. Modern France (1789-1895). By André Lebon. With 26 Illustrations and a Chronological Chart of the Literary, Artistic, and Scientific Movement in Contemporary France. (Story of the Nations. Vol 47) Large cr. 8vo, cloth **5/-**

LEE. Studies in the Eighteenth Century in Italy. By Vernon Lee New Edition, with a new Preface, a Photogravure Frontispiece, and 40 other Illustrations selected by Dr. Guido Biagi, of the Laurentian Library, Florence. Super royal 8vo, half-bound. net **21/-**

LEYDS The First Annexation of the Transvaal By W. J Leyds, LL.D., formerly State Secretary of the South African Republic Demy 8vo, cloth. net **21/-**

LILLY. Renaissance Types. By W S. Lilly Demy 8vo, cloth. **16/-**

LITTLE. Mediæval Wales, Chiefly in the Twelfth and Thirteenth Centuries By A. G. Little, M A; F.R.Hist S. With Maps and Plans. Cr 8vo, cloth. net **2/6**

LONERGAN. Forty Years of Paris. By W F. Lonergan. With 32 Portraits of Leading Frenchmen Demy 8vo, cloth net **10/6**

McCARTHY. Modern England (Vol. I.). Before the Reform Bill By Justin McCarthy, M.P Author of "The History of Our Own Times," &c With 31 Illustrations. (Story of the Nations. Vol. 50) Large cr. 8vo, cloth. **5/-**

—— Modern England (Vol. II.). From the Reform Bill to the Present Time. By Justin McCarthy, M P Second Edition With 46 Illustrations (Story of the Nations Vol. 52) Large cr. 8vo, cloth. **5/-**

MACKINTOSH. Scotland : From the Earliest Times to the Present Day. By John Mackintosh, LL.D., Author of "History of Civilisation in Scotland," &c. Fifth Impression. With 60 Illustrations and Maps. (Story of the Nations. Vol. 25)   Large cr 8vo, cloth.   5/-

MAHAFFY. Alexander's Empire. By John Pentland Mahaffy, D.D. With Collaboration of Arthur Gilman, M A   With 43 Illustrations and Maps   (Story of the Nations. Vol. 5.)   Eighth Impression. Large cr. 8vo, cloth.   5/-

—— An Epoch in Irish History : Trinity College, Dublin, Its History and Fortunes (1591-1660). By J. P Mahaffy, D D , Mus. Doc. Dublin ; Hon. D C.L , Oxon. , sometime Professor of Ancient History in the University of Dublin. Demy 8vo, cloth.   16/-
   Cheap Edition. Demy 8vo, cloth   net   7/6

—— The Particular Book of Trinity College, Dublin. A facsimile in collotype of the original copy. Edited by J P. Mahaffy, D D. A Companion Volume to "An Epoch in Irish History." Demy 4to.   net 63/-

—— The Progress of Hellenism in Alexander's Empire By John Pentland Mahaffy, D.D   Large cr 8vo, cloth.   net   5/-

—— The Silver Age of the Greek World. By J. P Mahaffy. Large cr. 8vo, cloth.   net 13/6

MARIO. The Birth of Modern Italy. The Posthumous Papers of Jessie White Mario   Edited with Introduction, Notes, and Epilogue, by the Duke Litta-Visconti-Arese. Illustrated. Demy 8vo, cloth. net 12/6

MASPERO. New Light on Ancient Egypt. By G. Maspero, Director-General of the Service of Antiquities in Egypt. Translated by Elizabeth Lee. Illustrated. Demy 8vo, cloth.   net 12/6

MASSEY. Ancient Egypt, the Light of the World. A Work of reclamation and Restitution in Twelve Books. By Gerald Massey. With Diagrams. 2 vols. Super royal 8vo, cloth.   net 42/-

MASSON. Mediæval France. From the Reign of Hugues Capet to the Beginning of the Sixteenth Century. By Gustave Masson, B A. Fifth Edition. With 48 Illustrations and Maps. (Story of the Nations. Vol. 16.)   Large cr. 8vo, cloth.   5/-

MAURICE. Bohemia : From the Earliest Times to the Fall of National Independence in 1620 ; with a Short Summary of later Events. · By C. Edmund Maurice. Second Impression. With 41 Illustrations and Maps. (Story of the Nations. Vol. 43.)   Large cr. 8vo, cloth   5/-

MILFORD. Haileybury College. By Rev L. S Milford. Illustrated.   net   7/6

MILLER The Balkans : Roumania, Bulgaria, Servia and Montenegro. By William Miller, M.A., Oxon. New Edition, with a new chapter containing their History from 1896 to 1908. With 39 Illustrations and Maps. (Story of the Nations. Vol 44.) Large cr. 8vo, cloth.   5/-

—— Mediæval Rome : From Hildebrand to Clement VIII. 1073-1535. By William Miller, M.A. With 35 Illustrations. (Story of the Nations. Vol. 57) Large cr. 8vo, cloth.   5/-

MONARCH SERIES, THE.
   Humorous Rhymes of Historical Times. By Roland Carse. With Illustrations in colour and black and white by W. Heath Robinson. Size 8½ in. by 11 in. (For titles of volumes see under "Carse.")

MOORE. The Story of the Isle of Man. By A. W. Moore, M.A. Illustrated. Cr. 8vo, cloth.   1/-

MORFILL. Poland. By W. R. Morfill, M.A., Professor of Russian and Slavonic Languages in the University of Oxford. Third Impression. With 50 Illustrations and Maps. (Story of the Nations. Vol. 33) Large cr. 8vo, cloth.   5/-

—— **Russia.** By W. R Morfill, M.A Fourth Edition. With 60 Illustrations and Maps (Story of the Nations. Vol. 23.) Large cr. 8vo, cloth.   5/-
War Edition. Brought up to date and with Supplementary Chapters on the Present Situation, and Large War Map. Cloth   5/-

MORRISON The Jews Under Roman Rule. By W. D. Morrison. Second Impression With 61 Illustrations and Maps. (Story of the Nations. Vol. 24) Large cr. 8vo, cloth.   5/-

MURRAY. Japan. By David Murray, Ph D., LL D., late Adviser to the Japanese Minister of Education Third Edition With 35 Illustrations and Maps. (Story of the Nations. Vol 37) Large cr. 8vo, cloth   5/-
War Edition, with New Chapter by Joseph H Longford, formerly British Consul at Nagasaki, and Large War Map. Cloth.   5/-

NEEDHAM Somerset House, Past and Present. By Raymond Needham and Alexander Webster With Photogravure Frontispiece and many Illustrations. Demy 8vo, cloth.   21/-

NEGRI. Julian the Apostate A Historical Study. By Gaetano Negri Translated by the Duchess Litta Visconti Arese. With an Introduction by Professor Pasquale Villari. Illustrated 2 vols. Demy 8vo, cloth.   net 21/-

O'BRIEN Irish Memories. By R Barry O'Brien, Author of "The Life of Charles Stuart Parnell." With Plans. Cr 8vo, cloth net   3/6

O'CONNOR. The Parnell Movement: Being the History of the Irish Question from the Death of O'Connell to the Suicide of Pigott. By T. P. O'Connor, M P. Cr. 8vo. Paper covers, 1/- ; cloth boards   2/-

OMAN. The Byzantine Empire. By C W. C. Oman, M A , F S A , Oxford Third Edition. With 44 Illustrations and Maps. (Story of the Nations. Vol. 30.) Large cr. 8vo, cloth.   5/-

ORSI. Modern Italy (1748-1898) By Pietro Orsi, Professor of History in the R. Liceo Foscarini, Venice. Translated by Mary Alice Vialls. With over 40 Illustrations and Maps. (Story of the Nations Vol. 54.) Large cr 8vo, cloth.   5/-

PAIS Ancient Italy Historical and Geographical Investigations in Central Italy, Magna Græcia, Sicily, and Sardinia. By Ettore Pais, Professor in the University of Rome, formerly Director of the Naples Museum. Translated by C. D Curtis. Demy 8vo, cloth. net   21/-

Patriot Parliament of 1689, with its Statutes, Votes and Proceedings, The. (New Irish Library. Vol. 1) See under "Thomas Davis."

POTT. A Sketch of Chinese History. By the Rev F. L. Hawks Pott, D.D Demy 8vo, cloth.   net   6/-

PUSEY. The Past History of Ireland. By S. E. Bouverie-Pusey. Small cr 8vo.   Paper covers   1/-

RAGOZIN Assyria From the Rise of the Empire to the Fall of Nineveh. (Continued from "Chaldea") By Zénaïde A Ragozin. Sixth Edition. With 81 Illustrations and Maps. (Story of the Nations. Vol 13) Large cr. 8vo, cloth.   5/-

—— **Chaldea:** From the Earliest Times to the Rise of Assyria Treated as a General Introduction to the Study of Ancient History. By Zénaïde A. Ragozin. Seventh Impression. With 80 Illustrations and Maps (Story of the Nations. Vol 11) Large cr. 8vo, cloth.   5/-

STORY OF THE NATIONS, THE. The volumes occupy about
400 pages each, and contain respectively, besides an Index
and Coloured Map, a great many Illustrations. The size is large cr.
8vo. There are published now (Autumn, 1908) 65 volumes, which
are to be had in the following bindings —

Ordinary Edition. Fancy cloth, gold lettered.   5/-

Half morocco, gilt.   net 10/6

Subscription Edition   Special cloth binding. On Subscription only.

Subscription Edition —A set of 65 volumes, newly printed on specially
prepared paper, and containing 2,500 full-page and other Illustrations. Now offered cloth bound for a preliminary payment of 15s,
and 18 subsequent monthly payments of 10s each, or a cash payment of £9 5s 3d. , or bound in half morocco, for a preliminary
payment of 25s. and 17 further payments of 20s each, or a cash
payment of £17 7s. Delivered free in the London Postal district.

LIST OF VOLUMES.

[For full Titles see under Authors' names]

(1) **Rome :** From the Earliest
Times to the End of the
Republic. By Arthur Gil-
man, M A.

(2) **The Jews.** By Prof. James
K. Hosmer.

(3) **Germany.** By S. Baring-
Gould, M.A.

(4) **Carthage.** By Professor
Alfred J. Church, M A.

(5) **Alexander's Empire** By
John Pentland Mahaffy,
D.D.

(6) **The Moors in Spain.** By
Stanley Lane-Poole.

(7) **Ancient Egypt.** By Prof
George Rawlinson, M.A

(8) **Hungary.** By Professor
Arminius Vambéry.

(9) **The Saracens :** From the
Earliest Times to the Fall
of Bagdad. By Arthur
Gilman, M A.

(10) **Ireland.** By the Hon.
Emily Lawless.

(11) **Chaldea.** From the Earliest
Times to the Rise of Assyria.
By Zénaïde A. Ragozin.

(12) **The Goths.** By Henry
Bradley.

(13) **Assyria :** From the Rise of
the Empire to the Fall of
Nineveh. (Continued from
" Chaldea.") By Zénaïde
A Ragozin.

(14) **Turkey.** By Stanley Lane-
Poole.

(15) **Holland.** By Prof. J E.
Thorold Rogers.

(16) **Mediæval France.** By
Gustave Masson, B.A.

(17) **Persia.** By S G. W Benjamin.

(18) **Phœnicia.** By Prof. George
Rawlinson, M.A

(19) **Media, Babylon and
Persia ·** From the Fall of
Nineveh to the Persian
War. By Zénaïde A
Ragozin.

(20) **The Hansa Towns.** By
Helen Zimmern.

(21) **Early Britain,** By Prof.
Alfred J. Church, M.A.

(22) **The Barbary Corsairs.**
By Stanley Lane-Poole

(23) **Russia.** By W R Morfill,
M A.

(24) **The Jews under Roman
Rule.** By W D, Morrison

(25) **Scotland.** By John Mackintosh, LL D

(26) **Switzerland.** By Lina
Hug and R. Stead

(27) **Mexico.** By Susan Hale.

(28) **Portugal.** By H. Morse
Stephens, M.A.

(29) **The Normans.** By Sarah
Orne Jewett.

(30) **The Byzantine Empire.**
By C W. C Oman, M A

(31) **Sicily** Phœnician, Greek,
and Roman. By Prof. E
A. Freeman.

STORY OF THE NATIONS, THE.—*continued.*

(32) **The Tuscan Republics,** with Genoa. By Bella Duffy.

(33) **Poland.** By W R. Morfill.

(34) **Parthia.** By Prof. Geo. Rawlinson.

(35) **The Australian Commonwealth.** (New South Wales, Tasmania, Western Australia, South Australia, Victoria, Queensland, New Zealand.) By Greville Tregarthen

(36) **Spain:** Being a Summary of Spanish History from the Moorish Conquest to the Fall of Granada (711-1492 A D) By Henry Edward Watts.

(37) **Japan.** By David Murray, Ph.D , LL.D.

(38) **South Africa.** By George McCall Theal.

(39) **Venice.** By Alethea Wiel

(40) **The Crusades:** The Story of the Latin Kingdom of Jerusalem. By T. A. Archer and C L. Kingsford

(41) **Vedic India.** By Zénaïde A Ragozin.

(42) **The West Indies and the Spanish Main.** By James Rodway, F L S.

(43) **Bohemia** From the Earliest Times to the Fall of National Independence in 1620 , with a Short Summary of later Events. By C. Edmund Maurice.

(44) **The Balkans.** By W. Miller, M A.

(45) **Canada.** By Sir John Bourinot, C.M G.

(46) **British India.** By R. W. Frazer, LL.D.

(47) **Modern France.** By André Lebon.

(48) **The Franks.** By Lewis Sergeant.

(49) **Austria.** By Sidney Whitman.

(50) **Modern England before the Reform Bill.** By Justin McCarthy.

(51) **China.** By Prof. R. K. Douglas.

(52) **Modern England under Queen Victoria.** By Justin McCarthy.

(53) **Modern Spain, 1878-1898** By Martin A. S. Hume

(54) **Modern Italy, 1748-1898.** By Prof. Pietro Orsi.

(55) **Norway.** By Professor Hjalmar H Boyesen.

(56) **Wales.** By Owen Edwards.

(57) **Mediæval Rome, 1073-1535.** By William Miller.

(58) **The Papal Monarchy:** From Gregory the Great to Boniface VIII. By William Barry, D D

(59) **Mediæval India under Mohammedan Rule.** By Stanley Lane-Poole.

(60) **Parliamentary England:** From 1660-1832. By Edward Jenks.

(61) **Buddhist India** By T. W. Rhy Davids

(62) **Mediæval England.** By Mary Bateson.

(63) **The Coming of Parliament.** (England 1350-1660) By L. Cecil Jane.

(64) **The Story of Greece** (from the Earliest Times to A D 14) By E. S. Shuckburgh.

(65) **The Story of the Roman Empire** (B C 29 to A.D. 476). By H. Stuart Jones.

THEAL. The Beginning of South African History. By Dr. George McCall Theal. With Maps and Illustrations. Demy 8vo, cloth.   **16/-**

—— **A Little History of South Africa.** By Dr. George McCall Theal. Third Edition. Cr. 8vo.   **1/6**

—— **South Africa.** (The Cape Colony, Natal, Orange Free State, South African Republic, Rhodesia, and all other Territories south of the Zambesi.) By Dr. George McCall Theal, D.Lit., LL.D. Ninth Impression (Sixth Edition). With 39 Illustrations and Maps. (Story of the Nations. Vol. 38) Large cr. 8vo, cloth.   **5/-**

THOMAS. Roman Life under the Cæsars. By Emile Thomas. Numerous Illustrations. Small demy 8vo, cloth. 7/6

TREGARTHEN. The Australian Commonwealth. (New South Wales, Tasmania, Western Australia, South Australia, Victoria, Queensland, New Zealand.) By Greville Tregarthen Fourth Impression. With 36 Illustrations and Maps. (Story of the Nations. Vol. 35) Large cr. 8vo, cloth. 5/-

TROWBRIDGE. Court Beauties of Old Whitehall. By W R H Trowbridge. With a Photogravure Frontispiece and many other Illustrations. Demy 8vo, cloth. net 15/-

—— Mirabeau, the Demi-God Being the True and Romantic Story of his Life and Adventures. By W. R H. Trowbridge. With a Photogravure Frontispiece and 32 other Illustrations. Demy 8vo, cloth net 15/-

—— Seven Splendid Sinners By W. R H Trowbridge With a Photogravure Frontispiece and other Illustrations. Demy 8vo, cloth. net 15/-

TURQUAN The Sisters of Napoleon. Edited from the French of Joseph Turquan by W. R H. Trowbridge. Illustrated. Demy 8vo, cloth. net 15/-

VAMBÉRY. Hungary : In Ancient, Mediæval, and Modern Times. By Prof Arminius Vambéry With Collaboration of Louis Heilprin. Seventh Edition. With 47 Illustrations and Maps. (Story of the Nations. Vol 8) Large cr. 8vo, cloth 5/-

VILLARI. The Barbarian Invasions of Italy. By Prof Pasquale Villari Translated by Linda Villari. With Frontispiece and Maps 2 vols Demy 8vo. 32/-

—— The History of Florence. (The First Two Centuries of Florentine History) By Prof. Pasquale Villari. Translated by Linda Villari. Illustrated. Demy 8vo, cloth. 7/6

Also in Unwin's Half-Crown Standard Library 1 vol., cloth. net 2/6

—— Studies Historical and Critical. By Professor Pasquale Villari, Author of "Girolamo Savonarola," &c. With 7 Photogravure Plates. Demy 8vo, cloth net 15/-

VOIGT Fifty Years of the History of the Republic in South Africa (1795-1845) By J. C. Voigt, M.D. With Coloured Maps, Sketches, and Diagrams. Maps and Plans 2 vols. Demy 8vo. net 25/-

WATTS. Spain · Being a Summary of Spanish History from the Moorish Conquest to the Fall of Granada (711-1492, A D). By Henry Edward Watts Third Edition. With 36 Illustrations and Maps. (Story of the Nations. Vol. 36) Large cr 8vo, cloth. 5/-

WEBSTER (Alexander). See " Needham."

WELSH PEOPLE, THE : Their Origin, Language, and History Being Extracts from the Reports of the Royal Commission on Land in Wales and Monmouthshire. Edited, with Additions, Notes and Appendices, by John Rhys, Principal of Jesus College, and Professor of Celtic in the University of Oxford, and David Brynmor Jones, K.C., M.P. Second Edition, Revised. Demy 8vo, cloth. 16/-

Also a cheap Edition. Large cr. 8vo, cloth. net 5/-

WHITMAN. Austria. By Sidney Whitman With the Collaboration of J R. McIlraith. Third Edition. With 35 Illustrations and a Map. (Story of the Nations. Vol. 49) Large cr. 8vo, cloth. 5/-

WHITTY. St. Stephen's in the Fifties. By E. M. Whitty. With an Introduction by Justin McCarthy And Notes by H. M. Williams. With Frontispiece. Demy 8vo, cloth   net 10/6
   Also in Reformer's Bookshelf. Large cr. 8vo, cloth   3/6

WIEL. Venice. By Alethea Wiel. Fourth Edition. With 61 Illustrations and Maps. (Story of the Nations. Vol. 39.) Large cr. 8vo, cloth.   5/-
   Also Tourist Edition in Baedeker Binding.   5/-

WILKINSON. The Personal Story of the Upper House. See under "Biography."

ZIMMERN. The Hansa Towns. By Helen Zimmern Third Edition. With 51 Illustrations and Maps. (Story of the Nations. Vol 20.) Large cr. 8vo, cloth.   5/-

—— **Heroic Tales.** Retold from Firdusi the Persian. By Helen Zimmern With two etchings by L. Alma-Tadema, R.A., and a Prefatory Poem by Edmund W Gosse. Third Edition Cr. 8vo, cloth.   5/-

—— **Old Tales from Rome.** By Alice Zimmern, Author of "Old Tales from Greece." Cr. 8vo, cloth. Fully illustrated.   5/-

---

POLITICS, ECONOMICS, FREE TRADE, &c.

ALBRIGHT. The Churches and the Liquor Traffic. By Mrs W. A Albright Cr 8vo, paper cover.   net   6d.

ARONSON. The Working of the Workmen's Compensation Act, 1906. By V. R Aronson, Barrister-at-law Demy 8vo, cloth. net 15/-

BAMFORD'S Passages in the Life of a Radical. Edited, and with an Introduction, by Henry Duckley ("Verax") 2 vols (Reformer's Bookshelf.) Large cr 8vo, cloth   7/-

BARNETT. Towards Social Reform. By A S. Barnett, M.A, Canon of Westminster. Cr 8vo, cloth.   net   5/-

BENTLEY. The Process of Government. A Study of Social Pressures. By Arthur F Bentley Demy 8vo, cloth.   net 12/6

BLISS (Rev E. M.). Turkey and the Armenian Atrocities. See under "History."

BLUNT. Atrocities of Justice under British Rule in Egypt. By Wilfred Scawen Blunt Paper cover   net   1/-

BOWACK. Another View of Industrialism. By William Mitchell Bowack Large cr 8vo, cloth.   net   6/-

BOWEN The Statutes of Wales. Collected, arranged and edited by Ivor Bowen, Barrister-at-law, of the South Wales Circuit. Demy 8vo, cloth.   net 21/-

BOWLES. National Finance An Imminent Peril. By Thomas Gibson Bowles Paper cover.   6d.

—— **National Finance.** In 1908 and after. By Thomas Gibson Bowles. Paper Boards   net   1/-

—— **The Public Purse and the War Office.** By T. Gibson Bowles. Royal 8vo, paper cover   net   6d.

BOXALL. The Awakening of a Race. By George E. Boxall. Large cr 8vo, cloth   net   7/6

BRADLAUGH (Charles). A Record of his Life. See under "Biography"

BRAY. The Town Child. By Reginald A Bray, L.C.C, Author of "The Children of the Town" in "The Heart of the Empire," "The Boy and the Family" in "Studies of Boy Life," &c. Demy 8vo, cloth. **net** 7/6

BRIGHT. Is Liberty Asleep. Glances—Historical and Political. By Allan H. Bright. Cr. 8vo, paper covers. 1/-

British Industries Under Free Trade. Essays by various writers. Edited by Harold Cox. Large cr. 8vo, cloth. 6/-

Also (Reformer's Bookshelf) cloth 3/6

BROWN (Ch. R.). The Social Message of the Modern Pulpit. By Charles Reynolds Brown, Pastor of the First Congregational Church, Oakland, California. Cr 8vo, cloth **net** 5/-

BROWN (F.). Political Parables. By the *Westminster Gazette* Office-Boy (Francis Brown) Small royal 8vo. Paper, net 1/-, cloth, net 2/6

BROWNE (H. M.). Balfourism. A Study in Contemporary Politics By H Morgan Browne **net** 6d.

BUCKMASTER. A Village Politician. Edited by J C. Buckmaster With an Introduction by the Right Hon. A J. Mundella, M.P Large cr. 8vo, cloth. 3/6

Burden of Armaments, The. A Protest of the Cobden Club. Cr. 8vo, cloth. 3/6

CADBURY. Women's Work and Wages. A Phase of Life in an Industrial City. By Edward Cadbury, M Cécile Matheson, and George Shann, M A., F.R G.S Large cr. 8vo, cloth 6/-

CALLAHAN. Cuba and International Relations. A Historical Study in American Diplomacy. By James Horton Callahan, Ph D. Demy 8vo, cloth. **net** 12/6

CARLILE. The Continental Outcast : Land Colonies and Poor Law Relief. By the Rev. W Carlile, Hon. Chief Secretary, and Victor W. Carlile, Hon. Organising Secretary, of the Church Army With 8 Illustrations. Cr. 8vo Paper, net 1/- ; cloth, net 2/-

COBDEN. The Political Writings of Richard Cobden. New Edition. With Preface by Lord Welby and Introductions by Sir Louis Mallet and William Cullen Bryant. With Frontispieces. 2 vols. (Reformer's Bookshelf) Large cr. 8vo, cloth. 7/-

—— **Richard Cobden and the Jubilee of Free Trade.** By P Leroy-Beaulieu, Henry Dunckley ("Verax"), Dr. Theodor Barth, the Right Hon Leonard Courtney, M P, and the Right Hon Charles Villiers, M P With introduction by Richard Gowing Uniform in style with the Jubilee Edition of "Richard Cobden' Cr. 8vo, cloth. 3/6

—— **Cobden as a Citizen.** A Chapter in Manchester History Being a facsimile of Cobden's pamphlet, "Incorporate Your Borough!" with an Introduction and a complete Cobden Bibliography. By William E. A. Axon. **net** 21/-

—— **Speeches on Questions of Public Policy.** By Richard Cobden. Edited by John Bright and James E. Thorold Rogers With a Preface by James E Thorold Rogers, and Appreciations by J E. Thorold Rogers and Goldwin Smith, and 2 Photogravure Portraits Fifth Impression 2 vols. Large cr. 8vo, cloth (Uniform with the Jubilee Edition of Morley's "Life of Cobden.") 7/-

COLLET. Taxes on Knowledge: The Story of their Origin and Repeal. By Collet Dobson Collet With an Introduction by George Jacob Holyoake. Large cr. 8vo 2 vols 16/-

Also 2 vols.. cloth. 7/-

COX. Mr. Balfour's Pamphlet: A Reply. By Harold Cox. Medium 8vo, paper covers.   net   2d.

—— The Policy of Free Imports. By Harold Cox. A Paper read at Liverpool on February 16th, 1903, to the New Century Society. Large cr. 8vo   Paper covers, 1d.; cloth, net   6d.

—— Protection and Employment. By Harold Cox, formerly Secretary of the Cobden Club. Paper covers.   6d.

CROMPTON. Our Criminal Justice. By Henry Crompton. With an Introduction by Sir Kenelm Digby, K.C.B.   net   6d.

DANSON. Economic and Statistical Studies, 1840-1890. By John Towne Danson. With a brief memoir by his daughter, Mary Norman Hill, and an Introduction by E. C K. Gonner, M.A., Brunner, Professor of Economic Science, Liverpool University. With a Photogravure Frontispiece, 2 other Portraits, and 31 Plates. Small royal 8vo, cloth.   net 21/-

DAVENPORT. Value and Distribution. A Critical and Constructive Study. By Herbert Joseph Davenport, Associate Professor of Political Economy in the University of Chicago. Demy 8vo, cloth.
                                                                         net 15/-

DAWSON. The Evolution of Modern Germany See under "Travel"

DEWSNUP. American Railway Organization and Working. Lectures by Prominent Railway Men. Edited by Ernest R. Dewsnup. Large cr. 8vo, cloth.   net   9/-

DIETZEL. Retaliatory Duties. By H. Dietzel. Professor at the University of Bonn Translated by D W Simon, D D., and W. Osborne Brigstocke, Member of the Unionist Free Trade Club · Cr. 8vo, cloth.   net   2/6

ELIAS. The Political Advertiser. By Frank Elias. Illustrated. Fcap. 4to, paper covers.   net   1/-

ELLIOTT Corn Law Rhymes and Other Verses. By Ebenezer Elliott. 12mo   Paper covers, 2d.; cloth limp   6d.

ESCOTT. The Story of British Diplomacy: Its Makers and Movements. By T. H. S. Escott, Author of "Society in the Country House," &c., &c. With a Photogravure Frontispiece. Demy 8vo, cloth.   16/-

Failure of Lord Curzon, The. A Study in Imperialism. An Open Letter to the Earl of Rosebery. By "Twenty-eight Years in India." Cr. 8vo, cloth   net   2/6

GEBUZA. The Peril in Natal. By Gebuza. Demy 8vo, paper covers.
                                                                         net   3d.

GOMME. The Governance of London. Studies of the place of London in English Institutions By G Lawrence Gomme, F.S A., Clerk to the London County Council. With Maps. Demy 8vo, cloth.   net 15/-

GOULD. The Modern Chronicles of Froissart. Told and Pictured by Sir F Carruthers Gould. With special Cover Design, Decorated Title, and 44 Illustrations. Fifth Impression. Fcap 4to.   3/6

—— Froissart in 1902. Told and Pictured by Sir F. Carruthers Gould. With special Cover Design and Coloured Frontispiece Fcap 4to.   3/6
Also a *Fine Edition* (limited to 50 copies) on Japan paper, numbered and signed.   net 21/-

—— F C G 's Froissart, 1903-1906. Told and Pictured by Sir F. Carruthers Gould. With special Cover Design, and 50 Illustrations. Fcap. 4to, cloth.   net   2/6
Also a *Fine Edition* (limited to 50 copies) on Japan paper, numbered and signed.   net 21/-
See also "Lawson"

GOULD. The Gould-en Treasury. With 34 Illustrations by Sir F. Carruthers Gould. Fcap. 4to   Paper, net 1/- ; cloth, net   2/6

GRANT. Free Food and Free Trade. By Daniel Grant, Ex-M.P.
Paper covers.   2d.

HALDANE Army Reform and Other Addresses. By the Right
Hon. Richard Burton Haldane, M.P Large cr. 8vo, cloth.   net   7/6

Heart of the Empire, The. Studies in Problems of Modern City Life in
England. Large cr. 8vo, cloth.   net   7/6
Cheap Edition, cloth.   net   3/6

HIRST. National Credit and the Sinking Fund: How to make
£500,000,000. By Francis W. Hirst. Paper covers.   6d.

HOBHOUSE. Democracy and Reaction. By L. T. Hobhouse Cr.
8vo, cloth.   5/-
Also a revised Edition in paper covers.   net   1/-

—— The Labour Movement. By L. T. Hobhouse, M A. (Reformer's
Bookshelf), large cr 8vo, cloth.   3/6
Also a New and Cheaper Edition. Cr. 8vo, paper covers.   net   1/-

HODGSON To Colonise England. A Plea for a Policy. By W B.
Hodgson, C F. G. Masterman and Other Writers Edited by A.
G. Gardiner Cr. 8vo   Paper, net 2/6 , cloth, net   3/6

HOGAN The Gladstone Colony. By James Francis Hogan, M.P.
Demy 8vo, cloth.   7/6
Also (Reformer's Bookshelf), cloth   3/6

HOLYOAKE. Sixty Years of an Agitator's Life : George Jacob Holyoake's Autobiography. 2 vols (Reformer's Bookshelf) cloth.   7/-
Also in 1 vol. (Unwin's Half-Crown Standard Library)   net   2/6

—— The History of Co-operation. Its Literature and its Advocates.
By G. J. Holyoake Illustrated. 2 vols. Demy 8vo, cloth   net   21/-
Also a Popular Edition in 1 vol. Illustrated. Large cr. 8vo,
cloth.   net   7/6

—— Bygones Worth Remembering. See under "Biography."
—— Public Speaking and Debate. A Manual for Advocates and
Agitators. By George Jacob Holyoake. New Edition
Paper covers, net 1/- ; cloth, net   2/-

HOWE. The City, the Hope of Democracy. By Frederic C. Howe,
Ph D. Large cr. 8vo, cloth.   net   7/6
—— The British City. By F. C. Howe, Author of " The City, the Hope
of Democracy." Large cr. 8vo, cloth.   net   7/6

HOWELL. Labour Legislation, Labour Movements, and Labour
Leaders. By George Howell. Demy 8vo, cloth   10/6
Also 2 vols Large cr. 8vo, cloth. (Reformer's Bookshelf)   7/-

Hungry Forties, The. An Account of Life under the Bread Tax
from the Letters of Living Witnesses. With an Introduction by
Mrs Cobden Unwin Illustrated. Large cr. 8vo, cloth.   6/-
Also (Reformer's Bookshelf), cloth.   3/6
People's Edition. Paper covers.   6d.

JEPHSON. The Sanitary Evolution of London. By Henry Jephson.
Demy 8vo, cloth.   net   6/-

JERNIGAN. China's Business Methods and Policy. By T. R
Jernigan, Ex-Consul-General of the United States of America at
Shanghai. Demy 8vo, cloth.   net   12/-

KING. Electoral Reform. An Inquiry into our System of Parliamentary Representation. By Joseph King. Cr. 8vo, cloth.   net   2/6

SCHREINER. The Political Situation. By Olive Schreiner and C. S. Cronwright Schreiner. Cr 8vo, cloth.　　　1/6

SHAW. Municipal Government in Continental Europe. By Albert Shaw. Demy 8vo, cloth.　　　net　7/6

—— Municipal Government of Great Britain. By Albert Shaw. Demy 8vo, cloth.　　　net　7/6

SIBLEY. Criminal Appeal and Evidence. By N. W. Sibley, B.A., LL.M. Trin. H. Camb. and B A. London; Barrister-at-Law of Lincoln's Inn; Joint Author of "International Law as Interpreted during the Russo-Japanese War," and "The Aliens Act, 1905." Demy 8vo, cloth　　　net　15/-

SMALL. General Sociology: An Exposition of the Main Development in Sociological Theory, from Spencer to Ratzenhofer. By Albion W. Small, Professor and Head of the Department of Sociology in the University of Chicago. Demy 8vo, cloth.　　　net　18/-

—— Adam Smith and Modern Sociology. A Study in the Methodology of the Social Sciences. By Albion W. Small, Professor and Head of the Department of Sociology in the University of Chicago. Cloth.　　　net　5/6

SMITH (Goldwin). My Memory of Gladstone. See under "Biography."

SMITH. International Law as Interpreted during the Russo-Japanese War. By F E. Smith, B C.L., and N. W. Sibley, LL.M. Second Edition, Revised. Royal 8vo, cloth.　　　net　25/-

SPELLING. Bossism and Monopoly. By T. C. Spelling. Large cr. 8vo, cloth.　　　net　7/6

STEAD. Peers or People? The House of Lords Weighed in the Balances and Found Wanting. An Appeal to History. By W T. Stead. Cr. 8vo.　　　Paper boards, net 2/6; cloth, net　3/6

STEVENI. The Scandinavian Question. By William Barnes Steveni. With a Map. Large cr. 8vo, cloth　　　net　3/6

STOPES. The Sphere of "Man" in Relation to that of "Woman" in the Constitution. By Mrs. C. C. Stopes, Author of "British Freewomen." Large cr. 8vo, paper covers　　　net　6d.

SVENSKE Sweden's Rights and the Present Political Position. By Anders Svenske. Cloth.　　　net　2/6

TAYLOR. Side-Lights on Protection. The History of a Vanished Industry. By Austin Taylor, M.P. Paper covers.　　　6d.

TWAIN King Leopold's Soliloquy. A Defence of his Congo Rule. By Mark Twain. With a Preface and Appendices by E. D. Morel, Author of "Red Rubber." Cr. 8vo.　Paper, net 1/-; cloth, net　1/6

VILLARI. Russia Under the Great Shadow. By Luigi Villari. With 84 Illustrations. Demy 8vo, cloth.　　　net 10/6

VILLARI (Pasquale). Niccolo Machiavelli. See under "Biography."

VILLIERS (B.). The Opportunity of Liberalism. By Brougham Villiers. Paper covers　　　net　1/-

—— The Case for Woman's Suffrage. A volume of essays by Mrs. Henry Fawcett, Mrs. Pankhurst, J. Keir Hardie, M P., Miss Eva Gore Booth, Miss Ll. Davies, Miss Margaret McMillan, and others. Edited with an Introduction by Brougham Villiers. Cr. 8vo. Paper boards, net 2/6; cloth, net　3/6

—— The Socialist Movement in England. By Brougham Villiers, Author of "The Opportunity of Liberalism." Demy 8vo, cloth net 10/6

VILLIERS (Ch. P.). Fiscal Reformation Sixty Years Ago : Passages from the Speeches of the Rt. Hon. Charles Pelham Villiers, M P. foi Wolverhampton, 1835-1898. Selected by Wilbraham Villiers Cooper. Paper covers. 1/-

WATSON The National Liberal Federation from its Commencement to the General Election of 1906. By R. Spence Watson, LL D., President of the Federation 1890-1902. With a Photogravure Frontispiece from a Portrait by Sir George Reid, and an Introduction by the Right Honourable Augustine Birrell. Cr 8vo, cloth. net 5/-

WELBY and MALLET. Cobden's Work and Opinions. By Lord Welby and Sir Louis Mallet Imitation Calf covers net 3d.

WHITE. The Inner Life of the House of Commons : Selected from the Writings of William White, with a Prefatory Note by his Son, and an Introduction by Justin McCarthy. 2 vols. (Reformer's Bookshelf.) Cr. 8vo, cloth. 7/-

WILKINSON The Personal Story of the Upper House. See under "Biography."

[For reference see also "Biography" and "History."]

GEOGRAPHY, TRAVEL, MOUNTAINEERING, &c.

ADAMS. The New Egypt. By Francis Adams Large cr 8vo, cloth. 5/-

ANGLO-ITALIAN LIBRARY, THE. Each volume fully illustrated Large cr. 8vo, cloth. net 5/-

With **Shelley** in Italy. A Selection of Poems and Letters relating to His Life in Italy. Edited, with an Introduction, by Anna Benneson McMahan

With **Byron** in Italy. A Selection of Poems and Letters relating to His Life in Italy Edited by Anna Benneson McMahan

Romola. By George Eliot A Historically Illustrated Edition. Edited, with Introduction and Notes, by Guido Biagi, Librarian of the Laurentian and Riccardi Libraries, Florence. 2 vols. The four volumes may also be obtained in Florentine white vellum binding. Price 10/6 net each

BAKER. Moors, Crags, and Caves of the High Peak and the Neighbourhood. By Ernest A Baker, M A. With about 40 Illustrations and 2 Maps. Demy 8vo, cloth. net 6/-

BANFIELD. The Confessions of a Beachcomber. Scenes and Incidents in the Career of an Unprofessional Beachcomber in Tropical Queensland. By E J. Banfield. With a Map and 48 Illustrations. Demy 8vo, cloth. net 15/-

BINDLOSS (Harold). Wide Dominion. See Overseas Library. No. 7

BLOND (Mrs. Aubrey Le). See under "Le Blond"

BOISSIER. The Country of Horace and Virgil. By Gaston Boissier. Translated by D. Havelock Fisher. Large cr. 8vo, cloth. 7/6

—— **Rome and Pompeii.** By Gaston Boissier. Translated by D. Havelock Fisher. (The only authorised version in English of "Les Promenades Archæologiques.") Maps and Plans. Large cr. 8vo, cloth. 7/6

Also in Unwin's Half-Crown Standard Library. Cloth. net 2/6

BUCHANAN The Real Australia. By A. J. Buchanan. Cr. 8vo. **6/-**

BULFIN (W.). Tales of the Pampas. See Overseas Library. No. 10.

CADDICK. A White Woman in Central Africa. By Helen Caddick. 16 Illustrations. Cr. 8vo, cloth. **6/-**

CAIRD. Romantic Cities of Provence. By Mona Caird, Author of "The Pathway of the Gods," &c., &c. Illustrated with Sketches by Joseph Pennell and Edward M Synge. Small royal 8vo, cloth **net 15/-**

CAYLEY. The Bridle Roads of Spain (Las Alforjas.) By George John Cayley. New edition. With an Introduction by Martin Hume, M.A., and Recollections of the Author by Lady Ritchie and Mrs. Cobden Sickert, and a Photogravure Frontispiece. La. cr. 8vo, **net 7/6**

CESARESCO. Lombard Studies. By Countess Evelyn Martinengo Cesaresco. Photogravure Frontispiece and many other Illustrations Demy 8vo, cloth. **16/-**

CLIFFORD (Hugh). A Corner of Asia. See Overseas Library. No. 5.

CONWAY. Climbing and Exploration in the Karakoram-Himalayas. By Sir William Martin Conway, M.A., F.S.A., F.R.G.S. 300 Illustrations by A. D. McCormick, and Maps. Super royal 8vo, cloth. **net 31/6**

Supplementary Volume. With Frontispiece of the Author. Super royal 8vo, cloth. **net 15/-**

CONWAY AND COOLIDGE'S CLIMBERS' GUIDES. Edited by Sir William M. Conway and Rev. W A B Coolidge. Gilt lettered, with pocket, flap, and pencil. 32mo, limp cloth, each. **10/-**

(1) The Central Pennine Alps. By Sir William Martin Conway.

(2) The Eastern Pennine Alps. By Sir William Martin Conway

(3) The Lepontine Alps (Simplon and Gotthard). By W. A B Coolidge and Sir William M. Conway.

(4) The Central Alps of the Dauphiny. By W. A. B Coolidge, H Duhamel, and F. Perrin. Second Edition. Thoroughly revised Small 8vo, cloth. 7/6 net.

(5) The Chain of Mont Blanc. By Louis Kurz.

(6) The Adula Alps of the Lepontine Range. By W A B Coolidge.

(7) The Mountains of Cogne. By George Yeld and W. A B Coolidge With Map.

(8) The Range of the Todi. By W. A B. Coolidge.

(9) The Bernese Oberland. Vol 1. From the Gemmi to the Monchjoch. By G. Hasler

(10) The Bernese Oberland. Vol 2. From the Monchjoch to the Grimsel. By W. A. B Coolidge.

(11) The Bernese Oberland. Vol. 3. The West Wing. By H. Dubi.

(12 & 13) The Bernese Oberland. Vol. 4 (Parts 1 and 2). From the Grimsel to the Uri Rothstock. By H. Dübi.

Also a Series of Six Coloured Maps of the Alps of the Dauphiny, mounted on linen, and strongly bound in cloth case, the set **4/6**

COOLIDGE (W. A. B.). See under Conway and Coolidge's Climbers' Guides.

CORNABY. China under the Searchlight. By W A Cornaby. Cr. 8vo, cloth. **6/-**

CORNISH. The Panama Canal To-day. By Vaughan Cornish. Cloth **6/-**

DAVENPORT. China from Within : A Study of Opium Fallacies and Missionary Mistakes. By Arthur Davenport. Cr. 8vo, cloth. **6/-**

DAVIDSON. Present-Day Japan. By Augusta M. Campbell Davidson,
M A Fully Illustrated. Medium 8vo, cloth. 21/-
Cheap Edition (Modern Travel Series), cloth. 5/-

DAVIS. The Congo and the Coasts of Africa. By Richard
Harding Davis. Illustrated. Large cr. 8vo, cloth net 6/-

DAWSON. The Evolution of Modern Germany. By W Harburt
Dawson, Author of "German Life in Town and Country." net 21/-

DEASY, In Tibet and Chinese Turkestan. By Captain H H P
Deasy. Being the Record of Three Years' Exploration. With
Appendices, Maps, and 80 Illustrations. Demy 8vo, cloth gilt net 21/-
Also a Cheap Edition. net 6/-

DIGBY. "Prosperous" British India. By William Digby, C I E
With Diagrams and Maps Demy 8vo, cloth. 12/6

DUTT. The Norfolk and Suffolk Coast. By W. A. Dutt With
about 40 Illustrations. Cr 8vo, cloth. 6/-

ECKENSTEIN. The Karakorams and Kashmir : The Story of a
Journey. By Oscar Eckenstein. Cr. 8vo, cloth gilt 6/-

ELIOT. Romola By George Eliot. A historically illustrated edition.
Edited, with Introduction and Notes, by Guido Biagi, Librarian of
the Laurentian and Riccardi Libraries, Florence With 160 Illustrations 2 vols. (The Anglo-Italian Library) each, net 5/-

ENOCK. The Andes and the Amazon. Life and Travel in Peru.
By C. Reginald Enock, F.R.G S. With a Map and numerous
Illustrations. Medium 8vo, cloth. 21/-

—— **Peru** Its Former and Present Civilization, Topography and
Natural Resources, History and Political Conditions, Commerce
and Present Conditions. By C Reginald Enock, F R G.S. With
an Introduction by Martin Hume, a Map, and numerous Illustrations. (The South American Series) Demy 8vo, cloth. net 10/6

—— **Mexico.** By C. Reginald Enock, F.R.G.S. (Volume 3 of the South
American Series) Demy 8vo, cloth. net 10/6

Everyday Life in Cape Colony. By a late Resident. Illustrated.
Cr. 8vo, cloth 3/6

FARGE. An Artist's Letters from Japan. See under "La Farge"

**FINDLAY. Big Game Shooting and Travel in South and East
Africa.** By Frederick R N. Findlay Fully Illustrated, and with
Map. Medium 8vo. net 15/-

FITZ-GERALD. Climbs in the New Zealand Alps : Being an Account
of Travel and Discovery. By E A. Fitz-Gerald, F R G S. Cloth,
size 9½ by 6½. net 31/6

FOREMAN. The Philippine Islands. A Political, Ethnographical,
Social and Commercial History of the Philippine Archipelago
By John Foreman, F.R G.S. With Maps and Illustrations. Royal
8vo, cloth. net 25/-

GAGGIN (John). Among the Man-Eaters. See Overseas Library. No. 8.

GRAHAM (Cunninghame). The Ipane. See Overseas Library. No. 1.

GRIBBLE. The Early Mountaineers : The Stories of their Lives. By
Francis Gribble Fully Illustrated. Demy 8vo, cloth gilt. 21/-

HALL Pre-Historic Rhodesia An Examination of the Ethnological
and Archæological Evidences as to the Origin and Age of the Rock
Mines and Stone Buildings, with a Gazetteer of Mediæval South-
East Africa. By R. N Hall. With Illustrations, Maps and Plans.
Medium 8vo, cloth. net 12/6

HARDY. John Chinaman at Home. By the Rev. E. J. Hardy.
Author of "How to be Happy though Married." With 36
Illustrations. Demy 8vo, cloth net 10/6
Cheap Edition (Modern Travel Series), cloth. 5/-

HARVIE-BROWN. Travels of a Naturalist in Northern Europe. By J. A. Harvie-Brown. See under "Natural History."

HAWKESWORTH. Australian Sheep and Wool. A Practical and Theoretical Treatise. By Alfred Hawkesworth, Lecturer in Charge of "Sheep and Wool" Department, Technical College, Sydney. Second Edition, Revised and Enlarged. With 55 Illustrations. Demy 8vo, cloth.   net   7/6

HERRING. Among the People of British Columbia: Red, White, Yellow and Brown. By Frances E. Herring. Fully Illustrated from Original Photographs. Cr 8vo, cloth.   net   6/-

—— In the Pathless West. By Frances E. Herring. With 14 Illustrations. Cr. 8vo, cloth   net   6/-

HEYWOOD. Guide to Siena. History and Art. By William Heywood and Lucy Olcolt. Cr. 8vo, cloth.   net   6/-

HILL. Cuba and Porto Rico: With the other Islands of the West Indies. By Robert T. Hill. 500 pages, with 250 Illustrations and Maps. Demy 8vo.   16/-

HINDLIP. British East Africa Past, Present, and Future. By Lord Hindlip, F R G S., F Z S. Cr 8vo, cloth   net   3/6

—— Sport and Travel: Abyssinia and British East Africa. By Lord Hindlip, F R.G.S, F.Z S. With Maps and more than 70 Illustrations. Demy 8vo, cloth   net   21/-

HOBBES. Imperial India: Letters from the East By John Oliver Hobbes. Cr 8vo.   Paper covers, 1/- ; cloth   2/-

HOBSON. Canada To-Day By J. A. Hobson, M A., Author of "The Evolution of Modern Capitalism," &c. Cr. 8vo, cloth.   net   3/6

HONEYMAN. Bright Days in Merrie England. By C. Van Doren Honeyman Cr. 8vo, cloth.   6/-

INDICUS. Labour and other Questions in South Africa. By "Indicus." Cr. 8vo, cloth.   3/6

JAVELLE. Alpine Memories. By Emile Javelle. Small demy, cloth.   7/6

JEBB. By Desert Ways to Baghdad. By Louisa Jebb. With many Illustrations from Photographs taken by the Author. Demy 8vo, cloth.   net   10/6

JERNIGAN. China's Business Methods and Policy. See under "Politics."

JOHNSON. Tramps Round the Mountains of the Moon and through the Back Gate of the Congo State By T. Broadwood Johnson, M A, of the Uganda Mission. With 30 Illustrations from Photographs Large cr. 8vo, cloth.   6/-

KERR From Charing Cross to Delhi By S. Parnell Kerr. With 65 Illustrations Demy 8vo, cloth.   net   10/6

KING. Mountaineering in the Sierra Nevada. By Clarence King. Cr. 8vo, cloth.   net   6/-

KURZ (Louis). See under Conway and Coolidge's Climbers' Guides.

LA FARGE An Artist's Letters from Japan. With many Illustrations. Demy 8vo, cloth.   16/-

LE BLOND. Adventures on the Roof of the World. By Mrs. Aubrey Le Blond (Mrs. Main). With over 100 Illustrations. Demy 8vo, cloth.   net   10/6
Cheap Edition (Modern Travel Series), cloth.   5/-

—— True Tales of Mountain Adventure for Non-Climbers, Young and Old. By Mrs. Aubrey Le Blond (Mrs. Main). With numerous Illustrations and Frontispiece. Demy 8vo, cloth.   net   10/6
Cheap Edition (Modern Travel Series) cloth.   5/-

LE BLOND. Mountaineering in the Land of the Midnight Sun. By Mrs. Aubrey Le Blond (Mrs. Main) With many Illustrations and a Map. Demy 8vo, cloth. net 10/6

LENTHERIC. The Riviera, Ancient and Modern. By Charles Lentheric. Translated by C. West. With 9 Maps and Plans. Large cr. 8vo, cloth. 7/6

LITTLE. In the Land of the Blue Gown. By Mrs Archibald Little, Author of "Intimate China." With over 100 Illustrations. Medium 8vo. net 21/-
Also a Cheaper Edition. Cloth. net 7/6

—— Round About My Peking Garden. By Mrs Archibald Little. Author of "Li Hung Chang, His Life and Times," "A Marriage in China," &c., &c. Fully Illustrated. Demy 8vo, cloth net 15/-

LLOYD. In Dwarf-Land and Cannibal Country. By Albert B. Lloyd. Illustrated and with 3 Maps. Demy 8vo. net 21/-
Also a Cheaper Edition. Cloth. net 7/6

—— Uganda to Khartoum Life and Adventure on the Upper Nile. By Albert B. Lloyd. With a preface by Victor Buxton. With a Map and 81 Illustrations. Demy 8vo, cloth. net 10/6

LUMSDEN. Through Canada in Harvest Time : A Study of Life and Labour in the Golden West. By James Lumsden. Fully Illustrated, and with Map Large cr. 8vo, cloth gilt. 6/-

MAC (J.) Little Indabas. See Overseas Library. No 9.

MACDONALD. In Search of El Dorado · A Wanderer's Experiences. By Alexander Macdonald. With 32 Illustrations. Demy 8vo, cloth net 10/6
Cheap Edition (Modern Travel Series), cloth. 5/-

McMAHAN. Byron in Italy. A Selection of Poems and Letters relating to His Life in Italy. Edited by Anna Benneson McMahan. With more than 60 Illustrations from Photographs. Large cr., 8vo, cloth. net 5/-

—— With Shelley in Italy A Selection of Poems and Letters relating to His Life in Italy Edited, with an Introduction, by Anna Benneson McMahan With 64 Illustrations from Photographs. Large cr 8vo, cloth. net 5/-

MALLIK. Impressions of a Wanderer. By Manmath C Mallik, of the Middle Temple, Barrister-at-Law. Crown 8vo, cloth net 5/-

MILLER. Travels and Politics in the Near East By William Miller, Author of "The Balkans." With 100 Illustrations and a Map. Demy 8vo, cloth. 21/-

MODERN TRAVEL SERIES, THE Each Volume Illustrated. Large cr. 8vo, cloth 5/-

(1) **True Tales of Mountain Adventure.** By Mrs Aubrey le Blond (Mrs. Main). With many illustrations from photographs by the Author.

(2) **In Search of El Dorado.** A Wanderer's Experiences. By Alexander Macdonald, F.R.G S With an Introduction by Admiral Moresby. With 32 Illustrations

(3) **Adventures on the Roof of the World.** By Mrs Aubrey le Blond (Mrs Main) With more than 100 illustrations.

(4) **John Chinaman at Home.** By the Rev. E. J. Hardy, Author of "How to be Happy though Married," lately Chaplain to H M. Forces at Hong Kong With 36 Illustrations.

(5) **Present Day Japan.** By A. M. Campbell Davidson With 32 Illustrations.

(6) **Links in my Life on Land and Sea.** By Commander J. W. Gambier, R.N. With a Frontispiece.

de **MONTAGNAC (Noel). Negro Nobodies.** See Overseas Library. No. 6.

MOSSO. Life of Man on the High Alps : Studies made on Monte Rosa By Angelo Mosso Translated from the Second Edition of the Italian by E. Lough Kiesow, in Collaboration with F Kiesow. With numerous Illustrations and Diagrams. Royal 8vo, cloth. 21/-

MUMMERY, Mes Escalades Dans les Alpes et le Caucase. Par A. F. Mummery. Traduit de l'Anglais par Maurice Paillon. With a new Preface and Notice on Mummery as a Climber. Illustrated by a Portrait of the Author in Collotype, 24 full-page Plates, and 4 Maps Paper covers. net 9/-

—— **My Climbs in the Alps and Caucasus.** By A. F. Mummery. With Photogravure, Coloured and Half-Tone Illustrations by Joseph Pennell and others. New Edition, with Introductions by Mrs. Mummery and T A Hobson. Super-royal 8vo, cloth net 21/-

NORMAN. The Peoples and Politics of the Far East. Travels and Studies in the British, French, Spanish, and Portuguese Colonies, Siberia, China, Japan, Korea, Siam, and Malaya By Sir Henry Norman, M.P. With many Illustrations. Sixth Impression. Small demy 8vo, cloth 7/6

—— **The Real Japan.** By Sir Henry Norman, M.P. Profusely Illustrated. Large cr. 8vo net 5/-

NORMAN-NERUDA, The Climbs of Norman-Neruda. Edited, with an Account of his last Climb, by May Norman-Neruda. Demy 8vo, cloth 21/-

OBER. A Guide to the West Indies and Bermudas. By F. A. Ober. With Maps and many Illustrations. Small cr. 8vo, cloth. net 8/6

OGILVIE. My Life in the Open. By Will H. Ogilvie, Author of " Fair Girls and Gray Horses." With Portrait, Large cr. 8vo, cloth. net 5/-

OLCOTT. Guide to Siena. See Heywood

OVERSEAS LIBRARY, THE. At the End of this Section.

PARIS-PARISIEN A Complete Guide to Paris. French Text. I.—What to See II.—What to Know. III.—Parisian Ways. IV.— Practical Paris Large demy 12mo, limp leather. 6/-

PINNOCK. Wander Years Round the World. By James Pinnock. With over 70 Illustrations and about 20 special Maps. Demy 8vo cloth. net 21/-

PULLEN-BURRY. Jamaica as it is. By B. Pullen-Burry. With a Map and 8 Illustrations. Cr. 8vo, cloth. net 6/-

—— **Ethiopia in Exile : Jamaica Revisited.** By B. Pullen-Burry. Cr. 8vo, cloth. 6/-

QUIN (Ethel). Well-Sinkers. See Overseas Library. No. 4.

REY The Matterhorn. By Guido Rey Illustrated by Edoardo Rubino. With a Preface by Edmondo de Amicis. Translated from the Italian by J. E. C Eaton. With 14 Coloured Plates, 23 Pen Drawings, and 11 Photographs. Super royal 8vo, cloth. net 21/-
Fine Paper Edition (Limited to Fifteen Copies) Price on application

RODGERS. The Scenery of Sherwood Forest. With some Account of the Eminent Families once resident there, and an Essay on Robin Hood By Joseph Rodgers. With Illustrations of the Magnificent Trees and Characteristic Scenery, from Drawings by the Author, and with Portraits in Photogravure. Super royal 8vo, cloth. net 21/-

RODWAY (James). In Guiana Wilds. See Overseas Library. No 3.

ROOSEVELT. Ranch Life and the Hunting Trail. By Theodore Roosevelt, late President of the United States. Illustrated by Frederick Remington. Royal 8vo, cloth.   10/6

SCIDMORE. Java: The Garden of the East. By Eliza Ruhamah Scidmore. With nearly 40 full-page Illustrations. Cr. 8vo.   7/6

—— Winter India. By Eliza Ruhamah Scidmore. Fully Illustrated. Medium 8vo, cloth.   net 10/6

SCOTT-ELLIOTT. Chile. By G. F Scott-Elliott, F R.G S With an Introduction by Martin Hume. Illustrated. (The South American Library. Vol 1) Demy 8vo, cloth.   net 10/6

SEARELLE. Tales of the Transvaal. By Luscombe Searelle. Illustrated by P Frenzeny, and after Photographs. 8vo, cloth.   2/6

SEYMOUR Saunterings in Spain—Barcelona, Madrid, Toledo, Cordova, Seville, Granada. By Major-General Seymour. Illustrated. Demy 8vo, cloth.   net 10/6

SIBREE. Madagascar before the Conquest. By James Sibree. Illustrated. With Map. Demy 8vo, cloth.   16/-

SMITH. Budapest. The City of the Magyars. By T. Berkeley Smith. Fully Illustrated. Cr. 8vo, cloth.   net 5/-

THE SOUTH AMERICAN SERIES. Edited by Martin Hume. Each Volume Illustrated. Demy 8vo, cloth.   net 10/6
    Vol. 1. Chile. By G. F. Scott-Elliot, F R G S
    Vol. 2. Peru By C. Reginald Enock, F R G S.
    Vol 3. Mexico By C Reginald Enock, F R.G S.

STEAD. Japan, Our New Ally By Alfred Stead With an Introduction by the Marquis Ito. Fully Illustrated Cr 8vo, cloth. net   6/-

STEIN Sand-Buried Ruins of Khotan. By M. Aurel Stein, Indian Educational Service. With over 120 Illustrations and a Photogravure Frontispiece and large Map Medium 8vo, cloth   net 21/-

STRASBURGER Rambles on the Riviera By Eduard Strasburger, F R.S, D.C L Oxon. With 87 Coloured Illustrations by Louise Reusch. Demy 8vo, cloth   net 21/-

STRATILESCO From Carpathian to Pindus: Pictures of Roumanian Country Life. By Tereza Stratilesco. With two Maps and many illustrations Demy 8vo cloth   net 15/-

STREET. A Philosopher in Portugal. By Eugène E. Street, F.S A. Cr. 8vo, buckram.   net 5/-

SUTCLIFFE. By Moor and Fell. Landscape and Lang-Settle Talk in West Yorkshire. By Halliwell Sutcliffe, Author of " Ricroft of Withens," &c. With many Illustrations Cr 8vo, cloth.   6/-

SYMONDS Days Spent on a Doge's Farm By Margaret Symonds (Mrs Vaughan) With a Photogravure Frontispiece and many other Illustrations from Sketches and Photographs. New Edition. Demy 8vo, cloth.   net 10/6

TAINE. Journeys through France. Being the Authorised Translation of " Carnets de Voyage." By Adolphe Hippolyte Taine. Cr 8vo, cloth.   7/6

TAYLOR Vacation Days in Hawaii and Japan. By Charles M. Taylor. Illustrated Large cr. 8vo, cloth.   net 7/6

TOWNSEND. Along the Labrador Coast. By Charles Wendell Townsend, M D. With 40 Illustrations and a Map. Large cr. 8vo, cloth.   net 5/-

TURNBULL. Tales from Natal. By A. R. R. Turnbull. Cr. 8vo, cloth   3/6

TURNER. Siberia: A Record of Travel, Climbing, and Exploration. By Samuel Turner, F.R.G.S. With more than 100 Illustrations and 2 Maps Demy 8vo, cloth.   net 21/-

VANDERLIP. In Search of a Siberian Klondike. By Washington B Vanderlip and H B. Hulbert. With 48 Illustrations, Large cr. cloth.   net 7/6

VILLARI. Russia Under the Great Shadow. By Luigi Villari, Author of "Giovanni Segantini," "Italian Life in Town and Country," &c. With 84 Illustrations. Demy 8vo, cloth.   net 10/6

—— Fire and Sword in the Caucasus By Luigi Villari. Illustrated. Demy 8vo, cloth.   net 10/6

WALLIS. The Advance of our West African Empire. By Captain Braithwaite Wallis Fully Illustrated. Medium 8vo, cloth.   21/-

WATSON (JOHN). Woodlanders and Field Folk. Sketches of Wild Life in Britain. See "Natural History."   net 5/-

WEBSTER. Through New Guinea and the Cannibal Countries. By H. Cayley-Webster. Very fully Illustrated from Photographs, and with Maps, Diagrams, and Photogravure Frontispiece. Medium 8vo, cloth gilt.   21/-

WELLBY. Through Unknown Tibet. By Captain M. S. Wellby. Photogravure and many other Illustrations, also Maps and Appendices of Flora, &c Medium 8vo, cloth gilt   21/-

WERNER (A.). Captain of the Locusts. See Overseas Library. No 2.

WILSON The Climber's Note Book. By Claude Wilson, M.D. Waistcoat pocket size. Buckram, gilt.   net 1/-

de WINDT Through Savage Europe. By Harry de Windt, Author of "Siberia as it is," "From Paris to New York by Land," &c., &c. With more than 90 Illustrations. Demy 8vo, cloth.   net 10/6

WOODS Washed by Four Seas. By H. C. Woods, F R G S, formerly of the Grenadier Guards. With an Introduction by Sir Martin Conway, 66 Photographs and a Map Demy 8vo, cloth.   net 7/6

WORKMAN. In the Ice World of Himalaya. By Fanny Bullock Workman and William Hunter Workman. With 4 large Maps and nearly 100 Illustrations Demy 8vo, cloth gilt.   16/-

Cheap Edition, with 2 Maps and 65 Illustrations.   6/-

—— Through Town and Jungle: Fourteen Thousand Miles Awheel among the Temples and People of the Indian Plain. By William Hunter Workman and Fanny Bullock Workman. With Map and 202 Illustrations. Super royal 8vo, cloth.   net 21/-

WRIGHT A Handbook of the Philippines. By Hamilton M. Wright Illustrated. Cr. 8vo, cloth.   net 7/6

YELD. Scrambles in the Eastern Graians. By George Yeld. Editor of the *Alpine Journal.* Illustrated, and with a Map. Large cr. 8vo.   7/6

Yorkshire Ramblers' Club Journal, The. Edited by Thomas Gray. Illustrated. 8vo, paper covers.   net 2/-

ZIMMERMAN Spain and her People. By Jeremiah Zimmerman. With many Illustrations. Demy 8vo, cloth.   net 8/6

ZURBRIGGEN. From the Alps to the Andes. Being the Autobiography of a Mountain Guide. By Mattias Zurbriggen. Translated by Mary Alice Vialls. Fully Illustrated. Demy 8vo, cloth.   net 10/6

[For reference see also "History."]

OVERSEAS LIBRARY, THE. Decorative Cover by W. H. Cowlishaw. Cr. 8vo. Paper covers, 1/6, cloth, each 2/-

(1) **The Ipane.** By R. B. Cunninghame Graham.

(2) **The Captain of the Locusts,** and Other Stories By A. Werner.

(3) **In Guiana Wi.ds.** By James Rodway

(4) **The Well-Sinkers.** By Ethel Quin.

(5) **A Corner of Asia.** By Hugh Clifford.

(6) **Negro Nobodies.** By Noel de Montagnac

(7) **A Wide Dominion.** By Harold Bindloss.

(8) **Among the Man-Eaters.** By John Gaggin.

(9) **Little Indabas.** By J Mac.

(10) **Tales of the Pampas.** By W. Bulfin.

NATURAL HISTORY, SCIENCE, &c.

BASTIAN. The Nature and Origin of Living Matter. By H Charlton Bastian, M.A, M D. (London), F R.S, F.L.S, Emeritus Professor of the Principles and Practice of Medicine, and of Clinical Medicine at University College, London. With 76 Illustrations. Medium 8vo, cloth. net 12/6

BEAVAN. Animals I Have Known. By Arthur H. Beavan. With about 50 Illustrations Cr 8vo, cloth. 5/-
Cheap Edition. (Unwin's Nature Books. Vol. 10.) Cloth. 2/-
—— Birds I Have Known. By Arthur H. Beavan. With 39 Illustrations. Cr 8vo, cloth. 5/-
Cheap Edition. (Unwin's Nature Books. Vol 9) Cloth 2/-
—— Fishes I Have Known. By Arthur H. Beavan. With about 40 Illustrations. Cr 8vo, cloth 5/-
Cheap Edition. (Unwin's Nature Books. Vol 11) Cloth 2/-

BELL Health at its Best v Cancer and other Diseases By Robert Bell, M.B, M.D, F.F P.S, &c, formerly Senior Physician to the Glasgow Hospital for Women, Author of "Cancer: Its Cause and Treatment without Operation," &c, &c. Cr. 8vo, cloth. net 5/-

BLIND. The Ascent of Man. An Edition de Luxe, limited to 250 Copies By Mathilde Blind. With an Introduction by Alfred Russel Wallace Heliogravure Medallion Portrait printed on Japan paper. Fcap 4to. 10/6

BOXALL. The Evolution of the World and of Man. By G. E. Boxall Cr. 8vo, cloth. 5/-

BRIGHTWEN. Glimpses into Plant Life: An Easy Guide to the Study of Botany. By Mrs. Brightwen. Illustrated Cr 8vo, cloth. 3/6
Cheap Reissue (Unwin's Nature Books. Vol. 4) Cloth. 2/-
—— Inmates of my House and Garden. By Mrs Brightwen. With 32 Illustrations by Theo Carreras. Crown 8vo, imitation leather, in box. 5/-
Also a Cheap Edition. (Unwin's Nature Books. Vol 3.) Cloth. 2/-
—— More about Wild Nature. By Mrs. Brightwen. With Portrait of the Author and many other full-page Illustrations. Cr 8vo, imitation leather, gilt lettered, gilt edges, in box. 5/-
Also a Cheap Edition. (Unwin's Nature Books. Vol. 2.) Cloth. 2/-
—— Quiet Hours with Nature. By Mrs. Brightwen. Fully Illustrated. Cr. 8vo, cloth. 5/-
Also a Cheap Edition (Unwin's Nature Books. Vol. 7) Cloth 2/-

BRIGHTWEN. Wild Nature Won by Kindness. By Mrs. Brightwen. Revised Edition, with additional Illustrations. Cr. 8vo, imitation leather, gilt lettered, gilt edges, in box. 5/-

Also a Cheap Edition. (Unwin's Nature Books. Vol. 1.) Cloth. 2/-

—— **Last Hours with Nature.** By Mrs. Brightwen, F.Z S., F.E.S, Edited by W. H Chesson With Illustrations. Cr. 8vo, cloth. net 2/6

THE BRIGHTWEN SERIES See "Unwin's Nature Books'

CESARESCO The Psychology and Training of the Horse. By Count Eugenio Martinengo Cesaresco. With Photogravure Frontispiece Demy 8vo, cloth. net 10/6

CHAMBERLAIN Methods in Plant Histology By Charles J. Chamberlain, A M , Ph D. With many Illustrations from Photomicrographs. Demy 8vo, cloth. net 10/6

DITTRICH. The Horse: A Pictorial Guide to its Anatomy. 110 Drawings (reproduced by Photo. Lithography) by Hermann Dittrich, with Explanatory Notes by Prof. Ellenberger and Prof. Baum. In portfolio, 4to net 30/-

FLAMMARION. Astronomy for Amateurs By Camille Flammarion. Authorised Translation by Francis A. Welby. With 84 Illustrations Cr. 8vo, cloth. 6/-

—— **Mysterious Psychic Forces.** An Account of the Author's Investigations in Psychical Research, together with those of other European Savants. By Camille Flammarion. With 21 Illustrations. Demy 8vo, cloth. net 8/6

GEEN. What I Have Seen While Fishing. By Philip Geen. See under "Varia"

GUYER. Animal Micrology Practical Exercises in Microscopical Methods. By Michael F. Guyer, Ph D. Demy 8vo, cloth. net 9/-

HARTING. Recreations of a Naturalist By J. E. Harting. With numerous Illustrations. Demy 8vo, cloth. net 15/-

HARVIE-BROWN Travels of a Naturalist in Northern Europe. By J. A. Harvie-Brown, F.R S.E., F.Z S. With 4 Maps, 2 Coloured Plates, and many Illustrations. 2 vols. Small royal 8vo, cloth. net 63/-

HULME That Rock Garden of Ours. By F. E. Hulme, F.L.S., F.S A. With Coloured Illustrations. Demy 8vo, cloth. net 10/6

INGERSOLL. The Wit of the Wild. By Ernest Ingersoll. Illustrated. Cr 8vo, cloth. net 5/-

IRVING. How to Know the Starry Heavens. An Invitation to the Study of Suns and Worlds. By Edward Irving. With Charts, Coloured Plates, Diagrams, and many Engravings or Photographs. Demy 8vo, cloth net 8/6

LOEB Studies in General Physiology By Jacques Loeb. With numerous Illustrations. 2 vols , royal 8vo, cloth. net 31/6

MILLS. The Dog Book: The Origin, History, Varieties, Breeding, Education, and General Management of the Dog in Health, and his Treatment in Disease. By Wesley Mills, M.A., M.D , D.V S , &c. With 43 full-page Cuts, one Coloured Plate, and numerous other Illustrations. Large cr 8vo, cloth. 10/6

NEWMAN. Bird Skinning and Bird Stuffing. By Edward Newman. Cr 8vo 1/-

OPPENHEIM. The Face and How to Read it By Annie Isabella Oppenheim, F B P.S Illustrated. Cr. 8vo, cloth. net 2/6

PARSONS. The Nature and Purpose of the Universe. By John Denham Parsons. Demy 8vo, cloth. net 21/-

PIKE. In Bird-Land with Field-Glass and Camera. By Oliver G. Pike. With over 80 Photographs of British Birds. Photogravure Frontispiece. Cr. 8vo, cloth gilt. 6/-

Cheap Reissue (Unwin's Nature Books. Vol. 5) Cr 8vo cloth. 2/-

RICHMOND. In My Lady's Garden. By Mrs. Richmond (late Garden Editor of *The Queen*). With a Coloured Frontispiece and other Illustrations Demy 8vo, cloth. net 10/6

RUDAUX. How to Study the Stars. By L. Rudaux. Profusely Illustrated. Cloth. net 5/-

SCHMIDT. Pain: Its Causation and Diagnostic Significance in Internal Diseases. By Dr Rudolph Schmidt. Translated and Edited by Karl M Vogel, M.D., and Hans Zinsser, A M., M D., Demy 8vo, cloth net 12/6

SNELL. The Camera in the Fields. A Practical Guide to Nature Photography. By F. C. Snell. With 80 Illustrations. Cr. 8vo, cloth 5/-

Cheap Re-issue. (Unwin's Nature Books. Vol 12.) 2/-

—— **Nature Studies by Night and Day.** By F. C. Snell. With about 90 Photographs taken direct from Nature. Cr. 8vo, cloth. 5/-

SOLLAS. The Age of the Earth, and other Geological Studies. By W. J. Sollas, LL D., D. Sc., F.R.S., Professor of Geology in the University of Oxford. Illustrated. Demy 8vo, cloth. net 10/6

Cheap Edition. Large cr. 8vo, cloth. net 6/-

STRACHEY. Cat and Bird Stories from "The Spectator." With an Introduction by John St Loe Strachey Cr. 8vo, cloth. 5/-

—— **Dog Stories from "The Spectator."** With an Introduction by J. St Loe Strachey Cr 8vo, cloth 5/-

STUTTARD. The Butterfly : Its Nature, Development, and Attributes By John Stuttard Illustrated Fcap. 8vo, limp cloth. 1/-

THOMPSON The Mental Traits of Sex. An Experimental Investigation of the Normal Mind in Men and Women. By Helen Bradford Thompson, Ph.D. With many Diagrams. Large cr. 8vo, cloth. net 6/-

UNWIN. Future Forest Trees. The Importance of German Experiments in the Introduction of North American Trees. By A. Harold Unwin, D. Oec. Publ. (Munich). With 4 Illustrations. Demy 8vo, cloth. net 7/6

UNWIN'S NATURE BOOKS (Formerly The Brightwen Series.) Each volume fully Illustrated. Cr. 8vo, cloth each 2/-

(1) Wild Nature Won by Kindness. By Mrs. Brightwen.

(2) More about Wild Nature. By Mrs. Brightwen.

(3) Inmates of my House and Garden. By Mrs. Brightwen.

(4) Glimpses into Plant Life. By Mrs Brightwen.

(5) In Birdland with Field-Glass and Camera. By Oliver G. Pike.

(6) Bird Life in Wild Wales. By J A. Walpole-Bond

(7) Quiet Hours with Nature. By Mrs. Brightwen.

(8) Nature's Story of the Year. By Charles A. Witchell.

(9) Birds I Have Known. By Arthur H. Beavan.

(10) Animals I have Known. By Arthur H Beavan.

(11) Fishes I Have Known. By Arthur H Beavan

(12) The Camera in the Fields. By F. C. Snell.

WALPOLE-BOND. Bird Life in Wild Wales. By J. A. Walpole-Bond. With 60 Illustrations from photographs by Oliver G. Pike. Large cr. 8vo, cloth.   7/6

Cheap Re-issue. (Unwin's Nature Books. Vol. 6)   2/-

WESTELL. British Bird Life. By W. Percival Westell, M.B.O.U., F.R.H.S, &c. With over 60 Illustrations. With an Introduction by Sir Herbert Maxwell, Bart. Large cr. 8vo, cloth.   5/-
Cheap Edition, Large cr. 8vo, cloth.   3/6

WATSON. Woodlanders and Field Folk. Sketches of Wild Life in Britain. By John Watson, author of "Poachers and Poaching," and Blanche Winder. Illustrated. Large cr 8vo, cloth.   net   5/-

WITCHELL. Nature's Story of the Year. By Charles A. Witchell. Fully Illustrated. Cr. 8vo, cloth.   5/-

Cheap Re-issue. (Unwin's Nature Books. Vol. 8) Cr. 8vo, cloth.   2/-

---

RELIGION and EDUCATION.

ALLARDYCE. Stops ; or, How to Punctuate. A Practical Handbook for Writers and Students By Paul Allardyce. Fcap. 8vo, cloth.   1/-

BADHAM. St. Mark's Indebtedness to St. Matthew. By F. P. Badham. Cr 8vo, cloth   3/6

BENSON. The Religion of the Plain Man. By Father Robert Hugh Benson. Cr. 8vo, cloth.   net   2/6

BERRY. How to Become a Teacher. By T. W. Berry. Fcap. 8vo, cloth   1/-

BLYTH. The Last Step to Religious Equality. By Edmond Kell Blyth. Cr. 8vo, paper covers.   6d.

BOUSSET. What is Religion ? By Professor W. Bousset. Translated by F. B. Low. Cr 8vo, cloth   net   5/-

—— The Faith of a Modern Protestant. By Professor W. Bousset. Translated by F. B. Low. Cr. 8vo, cloth.   net   2/6

BRAY. The Town Child. By Reginald A. Bray, L.C.C., Author of "The Children of the Town" in "The Heart of the Empire," "The Boy and the Family" in "The Studies of Boy Life," &c. Demy 8vo, cloth.   net   7/6

BRIDGETT. A History of the Holy Eucharist in Great Britain. By T. E Bridgett, C.S S R. A New Revised and Illustrated Edition. Edited, with notes, by Herbert Thurston, S.J. Royal Folio, cloth. net   21/-

BROWN. The Social Message of the Modern Pulpit. By Charles Reynolds Brown. Cr 8vo, cloth.   net   5/-

BURTON. The Life of Christ. An Aid to Historical Study, and a Condensed Commentary on the Gospels. By Ernest de Witt Burton and Shailer Mathews, Professors in the University of Chicago. Large cr. 8vo, cloth.   net   5/-

CAMPBELL. Thursday Mornings at the City Temple. By the Rev. R. J. Campbell, M A. Cr. 8vo, cloth.   net   5/-

COX. The Bird's Nest, and Other Sermons for Children of all Ages. By Samuel Cox, D.D. Fourth Edition, imp. 16mo, cloth.   3/6

—— Expositions. By Samuel Cox, D D. In 4 vols. Demy 8vo, cloth, each.   7/6

DILLON The Original Poem of Job. Translated from the Restored Text. By E. J. Dillon, Doc. Orient. Lang, Author of "The Sceptics of the Old Testament," &c. To which is appended "The Book of Job According to the Authorised Version." Crown 8vo, cloth   5/-

ELPHINSTONE. The Power of Character, and Other Studies. By Lady Elphinstone. With a Preface by Canon J. G. Tetley Cr. 8vo, cloth.   net   3/6

FOSTER (G. B). The Finality of the Christian Religion. By George Burman Foster, Professor of the Philosophy of Religion, Chicago Demy 8vo, cloth.   net 13/-

GARDINER. The Bible as English Literature. By J. H. Gardiner. Cr. 8vo, cloth   net   5/-

GEORGE Seventeenth Century Men of Latitude. Precursors of Liberal Theology By E. A. George. With Portraits. Cr. 8vo, cloth.   net   3/6

GILMAN. University Problems in the United States. By Daniel Coit Gilman, LL.D. Demy 8vo, 320 pp, cloth.   10/6

HALL. Christian Belief Interpreted by Christian Experience. By Charles Cuthbert Hall. With an Introductory Note by the Vice-Chancellor of the University of Bombay. Demy 8vo, cloth.   net   6/6

HARDY. Doubt and Faith. By Rev. E. J. Hardy, M.A. Cr. 8vo, cloth.   6/-

HARPER. Religion and the Higher Life. By William Rainy Harper, D D., LL D. Large cr. 8vo, cloth.   net   6/-

—— The Trend in Higher Education in America. By William Rainy Harper, D D, LL.D. Cr. 8vo, cloth.   net   7/6

HENSON. Christ and the Nation. Westminster and other Sermons. By H. Hensley Henson, Canon of Westminster, and Rector of St. Margaret's. Cr. 8vo, cloth.   net   5/-

HERBERT (George). A Country Parson. See under "Philosophy, Essays," &c.

—— The Temple. Sacred Poems. By George Herbert. Facsimile Reprint of the First Edition (1633). With an Introduction by J H. Shorthouse, Author of "John Inglesant" Fcap 8vo   net   3/6

HILL. The Aspirate ; or, the Use of the Letter " H " in English, Latin, Greek, and Gaelic. By Geoffry Hill, M.A. Cr 8vo, cloth   net   3/6

HORTON. Revelation and the Bible. By R F. Horton, M.A , D D. Third Edition. Cr 8vo, cloth.   3/6

—— Inspiration and the Bible: An Inquiry. By R F. Horton, M.A., D D. Crown 8vo, cloth.   3/6
Popular Edition, cr. 8vo.   Paper, net, 1/- ; cloth, net   2/-

HOWARD A History of Matrimonial Institutions. By George Elliott Howard, Ph.D See under "History"

HYDE. The Religious Songs of Connacht. By Douglas Hyde, LL D., M.R.I.A., Author of "A Literary History of Ireland," "Love Songs of Connacht," &c. 2 vols Cr 8vo, cloth.   net 10/-

JEPHSON. Christian Democracy. A Church for Our Day. By Julie Jephson. Cr. 8vo, paper covers.   6d.

KING. The Psychology of Child Development. By Irving King. With an Introduction by John Dewey. Cr. 8vo, cloth.   net   5/-

KO. Elementary Handbook of the Burmese Language. By Taw Sein Ko, M.R A.S , F A I , F.S.A. Boards.   net   3/9

KRUGER. The Papacy : The Idea and its Exponents. By

LEIGH. Our School Out-of-Doors. By the Hon M. Cordelia Leigh, Author of "Simple Lessons from Nature," &c. Illustrated. Cr. 8vo, cloth. 2/-

LUCAS and ABRAHAMS. A Hebrew Lesson-Book. By Alice Lucas and Israel Abrahams. Cr 8vo, cloth net 1/-

MACPHAIL. Essays in Puritanism. By Andrew Macphail. Large cr. 8vo, cloth. 6/-

MARK. The Teacher and the Child. Elements of Moral and Religious Teaching in the Day School, the Home, and the Sunday School. By H Thiselton Mark, Master of Method, the Owens College, Manchester With Frontispiece. Cr 8vo, cloth - net 1/-

MARTIN'S Up-To-Date Tables: Weights, Measures, Coinage. For Use throughout the Empire. By Alfred J Martin, F.S I. With 18 Diagrams and 3 Maps. Demy 16mo, cloth. net 2/6

——Up-to-Date Beginners' Table Book. For Schools and Home Teaching Twenty-ninth Thousand. In paper covers 1d.

MATHEWS The Messianic Hope in the New Testament. By Shailer Mathews. Demy 8vo, cloth. net 10/6

MAZZINI (Joseph). See Stubbs.

NEGRI. Julian the Apostate. By Gaetano Negri. See under "Biography"

OMAN The Mystics, Ascetics, and Saints of India. By John Campbell Oman Fully Illustrated Medium 8vo, cloth. net 14/-

Cheaper Edition. Demy 8vo, cloth. net 7/6

—— The Brahmans, Theists and Muslims of India. By John Campbell Oman, D Lit. Illustrated Medium 8vo, cloth. net 14/-

—— Cults, Customs, and Superstitions of India. Being a Revised and Enlarged Edition of 'Indian Life, Religious and Social.' By J. Campbell Oman, D.Lit., M.R.A.S. Illustrated. Demy 8vo, cloth. net 14/-

PARKER. The Complete Works of Theodore Parker. Crown 8vo, cloth each 5/-

(1) A Discourse of Matters Pertaining to Religion.	(8) Social Classes in a Republic.
(2) The World of Matter and the Spirit of Man.	(9) Prayers, Poems and Parables.
	(10) Lessons from the World of Matter and of Man.
(3) The American Scholar.	(11) Theism and Atheism.
(4) The Transient and Permanent in Christianity.	(12) The Divine Presence.
	(13) The Slave Power.
(5) Ten Sermons on Religion.	(14) The Law of God and the Statutes of Man.
(6) Historic Americans	
(7) The Sins and Safeguards of Society	(15) The Rights of Man in America.
	(16) A Minister's Experience.

PAULSEN. German Education, Past and Present. By Friedrich Paulsen, Ph D. Translated by T. Lorenz, Ph D Crown 8vo, cloth. net 5/-

PFLEIDERER. Religion and Historic Faiths. By Otto Pfleiderer, D D., Professor of Theology in the University of Berlin Crown 8vo, cloth net 5/-

—— Christian Origins By Otto Pfleiderer, D.D. Crown 8vo, cloth. net 5/-

—— The Development of Christianity. By Otto Pfleiderer. Cr 8vo, cloth. net 5/-

PHILPOTT. London at School · The Story of the School Board, 1870—1904. By Hugh B Philpott. Illustrated. Cr. 8vo, cloth. 6/-

PIKE. Wesley and his Preachers. By G. Holden Pike. See under "Biography."

RAVENSTEIN. A Pocket German-English Conversation-Dictionary By G. E Ravenstein. (Meyer's Sprachfuhrer) 500 pages. 16mo, cloth net 2/6

ROBINSON. The Golden Sayings of the Blessed Brother Giles of Assisi. Newly Translated and Edited, together with a Sketch of his Life, by Father Paschal Robinson, of the Order of Friars Minor. With 6 Illustrations. Crown 8vo, cloth. net 5/-

SABATIER. Modernism. The Jowett Lectures of 1908. By Paul Sabatier With a Preface and Notes, and the full text of the Encyclicals *Pieni l' Anmio, Lamentabili*, and *Pascendi Dominici Gregis* Translated by C. A Miles. Crown 8vo, cloth. net 5/-
—— Disestablishment in France. See under "Politics"

SELLECK. The New Appreciation of the Bible. A Study of the Spiritual Outcome of Biblical Criticism. By W C. Selleck, D D. Crown 8vo, cloth net 6/6

STUBBS. "God and the People!" The Religious Creed of a Democrat. Being Selections from the Writings of Joseph Mazzini. By Charles William Stubbs (Dean of Ely) Second Edition. Cr 8vo. 3/6

TYRRELL. The Programme of Modernism. A Reply to the Encyclical *Pascendi* of Pius X. Translated from the second Italian Edition (with the author's latest additions), by George Tyrrell, M A. With an Introduction by A. L. Lilley, M A., Vicar of St. Mary's, Paddington Green. Crown 8vo, cloth. net 5/-

UNWIN'S THEOLOGICAL LIBRARY.
Crown 8vo, cloth. Each Volume. net 5/-
1 Modernism. The Jowett Lectures of 1908. By Paul Sabatier.
2 What is Religion ? By Professor W. Bousset.
3 The Bible as English Literature. By Professor J. H. Gardiner.
4 The Programme of Modernism. A Reply to the Encyclical Pascendi of Pius X.
5 Christian Origins. By Professor Otto Pfleiderer.
6 Religion and Historic Faiths. By Professor Otto Pfleiderer.
7 The Development of Christianity. By Otto Pfleiderer.

WAGNER. Courage. By Charles Wagner, Author of "The Simple Life," &c. Medium 12mo. Paper, net 1/- ; cloth, net 2/-
—— Towards the Heights. By Charles Wagner. Medium 12mo. Paper, net 1/- , cloth, net 2/-

WARING. Christianity and its Bible. By Henry F. Waring. Large cr. 8vo, cloth. net 4/6

WILLIAMS. Psalms and Litanies, Counsels and Collects for Devout Persons. By Rowland Williams, D D New Edition Cr 8vo, cloth. 3/6
—— Stray Thoughts from the Note-Books of Rowland Williams, D.D. New Edition Cr 8vo, cloth. 3/6

WORSLEY. Concepts of Monism. A Critical Comparison of all Systems of Monism, both Asiatic and European By A Worsley. Demy 8vo, cloth net 21/-

See also under "Biography" for Oliver Cromwell, Robert and Mary Moffat, Dr. Parker, Girolamo Savonarola, Wesley, and others. Also Japp ["Master Missionaries,"] &c.

DOMESTIC LITERATURE.

BOLAND. The Century Invalid Cookery Book. By Mary A Boland. Edited by Mis Humphrey ("Madge" of *Truth*). Cr. 8vo, cloth.   3/6

DAVIES. The Housewife's What's What. A Hold-All of Useful Information for the House By Mary Davies Large cr 8vo, cloth net   6/-
Populai Edition, laige cr 8vo, cloth   net   2/6

FORSTER. Chelsea Window Gardening; or, Some Notes on the Management of Pot Plants and Town Gardens. By L. M Foister. Cr. 8vo, paper covers.   2d.

GUARRACINO. "Please, M'm, the Butcher!" A Complete Guide to Catering for the Housewife of Moderate Means, with Menus of all Meals for a Year, numerous Recipes, and Fifty-two additional Menus of Dinners without Meat. Illustiated. By Beatrice Guarracino. Large cr 8vo, cloth.   net   6/-
Cheap Edition, cloth.   net   2/6

HARDY. The Business of Life: A Book for Everyone. By the Rev. E J Haidy, M.A Square imperial 16mo, cloth.   3/6
Presentation Edition, bevelled boards, gilt edges, in box.   7/6

—— The Five Talents of Woman: A Book for Girls and Young Women. By the Rev E. J. Hardy, M.A. Popular Edition, small cr 8vo, cloth.   3/6
Presentation Edition, bevelled boards, gilt edges, in box.   7/6

—— How to be Happy though Married: Being a Handbook to Mairiage By the Rev. E. J. Hardy, M.A Presentation Edition, imperial 16mo, white vellum, cloth, extra gilt, bevelled boards, gilt edges, in box.   7/6
Popular Edition, cr 8vo, cloth, bevelled boards   3/6
Large cr. 8vo, gieen cloth with white label, flat back.   net   2/6
New Edition, 83ɪd thousand, small cr. 8vo, cloth.   net   1/-
Small cr 8vo, paper cover.   1/-
Also a Sixpenny Edition.   6d.

—— How to Get Married. By the Rev. E. J. Hardy, Author of "How to be Happy though Married. Cr. 8vo, paper covers.   net   1/-

—— "Manners Makyth Man." By the Rev. E. J. Hardy, M.A. Piesentation Edition, imperial 16mo, cloth, bevelled boards, gilt edges, in box.   7/6
  cloth,   6/-
Popular Edition, small squaie 8vo, cloth.   3/6

—— The Sunny Days of Youth: A Book for Boys and Young Men. Square imperial 16mo, cloth   3/6
Presentation Edition, elegantly bound, bevelled boards, gilt edges, in box.   7/6

HARLAND and HERRICK. The National Cook-Book: A Thousand Recipes carefully piepaied in the light of the Latest Methods of Cooking and Serving. By Marian Hailand and Christine Terhune Herrick. 12mo, cloth.   7/6

HUMPHREY. Manners for Girls. By Mrs. Humphrey. Long 8vo, cloth, decorated cover.   1/-

PINK. Gardening for the Million. By Alfred Pink. Large cr. 8vo, cloth. net 2/6

—— **Recipes for the Million: A Handy-Book for the Household.** By Alfred Pink. Twelfth Thousand. Cr. 8vo, cloth. 2/6

Quickest Guide to Breakfast, Dinner, and Supper, The. By Aunt Gertrude. Paper boards. 1/-

READ. The Way to Keep Well. Practical Home Hints on Common Ailments. By C. Stanford Read, M.B. (Lond.), London County Council Lecturer. Cr. 8vo, cloth. net 2/6

RONALD. The Century Cook-Book. By Mary Ronald. Fully Illustrated. Demy 8vo, cloth. 7/6

—— **Luncheons: A Cook's Picture Book.** A Supplement to "The Century Cook-Book." With many Illustrations. By Mary Ronald. Large cr. 8vo, cloth. net 6/-

TUCKER. Mother, Baby, and Nursery: A Manual for Mothers. By Genevieve Tucker, M.D. Illustrated. Large cr. 8vo, cloth. Paper covers, 1/-; cloth. 3/6

WHADCOAT. Every Woman's Own Lawyer. A Legal Adviser for Ladies. By Gordon Cuming Whadcoat, Solicitor, Author of "The Balance," and other novels. Cr. 8vo, cloth. net 3/4

WOOD. Quotations for Occasions. Compiled by Katharine B. Wood. Large cr, 8vo cloth. 3/6

BOOKS for CHILDREN.

BRENTANO. New Fairy Tales from Brentano. By Kate Freiligrath Kroeker. A New Edition. With Coloured Frontispiece and eight Illustrations by F. C. Gould. Fcap. 4to, cloth. 3/6

BYLES. The Boy and the Angel: Discourses for Children. By Rev. John Byles. Cr. 8vo, cloth. 3/6

—— **The Legend of St. Mark: A New Series of Sunday Morning Talks to Children.** By Rev. John Byles. Crown 8vo, cloth. 3/6

CHILDREN'S LIBRARY, THE. Illustrated. Fcap. 8vo. The following in cloth, Pinafore binding, floral edges. each 2/6

BASILE. The Pentamerone; or, the Story of Stories. By Giambattista Basile. Translated from the Neapolitan by John Edward Taylor. New Edition, revised and edited by Helen Zimmern. Illustrated by George Cruikshank.

BECKMAN. Pax and Carlino. By Ernest Beckman.

COLLODI. The Story of a Puppet. By C. Collodi. Translated from the Italian by M. A. Murray. Illus-trated by C. Mazzanti.

DAUDET. The Pope's Mule, and Other Stories. By Alphonse Daudet. Trans-lated by A. D. Beavington-Atkinson and D. Havers. Illustrated by Ethel K. Martyn.

DEFOE. The Adventures of Robinson Crusoe. Edited with Illustrations by George Cruikshank.

DROSINES. Stories from Fairyland. By Georgios Drosines. Illustrated by Thomas Riley.

CHILDREN'S LIBRARY, THE—*continued.*

EIVIND. Finnish Legends. Adapted by R. Eivind. Illustrated from the Finnish text.

EVANS, Sea Children. By S. Hope Evans. Illustrated.

HAUFF. The Little Glass Man, and Other Stories. Translated from the German of Wilhelm Hauff Illustrated by James Pryde.

HUEFFER. The Feather. By Ford H. Hueffer. Frontispiece by Madox Brown.

HUGESSEN. The Magic Oak Tree, and Other Fairy Stories. By Knatchbull Hugessen (Lord Brabourne), Author of "Prince Marigold," "Queer Folk" &c

MORRIS. Cornish Whiddles for Teenin' Time, By Mrs Frank Morris. Illustrated by Arch K Nicolson.

WILLIAMS. Tales from the Mabinogion. By Meta Williams.

Popular Re-issue, Fcap. 8vo, decorated bindings Illustrated. each 1/-

BROOKFIELD, Æsop's Fables for Little People. Told by Mrs. Arthur Brookfield. Pictured by Henry J. Ford.

BECKMAN. Pax and Carlino. By Ernest Beckman. Illustrated by Florence K Upton

CAPUANA. Once Upon a Time. By Luigi Capuana. Illustrated by C. Mazzanti.

COLLODI. The Story of a Puppet; or, The Adventures of Pinocchio Illustrated by C. Mazzanti.

DAUDET. La Belle Nivernaise. By Alphonse Daudet. Illustrated by Montegut.

DROSINES. Stories from Fairyland. By Georgios Drosines. Illustrated by Thomas Riley.

HOFFMANN. Nutcracker and Mouse King, and Other Stories. By E. T A. Hoffmann. Translated from the German by Ascott R. Hope

HUEFFER. The Brown Owl. By Ford H. Hueffer Illustrated by Madox Brown.

MOLESWORTH. An Enchanted Garden. By Mrs. Molesworth. Illustrated by J W. Hennessey.

O'GRADY. Finn, and His Companion. By Standish O'Grady. Illustrated by Jack B Yeats.

VOLKHOVSKY The China Cup, and Other Stories. By Felix Volkhovsky. Illustrated by Malischeff.

YEATS. Irish Fairy Tales. Edited by W. B. Yeats. Illustrated by Jack B. Yeats. 3

CHILDREN'S STUDY, THE. Long 8vo, cloth, gilt top, with Photogravure Frontispiece. each 2/6

(1) Scotland. By Mrs. Oliphant.

(2) Ireland. Edited by Barry O'Brien.

(3) England. By Frances E. Cooke.

(4) Germany. By Kate Freiligrath Kroeker.

(5) Old Tales from Greece. By Alice Zimmern, Author of "Old Tales from Rome."

(6) France. By Mary Rowsell.

(7) Rome. By Mary Ford.

(8) Spain. By Leonard Williams

(9) Canada. J. N. McIlwraith.

COX. The Brownies in the Philippines. By Palmer Cox. Large 4to. Copiously illustrated. 6/-

DEFOE. The Adventures of Robinson Crusoe. By Daniel Defoe. Newly Edited after the Original Editions. 19 full-page Illustrations by Kauffmann. Large cr 8vo, cloth extra, gilt edges. 5/-

DODGE, The Disdainful Maiden, A Fairy Story. By W. Phelps Dodge, Author of "Piers Gaveston," &c. Parchment, grey covers, cr. 12mo 2/-

FARROW   The Adventures of a Dodo. By G. E. Farrow, Author of "The Wallypug of Why," &c. With 70 Illustrations by Willy Pogany. Crown 8vo, cloth   3/6

GOULD. Tales Told in the Zoo. By F. Carruthers Gould and his son, F. H Carruthers Gould. Fully Illustrated by "F. C. G." Cr. 4to.   6/-

GRACE. Tales from Spenser By R. W. Grace. With 12 Illustrations Cr. 8vo, cloth.   5/-

JEPSON. The Lady Noggs, Peeress. By Edgar Jepson, Author of "The Admirable Tinker." Children's Edition. With 16 Illustrations by Lewis Baumer. Large crown 8vo, cloth.   6/-

MACDONALD. The Secret of the Sargasso. By Robert M. Macdonald. Profusely Illustrated. Large cr. 8vo.   5/-

—— Chillagoe Charlie. By Robert M. Macdonald. Profusely Illustrated Large cr. 8vo.   5/-

McMANUS. The True Mother Goose. Songs for the Nursery; or, Mother Goose's Melodies for Children. With Notes and Pictures in two colours, by Blanche McManus Cr. 4to, cloth.   net   3/6

MONARCH SERIES, THE Humorous Rhymes of Historical Times. By Roland Carse. Illustrations in colour and black and white by W. Heath Robinson. Size 8½ in by 11 in. See under "History."

NESBIT. The House of Arden. By E Nesbit. With 32 Illustrations by H R Millar. Large crown 8vo.   6/-

—— The Phœnix and the Carpet. By E. Nesbit. With 48 Illustrations. Large crown 8vo.   6/-

—— Five Children and It. By E. Nesbit. With 46 Illustrations by H. R Millar. Cr 8vo, cloth.   6/-

—— Nine Unlikely Tales for Children. By E. Nesbit. With 27 Illustrations.   6/-

—— The Story of the Treasure Seekers. By E. Nesbit. Fifth Impression. With 15 Illustrations by Gordon Browne and 2 by Lewis Baumer. Large cr. 8vo, cloth.   6/-

—— New Treasure Seekers. By E. Nesbit. With about 40 Illustrations by Gordon Browne and Lewis Baumer. Cr 8vo, cloth   6/-

—— The Would-be-Goods. Being the Further Adventures of the Treasure Seekers By E Nesbit. With 18 Illustrations. Cr. 8vo, cloth gilt.   6/-

—— The Enchanted Castle. By E. Nesbit. With 48 Illustrations by H R Millar. Large crown 8vo, cloth   6/-

—— The Story of the Amulet. By E. Nesbit. With 48 Illustrations by H R. Millar. Large crown 8vo, cloth.   6/-

ROWBOTHAM Tales from Plutarch. By F. Jameson Rowbotham Fully illustrated. Cr. 8vo, cloth.   5/-

SELLON. Only a Kitten, and Other Stories. By E. Mildred Sellon. Cr. 8vo, cloth   3/6

SIDNEY. Five Little Peppers and How they Grew. By Margaret Sidney. Illustrated.   6/-

THOMAS. The Welsh Fairy Book. By W. Jenkyn Thomas. With a Coloured Frontispiece and about 200 Illustrations by Willy Pogany. Small Demy 8vo, cloth.   6/-

TURNER. That Girl. By Ethel Turner (Mrs. Curlewis). With 25 Illustrations. Large cr. 8vo, cloth.   6/-

THE NEW IRISH LIBRARY. Edited by Sir Charles Gavan Duffy, K C M.G , Assisted by Douglas Hyde, LL.D., and R. Barry O'Brien. Small cr. 8vo   Paper covers, 1/- each ; cloth,

(1) **The Patriot Parliament of 1689, with its Statutes, Votes and Proceedings.** By Thomas Davis.

(2) **The Bog of Stars, and** Other Stories of Elizabethan Ireland. By Standish O'Grady.

(3) **The New Spirit of the Nation.** Edited by Martin MacDermott.

(4) **A Parish Providence.** By E M. Lynch.

(5) **The Irish Song Book.** Edited by Alfred Perceval Graves.

(6) **The Story of Early Gaelic Literature.** By Douglas Hyde, LL D.

(7) **Life of Patrick Sarsfield.** By Dr. John Todhunter.

(8) **Owen Roe O'Neill.** By J. F. Taylor, K.C.

(9) **Swift in Ireland.** By Richard Ashe King, M A.

(10) **A Short Life of Thomas Davis.** By Sir Charles Gavan Duffy.

(11) **Bishop Doyle.** By Michael MacDonagh.

(12) **Lays of the Red Branch.** By Sir Samuel Ferguson.

THE WELSH LIBRARY. Edited by Owen M. Edwards, Author of "Wales" Each volume fcap. 8vo   Paper covers, 1/- , cloth, 2/-

Vols. 1-3 **The Mabinogion.** Translated from the Red Book of Hergest by Lady Charlotte Guest. 3 vols.

Vol 4. **The Works of John Dyer.** Edited by Edward Thomas, M.A , Author of " Horæ Solitariæ."

In preparation

A Short History of Welsh Literature. By Owen M. Edwards.

The Works of George Herbert Edited by Miss Louise I Guiney.

Henry Vaughan.

Mrs. Hemans' Welsh Melodies.

THE INTERNATIONAL. A Review of the World's Progress. Edited by Rodolphe Broda. Published Monthly. Royal 8vo.   net   1/-

M. A. B. (Mainly about Books). An Illustrated Monthly Guide to the best New Books.   1d.

THE LITERARY "U" PEN. In book box.   1/-
" A smooth-running Pen with quill-like action "

UNWIN'S SHILLING NOVELS. A new series of high-class Novels by Popular Writers. Bound in Picture Wrappers.   Each **net**   1/-

(1) **In Summer Shade.** By Mary E Mann

(2) **Lady Mary of the Dark House.** By Mrs. C. N. Williamson.

(3) **The Shulamite** By Alice and Claude Askew.

(4) **"Mr. Thomas Atkins."** By the Rev. E. J Hardy.

(5) **The Blue Lagoon.** By H de Vere Stacpoole.

(6) **The Lady Noggs, Peeress.** By Edgar Jepson

(7) **The Canon in Residence.** By Victor L. Whitechurch.

(8) **De Omnibus.** By the Conductor (Barry Pain).

BAEDEKER'S GUIDE BOOKS

(List of Volumes in English.)

Published Prices are NET.

Austria-Hungary including *Dalmatia and Bosnia.* With 33 Maps and 44 Plans. Tenth edition. 1905. Net 8s.

The Eastern Alps including the Bavarian Highlands, Tyrol, Salzburg, Upper and Lower Austria, Styria, Carinthia, and Carniola. With 61 Maps, 10 Plans, and 8 Panoramas. Eleventh edition. 1907. Net 10s.

Belgium and Holland including the *Grand-Duchy of Luxembourg.* With 15 Maps and 30 Plans. Fourteenth edition. 1905. Net 6s.

The Dominion of Canada, with *Newfoundland* and an Excursion to *Alaska.* With 13 Maps and 12 Plans. Third edition. 1907. Net 6s.

Constantinople and Asia Minor, see *Special List.*

Denmark, see *Norway, Sweden and Denmark.*

Egypt, *Lower* and *Upper Egypt, Lower* and *Upper Nubia* and the *Sudân.* With 24 Maps, 76 Plans, and 59 Vignettes. Sixth edition. 1908. Net 15s.

England, see *Great Britain.*

France :

Paris and its Environs, with Routes from London to Paris. With 14 Maps and 38 Plans. Sixteenth edition. 1907. Net 6s.

Northern France from Belgium and the English Channel to the Loire excluding Paris and its Environs. With 13 Maps and 40 Plans. Fourth edition. 1905. Net 7s.

Southern France from the Loire to the Pyrenees, the Auvergne, the Cévennes, the French Alps, the Rhone Valley, Provence, the French Riviera and Corsica. With 33 Maps and 49 Plans. Fifth edition. 1907. Net 9s.

Germany :

Berlin and its Envir. With 5 Maps and 20 Plans. Third edition. 1908. Net 3s.

Northern Germany as far as the Bavarian and Austrian frontiers With 49 Maps and 75 Plans. Fourteenth edition. 1904. Net 8s.

Southern Germany (Wurtemberg and Bavaria). With 30 Maps and 23 Plans. Tenth edition. 1907. Net 6s.

The Rhine from Rotterdam to Constance, including the Seven Mountains, the Moselle, the Volcanic Eifel, the Taunus, the Odenwald and Heidelberg, the Vosges Mountains, the Black Forest, &c With 52 Maps and 29 Plans. Sixteenth edition. 1905. Net 7s.

Great Britain, *England, Wales and Scotland.* With 22 Maps, 58 Plans, and a Panorama. Sixth edition. 1906. Net 10s.

London and its Environs. With 9 Maps and 19 Plans. Sixteenth edition. 1909. Net 6s.

Greece, the *Greek Islands* and an Excursion to *Crete.* With 16 Maps, 30 Plans, and a Panorama of Athens. Fourth edition. 1909. Net 8s.

Holland, see *Belgium and Holland.*

Italy :

I. Northern Italy, including Leghorn, Florence, Ravenna and routes through Switzerland and Austria. With 30 Maps and 40 Plans. Thirteenth edition. 1906. Net 8s.

II. Central Italy and Rome. With 19 Maps, 55 Plans, a view of the Forum Romanum, and the Arms of the Popes since 1417. Fifteenth edition. 1909. Net 7s. 6d.

III. Southern Italy and Sicily, with Excursions to Malta, Sardinia, Tunis, and Corfu. With 30 Maps and 28 Plans. Fifteenth edition. 1908. Net 6s.

Italy from the Alps to Naples. With 25 Maps and 52 Plans. Second edition. 1909. Net 8s.

Norway, Sweden and Denmark including an Excursion to *Spitsbergen.* With 37 Maps, 22 Plans, and 3 Panoramas. Eighth edition. 1903. Net 8s.

Palestine and Syria, including the principal routes through *Mesopotamia* and *Babylonia.* With 20 Maps, 52 Plans, and a Panorama of Jerusalem. Fourth edition. 1906. Net 12s.

Portugal, see *Spain and Portugal.*

Riviera, see *Southern France.*

Russia, see Special List.

Scotland, see *Great Britain.*

Spain and Portugal with Excursions to *Tangier* and the *Balearic Islands.* With 9 Maps and 57 Plans. Third edition. 1908. Net 16s.

Switzerland and the adjacent portions of Italy Savoy and Tyrol. With 69 Maps, 18 Plans, and 11 Panoramas. Twenty-second edition. 1907. Net 8s.

Tyrol, see *The Eastern Alps.*

The United States, with Excursions to *Mexico Cuba. Porto Rico* and *Alaska* With 33 Maps and 48 Plans. Fourth edition 1909. Net 15s.

THE ORDNANCE SURVEY MAPS.

MR. T. FISHER UNWIN has pleasure in announcing that he has been appointed by His Majesty's Government sole wholesale agent for the Small Scale Ordnance Survey and Geological Maps of the United Kingdom.

UTILITY OF THE MAPS.—For general views of the structure of the country, the distribution and relation of mountains, plains, valleys, roads, rivers, and railways, the Ordnance Maps, practically the result of generations of work, are unsurpassed. Being Government publications they are the official maps from which all others have to be prepared.

LUCIDITY AND RELIABILITY.—Owing to the exceedingly fine draughtsmanship and engraving of Ordnance Maps, and the good paper they are printed upon, they will be found perfectly legible. They give a vast amount of information, yet they are easy to read and understand. They are being constantly revised and brought up to date, and may be regarded as of unimpeachable accuracy.

CONVENIENT FORM OF THE MAPS.—The maps can be obtained folded in such a way that they will go easily into the pocket, and need not be opened to their full extent for inspection, but can be examined a section at a time, like the pages of a book. This greatly facilitates outdoor reference in stormy weather.

DIFFERENT SCALES AND CHARACTERISTICS.—The maps are on the scales of 1, 2, 4, 10, and 15 miles to the inch. The one-mile-to-the-inch maps are ideal for pedestrian and cross-country purposes, being on a large and legible scale, with great wealth of topographical detail. The two-mile-to-the-inch maps in colour are the standard maps for all-round touring purposes, especially as road maps for motoring, cycling and walking. Special attention is directed to the new sheets of this scale on the "Layer system." The four miles, ten miles, and fifteen-miles-to-the-inch maps are practically indispensable to motorists and cyclists travelling long distances. They are also specially suitable as wall maps for educational purposes.

CATALOGUE.—The complete Catalogue containing full details of prices, with directions for ordering maps, will be sent post free to any address on request.

Indian Government Publications.

MR. T. FISHER UNWIN has been appointed Agent by the Secretary of State for India for the sale of these publications. They include a variety of works on Indian History and Archæology, Architecture and Art, Botany and Forestry; Grammars of the different Indian Languages— Dafla, Kurukh, Lepcha, Lais, &c.; and the valuable series of maps of the Indian Ordnance Survey.

Catalogues will be sent on application.

Lightning Source UK Ltd.
Milton Keynes UK
UKHW022258080223
416651UK00001B/467